THE
MEDICI

PAUL STRATHERN

THE
MEDICI

POWER, MONEY, *and* AMBITION
in the ITALIAN RENAISSANCE

PEGASUS BOOKS
NEW YORK LONDON

THE MEDICI

Pegasus Books Ltd
80 Broad Street, 5th Floor
New York, NY 10004

First Pegasus Books hardcover edition March 2016

ISBN: 978-1-60598-966-2

10 9 8 7 6 5 4 3 2 1

Printed in the United States of America
Distributed by W. W. Norton & Company, Inc.

Contents

Part 4: The Pope and the Protestant

Part 5: The Battle for Truth

To Kathleen

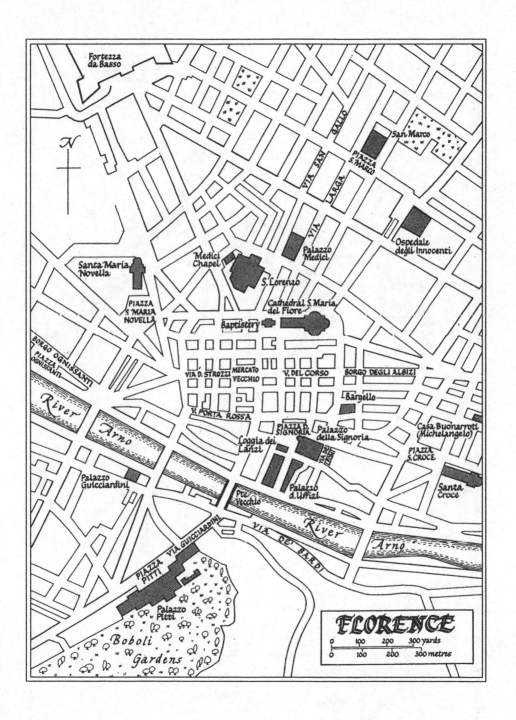

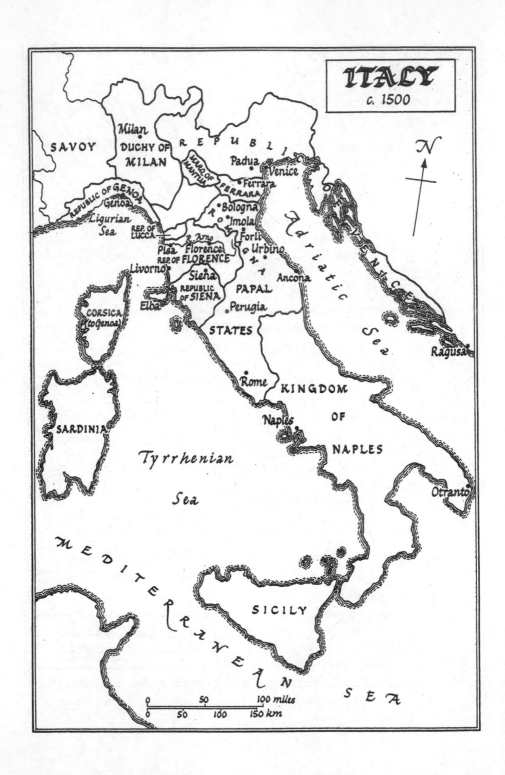

ITALY
c. 1500

N

SAVOY

Milan
DUCHY OF
MILAN

REPUBLI

MARD OF
MANTUA

Padua

Ferrara

Venice

MARD OF
FERRARA

REPUBLIC OF GENOA

Genoa

Ligurian
Sea

REP. OF
LUCCA

R. Arno

Bologna

Imola

Forli

R. Arno

Urbino

Pisa Florence

REP. OF FLORENCE

Livorno

Siena

Ancona

REPUBLIC
of SIENA

Elba

PAPAL

Perugia

STATES

CORSICA
(to Genoa)

Rome

KINGDOM

OF

Naples

NAPLES

SARDINIA

Tyrrhenian

Sea

Adriatic Sea

OF VENICE

Ragusa

Otranto

MEDITERRANEAN SEA

SICILY

0   50   100 miles
0   50   100   150 km

Illustrations

Santa Maria del Fiore, dome built by Filippo Brunelleschi
   (*akg-images/Rabatti-Domingie*).
David with Goliath's Head by Donatello, *c.* 1430, Museo Nazionale del Bargello
   (*akg-images/Erich Lessing*).
Detail from *Confirmation of St Francis of Assisi's Rules of the Order of the Pope
   Honorius III* by Ghirlandaio, *c.* 1483–85, Cappella Sassetti, S. Trinità, Florence
   (*akg-images/Rabatti-Domingie*).
Portrait of Pico della Mirandola, Gioviana Collection, Galleria degli Uffizi,
   Florence (© *1990 Gioviana Collection, Galleria degli Uffizi/Photo Scala; courtesy of the
   Ministero Beni e Att. Culturali*).
Girolamo Savonarola, painting by Fra Bartolomeo, Museo di San Marco,
   Florence (*akg-images/Erich Lessing*).
Execution of Savonarola on the Piazza della Signoria (1498), anonymous painting,
   contemporary, Museo di San Marco, Florence (*akg-images/Rabatti-Domingie*).
David by Michelangelo Buonarroti, Galleria dell'Accademia, Florence
   (*akg-images/Erich Lessing*).
Niccolò Machiavelli, painting by Santi di Tito, Palazzo Vecchio, Florence
   (*akg-images/Rabatti-Domingie*).
Three Landsknechte by W. Huber, 1515 (*akg-images*).
Castel Sant'Angelo, Rome, copperplate engraving by Matthäus Merian, *c.* 1650
   (*akg-images*).
The Siege of Florence by Giorgio Vasari, *c.* 1560, Palazzo Vecchio, Florence
   (*akg-images/Rabatti-Domingie*).
Alessandro de' Medici, portrait by Agnolo Bronzini, Museo Mediceo, Florence
   (© *1990 Museo Mediceo/Photo Scala, Florence; courtesy of the Ministero Beni e Att.
   Culturali*).
Cosimo I Medici, bronze sculpture by Benvenuto Cellini, 1545–48, Museo
   Nazionale del Bargello, Florence (*akg-images/Rabatti-Domingie*).
Catherine de Médicis, sixteenth-century painting, French School, Musée du
   Louvre, Paris (*akg-images/Erich Lessing*).
Galileo Galilei, coloured drawing by Ottavio Leoni, Biblioteca Marucelliana,
   Florence (*akg-images*).
Bust of Gian Gastone de' Medici, Galleria degli Uffizi, Florence (© *1990 Galleria
   degli Uffizi/Photo Scala; courtesy of the Ministero Beni e Att. Culturali*).

The Medici

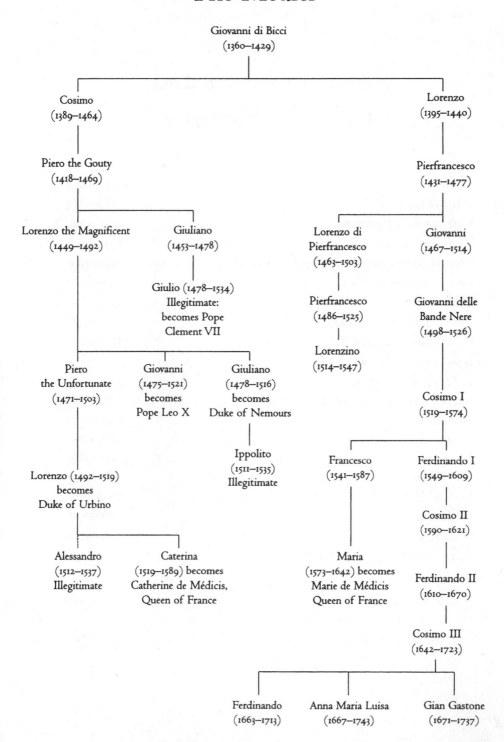

Giovanni di Bicci
(1360–1429)

Cosimo
(1389–1464)

Lorenzo
(1395–1440)

Piero the Gouty
(1418–1469)

Pierfrancesco
(1431–1477)

Lorenzo the Magnificent
(1449–1492)

Giuliano
(1453–1478)

Lorenzo di
Pierfrancesco
(1463–1503)

Giovanni
(1467–1514)

Giulio (1478–1534)
Illegitimate:
becomes Pope
Clement VII

Pierfrancesco
(1486–1525)

Giovanni delle
Bande Nere
(1498–1526)

Lorenzino
(1514–1547)

Piero
the Unfortunate
(1471–1503)

Giovanni
(1475–1521)
becomes
Pope Leo X

Giuliano
(1478–1516)
becomes
Duke of Nemours

Cosimo I
(1519–1574)

Ippolito
(1511–1535)
Illegitimate

Francesco
(1541–1587)

Ferdinando I
(1549–1609)

Lorenzo (1492–1519)
becomes
Duke of Urbino

Cosimo II
(1590–1621)

Alessandro
(1512–1537)
Illegitimate

Caterina
(1519–1589) becomes
Catherine de Médicis,
Queen of France

Maria
(1573–1642) becomes
Marie de Médicis
Queen of France

Ferdinando II
(1610–1670)

Cosimo III
(1642–1723)

Ferdinando
(1663–1713)

Anna Maria Luisa
(1667–1743)

Gian Gastone
(1671–1737)

Medici Leaders and Rulers in Florence

If you take a view of the princes of the Medici in a group, you will feel reverence and respect at one part of the picture and be struck with amazement and horror at the remainder. To revere and know them you must consider their generosity, their benefactions, their policy, and their scientific institutions. To view them with horror and amazement, you need only listen to the undoubted outrages of their private lives.

John Boyle, Earl of Cork and Orrery,
friend of the poet Alexander Pope and
an early British resident of Florence in 1755

Prologue: High Noon

IT IS SUNDAY 26 April 1478 in Florence, and the church bells ring out from the towers above the rooftops of the city. Lorenzo the Magnificent, accompanied by his circle of favourites, is making his way through the colourful crowds towards the cathedral of Santa Maria del Fiore.

The twenty-nine-year-old Lorenzo is the head of the Medici family, which along with its allies and powerful political machine controls the affairs of Florence beneath the veneer of republican democracy. Here, amidst the wealth and extravagance of Italy's most progressive city, the ancient God-obsessed world of the medieval era is slowly giving way to a new self-confident humanism. The Medici Bank is by now the most successful and respected financial institution in Europe, with offices and agents in all major commercial centres from London to Venice. Even the recent loss of the lucrative papal business to their Florentine rivals, the Pazzi family, is seen only as a minor setback; the profits from the Medici Bank have made Florence one of the architectural and cultural wonders of Europe, enabling the family to commission such artists as Donatello, Botticelli and Leonardo da Vinci. Yet even amongst such geniuses, it is Lorenzo himself who epitomises the new humanism of the Renaissance. Not for nothing is he popularly known as 'il magnifico'; he is the prince of Florence in all but name, and his supporters seek him as godfather to their firstborn male children. Lorenzo sees his rule as a celebration: the people are courted with festivities and carnivals. When commissioning great works of art, his taste is evident; he understands the artists he employs, encouraging them to excel in their own characteristic way — and they respect him as an equal in matters of art. He himself is an accomplished musician, athlete and swordsman; he is also well versed in

Fig 1 Lorenzo de' Medici

philosophy, and on the way to establishing himself as one of the finest
Italian poets of his time; yet for all this, he prides himself on being a
man of the people: his apparel is less ornate than that worn by many
other Florentine notables. Indeed, apart from the aura pertaining to his
implicit power, his appearance is somewhat unprepossessing; the
best-known portrait of him — a painted terracotta bust by Verrocchio
— depicts a surprisingly coarse-featured frowning figure: he has the prominent Medici nose and protruding lower jaw, heavy-lidded eyes and wide,
but curiously unsensual, narrow-lipped mouth. It is difficult to detect
the exceptional man behind such features in repose, though doubtless
when enlivened by the power of his personality they exuded that
compelling magnetic quality which made him so sexually attractive, and

which also attracted the fond admiration of philosophers, artists and even the people.

As the bells ring out over the city, Lorenzo and his entourage reach the end of the Via Larga and move towards the cathedral square. Before them, Brunelleschi's dome rises against the sky; this dome is perhaps the finest architectural achievement of early Renaissance Europe, outspanned only by the dome of the Pantheon in Rome, which had been built more than a thousand years previously: only now is Europe beginning to catch up with the greatness of its past. Lorenzo and his friends enter the cool, dimmed interior of the cathedral.

Back on the Via Larga, Lorenzo's younger brother Giuliano is hurrying to catch up with him, limping from a bout of painful sciatica. He is accompanied by Francesco de' Pazzi and his friend Bernardo Bandini, and as they walk down the street Francesco rests a comradely arm around Giuliano's shoulder, helping him to overcome his limp, assuring him there is no need to hurry. He gives Giuliano a playful squeeze, noting that he is not wearing any chainmail body-armour beneath his colourful doublet. When they reach the church, Giuliano sees that his brother Lorenzo is already up by the High Altar, surrounded by his friends and two priests, one of whom Giuliano recognises as a tutor to the Pazzi family. The service begins and Giuliano de' Medici decides to remain by the door with Francesco de' Pazzi, Bernardo Bandini and his companions. The sung responses of the choir ring out in the high, echoing interior of the cathedral beneath the towering dome, then the chanting voices fall silent and the priest conducting the service prepares to celebrate High Mass. The sacristy bell tinkles above the murmuring conversations taking place amongst the informally assembled congregation, and their voices too fall silent as the priest elevates the Host before the High Altar.

The moment the priest raises the Host, two separate incidents take place simultaneously. By the door, Bernardo Bandini whips out a dagger, turns and plunges it into Giuliano de' Medici's head with such force that Giuliano's skull is split open with a spray of blood. Next, Francesco de' Pazzi begins stabbing in a frenzy at Giuliano's falling body, slashing again and again, like a man possessed. Such is his mindless fury as he hurls himself forward onto the prostrate body of Giuliano that he is blinded with blood and even plunges his dagger into his own thigh.

At the same moment, up at the High Altar, the two priests standing behind Lorenzo have swiftly pulled out daggers from beneath their robes. One places a hand on Lorenzo's shoulder as he prepares to stab him in the back, but Lorenzo spins round and the tip of the descending dagger only slices through the skin of his neck. As he staggers back, he wrenches off his cloak, swirling it over his arm to form a shield, while with his other hand he rapidly draws his sword. The two priests retreat aghast, their daggers still raised. Immediately there is a mêlée of bodies around Lorenzo, with shouts and the slicing of steel as Lorenzo's attendant friends draw their swords, protecting him as he leaps over the altar rail and sprints for the safety of the open sacristy door. By now Bernardo Bandini has left Giuliano de' Medici for dead and is rushing through the congregation, his sword drawn. He attempts to cut off the fleeing Lorenzo, but Lorenzo's friend Francesco Nori hurls himself between them and Bandini runs him through with a single lunge, killing him instantly. Amidst the confusion another friend is wounded in the arm, and by the time Bandini can recover, Lorenzo and his friends are inside the sacristy, heaving the heavy bronze doors closed.

Lorenzo claps his hand to his neck; he can feel that the blood is flowing, but it is only a surface wound. Antonio Ridolfi, who is standing beside Lorenzo, impulsively launches himself forward, grabbing Lorenzo by the shoulders, appearing to kiss him on the neck; Lorenzo is aware of his friend sucking at his wound and then spitting out the blood – the priest's dagger point may have been poisoned. Even through the bronze doors they can hear the uproar that has broken out amongst the congregation, where there is a tumult of cries and shouts. Lorenzo starts forward, exclaiming, 'Giuliano? Is he safe?' His friends glance at one another: no one replies.

Amidst the pandemonium in the cathedral, Giuliano's assassins and the two priests melt away through the throng, while all kinds of rumours begin to spread amongst the crowd outside the cathedral. Some say the great dome has collapsed, and people begin running back through the streets for the safety of their homes; others clamour to get inside the cathedral; most cluster in bewildered groups, comforting the distressed and weeping. After a few minutes have elapsed and nothing further happens, Lorenzo's friends whisk him out through a side-door of the cathedral, bundling him down the street towards the safety of the Palazzo Medici.

Yet just a quarter of a mile away the other part of the plot is continuing according to plan. Archbishop Salviati, the leader of a second group of conspirators, has entered the Palazzo della Signoria, the civic palace, accompanied by fellow conspirator Jacopo Bracciolini and several of his companions. The archbishop asks to see the *gonfaloniere*, the titular ruler of the city state of Florence: he informs the attendant that he has an important message for Gonfaloniere Cesare Petrucci from Pope Sixtus IV. As the attendant mounts the stairway to the *gonfaloniere*'s quarters, the archbishop's retainers file silently through the front door of the palazzo. These retainers are an unlikely bunch for the retinue of an archbishop, their coarse fearsome faces barely softened by their pretences at disguise — they are in fact hired mercenaries from Perugia, all fully armed.

Gonfaloniere Petrucci is taking his midday meal with the members of the Signoria, his eight elected colleagues, when the attendant comes in and delivers his message. Gonfaloniere Petrucci asks that the archbishop be shown into the main reception chamber, whilst his companions can wait in the corridor; any further members of his retinue are to be admitted to the nearby Chancellery. As Gonfaloniere Petrucci turns to complete his meal, he is faintly aware of a distant clamour beyond the window in the streets.

When eventually Gonfaloniere Petrucci enters his reception chamber and takes the archbishop's hand, he notices that it is shaking: Salviati seems to be in an agitated state. As the archbishop begins delivering the pope's message, his voice breaks into a stammer so that it is barely intelligible; the blood drains from his face and he begins glancing towards the door. When Gonfaloniere Petrucci becomes suspicious and calls for the guards, the archbishop immediately makes a dash for the door, shouting to his companions in the corridor, telling them to summon the Perugian mercenaries.

But the Perugians are unable to respond: the Chancellery into which they have been admitted has doors that cannot be opened from the inside, and they can be heard hammering at the wooden doors, bellowing to be let out. As soon as Gonfaloniere Petrucci emerges into the corridor, the archbishop's companion Jacopo Bracciolini leaps towards him, drawing his weapon, but the *gonfaloniere* manages to catch him by the hair and hurls him to the ground. Grabbing the first implement he sees, the *gonfaloniere* begins wielding a metal cooking spit, scattering the archbishop and his companions. By now the Perugians sound as if they are breaking out of the locked Chancellery, prompting Gonfaloniere Petrucci and his colleagues to make a dash for the entrance to the tower, holding onto the heavy door as they begin frantically chaining it closed behind them. They then run up the stairs and begin tolling the bell, whose booming tones begin ringing out over the rooftops of the city: the customary warning, summoning all citizens to the Piazza della Signoria in times of emergency.

Soon the anxious crowds are gathering below in the large open piazza, as the bell continues to toll over the city. Suddenly Jacopo de' Pazzi, one of the leaders of the conspiracy, appears from a side-street leading a column containing several scores of armed men, who begin shouting: '*Popolo e Libertà!*' ('The People and Freedom'), the customary Florentine slogan of revolt against dictatorial government. The armed men ride about the square trying to encourage the crowd to join in, but they remain suspicious. Then, from high up in the tower, the *gonfaloniere* and his attendants begin hurling down stones at Jacopo de' Pazzi and his men, who quickly sense that the suspicions of the crowd are hardening into anger against them.

Meanwhile a group of several dozen armed men on horseback emerges from the side-street to the north of the square, which leads from the direction of the Palazzo Medici. These are Medici supporters, who make their way through the crowd towards the Palazzo della Signoria, where they dismount, unsheathing their weapons, and make their way through the door. Once inside, they storm upstairs and set upon the Perugians, quickly butchering them with their pikes and swords. After a matter of minutes, the Medici supporters emerge from the palazzo, carrying aloft on their pikes several severed Perugian heads dripping blood. Disheartened, Jacopo de' Pazzi and his men turn back, riding east out of piazza for the safety of the Palazzo Pazzi.

The entire city is in confusion, alive with rumour: there has been a conspiracy, Lorenzo has been stabbed, the Pazzi family are leading an army to invade the city . . . The gruesome sight of the Perugians' severed heads quickly inspires the crowd to bloodlust. In rage and fear, shouting groups begin running through the streets, seeking out members of the Pazzi family and their supporters, attacking real and imagined enemies, whilst others hurry towards the Palazzo Medici. Is Lorenzo alive or dead? Who is to lead them? Who is to save the city in its hour of danger? Lorenzo is prevailed upon to show himself on the balcony of the Palazzo Medici, where his appearance is greeted with cheers. Yet people in the crowd are alarmed, for Lorenzo's neck is bandaged and his tunic dramatically spattered with blood.

Lorenzo addresses the crowd from the balcony, telling them that there has been a conspiracy mounted by the Pazzi family, with the aim of overthrowing the legitimate government of the city. He assures the mass of faces below that the conspiracy has failed, and that although his brother Giuliano has been murdered by the conspirators, he himself is safe, only lightly wounded. There is no need for panic – all should remain calm; no one is to take the law into their own hands or attempt vengeance of any kind; the enemies of the city will be rooted out and dealt with by the authorities. But Lorenzo's attempt at calming the crowd has the opposite effect; relieved that they are safe, the mob is now determined to find scapegoats – the conspirators or their friends, or any of their allies. They scatter through the city in bands, baying for blood.

At the Palazzo Pazzi, Francesco de' Pazzi is discovered lying in bed, recovering from the knife-wound he had inadvertently inflicted on his own thigh. He is hauled naked from his bed, dragged through the streets to the Palazzo della Signoria and up the stairs to the *gonfaloniere*'s quarters. Here Gonfaloniere Petrucci takes charge, meting out rough justice: he orders Francesco de' Pazzi to be hanged forthwith. Naked as he stands, the gore dribbling from the gashed wound in his leg, a noose is cast over Francesco de' Pazzi's head; the other end of the rope is tied fast to the strong metal transom dividing one of the windows, and he is then bundled from the window. The crowd cheers and jeers at his swinging naked body, writhing in its death throes as it dangles in the air beneath the overhanging window. Next it is the turn of Archbishop Salviati, who is hauled before the *gonfaloniere* still wearing his purple robes; then, with a halter round his neck, and his hands bound firmly behind his back by a leather strap, he too is thrown from the window. The archbishop dangles from his noose, struggling frantically, his eyes starting from their sockets; desperately he tries to save himself, attempting to bite into the naked body swinging beside him as the upturned faces of the crowd howl with delight.

For the next few days mobs roam the city taking vengeance as they see fit. The two priests who had attempted to murder Lorenzo are discovered hiding in the Badia, the Benedictine abbey close to the Palazzo Pazzi;

they are immediately dragged into the street, their robes torn from their bodies, then castrated, before being hauled off to be hanged. There are many such gruesome examples of mob fury, as the victors vent their anger on the vanquished factions and old scores are settled; according to Machiavelli, writing less than half a century later in his *History of Florence*, there were 'so many deaths that the streets were filled with the parts of men'.

News of the failed Pazzi conspiracy soon spreads beyond Florence to Rome, where Pope Sixtus IV, who had backed the conspirators, is enraged – even more so when he learns that one of his archbishops has been publicly hanged, clad in his ecclesiastical robes. This is no less than sacrilege! A papal bull is issued excommunicating Lorenzo, who is described as 'the child of iniquity and the suckling of perdition'; this is accompanied by an interdict forbidding the celebration of Mass in any church throughout the entire Florentine Republic. After communicating with his ally, the King of Naples, and invoking their joint treaty, the pope then declares that Naples and the Papal States are going to war against Florence.

Back in Florence, Lorenzo the Magnificent is behaving with characteristic panache – he has decided that the defeat of the Pazzi conspiracy should be celebrated in style. He lets it be known to the appropriate government authority, the Council of Eight (the committee of political police and magistracy), that he wishes there to be a permanent artistic reminder of this triumph over the conspirators. Thereupon the Council of Eight summons Sandro Botticelli, Lorenzo's favourite artist, and offers him a generous commission: for forty golden florins he will paint, on the wall by the side-façade of the Palazzo della Signoria, a large fresco commemorating the recent events. In the customary Florentine manner for dealing with disgraced or traitorous citizens, this painting will contain eight full-length portraits of the leading Pazzi conspirators – those who have been caught will have nooses painted around their necks, indicating their punishment, whilst Bernardo Bandini, the man who first stabbed Lorenzo's brother Giuliano, and managed to escape, will be depicted upside down, hanging by his foot. Under each of these portraits Botticelli will paint the words of a short mocking verse, which will be composed by Lorenzo himself, specially for the occasion. In the verse beneath the upside-down Bandini, he will be described as:

A fugitive, who has not escaped the fates,
for on his return a far crueller death awaits.

Botticelli was approaching the height of his powers, and these portraits required all his skills. Custom dictated that they should be extremely realistic, portraying faces that were immediately recognisable to their former fellow citizens. Similarly, they should be depicted in clothes of the same colour and design as those they had habitually worn about the city. Archbishop Salviati was of course to be shown in full purple robes. It would take Botticelli all of twelve weeks before he finally finished this work, which must have been a masterpiece of its kind.

However, just seven months later the portrait of Archbishop Salviati would have to be obliterated, a requirement that was specifically inserted by Pope Sixtus IV into the peace treaty that was eventually negotiated between Florence and the Papal States. A few months after this, the portrait of Bandini would also have to be repainted. After the failure of the conspiracy, Bernardo Bandini had managed to escape to the coast, where he had succeeded in boarding a Venetian galley bound for Constantinople. Lorenzo was particularly keen to get his hands on the murderer of his beloved brother Giuliano, and a diplomatic request was despatched to the Turkish sultan, who ordered Bandini's arrest. He was then shipped back to Florence in chains, where he was hanged. Repainting the figure of Bandini in the mural was considered no small matter, but Botticelli was unable to fulfil this task; instead, the work was given to no less an artist than Leonardo da Vinci. In his notebooks there is a sketch of the hanging Bandini — almost certainly a preliminary drawing for the painting.

There would be no further alterations to this great fresco, unique in containing work by both Botticelli and Leonardo da Vinci, which would remain on the wall by the Piazza della Signoria for all to see. Here was art as celebration: a display of power and brilliance, which also stood as a warning to any who might contemplate opposing the Medici. It would remain in place for as long as the Medici ruled Florence.

Part 1
Origins of a Dynasty

I

Ancient Beginnings

THE MEDICI FAMILY is said to have been descended from a knight called Averardo, who fought for Charlemagne during his conquest of Lombardy in the eighth century. According to Medici family legend, Averardo was travelling through the Mugello, a remote valley near Florence, when he heard tell of a giant who was terrorising the neighbourhood. Averardo went in search of the giant, and challenged him. As they faced each other, the giant swung his mace. Averardo ducked and the iron balls from the giant's mace smashed into his shield; but eventually Averardo managed to slay the giant. Charlemagne was so impressed when he heard of Averardo's feat that he decreed that henceforth his brave knight could use his dented shield as his personal insignia.

The Medici insignia of red balls (or *palle*) on a field of gold is said to derive from Averardo's dented shield. Others claim that the Medici were, as their name suggests, originally apothecaries dispensing medicines to the public, and that the balls of their insignia were in fact pills. This story was always denied by the Medici, and their denial is supported by historical evidence, as the medical use of pills did not become commonplace until some time after the appearance of the Medici insignia. The most likely origin of their insignia is the sign that medieval money-changers hung outside their shops, depicting coins. Money-changing was the initial Medici family business.

The legendary knight Averardo settled in the Mugello, the fertile valley of the River Sieve, which runs through the mountains twenty-five miles by road to the north-east of Florence. Even today, the region remains a picturesque spot with vineyards and olive groves either side of the curving river, beneath steep wooded hills and the mountains beyond. This isolated region of less than twenty square miles must have had an exceptional gene pool: not only did it produce the multi-talented Medici, but also the families of geniuses as disparate as Fra Angelico, Galileo and Giotto. The Medici family came from the village of Cafaggiolo, and was always to retain strong links with this spot.

Some time before the turn of thirteenth century the Medici family appears to have left Cafaggiolo to try their luck in Florence. They were not the only country people to seek their fortune in Florence at around this time, and between the mid-twelfth and mid-thirteenth centuries the population of Florence is said to have increased fivefold to more than 50,000. Medieval methods of ascertaining the population were notoriously fanciful, which leaves such figures open to question. The census-taking methods of Florence were a case in point: births were registered by the simple method of counting beans – when a child was born, the family was expected to drop a bean into the local census box: black for a boy or white for a girl. However, we know that Florence experienced an unprecedented increase in population during this period, making it larger than Rome or London, though it remained smaller than the great medieval centres of Paris, Naples and Milan.

The Medici settled in the neighbourhood of San Lorenzo, clustered about the church of San Lorenzo, the earliest part of which had been consecrated in the fourth century. As a result, San Lorenzo would become the patron saint of the Medici, and some of the family's most illustrious sons would be named after him. From San Lorenzo it was just a few minutes' walk to the Mercato Vecchio (Old Market), the hub of the city's commercial life (now the large central Piazza della Repubblica). Here visitors came from miles around to buy the cloth for which the city was famous, with bolts of brightly coloured material laid out on the trestle stalls, cut to measure against the customer as he bargained. Early in the morning the streets leading to this large square would be filled with the carts of farmers bringing their wares to market, the squeals of driven pigs, bleating sheep, the mooing of milk cows. Amidst the cries of the sellers and animals, there were stalls selling freshly caught fish from the Arno, slices from hooked slabs of bloody meat, varieties of cheeses, wine from the barrel. Along the walls were neatly stacked piles of coloured vegetables and fruit — onions and withered greens in the spring; fennel and figs, cherries and oranges in summer; and in winter, meagre piles of earthy root vegetables. Amidst the throng of townsfolk and yokels, the mendicant friars in their threadbare robes begged from passers-by. The blare of a herald's trumpet, and the crowd would throng the entrance to the Via del Corso to watch a bloodied, stumbling criminal in rags and chains being whipped through the street amidst jeers, on his way to the Bargello and a public hanging on the morrow.

The first Medici mentioned in the records of Florence is one Chiarissimo, who appears on a legal document dated 1201. Little is known of exactly what happened to the family during this period; all we know for certain is that the Medici became money-changers and gradually prospered — to such an extent that by the end of the thirteenth century they had become one of the better-known business families in the city. Even so, the Medici were not regarded as one of the leading families, who were all either noble landowners or well-established merchants. Then in 1296 Ardingo de' Medici became the first member of the family to be chosen as *gonfaloniere*.

Florence was an independent republic, theoretically run on democratic lines. It was ruled by a nine-man council known as the Signoria, the chief of whom was the *gonfaloniere*, who presided for a period of two months. The *gonfaloniere* and his Signoria were selected by lottery from amongst members of the guilds. These lotteries were increasingly fixed, so that the Signoria generally represented whichever leading family, or families, held sway at the time. In 1299 Guccio de' Medici was the second member of the family to become *gonfaloniere*. Guccio must have shown his benefactors that the Medici could be relied upon, for in 1314 Averardo de' Medici became the third Medici *Gonfaloniere*.

Florence may have been lacking in power and historical greatness, compared with such cities as Paris and Milan, but it soon made up for this in the creation of wealth. This was mainly due to the new growth industry of the thirteenth-century — banking, which was to a large extent an Italian invention. (The English term derives from the Italian word *banco*, referring to the original counters on which the bankers conducted their trade.) At this time Italy was the main economic power in Europe, with the Genoese and the Venetians controlling the import of silk and spices

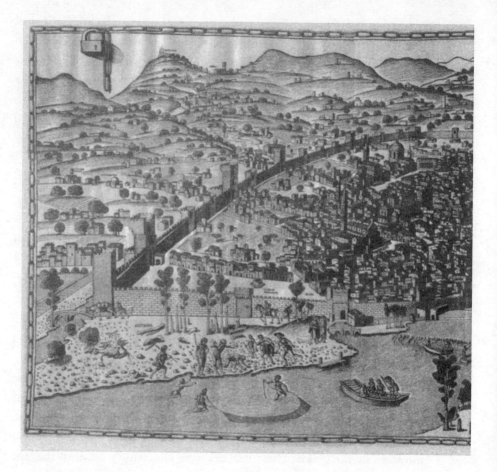

Fig 2 Florence around 1480

from the Orient. Marco Polo even records that in the last decade of the thirteenth century Genoese merchant ships were trading on the Caspian Sea; and as early as 1291 two Genoese galleys disappeared searching for a route to the Orient by way of West Africa. International trade was on the increase, despite hazardous rutted turnpikes and shipping routes raided by pirates. The overland journey from Florence across the Alps to the northern trading city of Bruges in Flanders, a distance of some 700 miles, usually took between two and three weeks. The less dangerous sea journey, via the port of Pisa and the Bay of Biscay, could take twice as long.

Goods such as cloth, wool and grain were supplemented by luxury goods from the Orient, which were mainly destined for the courts of

powerful noblemen and royalty. The setting up of banks in the main trading centres greatly facilitated this burgeoning international trade, and in
the process merchant bankers accumulated large assets at these centres,
which they soon began loaning out at interest, despite the Church's ban
on usury. Many banks managed to circumvent the Church's ban by maintaining that there was always a possibility of loss in their business; any
extra charge was merely a payment against 'risk', so this was not really
usury at all. Others claimed that they were not actually charging interest
on their loans – any increase in the size of the repayments was due entirely
to fluctuations in the exchange rate. Despite the spuriousness of its justi-
fications, banking soon became an accepted practice.

At the end of the thirteenth century the main banking centre was Siena, the smaller city over the mountains some forty miles south of Florence; but in 1298 the leading Sienese bankers, the Bonsignori family, went bankrupt. This was largely because they had loaned huge sums to royalty and powerful courts, the main borrowers in this market, whose requests were often impossible to refuse. The difficulty was that banks simply had no power to enforce these debts: such rulers were quite literally a law unto themselves, as the Sienese bankers found to their cost. Siena never recovered from the Bonsignori collapse, and Florence quickly took over the banking trade. This was soon dominated by three leading Florentine families: the Bardi, the Peruzzi and the Acciaiuoli, which became the greatest banking houses throughout Europe, with the Peruzzi house having a network of fifteen branches, stretching from Cyprus to London.

In its early heyday one of the symbols of Florence was a lion, which occasionally appeared stamped on commemorative medals, rather than the more usual Florentine lily. This lion was to become more than a fanciful symbol, for it was during this period that the city acquired its first real lions, probably through its trading link to the Levant. The lions were kept in a large cage on the Piazza San Giovanni, close to the cathedral, and these exotic creatures were a source of wonder and pride to the citizens; their occasional roars, which resounded through the streets, became regarded as omens by the superstitious population. Some time during the mid-fourteenth century the lions were moved to a site behind the Palazzo della Signoria, where their cage stood in the street still known as Via dei Leoni. Yet despite their popularity, and their central appearance in the life of the city, they were not adopted as the symbol for the city's most successful coinage, an honour that fell to the lily.

Florence's banking supremacy, and the trustworthiness of its bankers, led to the city's currency becoming an institution. As early as 1252 Florence had issued the *fiorino d'oro*, containing fifty-four grains of gold, which became known as the florin. Owing to its unchanging gold content (a rarity in coins of the period), and its use by Florentine bankers, the florin became accepted during the fourteenth century as a standard currency throughout Europe. This was a considerable advantage to bankers, who otherwise had to deal with flexible exchange rates between a range of different coinages.

It was during this period that the foundations of modern capitalism were laid, business practice was established, and banking evolved many of its skills. Double-entry bookkeeping was invented (first appearing in 1340); fiduciary money (that is, credit based on trust, and not matched by assets) was conjured up out of nothing; and payment by ledger transfers and bills of exchange was developed. Despite these advances, the Florentine bankers soon repeated the Sienese mistake, by opening loan accounts for King Robert of Naples and Edward III of England. In 1340 Europe suffered an economic depression, and the kings who were unable to repay their debts simply reneged on them. By this stage Edward III had embarked on what would come to be known as the Hundred Years War against France, and it was reckoned that he owed the Peruzzi bank 'the value of a realm'. As a result, the three leading banking families in Florence went bankrupt in quick succession.

Even before this catastrophe, the early fourteenth century had seen volatile times in the Florentine Republic, with political power frequently changing hands in violent fashion. The population was divided into two main parties, the Guelfs and the Ghibellines, and there were of course factions within these two parties. The Ghibellines drew their support mainly from the noble families, while the Guelfs were supported by the wealthy merchants and the *popolo minuto*, meaning 'the small people' – that is, the general public or working class. (Besides being disparaging, the term *popolo minuto* also contained an element of truth, mainly because the poorer classes endured a severely reduced diet, which restricted their growth: the *popolo minuto* were literally small people.)

Despite such political instability, the early fourteenth century saw Florence's first cultural golden age, with the city producing three of Italy's finest writers – Dante, Boccaccio and Petrarch – in just half a century. In a break with clerical tradition, they chose to write in Tuscan rather than Latin, and this not only established the Tuscan dialect as the standard form of Italian, but introduced a secular humanist element by dispersing literature beyond the language of the Church. This secular humanism was also reflected in the interests pursued by these authors. Petrarch, for instance, would become renowned for seeking out the manuscripts of ancient classical authors, which had long lain forgotten in monasteries throughout Europe. Boccaccio, on the other hand, would become notorious for his

Decameron, a sequence of sometimes obscene and often humorous tales depicting life as it was actually lived amongst the people of the time, rather than the way the authorities (particularly the Church) considered it ought to be lived. The two finest artists of the period, Giotto and Pisano, also lived in Florence and showed humanist inclinations, with their figures breaking away from the medieval formalism of the day to assume a more modern, lifelike manner with recognisable expressions of emotion. Such luminaries brought Florentine culture to the brink of the Renaissance; but before this could develop further, Europe was struck by the greatest disaster in its history.

The economic depression of the early 1340s was followed by the catastrophe of the Black Death. This arrived in Europe from China, by way of Genoese ships from the Black Sea, in 1347. Contemporary chroniclers, confirmed by recent research, record that during the next four years around one-third of Europe's population was wiped out by the plague. Owing to bad sanitation and ignorance of how the disease spread, the situation was worst in the cities, where families suspected of having the plague were sometimes simply bricked up in their homes and left to die. Those who could afford to do so fled from Florence into the surrounding Tuscan countryside; of those who remained behind, well over half perished. Not surprisingly, the first stirrings of the new humanism were quickly replaced by superstitious morbidity; yet the comparative social stasis of medieval Europe had begun to crumble, and fundamental change was inevitable.

The Medici family in Florence had by now expanded to include some twenty or thirty nuclear families. The affiliation of these families, recognisable by name, would have been looser than that of a single family, more akin to that of a clan, with its own internal rivalries but overall group loyalty. The Medici appear to have taken advantage of the vacuum left by the bankruptcy of the three leading Florentine banking families, with several Medici going into banking, establishing their own separate small enterprises. Brothers or cousins would have joined together as partners to provide shares of the original capital, often working together in the daily running of the bank, which would have involved such business as foreign-currency exchange, small deposits, and seasonal loans to wool traders, weavers and the like. At least two of these enterprises were sufficiently canny, or lucky, to survive the economic ravages of the Black Death, and were thus able to consolidate the Medici power base. The Medici now provided the city with more than the occasional *gonfaloniere*. Giovanni de' Medici (a direct descendant of the first-documented Chiarissimo) departed from the usual Medici preserve of civil affairs, and became a military leader. Keen to demonstrate his prowess, in 1343 he encouraged the Florentines into a war against the small city state of Lucca, some forty miles to the west. Giovanni tried to take Lucca, failed, then laid siege to the town; but the campaign turned into a fiasco, and on his return to Florence Giovanni was executed. After this, the Medicis stuck to civil affairs – yet on occasion these could prove just as dangerous.

In 1378 Giovanni's cousin Salvestro de' Medici became *gonfaloniere*, and during his two-month period in office a revolt broke out amongst the wool-workers, who were known as the *ciompi* (after the sound that their distinctive wooden clogs made on the stone-slabbed streets). The *ciompi* revolt was ostensibly led by Michele di Lando, who fronted a mob of fellow wool-workers and artisans demanding the right to form their own guilds – and thus the right to vote, and at least theoretically have a chance of getting onto the ruling Signoria. Despite being *gonfaloniere*, Salvestro sympathised with the revolt, though it appears that he also saw it as an opportunity to advance the Medici cause. In order to stir up trouble and intimidate the noble faction that had balked the Medicis, Salvestro secretly threw open the prisons. What had begun as a protest quickly became a riot, with Salvestro and the other eight members of the Signoria forced to barricade themselves in the Palazzo della Signoria while the mob went on the rampage, looting the palaces of the nobles and merchants, setting fire to houses and roughing up members of the guilds. In a characteristic political homily, Machiavelli would later remark of these events in his *History of Florence*: 'Let no one stir things up in a city, believing that he can stop them as he pleases or that he is in charge of what happens next.'

Salvestro's house was spared, allegedly because of his sympathy with the protesters, though this caused some to believe that Salvestro may well have instigated the revolt. Even given the deviousness of Florentine politics, this seems unlikely, especially in the light of what followed. In the immediate aftermath of the disturbances a commune was set up by the mob, Salvestro was deposed as *gonfaloniere* and the mob-leader Michele di Lando was installed in his place. Despite the continuing atmosphere of instability, this state of affairs would last for more than two years, though in time Michele di Lando found himself more and more out of his depth, and took to consulting secretly with Salvestro about what to do next. The *ciompi* and their supporters eventually got wind of this, and fearing an undercover return of power to the old rulers, took to the streets, threatening to destroy the city rather than let this happen. Michele di Lando panicked and turned to Salvestro de' Medici, who proposed that they use their joint influence to call out the militia. It responded to their call, whereupon the mob backed down without a fight, dispersed and returned to their homes: the revolt was over.

The guild workers and the shopkeepers, as well as the nobles and merchants, had been horrified by the *ciompi* revolt; the new guilds formed by the *ciompi* were dissolved, and the nobles took firm control. Salvestro de' Medici and Michele di Lando would normally have been executed, but instead they were merely exiled, in recognition of the part they had played in ending the revolt. The exile of Salvestro put paid to the bid of the Medici clan to become a leading force in Florentine politics, and was also a severe blow to the family business, which was run only with difficulty from exile.

When Salvestro died in 1388, the main Medici banking business was taken over by his cousin Vieri. The new head of the Medici firm was not interested in politics and devoted himself entirely to building up the business, opening exchange offices in Rome and Venice and conducting an export–import trade through the river port of Pisa. Vieri was the first Medici to achieve any business success that extended beyond the city itself, and according to Machiavelli: 'All who have written about the events of this period agree, if Veri [sic] had been possessed of more ambition and less integrity, nothing could have stopped him from taking over as prince of the city.' As Machiavelli was writing 130 years after the event, his assessments are not always to be trusted; here he was almost certainly exaggerating, in order to glorify the Medici. Even so, the political integrity of the Medici clan, and its loyalty to the constitutional government of Florence, was certainly put to the test during this time, no matter the precise extent of their potential political power. Just over a decade after the *ciompi* revolt there was another revolt, this time by the *popolo magro*, literally, 'the lean people' – the distinction being that they were the near-starving unskilled underclass, rather than the powerless artisans of the *popolo minuto*. But when the mob took to the streets, all those excluded from power joined them in voicing their grievances. The mob still remembered how the Medici family had been sympathetic to their cause, and they called on the elderly Vieri to lead them; but Vieri tactfully declined this dangerous offer. According to Machiavelli, he told the disappointed mob 'to cheer up, for he was willing to act in their defence as long as they followed his advice'. He then led them to the Signoria, where he made an ingratiating speech to the council members. 'He pleaded that the ignorant behaviour of the mob was none of his doing, and besides, as soon as they'd come to him he'd brought them straight here, before the forces of law and order.' Miraculously, everyone concerned appeared satisfied with this performance: the revolutionaries dispersed, while the Signoria accepted Vieri's word, allowing him to return home, and there were no reprisals. Yet despite Vieri's skilful handling of this affair, the strain of it all had evidently been too much for him, because later that same year he died; and with Vieri the senior line of the Medici family vanished from history.

2

The Origins of the
Medici Bank

THE MEDICI FAMILY fortunes now passed into the hands of Giovanni di Bicci de' Medici, head of the Cafaggiolo branch of the family, so called because it retained property in the Medici's home village in the Mugello. Giovanni was born in 1360, the fourth son of Averardo detto Bicci, who was the owner of a smallholding in Cafaggiolo. Averardo was not rich, but was of sufficient social standing to marry into the aristocratic Spini family, though when he died in 1363 his property was divided up between his wife and five sons, leaving none of them well off.

Giovanni di Bicci was eighteen at the time of the *ciompi* revolt, and was almost certainly in Florence during the two-year period of the commune, which was covertly supported by his distant relative Salvestro de' Medici. Possibly as a consequence of this, Giovanni was to retain a secret sympathy for the *popolo minuto* all his life, although the ensuing political climate hardly favoured such sympathies. After the collapse of the commune, the old families quickly reasserted their authority: an oligarchy was set up by the powerful Albizzi, Capponi and Uzzano families, led by Maso degli Albizzi, and this situation would continue for the next thirty years. Despite the occasional disturbance, such as the one that Vieri de' Medici helped to defuse in 1393, this was a period of prosperity and comparative stability in Florence; the oligarchy was firm, but was not particularly unpopular.

The powerful families of the oligarchy were strongly opposed to the Medici and their allies, which may well have accounted for Vieri's unwillingness to become involved in politics, as much as any innate humility on his behalf. This unwillingness also extended to his remote cousin

Giovanni di Bicci. It is difficult to tell whether the political modesty of these two early Medici was instinctive, feigned, or simply a matter of clan loyalty, or even clan policy. Self-consciousness in the late fourteenth century was still firmly rooted in medieval mores: people tended to regard themselves as members of a family, rather than as individuals. According to such a way of thinking, these early Medici would naturally have sunk their individual political ambitions in the long-term ambitions of the family as a whole, accepting that political power would only be achieved by the family in more propitious times; meanwhile it was best to lay the foundations, firmly establishing the family and its wealth to an ever greater degree, in preparation. However, such foresight would appear to display an extremely well-developed sense of political ambition. Did the Medici harbour secret long-term ambitions for political power, or was their early accumulation of wealth merely an ambition in itself? From such a distance it is impossible to tell the secret machinations and plans of the Medici family at this stage.

Being a member of the Medici family certainly helped Giovanni di Bicci, for shortly after the *ciompi* revolt the new head of the family business, his uncle Vieri de' Medici despatched Giovanni to Rome where he was apprenticed to the local branch of Vieri's bank. Familial ties always played their part in businesses, especially in banking where trust was so essential. Even so, Giovanni evidently had an aptitude for the business, because within a few years he was made a junior partner, and three years later he became manager of the Rome branch. In that same year, 1385, he married Piccarda Bueri, who brought him a sizeable dowry of 1,500 florins, which he almost certainly used to invest in various personal business projects.

From all accounts, the Vieri business flourished through the 1380s, much of this being due to the success of the Rome branch under Giovanni di Bicci, which provided a large share of the profits. But by now Vieri was approaching seventy, a venerable age in late medieval times, and in the early 1390s he retired, dissolving his business. This gave Giovanni di Bicci the opportunity to set up the Rome branch as his own firm, and in accordance with the practice of the day he was obliged to take over the assets and liabilities of Vieri's Rome office. According to the State Archives in Florence, Giovanni lost 860 florins on the deal, which suggests either that the Vieri business had taken a recent downturn, or that Vieri indulged in some creative accounting before handing on the business to his manager. Six centuries later there is no extant evidence either way, as indeed there may not have been at the time.

On 1 October 1397 Giovanni established a head office in Florence, and this is generally accepted as the date for the founding of the great Medici Bank. Rome, with the Curia (the papal court) and all its attendants, certainly provided a good source of income, but Florence was the banking capital of Europe, providing the best opportunities for investment. Details of the founding of the Medici Bank and its early trading are revealed in the bank's *libro segreto* (literally, 'secret book'), which is preserved in the State Archives in Florence. This 'secret book' is in fact no more than the bank's private records, but its literal name gives a flavour of the romance and conspiracy of early banking.

The Medici Bank's initial capital was 10,000 florins, with the controlling 5,500 florins put up by Giovanni di Bicci, and the rest being provided by two partners who were not immediate members of the Medici family (though such partners were almost invariably related to the family by marriage). In its first year's trading the bank made around 10 per cent profit, and it was customary for such profits to be withdrawn from the bank so that they could be invested privately by the partners. Giovanni appears to have bought some farmland near his home village of Cafaggiolo, prudently diversifying his assets beyond the vicissitudes of the financial world.

Besides being pre-eminent in banking, Florence was also an important centre of the wool-processing industry, with cloth-trading links as far afield as Flanders and England. The well-established merchant families often had interests in both businesses, and in 1402 the Medici Bank put up 3,000 florins to finance a cloth-producing workshop. Later in the year, the records show that the Medici Bank opened an office in Venice, with Neri Tornaquinci as manager, so that it could benefit from the Venetian trade with the Orient (whose actual practice was strictly monopolised by the Venetians, though outsiders were able to profit from the ancillary commerce that grew around this trade). By now the Rome office had expanded, opening sub-offices in Naples and the port of Gaeta eighty miles south-east of Rome. Yet apart from financing another wool workshop in 1408, this was to be the limit of the Medici Bank's expansion during the first twenty years: Giovanni di Bicci was a cautious man and preferred to consolidate. This was a trait he shared with his predecessor as head of the Medici clan, his distant relative Vieri, and he certainly passed it on to his son; as bankers, the Medici made their money through caution and efficiency, rather than innovation. Contrary to banking lore, they did not invent the bill of exchange, though they may have had a hand in the invention of the holding company; their success was based almost exclusively on the use of tried-and-trusted techniques pioneered by others. The Medici Bank never underwent rapid expansion, and even at its height was not as extensive as any of the three great Florentine banks of the previous century, those owned by the Bardi, Peruzzi and Acciaiuoli families – the Medici did not believe in overstretching themselves. As the bank's profits increased, Giovanni di Bicci displayed further evidence of his essentially conservative nature by continuing to buy up farmland in the Mugello and in the Tuscan hills around Florence; and as he became more prosperous still, properties within the city itself. Giovanni not only founded the Medici Bank, and the Medici banking code of practice, but also laid the solid foundations of the extensive family fortune that was to become its power base.

The head of the Medici Bank soon became a prominent figure in Florence, and as early as 1401 Giovanni di Bicci served on the committee of leading citizens that was to judge the winner of an international competition to create new bronze doors for the Baptistery. This was the first instance of a Medici being involved in artistic patronage, though in this case the actual patron was the city itself. What part Giovanni di Bicci played in choosing the winner is not known – the artist who received the commission for the bronze doors was Lorenzo Ghiberti, a young Florentine sculptor who was later to become one of the founders of Renaissance art, just as Giovanni di Bicci was to become the founder of the Medici patronage that did so much to engender this movement. Yet at this stage the twenty-three-year-old Ghiberti was merely talented, and the forty-two-year-old banker was merely interested in making money. It is no exaggeration to say that this occasion launched Ghiberti on the road to greatness, but at the same time it may well have opened Giovanni di Bicci's eyes to something greater than the accumulation of riches.

Fig 3 Portrait of Giovanni
di Bicci by Bronzino

At this distance, and on such scant evidence as we have, it is difficult
to discern the finer points of Giovanni di Bicci's character. The best physical likeness we have of him is probably the portrait by Bronzino in the
Medici Museum in Florence, which is a detailed and perceptive painting,
giving many possible clues to the nature of its subject. The trouble is that
Bronzino was born more than seventy years after Giovanni died, which
leaves a question as to this portrait's veracity on the physical level, let alone
the psychological one. However, although painted at the height of Medici
aggrandisement, it is not a flattering portrait; it also bears a more than
passing resemblance to other likenesses, while the cast of its features uncannily echoes that of his son Cosimo. This suggests that there could be some
truth in the unverified story that the painting was copied from an earlier,
contemporary portrait for which Giovanni di Bicci may well have sat.
Bronzino depicts a shrewd, perhaps wise man, whose features retain an
element of peasant earthiness and cunning. The tilt of his chin indicates
a certain pride, and the eyes have a clear unwavering stare, but the finely
lined forehead suggests a man who worried deeply and constantly, while

the wide but thin lips hint at the repressed sensuality of an ascetic, calculating temperament. In other words, much the kind of man one would
expect from the little we know of his actual life: even if this portrait is
not 'true', it certainly seems fitting.

In 1402 Giovanni di Bicci became prior of the Florentine Arte del
Cambio (the guild of bankers and money-changers) and held a seat on
the ruling Signoria. This sounds very grand, though in actuality Giovanni's
bank in Florence was a distinctly humble affair — apart from its profits,
that is. During this period, a bank usually consisted of a single largish
room, divided by the *banco* or counter that gave it its name, and behind
the counter sat the clerks, together with the bookkeeper and his abacus.
Most banks had fewer than half a dozen employees, though according to
the Medici *libro segreto*, in 1402 the bank employed seventeen in all — five
at the head office in Florence, with the remaining dozen divided between
Rome, Venice, Naples and Gaeta. Bank clerks earned around fifty florins
a year, which was enough to live modestly — when one considers that with
an annual income of 200 florins a year a man could support a large family
and live in a sizeable town house with two servants, a horse and a donkey.
Employees in the Medici Bank, and other Florentine banks, were not always
promoted on merit, but often on account of their connections — either
within the family or to important personages outside it. And to cement
trust, branch managers were usually made junior partners in their particular branch — though despite this, things could still go wrong, as happened
in the Venice office of the Medici Bank where Neri Tornaquinci was
manager. His partnership agreement explicitly forbade him from doing
business with the Germans, whose business methods were considered backward and devious by the Italians. Evidently Neri was made a tempting
offer and decided to risk a loan to some German traders, whereupon the
Germans decamped back home across the Brenner Pass without repaying.
Neri was left with a large discrepancy in his accounts, which of course
made no mention of his illicit German venture. In a panic lest head office
should find out, Neri borrowed money which more than covered the debt
— so that the books for the Venice office actually showed a healthy profit.
Unfortunately, this money was borrowed at ruinous rates, and no matter
how desperately he tried, Neri was unable to generate sufficient profit
from the daily running of the bank to cover the interest and also balance

the books. According to the records, on 25 April 1406 Neri Tornaquinci was summoned to Florence, where Giovanni di Bicci dismissed him, and sued him for the missing money. Neri was forced to sell everything, including his home, but this was not enough to cover the debt, so he gamely set off north across the Alps to try and track down the Germans. It seems that he finally caught up with them in Poland, at Cracow, where he managed to collect part of the debt; but by now he was so far from home that he decided against sending the money back to Giovanni, and chose to begin a new life on the proceeds. Such a tale vividly illustrates the circumstances of banking in the early fifteenth century: as ever in commercial practice, risk and trust were finely counter-balanced, even for someone as cautious as Giovanni di Bicci.

Yet despite all his caution, Giovanni was not above the odd lapse of judgement himself. The explicit ban on trading with Germans, which was written into house contracts, suggests that Giovanni too may have had his fingers burned by Teutonic commercial enterprise; and even his major business connections were sometimes far-from-trustworthy characters. This was certainly the case with Baldassare Cossa, whom Giovanni befriended during his spell at the Rome office. Baldassare was descended from impoverished Neapolitan nobility, and as a young man had run off to sea, where he made a fortune as a pirate. Back on land he used this money to obtain a doctorate in law at the University of Bologna; he then bought himself a position in the Church, where he soon began to prosper. In 1402 he decided to buy a cardinal's hat, and approached Giovanni di Bicci for a loan of 10,000 ducats (approximately 12,000 Florentine florins). Astonishingly, Giovanni obliged – and this decision becomes even more surprising when one considers Baldassare Cossa's character. According to a contemporary writer, during Baldassare's nine years as cardinal legate at Bologna, his spiritual qualities were 'zero, or minus zero', and the cardinal's residence quickly became notorious for its 'two hundred maids, wives and widows, with many nuns'.

So why did the cagey Giovanni become involved with an unscrupulous profligate like Baldassare? Let alone 'loan' him such a large sum? The answer was simple: Giovanni took a gamble on Baldassare Cossa because he knew that he was in the running for the papacy, and Giovanni had worked long enough in Rome to understand that being banker to the pope was the biggest financial prize of all. If the Medici Bank could handle the financial affairs of the Curia, it could establish itself as one of the major commercial institutions in Europe. For eight long years Giovanni di Bicci befriended Badassare Cossa and acted as his banker, regularly corresponding with him and doing his best to limit Baldassare's extravagances, which remained a constant drain on the Medici Bank's resources. Then in 1410 it all paid off: Baldassare Cossa was elected pontiff, becoming Pope John XXIII, and the Medici Bank took over the handling of the Curia's finances.

By the early fifteenth century, banking had become an essential arm of the papal executive. Unlike any other European power of this period, most of its revenues were earned abroad, coming largely in the form of remittances from the vast number of sees throughout Europe. These sees extended to the very limits of the Western world – as far as Iceland and even Greenland (whose bishop paid in sealskins and whalebones, which were converted into cash in Bruges). Another form of income was the selling of holy relics, which often fetched an enormous price, as they had the power to transform an entire economy, turning the region that possessed them into a centre of pilgrimage. Even more lucrative was the trade in indulgences, which offered the purchaser the pope's pardon for his sins, the price increasing dependent upon the magnitude of the sin involved. Another constant source of revenue was the selling of appointments to holy office, which involved offices from the lowest rank up to and including that of cardinal.

The sums involved in this continent-wide commercial enterprise were enormous – porportionately far larger than those accumulated by any present-day multinational – and the bank that handled them would of course receive its commission, which would amount to a huge annual income. Whichever bank was chosen to handle the papal business would need to have proven expertise: it would have to deal with monies gathered from sources throughout Europe, and would also have to be utterly trustworthy, answering in utmost confidence to the pope alone. By the time Baldassare was appointed Pope John XXIII, Giovanni di Bicci had done enough to convince him that he was utterly competent, utterly trustworthy and, above all, utterly loyal.

Apart from dealing with such revenues, the Rome office of the Medici Bank had now also attracted trade from the cardinals, prelates and sundry advisers who made it their business to attend the Court of Rome. Yet curiously, according to the Medici records, the Rome branch of the bank spent more of its time lending money than receiving it. High office in the Church may have been rewarded with a high income, but seemingly it often involved even higher expenditure: the Medici accounts reveal that the accounts of many cardinals were frequently overdrawn, and to a considerable sum. Despite these loans, the Court of Rome branch yielded no less than 30 per cent on investment for Giovanni di Bicci and his partners. Indeed, this branch was responsible for over half the profits of the entire bank. According to the *libro segreto* for 1397–1420, the Court of Rome branch provided 79,195 florins profit, out of a total 151,820 florins. This easily exceeded the combined efforts of the branches in Florence, Venice, Naples, Gaeta, miscellaneous agents and the two wool workshops. Such sums may seem small in comparison to modern financial statistics, but this represented an annual income for Giovanni di Bicci of almost 1,900 florins – when a gentleman could live comfortably for a year on 200 florins, and a skilled craftsman had to support his entire family on an annual income of less than 100 florins.

Giovanni di Bicci's financial future, and that of the Medici Bank, seemed assured. But appearances could be deceptive, not least in matters concerning the papacy. This was the era of the Great Schism, when at one point there were no fewer than three rival claimants to the papal throne: John XXIII, Gregory XII and Benedict XIII. Fortunately, most clerical authorities were of the opinion that Pope John XXIII was at least the leading contender, though unfortunately such learned opinions cut little ice with King Ladislas of Naples, who backed Gregory XII. King Ladislas launched a military campaign against the neighbouring Papal States, and John XXIII was eventually forced to sign a humiliating treaty that involved paying King Ladislas the equivalent of 95,000 florins. John XXIII found himself financially embarrassed, and approached the papal bankers for a loan to cover this sum. After some agonising, Giovanni di Bicci decided that this further outlay was probably worth the risk, if only for the sake of keeping his investment in place. The fact that he could even consider loaning such a sum – nearly 20 per cent more than the entire profits from the Rome branch in more than twenty years – gives an indication of the level of assets which the canny Giovanni had already accumulated, though he too would probably have raised at least part of this sum in the form of loans. The Medici Bank was now involved in the risks as well as the benefits of high finance. Giovanni arranged for it to pay John XXIII 95,000 florins, but took the precaution of asking for some security. This John XXIII provided in the form of an ancient jewel-encrusted mitre and various pieces of gold plate removed from the papal treasury.

Yet there still remained the problem of John XXIII's two rivals, Gregory XII and Benedict XIII. The powerful Holy Roman Emperor Sigismund, whose rule extended through the German-speaking lands from Austria to the North Sea, decided that it was time to deal with the Great Schism once and for all, and in 1414 he called the Council of Constance, summoning all three papal claimants to put their case before him. In order to keep a close watch on his investment, Giovanni di Bicci ordered his eldest son Cosimo to accompany John XXIII on his journey north across the Alps to the lakeside German city of Constance, which was at the time Sigismund's imperial capital. Cosimo was twenty-five, and was already showing considerable promise as a banker; as we shall see, the trip to Constance on behalf of the Medici Bank was an undertaking of exceptional responsibility, and it was a mark of Giovanni's absolute confidence in his son that he chose Cosimo for the job.

According to entries in the *libro segreto* for this period, the Medici Bank now had two Rome branches: the Rome branch itself and the Court of Rome branch. Many historians have taken this geographical location literally, citing the need for two branches in Rome as evidence of the sheer volume of business done by the Medici Bank in the Eternal City. In fact, only one of these branches remained in Rome; the other branch accompanied the papal court (that is, the 'Court of Rome') on its journey to Constance, in order to take care of the pope's immediate financial needs. Meanwhile the original branch remained in Rome to deal with the all-important matter of the papal incomes from abroad.

The Council of Constance would prove to be the greatest social and political event of the early fifteenth century, and would attract leading figures from all over Europe. Here the up-and-coming young Cosimo de' Medici would have had the opportunity to meet representatives of all the major international banks and business families, such as the rising Fuggers of Augsburg and merchants from as far afield as Poland and Spain. Indeed, personal contacts made at this event would cement far-flung commercial relationships for many decades to come, in some cases providing the opportunity of a lifetime to meet the leaders of commercial enterprises whose names from then on would be relied upon as guaranteeing the trustworthiness of the bills of exchange, credit notes and other commercial documents that formed the lifeblood of the emergent capitalist world of western Europe. Yet the main and stated aim of the Council remained nothing less than to resolve once and for all the spiritual rule of Christendom. Besides settling the Great Schism, Sigismund also intended to iron out certain doctrinal differences that had arisen within his Holy Roman Empire. To this end, the Bohemian heretic Jan Hus was summoned, under the emperor's personal guarantee of safe passage, to justify his dissenting religious views, which included his opposition to the sale of papal indulgences. In the event, Hus's teachings were found to be unacceptable on no fewer than thirty counts, and Sigismund had him burned at the stake, regardless of his personal guarantee. The Council then turned to examine the cases put forward by the three rival popes: John XXIII who had arrived from Rome, Benedict XIII who had arrived from his seat in Avignon, and Gregory XII whose peripatetic court roamed northern Italy. When it came to John XXIII's turn to give evidence, he was disconcerted to find himself subjected to an investigation of the papal lifestyle, including accusations of a list of personal misdemeanours. Apart from the stock accusation of heresy (which could prove serious, as in the case of Hus), he was also accused of poisoning his predecessor Pope Alexander V, and of no fewer than seventy further charges – though in the end sixteen 'of the most indescribable depravity were dropped, out of respect not for the pope, but for public decency'. This was evidently no euphemism, as indicated by the eighteenth-century historian Edward Gibbon: 'The most scandalous charges were suppressed; the Vicar of Christ was only accused of piracy, murder, rape, sodomy and incest.' Rather than face any further scrutiny of his personal habits, Pope John XXIII promised to resign – on condition that his rivals did too; he then fled the city, disguised as an archer. This latter move betrayed no loss of nerve on John XXIII's behalf; on the contrary, it was a calculated act to deprive the Council of its power, for according to the doctrine of the Church, an ecumenical council was invalid without the pope in residence. But Sigismund was in no mood for such niceties, and ordered the Council to continue with its proceedings regardless; at the same time, he despatched his soldiers to apprehend John XXIII, who was taken prisoner and incarcerated in Heidelberg Castle.

Cosimo de' Medici was thus left high and dry in Constance. He quickly recognised the possible peril of his position, and set about making his own escape from the city; in so doing, not only did he evade any possible pursuers sent by the emperor, but he also managed to keep possession of a jewel-encrusted mitre that John XXIII had given him for safe-keeping prior to his own flight. Whether this was the same mitre that John XXIII had pledged against the 95,000 florins loaned to pay off the King of Naples is unclear; if it was, John XXIII must at some stage have redeemed it and paid back this loan. No transactions involving a jewel-encrusted mitre belonging to the papacy appear in the Medici Bank's *libro segreto* for this period: such transactions were probably too secret, even for the *libro segreto*.

The Emperor Sigismund now declared that Pope John XXIII was deposed. Back in Constance, the other popes were encouraged to drop their claims: Gregory XII was forced to abdicate, Benedict XIII was eventually deposed, and the Great Schism was finally healed by the election in 1417 of an entirely new pope, Martin V. The Emperor Sigismund announced that the former Pope John XXIII, now plain Baldassare Cossa, was being held for a ransom of 38,500 Rhenish guilders (the equivalent of 35,000 florins). Despite being incarcerated, ill and destitute, Baldassare managed to smuggle word to Cosimo that he was prepared to make him his heir, if he would raise the 35,000-florin ransom. Was there any point in throwing good money after bad? Cosimo decided there was: he went to Giovanni and tried to persuade him to pay up on John XXIII's behalf. Once again the sum involved was vast, this time equivalent to almost half the profits made by the entire Medici Bank during the twenty years since its foundation – though this time the risk was far greater: the future appeared bleak for Baldassare, who had no assets and little prospect of any future income. Yet still Giovanni di Bicci was willing to take the risk: Baldassare Cossa's ransom was paid in full to the Emperor Sigismund, and the disgraced former pope was set free.

Why should the normally careful Giovanni di Bicci once again have gambled so much on this now-worthless figure? Contrary to appearances, this was not an uncharacteristically risky move – there was no risk involved, for there was not even a prospect of getting the money back. Nor was the move inspired by personal loyalty, as far as it is possible to tell; despite Baldassare's habit of addressing Giovanni in his letters as 'My very dear friend', the arrangement between the two appears to have been one of purely commercial loyalty. Yet, as we shall see, this was one of the most astute moves Giovanni di Bicci made in his entire life (a period that included many moves in this category). And it is no accident that he was prompted to it by his son Cosimo, who was proving every bit as astute as his father.

3

Giovanni's Legacy

IN 1418, AFTER three years in his grim Heidelberg prison-quarters, Baldassare Cossa was released and made his way to Florence, where he was immediately offered hospitality by Giovanni di Bicci. At a stroke, the social standing of the Medici family was transformed; even if Baldassare was now merely a deposed former pope, Giovanni was nonetheless welcoming into his house a man who had once been the spiritual ruler of all Christendom. Likewise, the prestige of the Medici Bank rose throughout Europe: this enterprise was evidently as solid as a rock, if its senior partner could afford to indulge 35,000 florins on a mere business friend, with no prospect of recompense.

Yet Giovanni's shrewdness was also prompted by necessity. In acting as he did, he demonstrated the deep and unfailing loyalty of the Medici; had he not done so, the untrustworthiness of the Medici would have been broadcast throughout Europe by rival bankers, considerably lessening international trust in the Medici Bank. In the uncertain world of late medieval banking, such acts of betrayal were not forgotten for generations. But Giovanni's decision to stand by Baldassare was more than just a matter of far-sighted calculation, designed to influence future events – it was also very much calculated to influence the present. Once again, Giovanni was scheming for the big prize: he wanted to be banker to the new pope, Martin V, who happened to be living in Florence at the time, as Rome had been seized by Queen Joanna of Naples. Giovanni had quickly seen a way to make good use of this situation. Before paying Baldassare's ransom, Giovanni had informed him that this service was being rendered on one condition – that the former pope would come to Florence for a public reconciliation with Pope Martin V. The reconciliation duly took place, and Martin V was delighted at the prospect of his papacy remaining the first undisputed reign since 1378. He gave expression to his pleasure by appointing the ill and ageing Baldassare as Cardinal-Bishop of Tusculum (Frascati). In appreciation of Giovanni di Bicci's part in this reconciliation, the pope created him Count of Monteverde, a title that Giovanni politely declined to use, on the grounds that he wished to remain an ordinary citizen. However, no more concrete expression of Martin V's friendship was forthcoming; he remained wary of Giovanni, and there was also the matter of the priceless jewel-encrusted mitre that John XXIII had given away before fleeing Constance, which the pope was claiming as papal property. For the time being, the pope was unwilling to appoint Giovanni di Bicci as the papal banker, and thus the situation remained for the next two years.

In September 1420 Pope Martin V left Florence to take up residence in Rome, watched by a disappointed Giovanni – the pope had chosen the aristocratic Florentine family, the Spini, as his bankers. Although Giovanni was related to the Spini through his mother, this socially superior family remained old rivals of the Medici.

Baldassare had died the previous year. For once, he had remained as good as his word: the Medici were named executors of his will, and benefited considerably from this document. Though Baldassare had arrived back from his spell in Heidelberg Castle apparently penniless, he evidently still had a few savings salted away. Giovanni di Bicci inherited Baldassare's favourite holy relic: a finger of John the Baptist, which he had carried with him at all times, in the superstitious hope of warding off bad luck. As executors of Baldassare's will, the Medici were also responsible for building the ex-pope's tomb in the Baptistery in Florence, and for this Giovanni hired the sculptor Donatello and the architect Michelozzo, who produced one of the earliest tombs in the new Renaissance style. Inscribed on the tomb, as requested in Baldassare's will, were the words 'Ioannes Quondam Papa XXIII' ('John XXIII formerly pope'). When word of this reached Rome, Martin V was furious; he regarded John XXIII as having been only an anti-pope, and Giovanni was held responsible for this slight on the papacy. Not all of Giovanni di Bicci's decisions were faultless.

By this time the political situation in Florence had changed. The head of the ruling oligarchy, Maso degli Albizzi, had finally succumbed, at eighty-four, to the wave of plague that passed through the city in 1417. The most influential member of the oligarchy now became Niccolò da Uzzano, a reputable and aristocratic Florentine grandee, who had in fact combined with Giovanni di Bicci in persuading the reluctant Baldassare to affect a reconciliation with Pope Martin V. After this, Giovanni had done his best to cultivate his relationship with the powerful Niccolò, but despite responding to these overtures, Niccolò retained a deep suspicion of the Medici. The citizens of Florence were becoming restless under the ruling families, and the Medici family still retained their reputation as covert sympathisers with the *popolo minuto*, who were now referred to dismissively amongst the oligarchy as the *piagnoni* – literally 'whiners' or 'snivellers'. This was another term that contained its element of brutal social truth, for the uncouth lower orders were constantly snivelling rather than blowing their noses; in winter, their restricted diet and inadequate clothing meant they were perpetually suffering from colds and lung-racking coughs: the short people also had short lives.

In 1421 there was a move to elect Giovanni di Bicci as *gonfaloniere* – to which Niccolò da Uzzano immediately objected, citing Salvestro de' Medici's treacherous behaviour when he had been *gonfaloniere* during the *ciompi* revolt – which had taken place only forty-three years previously. In Niccolò's view, Giovanni di Bicci posed an even greater threat, for he was much more clever and persistent; he had been biding his time for years, gradually increasing his riches and his power base, quietly cultivating his popularity amongst the *popolo minuto* with gifts and largesse. Yet at the same time he had done his best to disguise his vast wealth by putting on the appearance of a modest unassuming lifestyle, in the same way as he had disguised his political ambitions by pretending that he was only interested in making money, whilst at the same time using his wealth to build up a network of Medici supporters that might one day be turned to political use. In the view of Niccolò da Uzzano, Giovanni had no intention of honouring the republican traditions of Florence, and if elected would use his power only for his own ends and those of his family. This was ironic, coming from such a source, as many Florentines recognised all too well; but in fact Niccolò was not altogether wrong. Despite these objections, however, Giovanni di Bicci was elected *gonfaloniere* in 1421. Though he did not gain permanent control of the city, this event can be taken as the first manifestation of the new Medici political influence, which was to end in them gaining complete control of the city for more than three centuries.

Three years later Giovanni di Bicci achieved another one of his goals, when the Spini family went bankrupt, leaving Pope Martin V without a banker. Giovanni quickly stepped in to fill the breach, and once again the Medici Bank had its licence to coin money. The *libro segreto* for this period contains some fascinating entries: the balance sheet of the Rome branch includes a long list of personal deposits *'a discrezione'* (that is, secret accounts paying interest, which was contrary to the Church's ban on usury). Individual deposits here ranged from 2,600 up to 15,000 florins, and depositors included no fewer than two cardinals, several prelates, the pope's closest confidant and the apostolic treasurer.

The year of 1420 had seen the death of Giovanni di Bicci's partner Benedetto de' Bardi, which had provided Giovanni with an opportunity to reorganise the bank's affairs. One of the woolshop partnerships was discontinued, and the Florence branch gained a new manager: Folco d'Adoardo Portinari (a descendant of Dante's Beatrice). Giovanni was now sixty, and decided to hand over the business to his sons Cosimo and Lorenzo; the bank's new capital was declared as 24,000 florins, with 16,000 florins being provided by the two Medici, and a further 8,000 florins by a member of the Bardi family. Giovanni continued his connection with the bank, though only behind the scenes – counselling, suggesting, warning. He now lived in a central but unpretentious house on the piazza in the shadow of the cathedral; this was just a 300-yard walk down what is now the Via Roma, to the Medici Bank's headquarters on the Via Porta Rossa. Most days he could still be seen taking this walk, usually accompanied only by his personal servant – unlike members of the leading families in the city, who seldom ventured out in public without their retinue, both for protection and as a mark of status. Giovanni di Bicci continued to maintain a modest lifestyle – partly through temperament and partly for political reasons. Only in the hot months of the summer would he spend any length of time at his country house in Cafaggiolo. He was never away from the city for long: besides his increasing behind-the-scenes political power, Giovanni had now begun to devote much of his time and money to patronage. In 1419 he had become involved in his first major project: he had been in charge of the public committee that commissioned the building of the Ospedale degli Innocenti, the city's foundling home. Two years later, in company with seven other neighbourhood families, Giovanni commissioned the rebuilding of the church of San Lorenzo, which had originally been consecrated by St Anselm in 393 and was already in a bad state of disrepair when it was damaged by fire in 1417. These ventures into patronage were to be part of the Medici bid for a social status to match their growing political influence, and they were selected with typical astuteness. The Ospedale degli Innocenti was particularly favoured by the *popolo minuto*, many of whom had been brought up here; the church of San Lorenzo was where all the Medici clan traditionally worshipped, its name being given to many of their sons: in building such places, they were also building their reputation.

The man commissioned to build the Ospedale degli Innocenti and redesign San Lorenzo was Brunelleschi, then the most prominent architect in Florence. Brunelleschi was an irritable, abrasive character whose hobby was writing vituperative sonnets to his enemies; but this secretive, ambitious man was also one of the pioneers of the Renaissance. It was he who rediscovered the rules of perspective, which had been lost since classical times, and his design for the portico of the Ospedale degli Innocenti is generally regarded as the first piece of Renaissance architecture. Its line is clean and classical, reflecting the architectural style of Ancient Rome; and its thin graceful columns were not simply decorative, but were used for structural support, a method that had not been tried since Roman times. The building of the Ospedale degli Innocenti and the rebuilding of San Lorenzo were major undertakings, which were to take Brunelleschi more than a decade, during which the canny patron and his difficult architect struck up an unlikely friendship.

But Giovanni soon had more pressing matters on his mind. Italian politics remained as turbulent as ever, with constant friction between Florence and its powerful expansionist neighbour Milan. In 1422, Filippo Maria Visconti, the Duke of Milan, signed a peace treaty with Florence, so that Milan could attack its western neighbour Genoa without interference; yet despite this treaty, Milan occupied Forlí, a small town in the Romagna that was nominally under the protection of Florence. The Florentine noble families — such as the Albizzi and Uzzano — were all for going to war, but the people, supported by the Medici, were in favour of moderation: the ordinary citizens were sick of paying taxes for such military adventures, which usually ended in disaster. Despite this popular feeling, the ruling Signoria was induced to vote for war, whereupon Giovanni di Bicci patriotically accepted the decision and assisted in the military preparations; the Medici may have been popular, but they did not yet control the city and its organs of government.

Just as Giovanni had feared, the war went badly, with Milan making increasing territorial gains during the first three years. However, although the distance between Milan and Florence is only 160 miles, these gains were not sufficient to end the war; such wars were largely fought by mercenaries, who favoured the minimum loss of life in their encounters with their fellow tradesmen, and were inclined to prolong any war for as long as their paymasters could afford it. After three years Venice entered the war on the side of Florence, thus heavily tilting the balance the other way. The mercenary combatants kept up a semblance of conflict for the next two years, until eventually Visconti of Milan was forced to sign a humiliating peace treaty in 1427.

Florence was now faced with the prospect of raising sufficient taxes to pay for this ruinously expensive war. According to Machiavelli: 'In this war the Florentines expended three millions and a half of ducats' – the equivalent of a staggering 4,200,000 florins. Previously the city had raised a large portion of its revenue from taxes by the *estimo* system, which was mainly used by those in power to inflict swingeing financial damage on their adversaries. What was estimated in the *estimo* was income, which meant that the landowners paid little; those with a large income did their best to conceal its full extent, and those with too small an income to conceal bore a disproportionately large burden. This had long been a cause of grievance among those who did not benefit from it – that is, the majority of the population.

It was soon realised there would be difficulty in collecting sufficient taxes to pay for the war. The only answer was to change the tax system, and a new method of taxation was now instituted: the *catasto* (or register of property), which was to be based on a citizen's entire wealth, rather than merely on his income. This wealth would be declared in a public register, which would list all possessions, as well as income from these possessions and from any other source; the register would be drawn up by inspectors, who could make use of suitably rewarded informers to ensure that the register bore some relation to reality. The *catasto* thus shifted the emphasis to taxing land and ostentatious riches, rather than more easily concealable income.

The *catasto* was highly popular with the people, though not with all their sympathisers. Unsurprisingly, the ever-cautious sixty-seven-year-old Giovanni di Bicci initially had reservations about the *catasto*, but when he saw which way the wind was blowing he soon appeared as one of its most enthusiastic backers. Eventually Rinaldo degli Albizzi, the leader of the oligarchy faction, was forced by public pressure to carry the new tax through, though he got little credit for this. By now Giovanni di Bicci had manoeuvred himself into a position where it was he who took much of the public credit for selflessly lending his support to this innovation.

Yet Giovanni's actions were not all machinations aimed at advancing the Medici cause; he also had a compassionate side. When word reached him, through the ever-extending tentacles of the international bankers' grapevine, that his disgraced Venetian manager Neri Tornaquinci was now reduced to living in abject poverty in Cracow, Giovanni at once ordered a remittance of thirty-six florins to be despatched to his former employee. Such small acts of kindness were common, and were invariably discreet; as well as aspiring to nobility, the Medici were also taking on some of its qualities and reponsibilities.

In 1428 Giovanni di Bicci fell ill; he was now sixty-eight, and he knew he was dying. He summoned his two sons Cosimo and Lorenzo to his bedside, and he is traditionally said to have given them the following advice: 'Never hang around the Palazzo della Signoria, as if it is the place where you do business. Only go there when you are summoned, and only accept the offices which are bestowed upon you. Never make a show before the people, but if this is unavoidable, let it be the least necessary. Keep out of the public gaze, and never go against the will of the people – unless they are advocating some disastrous project . . .' It is unlikely that Giovanni used these exact words at the time, but these were the ones that would pass into Medici legend. For many years the family would adhere to this advice; and if it did not, it would still be how they felt they were living – or at least how they felt they ought to be living. Giovanni had created a strong, formative self-image for the Medici; in keeping with this, his final request to his sons was that he should be buried quietly, with no ostentatious funeral.

Cosimo might even have obeyed this, but popular feeling demanded otherwise. The old man had brought great honour to Florence, and it was felt that he had used his influence for the benefit of the people, so they called for him to be buried with full honour. As astute as his father, Cosimo decided that perhaps after all it was time to make a public display, though its message would be suitably oblique: Giovanni di Bicci's public funeral would not be a blatant demonstration of Medici power, but a show of affectionate respect for an illustrious citizen who had died. Yet in the event, things soon took on their own momentum, with everyone wishing to be part of this celebration of the greater glory of Florence.

First an ancient tradition had to be observed, one that was said to date back as far as Etruscan times, before even the coming of the Roman Republic nearly 2,000 years previously. When the head of the family died, a hole was knocked through the wall of his home, and his body was then carried through this hole before being placed in its coffin at the head of the funeral procession. Giovanni di Bicci's body was placed in an open coffin, which was followed through the streets by two dozen members of the Medici family; behind them, in order of precedence, came all the foreign ambassadors residing in the city, followed by the *gonfaloniere* and the members of his Signoria, followed in turn by representatives of the guilds, and so it went on. Cosimo may have intended the message to be oblique, but to all who watched the long procession winding its way through the streets to the church of San Lorenzo, it was loud and clear: the Medici had arrived.

4

Cosimo Rising

COSIMO DI GIOVANNI de' Medici (that is, the son of Giovanni) was born in 1389. Little is known of his early life, apart from the fact that he was close to his younger brother Lorenzo; together they were educated at the monastery school of Santa Maria degli Angeli. Even at this early date, the school was known as a cradle of the new learning, which involved a revival of interest in the classical learning of Ancient Greece and Rome.

During the Dark Ages, much of this ancient learning had simply vanished from Europe; it was preserved only in the Middle East, where it would be enthusiastically taken up by Arabic scholars. In its early years, Islam encouraged philosophical and scientific speculation: to know how the world worked was to know the mind of God. In this way the works of Ancient Greek philosophers, especially the natural philosophers (that is, early scientists), spread throughout the Arabic Empire, which by the eighth century even extended far into Europe – occupying the whole of the Iberian peninsula, reaching into southern France and Italy. When in the thirteenth century great Arabic centres of learning, such as Cordoba and Seville in southern Spain, were retaken by Christian forces, many previously unknown works of the ancient philosophers were rediscovered by Christian scholars.

As a result, an entirely new attitude to learning was beginning to spread through Europe. This advocated a return to the study of the classical authors of Ancient Greece and Rome, at the expense of the scholasticism and comparative intellectual stasis of the medieval era. Rather than simply accepting the authority of Christian theology and an ossified version of Aristotle's philosophy, some contemporary scholars had begun to embrace a more questioning element in the Greek philosophers and Roman writers. As early as the thirteenth century translations of Arabic interpretations of Aristotle by such Muslim philosophers as Averroes and Avicenna had cast doubt on the accepted Christian version of Aristotle. Now previously unknown works by Aristotle himself began to appear, some of which developed his ideas in new directions; ironically the unimpeachable authority of Aristotle was being undermined by his own works. But the rediscovered works of the ancients for the most part included many other Ancient Greek and Roman authors – philosophers, poets, rhetoricians and historians – and these caused some to understand that there had once been an age that far outshone their own, one that emphasised the humanity of humankind, rather than its spirituality. As a result, there was now a new humanism in the air, which began to emphasise freedom of thought, rather than the selfless submission demanded by medieval philosopher-theologians. This humanism encouraged the exploration of human potential, and the expression of humanity, especially in literature, philosophy and all forms of art.

It had only been in his later years that Giovanni di Bicci had begun to understand that there was more to life than banking and its attendant risks. Money could be turned into the permanence of art by patronage, and in the exercise of this patronage one gained access to another world of timeless values, which appeared free from the corruption of the religious authorities, or the devious politics of power and banking. Cosimo, on the other hand, would be aware of this other world from his earliest years; his education made him a humanist, yet he also retained his father's astute character, and Giovanni made sure that this was thoroughly applied to the skills of banking. Cosimo must have shown exceptional promise to be entrusted by his cautious father with the task of looking after Pope John XXIII at the Council of Constance; this was no mean task for a twenty-five-year-old.

During his stay in Constance, Cosimo would have been able to make many useful contacts amongst the other international banking families who were present. However, his most important task had inevitably been to keep an eye on Pope John XXIII. Despite this, he seems to have been caught unawares by the pope's secret flight in disguise, his capture and

consequent incarceration in Heidelberg Castle. It is known that Cosimo
too fled Constance, probably in disguise, and somehow managed to take
with him such valuable assets as the disputed jewel-encrusted mitre.

At this point, the records vary. According to one version, Cosimo
returned straight away to Florence, a story that is supported by the fact
that he served briefly as a member of the nine-man Signoria in 1415 and
again in 1417. Yet according to a contemporary memoir, after fleeing from
Constance, Cosimo embarked upon a journey through northern Europe,
which lasted several years. At the time, the Medici had only a few correspondents in major financial centres such as Geneva, Lyons and Avignon;
they had not yet opened full branches of their bank outside Italy. It seems
very likely that Giovanni would have sent Cosimo on a tour of these
centres, to check up on the Medici correspondents and seek out the
prospects for further business. It would also seem likely that Cosimo visited
Bruges, in Flanders. According to Raymond de Roover, the great expert
on the Medici Bank, a correspondent was established in Bruges around
1416, followed shortly afterwards by one in London. Bruges was very much
the linchpin in northern-European finance; as a centre of the wool trade,
it had links reaching right across Europe from England to Italy. It also
had connections to the east with the Hanseatic League, whose city ports
monopolised trade in the Baltic and north Germany. It was in Bruges
during this period that bills of exchange would be traded in the little
square opposite an inn owned by the Van der Beurse family, giving rise to
the word 'bourse'. On his travels, Cosimo is also said to have begun buying
rare manuscripts, the first in what would one day become a priceless collection. Judging from the meticulous instructions he issued to his European
correspondents in later years concerning the purchase of manuscripts for
his collection, he certainly knew the ways of this far-flung market. The
most likely answer to these apparently conflicting accounts is that Cosimo
at first returned to Florence, and then took more than one shorter trip
to northern Europe.

Cosimo was certainly in Florence during early 1416, for it was then
that he married the niece of his father's partner, a young woman known
as Contessina de' Bardi. (Curiously, *contessina* seems to have been both the
name everyone called her and her title: meaning 'little countess' or 'daughter of the countess'.) In the usual custom of the period, Cosimo's marriage

was arranged by his father Giovanni, and it marks a distinct step up the social ladder for the Medici. The Bardi were one of the old banking families who had been ruined in the Florentine banking collapse of the 1340s; they had retained an element of their former social standing, but now had comparatively little money. Contessina de' Bardi brought as her dowry the old and slightly run-down family home, the Palazzo Bardi, which stood on the south bank of the River Arno. Immediately after his marriage, the twenty-seven-year-old Cosimo began refurbishing the palazzo, demonstratively decorating its outside with the Medici insignia: the shield and *palle*, or balls. Even at this early stage this simple insignia, which was to become so emblematic of Medici ambition and power, had developed variations. Originally the shield had contained anything up to a dozen *palle*. By the time Cosimo began using it on the Palazzo Bardi, the shield generally contained six balls. But this was only the usual figure, and the number would never be strictly formalised; shields containing five or even eight *palle* would continue to appear through the centuries.

Contessina would give birth to Cosimo's son and heir Piero within two years, though by then Cosimo was almost certainly away on his travels. A year or so later his father Giovanni would appoint him to the important post of permanent manager at the Medici Bank's branch in Rome; although the Medici had lost the papal account to the Spini family at this point, the Rome branch remained the major source of profit for the Medici enterprises. Precise annual accounts cannot be gleaned from the *libro segreto*, but it seems likely that several powerful cardinals retained secret deposit accounts *a discrezione*, and that this branch still contributed well over 50 per cent of the entire bank's profits.

What is certain is that during Cosimo's three years in Rome one of the bank's agents brought him a young Caucasian slave girl whom he had purchased in Venice, where she had been adjudged 'a sound virgin, free from disease and aged about twenty-one'. The girl was employed as Cosimo's household servant, and he called her Maddalena. Slavery was not uncommon amongst wealthy Italians after the Black Death, when servants became more difficult to obtain; in fifteenth-century Florence there would have been on average around 100 slaves distributed amongst the houses of the leading families, and other major Italian cities would have had similar numbers. These slaves were imported from the Levant and the Black

Sea region by Genoese and Venetian traders; Caucasian and Slavonic slaves were preferred to Turkic or Tartar ones because they worked harder, assimilated better and were generally considered 'less barbaric'. Most of these slaves were young and female, and were employed as household servants. As was customary with servants of the time in Italy, they usually shared the family dinner table and were looked upon as minor members of the family, with whom they often remained for life. Inevitably there were cases of maltreatment, but these appear to have been the exception; less unusual was the occurrence of slave-girl pregnancy. This was mostly attributed to the master of the house, and when it was not, there could be serious trouble – either for a young son or a hapless groom.

By all accounts, Cosimo de' Medici was not a promiscuous man, yet he certainly formed an attachment to his slave girl in Rome, who bore him a son called Carlo. This offspring would later be brought up with his two sons in Florence, an arrangement that was not regarded as exceptional at the time. Like many other such offspring, Carlo would be destined for the priesthood, and would not be employed in the family business. Although illegitimate children were taken into the family, at this time they never fully became members of it; the delineations were subtle, but very definite. Indicative of this was the choice of Carlo as the name for Cosimo's illegitimate offspring. The Medici were particularly restrictive concerning first names: Averardos, Lorenzos, Cosimos and Giovannis recur again and again through the generations in the family tree, but Carlo was not one of these names. The slave girl Maddalena appears to have been brought back to Florence, and judging from Cosimo's *catasto* returns was still working for (or being looked after by) the family as late as 1457, when she would have been over forty years old, a considerable age for a working woman of this period.

What Contessina made of all this is not recorded, though she would in all likelihood have simply tolerated Cosimo's behaviour as being typical of an Italian male of the period. Contessina is said to have been a plump, rather jolly lady who enjoyed her food and her growing young family (she would have a second son in 1421, called Giovanni). Previous commentators have tended to regard her as simply a housewife, a good mother to her children, who took little interest in her husband's business or the family's increasing political influence. Cosimo is said to have written to her seldom, and she is reputed to have borne his absences with equanimity. Admittedly, few of Contessina's letters survive, yet those that do paint a rather different picture. At one point she writes to Cosimo: 'This evening I have a letter from thee and have understood how much we are to pay for the barrels at Careggi . . . I have a letter from Antonio Martelli saying that he is sending nine bales of our linen cloth . . . give orders that they be put in a dry place.' This, and the few other letters, indicate that Contessina was deeply involved in running the ever-expanding Medici country estates, as well as the haberdashery side of the business, which maintained a healthy profit despite fluctuations in trade. Surviving letters to other family members reveal her close concern for Cosimo during his absences: 'They tell me he is putting on a bit of weight, which is a good sign.'

Cosimo's behaviour at this time is suggestive of a close supportive family; he may have inherited his father's canniness, but Giovanni's tendency to dry calculation and narrow-mindedness was softened in Cosimo's case. His intellect was broadened by his humanist education, but his emotional sympathies seem to have been broadened by his wife, who would maintain a close and very human presence in his life, even when she was not actually at his side. Contessina's taste almost certainly influenced Cosimo, its femininity helping to vivify and add colour to his more intellectual humanist side. In this way she would play a role in forming the taste of the man whose artistic discernment was to help transform an entire era – no small part to have played in the scheme of things.

In 1420, when Giovanni di Bicci retired, he handed over the running of the bank to his two sons, leaving Cosimo nominally in charge. The thirty-one-year-old Cosimo may only gradually have emerged from his father's shadow, but his mark on the bank's affairs was soon apparent; it was almost certainly influential figures cultivated by Cosimo in Rome who persuaded Martin V to reinstate the Medici as papal bankers when the Spini family went bankrupt. Cosimo now headed the major financial business in Florence, and eight years later, when Giovanni di Bicci died, would take over as head of the family and leader of its influential faction in Florentine politics. According to Machiavelli: 'Those who rejoiced at Giovanni's death, now regretted it, perceiving what manner of man Cosimo was.' His political skill quickly became evident. His brother Lorenzo was delegated to look after the everyday business of the bank, though Cosimo would continue to take all the important decisions. Meanwhile his loyal but ambitious cousin Averardo de' Medici would provide the political impetus and organisation backing the Medici cause. Cosimo had realised that there was no holding back now. There were strong forces aligned against the Medici, yet the family still had no real political power; either they must gain that power, or they were liable to be destroyed by their many enemies amongst the ruling oligarchy.

In 1430 Cosimo decided that the Medici should have a genuine palazzo of their own, rather than the inherited Bardi residence. He selected a site on the corner of the Via Larga, the main road leading north out of the city centre (now the Via Cavour), and then hired Brunelleschi, his father's chosen architect and now regarded as the leading architect of the time, to draw up a plan for the projected Palazzo Medici. Brunelleschi set to work, eventually producing a sumptuous and ambitious plan, which was widely regarded as a masterpiece. But Cosimo was strangely hesitant: having leaked details of this plan to test public opinion, he decided against Brunelleschi's design – as he had perhaps intended all along. Brunelleschi's plan was too ostentatious, he declared; a more modest design would be closer in accord with Medici taste. In the end he chose a design by an up-and-coming young architect called Michelozzo, whose drawings featured a more austere façade.

Yet inside, out of public view, it would be a very different matter. Cosimo commissioned the sculptor Donatello to produce a bronze statue of the biblical David, which would stand in the *cortile*, the inner courtyard – intended to impress all who had been favoured with an invitation to enter the Palazzo Medici. In commissioning the figure of David, Cosimo made a characteristically shrewd choice: the young David who slew the giant Goliath was widely recognised by Florentines as an emblem of their city – for them, David represented the triumph of justice over tyranny, an embodiment of the city's much-vaunted republican values. Here was an implicit declaration by Cosimo that, as ever, the Medici were on the side of the *popolo minuto*, that they had the interests of the people at heart. The choice of subject was also an implicit warning to the increasingly powerful oligarchy: this was how the Medici saw themselves, as upholders of a just republic against any who would seek to tyrannise it.

The sculptor Donatello had been born in Florence some forty-four years previously, making him slightly older than Cosimo, with whom he would become increasingly close over the years. His father had been a wool-comber who had taken part in the *ciompi* revolt. Donatello's wide-ranging study of ancient sculpture led him to absorb many of the humanist artistic ideals, although he was not in fact a humanist intellectual; he lived an untypically simple life for a well-known Florentine artist, with few possessions other than the tools of his trade. It may well have been Donatello, along with Cosimo's humanist friends, who persuaded his patron to start collecting antiques, many of which he restored for Cosimo. Around this time Cosimo commissioned Donatello to produce a bronze head of Contessina – further evidence of the regard in which he held his wife, and suggestive of her influence on his taste. Donatello's early sculptures were famed for their artistic realism, but as he entered middle age this realism began to take on an inner resonance that surpassed mere verisimilitude. The greatest example of this would be the *David* that he produced for the *cortile* of the Palazzo Medici, which would break fresh ground in a number of ways.

For a start, this was the first life-sized free-standing bronze statue to be created since the classical era – though here was an ancient technique remastered as never before. Transcending classical perfection, Donatello's *David* exhibited a very modern expressiveness: the outer form was inhabited by an unmistakably new inner humanity, while the dapper naked figure in his hat and tresses struck a highly unmilitary pose, left hand on hip, with his right hand resting on his large sword (see Figure 6, page 109) Donatello's *David* revelled in its naked male beauty, expressing an unambiguous subjective truth concerning its creator – namely, his homosexuality. But this was so much more than an expression of a forbidden sexuality, and the fact that Cosimo accepted this statue speaks volumes for his taste and understanding (as well as that of his family). The new humanism would break the mould of conventional medieval religiosity and sexual repression; it would see beauty as very much a human attribute, not merely the reflection of a sublimated spirituality. Despite this, one of the intellectual centres of this new humanism in Florence remained the monastery of Santa Maria degli Angeli, the home of Cosimo's old school. Here he would meet up with such figures as the monk Ambrogio Traversari, a brilliant scholar who accepted many commissions from Cosimo to translate his rare Greek, Latin and Hebrew manuscripts. Other intellectual figures combined professional lives with the pursuit of literature, such as the poet and civil servant Niccolò Tinucci, who was as renowned for his political acuity as for his verse (and kept Cosimo well supplied with inside information on government policy). The circle of scholars and humanists that Medici patronage was beginning to attract now extended beyond fine art into the realm of ideas.

Yet such progressive ideas inevitably provoked a conservative backlash, for not all were in favour of the new humanism. Rinaldo degli Albizzi, the arrogant leader of the old oligarchy families, despised this contemporary trend, regarding it as subversive as well as irreligious, despite its attraction to many priests and prelates. The old families were growing increasingly frustrated at the amounts they were having to pay under the new *catasto* tax system, for which Cosimo's father was held responsible, and they decided to make the *catasto* as unpopular as possible. To this end, they insisted that it should be applied not just in Florence, but should be extended to the other Tuscan towns under Florentine rule, towns that were normally left to settle their own tax affairs, as long as they supplied the required revenue to the Florentine exchequer. When the Florentine authorities decreed that from now on all towns would be subjected to the *catasto*, this caused huge resentment, to such an extent that there was even a rebellion in Volterra that had to be put down by the militia.

The old oligarchy families had been largely responsible for the war against Milan, which had dragged on so disastrously and been responsible for the introduction of the *catasto*. Despite this, they now saw a chance to redeem themselves. The independent city of Lucca, some forty miles to the west, had treacherously sided with Milan in the war, thus threatening Florence's link to the sea at Pisa. Rinaldo degli Albizzi and the ruling families now began to foment popular feeling for a war against Lucca, and the people were soon convinced – if a victorious Florence gained the spoils of war, there would be fewer taxes to pay.

The Medici had been outmanoeuvred. Cosimo had deep misgivings about the war – this was the last thing Florence needed. Yet when he was called upon to join the Committee of Ten, the council set up to oversee the conduct of the war, Cosimo felt that it was his patriotic duty to suppress his own mixed feelings and serve on the Committee, thus publicly demonstrating his support for the war. His more impetuous cousin Averardo de' Medici had fewer reservations, and took command of the troops in Pisa. The Medici had been manoeuvred into a position where they were fully committed to the war, alongside the ruling oligarchy.

In 1430 the Florentine army, under the command of Rinaldo degli Albizzi, began marching towards Lucca, which immediately appealed to Milan for help. Cosimo's initial misgivings about the wisdom of launching into a war against Lucca were confirmed when the ruler of Milan despatched his finest young *condottiere* (mercenary commander), Francesco Sforza, with his hired troops to defend Lucca. The Florentine troops encamped outside Lucca were soon forced to beat a tactical retreat in the face of Sforza's battle-hardened mercenaries, whereupon Sforza marched into the city, and for good measure deposed the ruling tyrant, setting up a republican government. Florence, which prided itself on being the great defender of republicanism, now had even less excuse for attacking Lucca: the Committee of Ten was in disarray, and the ruling Signoria dithered – the conduct of the war by committee was proving hopelessly ineffective. In the end the Florentines decided that their best course of action was to bribe Sforza with 50,000 florins to leave Lucca. In true mercenary fashion, Sforza's army duly accepted its extra pay – and left its previous, less generous Milanese paymasters to sort out their problems on their own. The financially prudent Cosimo was appalled and wrote that this was 'a needless expense, Sforza would have left Lucca in any case, because there had been an outbreak of plague amongst his soldiers, and he was running out of supplies'. Averardo de' Medici saw it differently, and pledged his support for Rinaldo degli Albizzi – though he also sent supportive letters to Cosimo.

The Florentine army marched back to the walls of Lucca and resumed its siege, but to little avail; the republican government of Lucca and its newly enfranchised citizens were prepared to defend their city with renewed enthusiasm. Rinaldo degli Albizzi returned to Florence and persuaded the Committee of Ten to adopt an ingenious plan, involving the architect Brunelleschi, along with Michelozzo and Donatello, who were despatched to Lucca to supervise engineering works. The plan was to dam the River Serchio, and then divert its waters so that they could be released down the hillside in a sudden torrent, washing away the ramparts of Lucca. The artists and architects set to work, directing the soldiers as they heaved in the mud, while the commander of the Lucca garrison looked on from the ramparts. Then night fell; overnight the dam would fill with water, and next morning the deluge would be unleashed on Lucca. But the commander of the Lucca garrison had hatched his own plan, and under cover of darkness he despatched his soldiers to destroy the other side of the dam, which released a deluge of water that washed away the entire Florentine camp.

When news of this farcical catastrophe reached Florence, Cosimo resigned in disgust from the Committee of Ten and left for Verona; he had no intention of being held responsible for the disastrous running of the war. Rinaldo degli Albizzi now saw his opportunity – with Cosimo out of the way, he would make sure that Florence was rid of the Medici for ever. He began stirring up popular feeling against the Medici, spreading rumours of their hypocrisy: the Medici were not interested in supporting the people, all they really wanted was to take over the city and establish a tyranny. Rinaldo was sure of the backing of most of the oligarchy families, but the Medici had powerful allies of their own. Giovanni di Bicci had long ago foreseen such difficulties, and had arranged the marriages of his sons well. Cosimo was married to a Bardi, and his younger brother Lorenzo's marriage to Ginevra Cavalcanti linked the Medici with both the powerful Cavalcanti and the Malespini families; also several of Cosimo's humanist friends were members of the old oligarchy families. If a move was to be made against the Medici, Rinaldo degli Albizzi had to be sure of overwhelming support. With this in mind he approached Niccolò da Uzzano, who years beforehand had opposed Giovanni's election as *gonfaloniere* and was now regarded as the leading elder statesman of the city. But Niccolò was not convinced by Rinaldo's arguments about the Medici taking over the city and establishing a tyranny, for he was well aware that the Albizzi had long had plans for setting up a tyranny of their own. Without Niccolò da Uzzano's support, an uneasy stalemate prevailed.

But within a year Niccolò da Uzzano was dead; Cosimo now returned to Florence to find a city in disarray. The exchequer had been emptied by the war effort, leaving Florence beleaguered by debts. Under such circumstances the leading families of Florence, bankers and others, were required to make 'enforced loans' to the city. These would be made at inflated interest rates, so that often the lenders would end up with a healthy profit. But it was evidently too late for such measures: Cosimo instructed the Medici Bank to loan the exchequer sufficient to cover at least the most pressing debts, though it was obvious to all concerned that neither this loan nor any interest on it was liable to be repaid. Leaked news of this move made Cosimo popular with a citizenry tired of high taxes, but it also confirmed the oligarchy in their suspicions of the Medici. The streets were rife with rumours of plot and counterplot.

These were dangerous times and the stakes were high; the prospect of death, ruin or exile faced the losers of the struggle, together with their family and their supporters. Meanwhile the whole of northern Italy was in a ferment – the Florentine war against Lucca had begun to act like a whirlpool, sucking in the major powers all around. Venice declared war on Milan, forcing it to end its assistance to Lucca, whereupon the powerful Genoese fleet set sail, seemingly intent on taking the vital Florentine port of Pisa, but was defeated by combined Venetian and Pisan warships. Then at last in April 1433 a peace was agreed, under which all parties were required to retreat to the status quo that had prevailed before the outbreak of war. Florence had waged war for three years, spent a fortune, and gained nothing – many would have to pay for this, and many were angry. No longer distracted by external affairs, the Florentines returned with a vengeance to internal matters, and the situation became inceasingly tense as the rival factions manoeuvred. At night, each of the powerful families remained locked in their palazzi, which now more than ever resembled private fortresses. The walls of most Florentine palazzi bordered directly onto the street, but during this period their windows would be high above ground level, and were always barred, while the large wooden iron-studded gates that opened into the inner entrance courtyard were built to withstand a siege. Under cover of darkness the streets witnessed a growing number of violent incidents, which would continue through the long, hot months of summer. Typical of these was the occasion when a 'scion of one of the leading conservative families', on his way home late from civic business at the Palazzo della Signoria, 'was set upon, seized by the hair, and struck in the face . . . by two citizens without surnames from the Medici quarter of San Giovanni'.

A war of nerves now began, and on a night early in May 1433 the doors of the Medici residence were daubed with blood, a demonstrative and chilling warning for all to see. Cosimo has frequently been characterised as a master schemer, but also as a man who lacked physical courage. Yet judging from the evidence, it is difficult to tell where prudence ended and cowardice began, especially in this instance. Cosimo immediately decided it was time to move out to the family estates in the Mugello, but this time he did not stay in his usual summer residence at Cafaggiolo; instead he retired to the nearby villa Il Trebbio, a small converted medieval fort, which he had recently had restored by Michelozzo.

With Cosimo out of the way, the path was now clear for Rinaldo degli Albizzi to make his next crucial move, and he immediately set about doctoring the ballots for the election of the new *gonfaloniere* and his ruling Signoria. After the election it emerged that seven out of the nine who were due to take up office in September were Albizzi supporters, and the new *gonfaloniere* Bernardo Guadagni was deemed firmly in the Albizzi pocket, having had his tax debts settled by the Albizzi so that he could stand (debtors were not permitted to hold public office). The Signoria had power of life and death over the citizens of Florence, and at a stroke it could bankrupt any enemy. Time was running out for Cosimo de' Medici, and there appeared to be little he could do about it.

Yet although Cosimo's political power was draining away by the minute, like a true Medici he was making sure that his financial power was draining elsewhere. Through the hot days of summer, he secretly directed the transfer of vast sums from the Medici Bank in Florence to the branches in Rome and Venice. The Medici Bank's *libro segreto* for this period makes intriguing reading, with the entries for 30 May 1433 revealing a peak of activity. On this day, the equivalent of 2,400 florins in gold Venetian ducats was spirited away from the Medici residence and placed in the hands of the Benedictine hermits at the ancient monastery of San Miniato al Monte, on a hill just south of Florence. Also on this day, 4,700 florins' worth of Venetian gold ducats was deposited with the Dominican friars at San Marco; at the same time, 15,000 florins were transferred from the Florence branch of the bank to the Venice branch – all this in one day! For good measure, Cosimo directed Lorenzo to transfer the stocks which the Medici held in the Florence commune to the Rome branch, so that whatever happened, Cosimo's investments could not simply be appropriated by his enemies.

Cosimo was making sure that the new Signoria would have nothing to seize if it ordered the confiscation of his assets. Pope Martin V had now been succeeded by Eugenius IV, who had retained the Medici Bank to handle the Curia's financial affairs, and not surprisingly the papal banker had many good friends in the Church. No government would have dared to raid the monasteries where Cosimo had transferred his gold, for fear of incurring the wrath of the Church. Yet these precautionary measures show that Cosimo was thinking of more than just his own capital assets: he was also making sure that he could lay his hands on sufficient funds outside the republic, in case any move against him resulted in a run on the Florence branch of the bank. The Medici Bank would not go bankrupt — come what may, it would retain its good name and the trust of its customers. The principles instilled in Cosimo by Giovanni would be maintained, whatever the circumstances. Yet such foresight could only be a precautionary measure, for Cosimo's survival would depend very much upon how he reacted to events as they unfolded. The events that now took place would prove pivotal in the fortunes of the Medici family, and for this reason it is worth following them in some detail.

5

The Moment of Truth

A T THE START of September 1433 the new *gonfaloniere* and his Signoria were duly installed in the Palazzo della Signoria, whereupon an official message was despatched to Cosimo de' Medici in the Mugello, requiring him to return forthwith to Florence and present himself before the Signoria for 'some important decisions to be made'. Cosimo at once set out for Florence 'though many friends dissuaded him from it', according to Machiavelli in his somewhat partisan *History of Florence*, whose description of the ensuing events drew heavily on eyewitness accounts spiced with generally accepted gossip. According to the equally biased diary of these events written down by Cosimo himself some time later, he arrived in Florence on 4 September and went straight away to see Gonfaloniere Bernardo Guadagni and the members of his Signoria at the Palazzo della Signoria. Cosimo at once brought up the worrying rumours that had been reaching him in the Mugello – namely, that the Signoria was planning a revolution in Florence, with the aim of seizing his property and destroying him. But, in Cosimo's words: 'When I told them what I had heard, they denied it, and told me to be of good cheer, as they hoped to leave the city in the same condition as they had found it when their time was up.' If he had any worries, he should voice them at the meeting of the Signoria in three days' time, which he was invited to attend.

Cosimo left, and proceeded to the premises of the bank in the nearby Via Porta Rossa, where he made arrangements for the trusted Lippaccio de' Bardi, Contessina's cousin, to take over as general manager of the entire Medici Bank and see it through any future events. Three days later, on the morning of 7 September, Cosimo duly arrived at the Palazzo della

Fig 4 Palazzo della Signoria (now Palazzo Vecchio)

Signoria, and was surprised to find that the Signoria was already in session. He was escorted up the stairs by the captain of the guard and his men-at-arms, but to his consternation they led him past the closed door where the meeting was taking place, and up the stairs into the tower. Here he was hustled up the dark stone steps to the very top of the 300-foot tower, and thrust into the poky cell popularly known by the citizens of Florence as the *alberghetto* (the little inn).

As Cosimo wrote: 'On hearing of this, the whole city rose up.' This is at best an exaggeration: what in fact happened was that Rinaldo degli Albizzi ordered his son and a band of armed followers to occupy the piazza in front of the palazzo, to make a show of strength and dissuade any potential protesters, or any attempts to rescue Cosimo. Inside the palazzo it was a different picture. The Signoria and the palace guard were in a panic, alarmed at the enormity of what they had done, and in the words of an eyewitness there were 'arms everywhere; some ran upstairs, some down, some talked, some shouted; everything was full of passion, excitement, and fear'. Eventually Rinaldo degli Albizzi managed to regain some sort of order, the *gonfaloniere* and his Signoria met and were prevailed upon to pass sentence on Cosimo. The prisoner was charged with 'attempting to raise himself above the rank of an ordinary citizen', an apparently innocuous charge, though in fact one of the most serious that could be brought against a citizen of the Florentine Republic, carrying the death penalty. Cited as confirmation of the charge against Cosimo was the palazzo that he was building for himself on the Via Larga; for despite Cosimo's precautions concerning the design, it was described as being far too ostentatious to house any ordinary citizen of the republic, and much more like the palace of a potential tyrant. The message implied in the charge was clear: Cosimo de' Medici was planning to take over the city — he was a traitor, and deserved a traitor's fate.

In the event, the Signoria proved too terrified to pass the death penalty that Rinaldo had demanded, and instead sentenced Cosimo to banishment from the city for five years. Meanwhile Cosimo crouched in his cell, peering apprehensively down at the clamour of armed men in the piazza far below; he did not know exactly what was happening, but feared the worst. By now his imagination was running away with him: they might not even execute him, but instead simply have him thrown from the top of the tower — such things had happened before.

When the jailer pulled open the cell door to read the prisoner his sentence, reliable sources report that Cosimo 'fell into a swoon'. This episode is not mentioned in Cosimo's diary, though he does describe other reactions to his sentence: 'This decision was at once made known to my brother Lorenzo, who was in the Mugello, and to Averardo, my cousin, who was at Pisa . . . Lorenzo came to Florence that same day, and the Signoria sent for him, but he, being warned why they wanted him, left at once, and returned to Il Trebbio. Averardo also left Pisa in haste, as they had given orders to seize him. Had they taken us all three, we should have been in evil plight.' Cosimo goes on to mention that: 'The news was also sent to Niccolò da Tolentino, captain of the Commune, who was my good friend.' The significance of this news would only later become apparent.

Cosimo remained incarcerated, while Rinaldo degli Albizzi persisted with his efforts to force the death penalty — or settle matters in his own way. During this terrifying period Cosimo did not eat for two days, fearing that his food would be poisoned; and his fears appear to have been justified, as it is now known that Rinaldo secretly paid two members of the guard to poison Cosimo at the earliest opportunity.

On 9 September Cosimo was stunned by the sound of the palazzo bell sounding above his head in the belfry of the tower. This large bell was known as the *vacca* (cow), on account of the mooing boom that rang out over the city when it was pealed to summon the citizens of Florence to the Piazza della Signoria in an emergency. This gathering of all citizens eligible to vote was known as a Parlamento – the Italian word aptly catches the aspects of both parley and parliament: this was a meeting where citizens spoke and voted on matters of crucial importance for the government of the city, including changes to the constitution. But this time Rinaldo degli Albizzi's armed men had mounted guard at each street leading into the wide piazza, and all citizens who were known to be Medici supporters (or even judged likely to support their cause) were turned back. Cosimo watched helplessly from his tiny cell window high in the tower of the palazzo; the Albizzi were evidently taking no chances, and according to Cosimo, only twenty-three people were allowed into the piazza to form the Parlamento.

In the customary manner, the members of the Signoria assembled on the raised stone terrace in front of the palazzo, and the *gonfaloniere* formally asked the assembled Parlamento to vote on whether a Balìa should be set up 'to reform the city for the good of the people'. The Balìa was a committee of 200 citizens, newly selected on each occasion, which was required to sanction all changes to the constitution of the city, or important decisions taken in the city's name. The twenty-three assembled yes-men of the Parlamento duly shouted 'Sì! Sì!', a Balìa was agreed upon and immediately the Albizzi faction began preparing the lists, making sure that when the Balìa met it would be packed with their men.

Machiavelli vividly brings to life how Cosimo remained confined in his cell, with one Federigo Malavolti as his jailer:

> In this place, hearing the assembly of the Councils, the noise of
> arms which proceeded from the piazza, and the frequent ringing
> of the bell to assemble the Balìa, he was greatly apprehensive for
> his safety, but still more lest his private enemies should cause him

to be put to death in some unusual manner. He scarcely took any food, so that in four days he ate only a small quantity of bread. Federigo, observing his anxiety, said to him, 'Cosimo, you are afraid of being poisoned, and are evidently hastening your end with hunger. You wrong me if you think I would be party to such an atrocious act. I do not imagine your life to be in danger, since you have so many friends both within the palace and without; but if you should eventually lose it, be assured they will use some other medium than myself for that purpose, for I will never imbue my hands in the blood of any, still less in yours, who never injured me; therefore cheer up, take some food, and preserve your life for your friends and your country. And that you may do so with greater assurance, I will partake of your meals with you.' These words were a great relief to Cosimo, who, with tears in his eyes, embraced and kissed Federigo, earnestly thanking him for so kind and affectionate conduct, and promising, if ever the opportunity were given him, he would not be ungrateful.

After this Cosimo slowly began to regain his composure, and when he was given his dinner Federigo brought in someone to keep him company and cheer him up, a local character called Il Farnagaccio (an affectionate nickname, loosely translated as 'The Crazy Guy'). Cosimo knew Il Farnagaccio well, and also knew that he was a friend of Gonfaloniere Guadagni, so while Federigo the jailer tactfully absented himself, Cosimo passed a piece of paper to Il Farnagaccio. Cosimo told him to go at once to the director of the Santa Maria Nuova Hospital; on receipt of the note, the director would give him 1,100 Venetian ducats. Il Farnagaccio was instructed to keep 100 ducats for himself, and then pass on the rest as discreetly as possible to Gonfaloniere Guadagni.

Meanwhile a stormy meeting of the Balìa was under way, for despite the strongest possible urging from Rinaldo degli Albizzi, they were reluctant to come to a decision, and many of the 200 hand-picked members were starting to have second thoughts about what was expected of them. Amidst an uproar of arguments the Balìa was beginning to separate into factions, and according to Machiavelli, some 'urged Cosimo's death, some his exile, some were silent, either out of compassion for him or out of fear'. Eventually order was restored, and the Balìa voted that Cosimo should be banished for ten years. Whilst apparently accepting this decision, Rinaldo degli Albizzi now decided that it was time to take matters into his own hands.

Though still imprisoned in his cell, Cosimo soon learned further news about what was happening outside the city: his 'good friend' Niccolò da Tolentino had acted according to prearranged instructions and immediately summoned his company of armed mercenaries; they had then marched from Pisa up the Po valley to Lastra, just six miles from the walls of Florence. Here they had halted, hoping for an uprising in the city, fearful that if they marched any closer they might precipitate the murder of Cosimo. By now the news of Cosimo's arrest had also spread through the mountains of the Romagna, above and beyond the Medici stronghold in the Mugello, and in response many of the local peasants had taken up arms and flocked to Lorenzo's support, gathering outside the fortified villa of Il Trebbio where he and his family had taken refuge. But Lorenzo was advised not to make a move on the city, for fear of what might befall Cosimo – though when Cosimo heard that his brother had heeded this advice, his fragile composure broke into exasperated rage. In his own words: 'Although this advice was given by relations and friends, and in all sincerity, yet it was not good, for had they advanced at once I should have been free, and he who was the cause of it all would have been undone.'

While Cosimo's would-be rescuers dithered, Rinaldo degli Albizzi moved into action, despatching armed men to round up and imprison a number of well-known Medici supporters, amongst whom was Cosimo's friend, the humanist poet and notary Niccolò Tinucci, who was immediately put to torture. After several gruesome hours on the rack, Tinucci finally broke down and was made to sign a confession, stating that Cosimo had intended to foment a revolution in Florence with the aid of foreign troops, after which he planned to install himself as tyrant. Here at last was incontrovertible evidence of treason, and Rinaldo degli Albizzi knew that for this offence there could be no question of banishment; this was undeniably a hanging offence.

But by now word of Cosimo's fate had spread far beyond the borders of the Florentine Republic and was meeting with an international response. Cosimo's services as a banker had proved indispensable to several foreign powers, who quickly made their feelings plain: the first to respond was the ruler of nearby Ferrara, who had good reason to be grateful to Cosimo for extensive loans and was outraged at this blow to his potential expenditure. A message in the strongest possible terms was despatched by fast messenger seventy miles down the road to Florence – but both Rinaldo degli Albizzi and Cosimo de' Medici were well aware that this could be ignored: Ferrara was not a major power.

Venice, on the other hand, was a more difficult proposition for Rinaldo. A branch of the Medici Bank had been established in the Venetian Republic as early as 1402, and by now the bank had become deeply involved in the far-flung trade of the Venetian Republic – dealing in wool from Valencia, and handling spice and amber shipped in from the Orient by Venetian merchants. The *libro segreto* for 1427 shows that the Venetian branch had a turnover equivalent to 50,568 florins, a colossal sum – generating a profit equivalent to 4,080 florins – that is, around 8 per cent). The merchants who dealt with the Medici Bank were among the leading families of the Venetian Republic, and a delegation consisting of three ambassadors was sent post-haste to Florence with orders to secure the immediate release of Cosimo de' Medici.

A similar response came from Rome, for Pope Eugenius IV was the son of a Venetian merchant and well knew of Cosimo's beneficial involvement in the city's commerce. More importantly, Cosimo was also the papal banker. Eugenius IV sent word to Florence ordering intervention on Cosimo's behalf by the local papal representative, who happened to be Ambrogio Traversari, Cosimo's humanist friend who had translated several of his rare manuscripts. When Traversari demanded to know why Cosimo had been imprisoned, he was informed of Niccolò Tinucci's confession that Cosimo was planning to take over the city with the aid of foreign troops. Not for one moment did Traversari believe this 'confession' by his fellow humanist and friend, and the three Venetian ambassadors were similarly unimpressed with such flimsy evidence – all were by now well aware of how it had been obtained.

A meeting of the *gonfaloniere* and his Signoria was called, but by this stage Gonfaloniere Guadagni had gratefully accepted his 1,000 ducats from Cosimo and decided it would be wiser to hedge his bets; while a number of others on the Signoria had accepted lesser bribes from the same source.

As Cosimo remarked in his diary: 'They had small intelligence, for they might have had 10,000 or more for allowing me to escape from peril.' Gonfaloniere Guadagni informed the Signoria that he was too ill to attend the meeting, and delegated his vote to another member (who also happened to have been bribed by Cosimo).

Rinaldo degli Albizzi was quick to recognise what was happening, and was also pressingly aware of the effect on the city of Niccolò da Tolentino and his mercenary troops waiting at Lastra. He knew he had to act quickly, and decisively, before all his support melted away, for if Cosimo got off scot-free, as now seemed possible, then it would be the Albizzi who would be fighting for their lives. On 28 September yet another meeting of the ruling Signoria was called, for Rinaldo knew that despite Cosimo's bribes, in the last resort the Albizzi still had a firm hold on seven members out of the nine. The Signoria decided once again that Cosimo should be banished, to Padua, for ten years, together with other leading members of the Medici family: Averardo to Naples for ten years, Lorenzo to Venice for five years, and others for varying terms. Futhermore, the Medici faction was to be excluded for ever from holding any public office in the city. At a stroke, the Medici power in Florence had been emasculated, and afterwards a grateful Rinaldo degli Albizzi assured the seven loyal members of the Signoria that they would be appointed to suitable sinecures as a reward.

On 3 October Cosimo de' Medici was led down from his cell and escorted by armed guards to face the Signoria, where his sentence was formally read out to him. Opinions differ as to precisely how Cosimo reacted to this. According to Machiavelli (a staunch supporter of the Medici): 'Cosimo received his sentence with a cheerful look.' On the other hand, the modern historian Christopher Hibbert (with no axe to grind) takes a different view: judging from his own interpretation of the conflicting reports, he describes Cosimo as being 'abject', commenting that his 'many virtues seem not to have included physical courage'.

But was there perhaps more to all this than meets the eye? In Cosimo's reply to the Signoria, he declared that he was willing to go into exile wherever they chose to send him, even 'to live among the Arabs, or any other people alien to our custom'. He went on: 'As disaster comes to me by your orders, I accept it as a boon, and as a benefit to me and my belongings.'

This certainly sounds like grovelling behaviour, yet it soon becomes clear that Cosimo was in fact pleading for his life, as is evident from his final request to the Signoria: 'Have a care that those who stand outside in the piazza with arms in their hands anxiously desiring my blood, should not have their way with me.' Adding, with a sting in the tail, that should he die: 'My pain would be small, but you would earn perpetual infamy.' Having cajoled the Signoria, he was now plainly warning them of the consequences, should he be 'accidentally' stabbed in the mêlée by one of the Albizzi supporters waiting outside as he was escorted across the piazza. He had guessed what Rinaldo degli Albizzi had in store for him, and there is every reason to believe that Cosimo had guessed right.

His words of warning evidently had their effect on the Signoria, for they realised that if Cosimo was assassinated there might be heavy bloodshed. Florence was already in turmoil, Niccolò da Tolentino and his mercenaries were liable to march on the city, and the ruling oligarchy would flood the streets with armed men. There was no telling how it would end. The Signoria gave instructions that Cosimo should be held at the Palazzo della Signoria until nightfall and the crowd in the piazza had dispersed. Under cover of darkness, and protected by the palace guards, he could then be smuggled through the streets to the northern gate in the city walls, the Porta San Gallo, from where he would be taken under armed guard the forty miles north-east to the border of the Florentine Republic. On 5 October 1433 Cosimo de' Medici was escorted up the high mountain pass below the snow-streaked peak of Mount Cimone as far as the frontier, where he rode on into exile.

Part 2
Out of the Darkness

6

The Medici in Exile

COSIMO DE' MEDICI had ultimately survived his long moment of truth. Things could have gone either way, yet by a mixture of astute calculation and luck he had succeeded in saving his life and business. But it seemed he had also failed, for he had been defeated by his old enemies in the oligarchy and had been evicted from his power base in Florence. Yet this apparent defeat would ultimately prove to be a pivotal victory for the Medici.

Florence was left in the hands of the Albizzi and their supporters amongst the oligarchy of old families, but from now on whoever ruled the city would be unable to rely on Medici money to bale out the exchequer. Rinaldo degli Albizzi was forced to muddle on as best he could, attempting to control a city that remained as divided as ever. The Medici supporters continued to plot, and Rinaldo was driven to coerce the ruling Signoria into increasingly despotic measures, with individual Medici supporters being banished for ten years on a regular basis.

In exile, Cosimo obtained permission to leave Padua and join his brother Lorenzo in Venice, from where he paid close attention to the events in Florence, but at the same time he took good care to distance himself from any moves made on his behalf. The Venetian authorities allowed him and his family to take up residence in the monastery of San Giorgio Maggiore, on the small island opposite the entrance to the Grand Canal, where Pope Eugenius IV had once been a monk. In recognition of the pope's effort to rescue him, Cosimo decided to build a new library for the monastery, and commissioned a design from his favoured architect Michelozzo.

A measure of the loyalty of Cosimo's artists to their patron can be seen from their behaviour when he was banished from Florence. Michelozzo and Donatello at once called a halt to the construction of the new Palazzo Medici — Donatello left for Rome to study the ancient sculptures that were now beginning to be unearthed amongst the ruins, and Michelozzo followed Cosimo into exile. Both these artists were Florentines and could easily have remained in the city, where they were very much a part of the flourishing humanist revival. At this stage, the influence of this revival was only just beginning to spread elsewhere and had not permeated into art and architecture. In following Cosimo into exile they not only isolated themselves from their home city and their humanist friends, but also from the circle of wealthy patrons amongst the oligarchy families who would have guaranteed them work and recognition amongst their own people.

By April 1434, just six months after Cosimo's banishment, popular feeling against the Albizzi was beginning to gather strength, to such an extent that even the banking families amongst the oligarchy were waiting to see which way things would turn out. Cosimo was pleased to hear that no one could be persuaded to furnish the empty city exchequer 'with so much as a pistachio nut'. During the summer war flared against Milan, and a Florentine army was defeated by Milanese mercenaries at the frequently disputed small city state of Imola. Despite all Albizzi attempts at rigging the next elections, Medici supporters were voted into all eight seats on the Signoria, and a Medici sympathiser was even selected as *gonfaloniere*. Rinaldo degli Albizzi was all for preventing the Signoria from taking office, but this would have been a drastic step, making a mockery of Florence's entire political system. Although the system was easily corrupted, in a covert manner, the citizens of Florence remained proud of it: their republican form of government, even with its pretence of a very limited democratic process, was what raised Florence above the tyrannies and political squalor of their neighbours. According to Machiavelli, even some of the ruling families thought that Rinaldo degli Albizzi's proposed action was 'too violent, and likely to be attended with great evil'. In an attempt to calm the situation, Rinaldo was approached by the man who had succeded Niccolò da Uzzano as the city's elder statesman, Palla Strozzi, an extremely rich and cultured man of great persuasive powers. Strozzi advised caution, and Rinaldo reluctantly acquiesced, but on one condition: the Signoria should make no attempt to overturn Cosimo de' Medici's sentence of exile and invite him to return. The Signoria agreed to this, and took office; but a month later, when Rinaldo was briefly called from the city on business, the Signoria sent word to Venice, asking Cosimo if he was willing to return.

The moment Rinaldo arrived back in the city a few days later, he was summoned to the Palazzo della Signoria. Mindful of what had happened to Cosimo de' Medici when he had obeyed such a call, Rinaldo ignored the Signoria and rode at once to the Palazzo Albizzi, where he put into action what had evidently been a prearranged plan in case of such an eventuality. He ordered his bodyguard of 500 armed men to take up strategic positions and occupy the church of San Pier Scheraggio (on the site now occupied by the Uffizi), which overlooked the Piazza della Signoria in front of the palazzo. At the same time, the gatekeeper of the Palazzo della Signoria was quietly offered as many gold ducats as his helmet could hold if he left the door unlocked; Rinaldo's plan was to storm the palazzo, overthrow the Signoria and occupy the seat of power.

But the Signoria had made their own preparations, and sent the palace guards out into the Piazza della Signoria to confront Rinaldo's men. Rinaldo realised that the guards could easily be overcome, but that this would involve serious bloodshed — for the moment there was a tense stand-off as the armed men faced each other across the piazza. Hearing about the prospect of Florentine blood being shed by Florentines, several of the oligarchy families became hesitant about supporting Rinaldo. Palla Strozzi, who had promised his 500-strong bodyguard in support of Rinaldo, turned up for a meeting with him in the nearby Piazza Sant'Apollinaire accompanied by just two personal bodyguards. Rinaldo and Strozzi had a short altercation, and Strozzi rode off, vowing to take no further part in the revolt. But Rinaldo was still confident of sufficient backing to overcome the Signoria, which was now under a state of siege in the palazzo.

Then the Signoria played its trump card. At the time, Pope Eugenius IV happened to be in Florence, residing at the monastery of Santa Maria Novella on the western side of the city. Eugenius IV had quarrelled with the Holy Roman Emperor Sigismund, and in the course of this conflict Milanese troops had marched on Rome. Thereupon the Roman populace had risen up against the pope, threatening his life, and Eugenius IV had been forced to flee through the streets in disguise, eventually making his way to Florence, where the authorities had housed him and his entourage of loyal cardinals in the extensive monastery of Santa Maria Novella. The Signoria now sent a message to Eugenius IV, appealing to him to arbitrate in the dispute that threatened to engulf the city. The pope, who had no wish to flee another city in turmoil, readily agreed and despatched Cardinal Vitelleschi, 'Rinaldo's most intimate friend', with an invitation to a meeting. (An indication of the divided loyalties which added a characteristic complexity to these manoeuvrings is given by the fact that Cosimo also referred to Cardinal Vitelleschi as 'very much my friend'; the pope too would have fallen into this category, despite the fact that he had chosen to take refuge amongst Cosimo's enemies.)

It took some time for Cardinal Vitelleschi to persuade Rinaldo, but he eventually agreed to meet Eugenius IV. By now it was late afternoon, and Rinaldo's men had been joined by several armed bands from the other oligarchy families. Rinaldo rode throught the streets to Santa Maria Novella at the head of his noisy swollen army. According to an eyewitness, his forces now consisted of so many men that 'the last of them had not left the piazza when the first reached the monastery' – a distance of more than quarter of a mile. Rinaldo went in to see the pope, while his increasingly rowdy troops camped in the piazza outside. Night was coming on, it was dinner time and they started to pass round the wine.

When Rinaldo encountered the pope, he found the pontiff in a state of extreme distress over the turmoil that was engulfing the city, though according to one report 'the infinite tears of the Pope issued from the same source as those of the crocodile'. Finally Eugenius IV prevailed upon Rinaldo to call off his revolt, while promising that he would ensure the Signoria took no retaliatory steps against Rinaldo and the oligarchy families. On his word as pope, there would be no banishments, no confiscations of property, not even any fines.

Rinaldo finally emerged in the early hours to find that most of his troops had dispersed and had gone home for the night. Indeed, there were so few troops remaining, and such was their drunken state, that Rinaldo thought it best to stay overnight with the pope, rather than risk travelling through the dark streets without proper protection.

By now the revolt was as good as over. The Signoria had sent word to the mountains, summoning a brigade of mercenaries in Florentine pay, and they entered the city under cover of darkness. Next day the *vacca* was tolled, summoning all enfranchised citizens to the Piazza della Signoria, which was made safe by the mercenary troops. The Signoria emerged from the palazzo, accompanied by the ever-reassuring figure of Cardinal Vitelleschi, and the assembled citizens were asked by the Signoria if they wished for a Balìa. This request was confirmed by an overwhelming shout of 'Sì!'; a Balìa of 350 citizens was selected and immediately voted for an official overturning of the Medici banishments.

The moment this news reached Cosimo, he set off from Venice, accompanied by the good wishes of the Venetian Republic, which were publicly manifested in an escort of 300 Venetian soldiers leading him to the border. News of Cosimo's crossing into Florentine territory two days later was greeted with national rejoicing, and his progress to Florence quickly became a triumphal procession, with crowds lining the roadside to cheer him. What was happening? This was not precisely clear – either to Cosimo or to anyone else. As so often happens in spontaneous popular manifestations of feeling, events had taken on an unforeseen momentum of their own. Yet there was no doubting that something crucial was taking place, for in the words of Machiavelli: 'Seldom has a citizen returning from a great victory been greeted by such a concourse of people, and with such demonstrations of affection, as was Cosimo on his return from exile.'

On 5 October Cosimo reached his villa at Careggi just outside Florence, where he and his entourage paused for a meal. By now so many people were thronging the streets of Florence, eagerly anticipating his return, that the Signoria sent word to Careggi begging Cosimo not to enter the city that afternoon, for fear of a disturbance. It is not clear precisely what nature of disturbance the Signoria feared – might the celebrations have turned into a vindictive settling of scores by the triumphant Medici supporters, or was the city perhaps still sufficiently divided to leave Cosimo in danger of assassination as he made his way through the crowded streets? Either way, Cosimo complied with the Signoria's request and postponed his departure for the city until after dark, when he was accompanied only by his brother Lorenzo and a high-ranking city official. Cosimo was let in quietly through a side-gate in the city walls east of the Bargello, and led through the streets to the Palazzo della Signoria, where he was put up for the night in one of the rooms normally occupied by a member of the Signoria.

First thing next morning Cosimo paid a courtesy visit to the pope, to thank him for his support, reaffirm his friendship and perhaps as a public demonstration that he had friends in high places. By now word had spread of Cosimo's arrival in Florence, and by the time he made his way home to the Palazzo Bardi, the crowds lining the streets cheered him 'in such a manner that one would imagine him to be their prince'.

In fact, there are several reports of Cosimo's return from exile, and these differ considerably, in the main through a process of selection. The pro-Medici Machiavelli stresses the great public welcome; others choose to focus on the fact that 'he crept back to the city very quietly'. It would seem probable that all these events took place, but there can be no doubt that Cosimo was returning to take control of the city.

Out of defeat had come victory: without Cosimo being banished, it is unlikely that the opportunity would have arisen for him to be acclaimed in such a fashion, and although no one said so in as many words, there could be no doubting that he was being welcomed back as a national saviour. He had now been publicly acknowledged as the ruler of Florence – both by its citizens and by the international powers who had previously, but ineffectually, tried to come to his rescue. The city was his for the taking – Florence appeared to be ready to accept a permanent and public ruler, but caution led him to hesitate. Now was the time he chose to remember his father's deathbed advice – 'avoid being conspicuous' – as well as the tradition of Florentine republicanism (and attendant self-delusion). Cosimo preferred the old ways, and subterfuge suited his character, as well as that of his city; he would rule, but he would not be seen to rule. It would be business as usual – only more so!

Yet a significant change had taken place. Although Cosimo would continue to maintain a scrupulously unpretentious demeanour, and encourage the political machinery of the city to go through the motions, there could be no doubting who now held the reins of power. Delegations from foreign powers would approach him personally, going immediately to his palazzo; likewise citizens wanting offical assurances would seek an audience with him, and there was even a special hour of the day set aside for this. It was probably around this time that Cosimo began receiving, and accepting, invitations from leading citizens to become godfather to their firstborn male heir. Such a method of ensuring loyalty appealed to him; it was not ostentatious, but it was binding.

The power of the oligarchy families was quickly broken by the Signoria, certainly at Cosimo's urging. Despite the pope's promises, Rinaldo and the leading members of the Albizzi faction were all banished from the city, which caused Rinaldo to have bitter parting words for Eugenius IV: 'I blame myself for having thought that you, who were expelled from your own city, could preserve me in mine.' The other families suffered similar harsh treatment, and even the seventy-year-old Palla Strozzi, who had done so much to make the Medici return possible, was sentenced to ten years in exile – effectively banishment for life. Strozzi's intellectual pursuits had often brought him into contact with Cosimo, and they had something of a friendship, but when Cosimo was asked to intervene, the coolness of his pleading on Strozzi's behalf spoke volumes. The Signoria understood, and Strozzi's banishment remained in place. Cosimo had recognised that the wealth and influence of the elder statesman would inevitably become a focus for hostility to Medici rule, and this was not the time for a tolerated opposition. After years of trouble and unrest, Cosimo wished to establish a period of firm government, bringing peace and prosperity to Florence; and this he proceeded to do, though once again this was effected with characteristic discretion. As one of his humanist friends remarked: 'whenever he wished to achieve something, he saw to it, in order to escape envy as much as possible, that the initiative appeared to come from others and not from him'.

Cosimo went to great pains to appear as nothing more than a citizen of the republic: a powerful one, but a citizen nonetheless, and one who was bound to respect the law just like any other citizen. He would set a public example by being far and away the highest taxpayer in the city, though in fact the income he declared for tax purposes was always considerably lower than his actual income; his public balance sheets were invariably padded with hugely inflated, or even fictitious, debts and no one was willing to question his accounting methods. On the other hand, his covert control over the tax-assessing and tax-gathering apparatus was complete, and the Medici party machinery made sure that this remained so. Anyone who proved troublesome could easily be ruined by a vindictive *catasto*, overestimating their taxable property and possessions, and this soon became Cosimo's favoured method of eliminating any opposition. Wealthy opponents were simply bankrupted, or assessed so ruinously that they were forced into voluntary exile, whereupon the trusted Medici party bosses snapped up the abandoned estates at bargain prices and distributed them amongst the faithful. The *pax* Medici came at a price.

Yet there were also a number of long-overdue reforms, introducing a certain measure of increased democracy into the arcane Florentine political system. The *popolo minuto* were rewarded for their loyalty, and regularly each year another hundred or so deserving members of this class would be given the right to vote in the elections for the Signoria — and thus at least theoretically become elegible for public office themselves.

In foreign affairs too, Cosimo used his considerable diplomatic powers to promote stability, as far as was possible in the treacherous and volatile world of Italian politics. The main power in northern Italy remained Milan, which was ruled by the formidable Filippo Maria Visconti, the Duke of Milan, who was constantly seeking to expand into Florentine territory. To make matters worse, the exiled Albizzi were now urging Milan to invade Florence and re-install them as friendly rulers. For the time being Florence managed to resist Milan only by maintaining an uneasy alliance with Venice and the ever-unstable Papal States.

In 1436, just two years after his return, Cosimo took a drastic step which was to have a lasting effect upon the city's foreign policy: he invited to Florence the powerful *condottiere* Francesco Sforza. This thirty-four-year-old military leader was the bastard son of a farmer from the Romagna, who had himself become a *condottiere*, taking on the name Sforza (meaning 'force'). Francesco had succeeded to his father's command, quickly gaining the respect of his tough mercenary troops and a reputation as the finest military leader in Italy. He had risen to such eminence through his skill on the battlefield and his ability to inspire the loyalty of his mercenary troops. Sforza had strong links with Milan, and even had ambitions to marry the Duke of Milan's illegitimate daughter, in the hope of succeeding to Filippo Maria Visconti's dukedom. Sforza was well aware of his growing political power, and had already begun to create a private kingdom of his own in the Romagna, taking over territory that officially belonged to the Papal States. By inviting Sforza to Florence, Cosimo thus risked antagonising both the Duke of Milan and the pope, yet he calculated that the gamble was worth it. Cosimo had learned from his father that in order to succeed it was sometimes necessary to ally one's fortunes with such powerful but unreliable characters – having had dealings with Baldassare Cossa, he knew the measure of such men, but he also understood that handling them required immense diplomatic skill.

Francesco Sforza was a figure of commanding physical presence, who had little time for social graces; he had broad, somewhat coarse features, but beneath his brusque, antagonistic manner lay a certain boyish charm. The middle-aged sophisticated Cosimo seems to have read the younger man at once: Sforza wanted to be liked, to be appreciated for himself, rather than for his fearsome military reputation. Cosimo charmed Sforza, treating him as if he were one of his brilliant young humanist protégés. This at first perplexed Sforza, who had never received such understanding and courteous treatment, but he was soon smitten with Cosimo. This is no exaggeration, for when Sforza returned from Florence to the Romagna he began writing regularly to Cosimo in his mixed Italian dialect, addressing him as '*Magnifice tanquam Pater carissime*' ('Magnificent and dearest almost father'). Cosimo had won a powerful and dangerous friend.

Cosimo de' Medici was now at the height of his powers, entering upon the period that earned him his place in history. From now on he would become more than an extremely skilful banker, more than a canny and manipulative ruler, more even than a generous and discerning patron. Such people have little cause to be remembered much beyond their time, but Cosimo would transcend himself, emerging as the richest man of his age, the founder of a dynasty, the man who encouraged the first flowering of the Renaissance. Yet who was this man who would indissolubly link the Medici name with one of the turning points of Western culture?

There are several contemporary portraits, most of which seem to flatter a somewhat nondescript appearance, though there are hints that beneath the veneer of social skill, Cosimo inherited elements of his father's awkward, driven temperament. Once again the most revealing portrait was painted posthumously: this is by Jacopo da Pontormo and was painted more than half a century after Cosimo's death (see colour plates). Here there is little attempt to flatter, or to deceive; it seems to be a balanced but shrewd psychological study, a final summing up of a remarkable man.

Its clear-eyed depiction has a distinct air of verisimilitude, and may well have drawn on some more realistic contemporary sketches that have not survived. Cosimo poses dressed in a plain but well-cut fur-lined scarlet gown, with his sallow-skinned, hollow-cheeked face turned away from the painter, revealing the prominent Medici nose and a large fleshy ear. But what is striking, and is even hinted at in some of the flattering contemporary portraits, is Cosimo's posture, which is slightly twisted, and looks more than a little uncomfortable.

In later life Cosimo would suffer from gout and arthritis, yet Pontormo's portrait seems to suggest something more than his later physical ailments, implying something deeply uneasy in his character. Most interesting of all are the hands, which are inelegantly grasped, one in the other, but at the same time emphatic; they draw attention to themselves by their very inability to achieve composure. This is not an aristocrat at ease with himself, his dynasty and his inherited surroundings – this is the son of a man who emerged from the people, a man secretly aware of his own fallibility, his ordinary humanity. Cosimo de' Medici may have inherited his father's driven nature, and he may have achieved much through ambition, but he was lucky too, and he understood his fortunate humanity as his greatest blessing. Such was the man who would do so much to promote the new humanism that was coming to life in Florence, and play such a leading role in the Renaissance to which it gave birth.

7

The Dawn of Humanism

A S WE HAVE seen, humanism had its origins in such figures as the fourteenth-century Florentine poet Petrarch, who died just fifteen years before Cosimo de' Medici was born. Petrarch had found his poetic temperament unsuited to the otherworldly spirituality required by medieval Christianity. In the writings of the classical authors of Ancient Greece and Rome he glimpsed an entirely different way of living, where instead of the denial of this life in favour of a life to come, he saw a cultivation of worldly sensibility, ambition and personal ability. Instead of seeing goodness in terms of aspiration to purely spiritual values, it was possible to aspire to a full expression of our humanity in this world.

Most of the original writings of the ancient authors had been lost after the fall of the Roman Empire and the onset of the Dark Ages, and what remained were mostly emasculated Christianised commentaries on these works. Petrarch devoted himself to searching out lost original manuscripts, and during his travels through Europe he discovered a number of important works, including several by the Roman author Cicero, who wrote of civic virtues and how to live a good life that would be of benefit both to the individual and the community at large. Here was a fresh, positive attitude towards life: a picture began to emerge of a great dynamic age that had preceded the decline of the Dark Ages, and with this came the realisation that it might be possible to re-create this age anew.

Despite the setback of the Black Death in the mid-fourteenth century, Florence had remained a centre of the new interest in the classics, which gave birth to humanism, and from which we derive the modern term the 'humanities'. The emphasis here, then as now, was on the wide range of intellectual understanding that lies between theology, on the one hand, and natural philosophy (science), on the other. Humanism, and the humanities, would encourage the understanding of the human, rather than the spiritual or technological aspects of learning. These were the first stirrings of the recognition of individual personality as a general human trait.

But it should be borne in mind that what took place was for the most part a long and gradual process. Many of the values that characterised medieval thought would not be shed either swiftly or completely; and the new humanism would develop within a pervasive and unquestioned Christian context. The earliest art, writing and architecture of the Renaissance were all religious, involving paintings of holy scenes, poems of a devout character, churches and so forth. Indeed, what has been viewed as the novelty of the emergent humanistic concepts was often little more than a gradual shift in nuances. This advent of an emergent Renaissance, and indeed the full flowering of the Renaissance itself, should be seen as slow, complex transformation rather than any sudden break into a completely new era. What had been the early inklings in the fourteenth century of Petrarch would in fact develop in several long stages, which took more than two centuries to reach their fulfilment.

One of the leading figures in Florentine humanist circles at the turn of the fifteenth century was Niccolò Niccoli, who would become an avuncular friend of the young Cosimo de' Medici. Niccoli, who was twenty-five-years older than Cosimo, was the son of one of the new wealthy wool merchants who had made their fortune in the Florentine recovery following the Black Death. Although Florence had lost nearly half its population to the plague, its recovery had been comparatively swift, in part because the disease had largely affected the poor and unskilled workers. Those with any money at all, and this included a wider cross-section of Florentine society than could be found in other less rich and less republican societies, had simply fled to the countryside.

Niccolò Niccoli would become one of the first arbiters of the taste that would shape the Renaissance, and his dedication to the discovery of ancient texts, and the propagation of their ideas, would become his obsession. Not long after he befriended the young Cosimo, they planned a trip to the Holy Land together to search for lost Ancient Greek manuscripts, but Cosimo's father Giovanni disapproved, and Cosimo was quickly apprenticed to the family banking business. It seems unlikely that Cosimo resented this for long; he would become an extremely able though distinctly cautious banker, very much in the mould of his father. Yet the humanist education he had received, and his early friendship with Niccolò Niccoli, must also have accorded with an element of his character, for as soon as Giovanni died, Cosimo devoted a large part of his considerable energies to humanist pursuits. Giovanni had been doing little more than carrying on a Florentine tradition of civic duty when he began patronising the building of churches in his retirement. Cosimo's activities, on the other hand, would be the fulfilment of a personal need; and the great amount of time, energy and money that he would devote to these activities would seem to indicate how much this need had been suppressed during the first forty years of his life.

To many Florentines, and certainly Giovanni di Bicci, Niccoli was a questionable influence. Dressed in his Ancient Roman toga, and parading all the affectations of 'sensibility', he cut a slightly absurd figure and appeared to be little more than a privileged individual squandering his inheritance. Yet there was a forceful and abrasive side to Niccoli, and allied with his friend, the elder statesman Palla Strozzi, he proved a formative influence on the University of Florence, which had been founded in 1321, but had sunk into a rut of medieval scholasticism. In 1397, Niccoli and Strozzi fulfilled Petrarch's long-standing wish that there should be a chair of Ancient Greek at the university, thus enabling the study of recently discovered manuscripts of Plato; to this end they appointed Manuel Chrysoloras, an emissary from the Byzantine Emperor in Constantinople who had settled in Italy, as professor of Greek. (Ancient Greek was not widely known in medieval times, and even Petrarch had never fully mastered the language, mainly because he could find no competent teacher.)

Niccoli's influence in Florence was all-pervasive, to such an extent that during the first three decades of the fifteenth century he presided over the intellectual life of the city almost like an unofficial minister of culture. Besides maintaining a fine house in Florence, he also paid agents to search out ancient manuscripts for him all over Europe – a costly business that eventually threatened him with bankruptcy. This was only averted when Cosimo discreetly came to his rescue, ordering Niccoli's bank drafts to be honoured without question, at any branch of the Medici Bank. This was fortunate, for Niccoli's sharp manner had won him few friends outside the humanist circle in Florence, and even here he became involved in several violent disageements. However, his most persistent arguments took place at home with his mistress Benvenuta, who had originally been the mistress of his younger brother; but according to a contemporary source, 'this syren' by means of her 'charms and allurements gained such an ascendancy over [Niccoli's] better principles' that he stole her from his brother. To his cost, Niccoli soon discovered that Benvenuta required higher standards of attention than his scholarly nature was willing, or able, to provide, and as a result the somewhat humdrum bachelor routine of his home life became transformed into a drama filled with operatic surprises.

Niccoli's fastidious taste prevented him from producing any original work of his own, for when setting down his ideas he became too aware of what he perceived to be his own inadequacies, though his writing would have lasting effect in its own oblique fashion. Niccoli was in the habit of making copies of the many rare manuscripts in his library. Those manuscripts that he was unable to acquire would frequently be loaned to him so that he could transcribe their contents — for the age of printing still lay in the future, and this was the only way to disseminate the contents of rare manuscripts. Ironically, it was this unoriginal activity that would leave Niccoli's most original and lasting mark: the clear, distinctive forward-leaning script that he developed to copy manuscripts would eventually be adopted by the first Italian printers after his death — it would become known as *italic*.

Niccoli's influence would spread beyond literary tastes, and would also prove formative in modelling the taste of artists such as Donatello and Brunelleschi, who met Niccoli at Cosimo's house. It was from Niccoli that Donatello acquired his passion for classical sculpture, and he also helped open Brunelleschi's eyes to the wonders of Ancient Rome, which still lay in ruins amidst the ramshackle medieval city that had grown up in its place. When Niccoli died in 1437, he bequeathed his library of 800 manuscripts to Cosimo. Niccoli had always regarded his collection as something of a public service, open to scrutiny by any scholar or artist willing to brave its owner's forthright questioning, and he knew that Cosimo would continue this tradition of openness. Four hundred of Niccoli's manuscripts would become the core of the Medici Library, which Cosimo founded in 1444, when he finally moved into the Palazzo Medici on the Via Larga; at the same time Cosimo added manuscripts from his own collection, and this became the first extensive public library in Europe. It was even possible to borrow original manuscripts, and Cosimo was constantly extending the library's contents. At one stage he would employ no fewer than forty-five copyists, who would produce more than 200 further manuscripts in the space of just two years. Cosimo would split the rest of Niccoli's manuscripts between his own private collection and the library that he had founded at San Giorgio Maggiore in Venice in gratitude for hospitality during his exile.

Another novelty of Cosimo's library was that it provided knowledge from a source other than the Church — here was the initial public manifestation of a new lay learning. Conversely, the manuscripts that Cosimo provided for the library at San Giorgio Maggiore, a religious institution, marked a broadening of knowledge available within the Church. Although the Church was losing its medieval monopoly on scholarship, there was initially no conflict here — both secular and sacred knowledge co-existed.

By far the most successful agent, whom Niccoli employed to search out manuscripts for him all over Europe, was Poggio Bracciolini, who would become another leading light of Cosimo's humanist circle, both as a writer and as a collector of manuscripts. Bracciolini was born in 1380, the son of a poor apothecary in the small town of Arezzo, forty miles south-east of Florence, and is said to have made his way to Florence at the age of eighteen, where he arrived all but penniless. Somehow he managed to talk his way into the university, where he studied law, but also found time to learn Greek, being one of the first to benefit from the newly appointed professor, Manuel Chrysoloras, who is now generally recognised as the founder of Greek studies in Italy. After Bracciolini's graduation in 1403, he obtained a post as a scrivener in the papal service, and when Baldassare Cossa became Pope John XXIII in 1410, he promoted Bracciolini to the post of chief writer of his letters and papal edicts. In 1414 Bracciolini accompanied Pope John XXIII to the fateful Council of Constance, and it was here that Bracciolini became a close friend of the young Cosimo de' Medici, who was also in the papal entourage.

After this, Bracciolini seems to have operated for several years as a sort of freelance manuscript hunter, roving the monasteries of Switzerland,

Germany and France in search of lost ancient works for various employers, including Niccolò Niccoli, and Cosimo de' Medici, who had recently started collecting books and ancient manuscripts. Despite Bracciolini's high-minded quest for knowledge, he was not above using underhand methods to obtain what he wanted; he would copy manuscripts, even when expressly forbidden to do so, and frequently bribed or cajoled reluctant abbots. When he happened upon unknown caches in dusty cloister cellars, he was not above having recourse to a hidden pocket in his cloak; no one was any the wiser, and back in Italy the cause of learning received a further boost, while the finder received a suitably lavish fee. In this way Bracciolini was able to continue with the well-heeled travelling style to which he was becoming accustomed; indeed, his appetite for ancient learning is said to have been matched only by his appetite for good food and beautiful women.

Amongst Bracciolini's finds was an entire hoard of forgotten ancient manuscripts found in the dungeon of a tower at the Swiss monastery of St Galen, though his most famous discovery was the unearthing in 1417 of a complete manuscript of *De Rerum Natura* by the first-century BC Roman author Lucretius, a work which had been lost since the fall of the Roman Empire and was known only through brief quotations in the works of others. *De Rerum Natura* (On the Nature of Things) is a long poem whose six books include a quasi-scientific explanation of the universe, much of it derived from Ancient Greek philosophers such as Democritus and Epicurus, who described a surprisingly modern universe made of atoms, governed by scientific laws, where the gods had no role to play. In *De Rerum Natura* Lucretius put forward the Epicurean view that human beings should pursue pleasure and avoid pain; philosophy was intended to cure humanity of its fear of death and the gods; and Religio appears as a monster whose gruesome visage peers down from a distant region of the sky. According to Lucretius, Epicurus had reached beyond 'the fiery ramparts of the world' and seen into the very core of nature's truth. Nearly one and a half millennia previously Lucretius had articulated much that still remained in embryo in the early humanist vision: here was an incitement for humanity to discover itself, and to discover the workings of a world free from metaphysical influence.

Bracciolini sent this manuscript of Lucretius to Niccoli in Florence, where he made a painstaking copy in his meticulous italic hand – a fortunate precaution, as the manuscript that Bracciolini discovered has since been lost, and all we know of its contents is from Niccoli's copy. In the year following this miraculous find, Bracciolini went to England for four years in the hope of making further discoveries, but was disappointed owing to the effect of the damp climate, which had rendered so many ancient manuscripts mouldy and unreadable. On his return to Italy he was pleased to rejoin the papal service, which enabled him to continue searching for manuscripts, as well as composing his own works. Unlike many papal appointments, this post did not require him to take holy orders; consequently, at the age of fifty-six he decided to settle down and married an eighteen-year-old girl, who would eventually bear him six children – to add to the fourteen illegitimate children he had already fathered.

Later Bracciolini returned permanently to Florence, where he took on a leading role in the humanist circle, becoming a close friend of Cosimo. In 1427 they even went on holiday together to Ostia, the port of Rome, where they dug amongst the ancient ruins, which at the time lay scattered and largely ignored. Further evidence of his close friendship with Cosimo is found during the period of the latter's exile, when Bracciolini sent him a series of supportive, if somewhat hypocritical letters, which are replete with philosophical advice such as: 'Be thankful that life has given you this opportunity to exercise such great virtue.' Interestingly, Bracciolini appears to have accepted that Cosimo would not be returning to Florence, consoling him: 'Whatever land fate takes you to, think of that as your country' – a sentiment that prompts the suspicion that this feeling must have been widespread in Florence at the time.

Bracciolini also advised Cosimo on how to build up his growing collection of manuscripts, and it was possibly on Bracciolini's advice that Cosimo hired Cyriac of Ancona, a renowned merchant and antique dealer. Cyriac had travelled through the Near East and North Africa copying down inscriptions he found amongst classical ruins and providing the first description of many ancient sites (centuries later, these would become primary sources for exploring archaeologists). Cosimo sent Cyriac on trading expeditions to Constantinople, the Holy Land and Egypt, during which he was also asked to seek out manuscripts, and it was this that prompted the historian Edward Gibbon to his celebrated, if somewhat rose-tinted, description of Cosimo in his prime: 'his riches were dedicated to the service of mankind;

he corresponded at once with Cairo and London; and a cargo of Indian spices and Greek books were often imported in the same vessel'.

Bracciolini must have made an endearing and entertaining companion for Cosimo, if his literary works are any guide to his character. These are amongst the finest of this early humanist period: they are stylish, witty and original, covering the whole range from bawdy tales to profound philosophical dialogues. In one of the latter, *On the Unhappiness of Princes*, Niccoli appears as the embodiment of classical taste, while Cosimo features as the worldly but high-minded banker. It has been said that, when crossed, Bracciolini was capable of producing some of the most notorious and vituperative polemics of a polemical age – his writings frequently satirised the corruption of the Church and the hypocrisy of priests who fathered illegitimate children (a topic on which he was undeniably an expert). Coincidentally, Bracciolini's distinctive handwriting would also leave its lasting impression: this he modelled on the precise script, with clearly separated words, that appeared in German manuscripts of the eleventh century. After this date writing had degenerated into the speedily executed but barely legible Gothic script favoured by bored copyist monks in medieval monasteries. As a result, Bracciolini's distinctive script also came to the notice of the early Italian printers in the following century, when it was used as a model for what is now known as roman type, which remains a much-favoured font to this day (being the type you are at present reading). At the age of seventy-three Bracciolini was profoundly moved when he was honoured by being elected as Chancellor of Florence, a move in which his friend Cosimo must surely have played a part. Six years later Braccioloni died, and Florence honoured the writer whose Latin was said to be as sweet as honey, and who preferred to work seated beside a beautiful woman 'in preference to a long-horned buffalo' (his fanciful notion of the conditions that prevailed in a medieval monastery).

The other leading figure amongst the humanist circle in Florence that Cosimo frequented was Marsilio Ficino, the son of his physician, who was born in 1433. Ficino was a strange figure: a small hunchback who walked with a limp, his inclinations were spiritual, but he occasionally displayed an explosive temper. Initially he studied medicine, but at the same time he also learned Greek and developed a profound interest in Plato, so much so that he would come to be regarded as Florence's leading expert on the philosopher and his works. Cosimo was particularly keen to read Plato, but could find no satisfactory translations of his work; as a result, he virtually adopted Ficino, establishing him in a cottage on his estate in the Mugello where he was to translate for Cosimo all of Plato's dialogues into Latin. In the summer, when Cosimo retreated from the heat of Florence to the cooler mountain air of the Mugello, he would invite Ficino to his villa in the evenings, where they would read and discuss Plato long into the night.

The way of life that Cosimo led left him particularly susceptible to philosophical problems. The usury upon which his bank prospered was still strictly speaking a mortal sin, and this worried him; similarly, the devious political machinations involved in the running of the city made him ponder the morality of his life. Beneath the prudent humanist façade lurked an increasingly guilt-ridden soul, and Plato's discussions of the immortality of the soul, of the ideal republic ruled by the philosopher-king and the qualities necessary for the good life, all affected Cosimo deeply.

Ficino would eventually produce his own neo-Platonic ideas on these subjects. In his view, the immortality of the soul depended on its participation during life in the divine properties of reason, unity and self-sufficiency. He saw the writings of the Ancient Greek philosophers as prefiguring the truth of the Christian religion, and strove to unite Plato's pagan philosophy with Christianity in a distinctly humanist religion. The Platonic ideas of beauty, truth and the absolute became central to Ficino's thinking, which resulted in his interpretations of these ideas becoming highly influential amongst the artistic and literary humanists of Florence. He famously wrote that beauty lay 'Not in the shadows of matter, but in the light and form; not in the darkling stuff of the body, but in its lucid proportion; not in the sluggardly sullied weight of the flesh, but in number and measure.' This could almost be a manifesto of the humanist artists.

Yet Ficino could not accept all manifestations of humanism; his ideas tended to the spiritual, and at the age of thirty he would become a priest. One winter's night, whilst reading a copy of Lucretius's *De Rerum Natura* in his cottage, he became so exasperated by its Epicurean worldliness that he flung it into the fire. Cosimo was not the only one troubled by the deep contradictions exposed by his attempt to live a new way of life.

8

East Meets West

JUST FOUR YEARS after his return from exile, Cosimo secured the
Florentine Republic's greatest international triumph. In 1439 the city
became host to the great Ecumenical Council, which had been called
to settle the differences between the Catholic Church of Rome and the
Orthodox Church of Constantinople (also known as Byzantium, now
Istanbul).

The split between the Roman and the Byzantine churches dated back
to the late Roman era, when the Christianised Empire had split into two.
The Greek Eastern Church had maintained a strict orthodoxy, insisting
that there should be no deviation from the original doctrines of
Christianity, whilst the Roman Western Church had to a certain extent
evolved through the centuries — as a result, neither church regarded the
other as practising true Christianity.

This division was further exacerbated in 1204 when the soldiers of
the Fourth Crusade arrived at Constantinople on their way to the Holy
Land. Amidst scenes of licentious mayhem, the crusaders raped and
pillaged their way through the city, setting a drunken prostitute on the
emperor's throne in the cathedral of Santa Sophia. After such a débâ-
cle, any prospect of unification between Rome and Constantinople
seemed remote, but two centuries later the Muslim army of the
Ottomans had conquered most of Turkey and now threatened
Constantinople itself. The Byzantine emperor John VIII Paleologus
appealed to the pope for help 'in the name of Christ'. Pope Eugenius
IV responded by suggesting that the leaders of the two churches should
meet to resolve their doctrinal differences, and the Byzantine emperor
agreed, setting sail with a 700-strong delegation, including twenty-three

bishops, for a meeting at the northern Italian city of Ferrara.

The Byzantine delegation arrived at Ferrara in January 1438. At the time, the city was freezing in the cold wind from the Alps, and the civic authorities found it all but impossible to house the large Roman delegation as well as the unexpectedly massive delegation from Constantinople. Pope Eugenius IV was essentially a monastic character, with little financial expertise, which had left him heavily in debt. Now as host he found himself expected to pay for the Byzantine emperor and his seemingly limitless entourage, which even included a menagerie of exotic pet animals. Initially Eugenius IV borrowed 10,000 florins from the Medici Bank, but this soon proved hopelessly inadequate and he was forced to borrow another 10,000 florins – yet even this was not enough. Without consulting his Medici bankers, the pope then managed to raise a further large loan, but only after he had been induced to pledge his entire medieval fortress at Assisi as security.

Cosimo de' Medici followed these proceedings closely from Florence; but when an outbreak of plague was reported in Ferrara, he decided it was time to act and despatched his brother Lorenzo with a message for the pope. This suggested that the great Ecumenical Council should be moved to the healthier climate of Florence, and to facilitate this move the city of Florence would be willing to pay 1,500 florins a month to help cover the expenses of the Ecumenical Council, for however long it chose to stay in session. Eugenius IV was well aware of Cosimo's motives behind this offer, for it was evident that moving the Council to Florence would bring him immense prestige in the city, while it would also cause a huge boom in trade, which would considerably benefit the local traders, to say nothing of the resident banks. But the pope had little choice, for the plague was liable to increase in virulence with the coming of hot weather, so the Council set out for Florence.

On this occasion, Cosimo decided to dispense with his characteristic caution and ensured that he was elected *gonfaloniere*, so that he could personally greet the delegations of the pope and the emperor as leader of the city. On the day the delegations were due to arrive, the streets were decked out with flags, the processional route was lined with liveried heralds bearing trumpets, and huge crowds gathered all along the way, packing the balconies and windows, even clambering onto the rooftops. But when the

Byzantine emperor and his long, trailing cortège at last entered the city, they were greeted by a sudden downpour, accompanied by fierce gusts of wind. Such was the force of the rain that the crowds soon ran for cover, the balconies emptied and the onlookers scrambled from the rooftops, leaving the bedraggled imperial procession to make its way through the torrent in the deserted streets. It was quickly led from the flag-decked processional route down a side-street to a nearby palazzo, where it sheltered in bedraggled disarray.

Despite this inauspicious start, the great Ecumenical Council soon got under way, and the contemporary Florentine book-dealer Vespasiano recorded in his vivid *Memoirso*: 'On a sober day the Pope with all the court of Rome, the Emperor of the Greeks and all the bishops and prelates assembled in Santa Maria del Fiore, where had been made a goodly arrangement for placing and seating the prelates of each church.' Amidst the vast echoing interior of the cathedral, beneath Brunelleschi's magnificent dome, the opening discussions began. In no time, the delegates were locked in debate on matters of crucial doctrinal importance. Should the bread used in the celebration of Mass be leaven (Catholic) or unleaven (Orthodox)? When the souls of the dead journeyed to their final destination in Heaven or Hell, did they first have to pass through Purgatory (Catholic) or not (Orthodox)? But the most divisive point of all concerned the Holy Trinity of 'the Father, the Son and the Holy Ghost': was the Holy Ghost generated by the Father *and* the Son (Catholic) or just by the Father (Orthodox)? Voices were raised and passions flared over the vexed matter of whether or not to accept the word *Filioque* ('and the Son').

Yet the main effect of the Council was felt outside the corridors and debating hall, in the streets themselves, where the citizens of Florence, and especially its artists, were presented with a hitherto unseen spectacle. Daily walking the streets of their city they saw all manner of bearded, exotically dressed prelates clad in opulent silk robes. Eyewitness acounts marvelled at the Greek archbishops who were dressed from head to toe in black robes, their heads topped with black stovepipe hats, over which were draped black veils, whilst from their shoulders hung brightly coloured cloaks with white-and-purple vertical stripes. According to Vespasiano, the delegates included 'certain Armenians, Jacobites [a heretical Monophysite sect from Macedonia], and Ethiopians were sent by Prester

John [the legendary Christian ruler in the East]'. There were certainly Ukrainians and Russians with Tartar servants, and other entourages included Moorish, Berber and black African attendants. Apparently at least one delegation had pet monkeys, while others had brought along exotically plumed singing birds in cages, as well as some tamed cheetahs – and all these would later begin appearing in paintings by Florentine artists. The visitors even had their effect on Florentine cooking, when it was noticed that the Byzantine emperor liked his eggs done in a particular way – cracked into a heated pan, stirred with a few herbs and spices, then turned onto his plate. In this way, Florentine cuisine discovered scrambled eggs.

During the summer evenings, when dinner had been taken and the theological wrangling set aside, private gatherings of scholars would take place in the palazzi where the Eastern delegates lodged. Of particular interest were those hosted by Archbishop Bessarion, a renowned theologian and philosopher who came from Trebizon on the Black Sea. Another leading light of these gatherings was Gemisthos Plethon, whose knowledge of Plato was unrivalled; Cosimo and his humanist friends listened in awe as Plethon expounded on Plato's theory of ideas. Human beings were like chained prisoners sitting in a dark cave facing the wall, and the world they saw consisted of mere shadows playing over the cave wall. Yet in order to achieve enlightenment and understand the truth they must turn away from this world of shadows and face the true reality of ideas that existed in the light outside the cave.

This was not how Cosimo lived: on the contrary, he had always been a very worldly man, paying meticulous attention to his banking ledgers, and constantly scheming to ensure that his political intentions were fulfilled. Yet something in Plato's idealism struck a chord in his personality, perhaps satisfying some profound unfulfilled spiritual need within him – possibly a remnant of that youthful enthusiasm for antiquity which he had been forced to abandon by his father. It was these gatherings of Byzantine philosophers that inspired Cosimo to commission Ficino's translation of the works of Plato into Latin, so that he could read them for himself. At the same time Cosimo began dreaming of founding a school much like that established by Plato in Athens more than 1,800 years previously. He would create a Platonic Academy in Florence, where the philosopher's ideas could be discussed and disseminated amongst like-minded intellectuals: these would be the torch-bearers of the new learning.

After four long, hot summer months of wrangling, the Ecumenical Council eventually agreed on a theological formula allowing the two churches to form a united Christendom – the schism that had lasted for six centuries was finally over. The pope would be recognised as the over-all head of the Church, and the Byzantines agreed to a compromise over the crucial question of the Holy Ghost. (This was only brought about because the Byzantines remained unsure of their own precise doctrinal position on this matter, mainly because the relevant codices had somehow been left behind in Constantinople.)

The final meeting of the Council was held on 6 July 1439, and here the documents sealing the two churches in a united Christendom were ceremoniously signed. According to Vespasiano: 'All Florence was there to witness this noble function.' On one side sat the pope and his delegation, 'on the other side was a chair covered with a silken cloth on which sat the Emperor, clad in a rich robe of damask brocade and a cap in the Greek fashion, on the top of which was a magnificent jewel. He was a very handsome man with a beard of the Greek cut.' First in Latin, and then in Greek, the proclamation was read out: 'Let the heavens rejoice and the earth exult, for the wall which divided the Western and Eastern Churches has fallen. Peace and concord have returned.' The Roman cardi-nals and the Greek archbishops clasped each other in fond embraces, before kneeling at the foot of the pope's throne.

After this, the Emperor John VIII Paleologus sailed back to Constantinople, to await the troops promised by the pope for the city's defence against the Turks. But when he arrived, and the terms of the agreement he had signed became public knowledge, the population rose up in anger against it and there were extensive riots. The people of Constantinople wanted nothing to do with the new agreement, which was anathema to their faith. As a result, the concord fell apart and the fate of Constantinople became inevitable: just over a decade later, in 1453, Sultan Mehmet the Conqueror and his vast Ottoman army arrived outside the walls and laid siege to the city. Eventually the great ramparts were breached and the Ottoman troops poured into Constantinople. During the three days of massacre that followed, the head of the last Byzantine emperor Constantine IX Paleologus was severed from his body with a scimitar and placed on a column amidst jeering crowds in the Hippodrome.

In fact, by this stage Constantinople had been reduced to a shadow of its former glorious self. Fearing the worst, much of the population had already fled, and amongst these were many scholars and philosophers who made their way to a new life in Italy. Archbishop Bessarion had been persuaded to remain behind in Italy after the Ecumenical Council, and the pope had made him a cardinal; now Italy became a refuge for Greek scholars, causing a craze for all things Greek. Soon upper-class children were being taught Ancient Greek, and the ability to converse in Greek was considered the height of intellectual fashion. In time, some in Florence began describing what was happening as a *rinascimento* (renaissance, or rebirth) of ancient learning.

The word *rinascimento*, as we understand it, first appeared in the writings of the sixteenth-century Florentine artist and biographer Vasari, though his context suggests that it had already been in growing use for some years. Not until the early nineteenth century would the word arrive in France, spreading to Britain and Germany in the mid-nineteenth century, as writers gained a historical understanding of what had taken place, and began to conceptualise this as a particular age.

This renaissance of knowledge in fifteenth-century Italy, and Florence in particular, was given further impetus by the many rare Greek manuscripts that were brought west by the scholars fleeing Constantinople. These covered all manner of subjects, including topics that remained unknown or forgotten in the West, ranging from philosophy to mathematics, from alchemy to astrology. All these subjects would undergo a revival: the coming age would see a flowering of both the rational and the irrational, of both sense and nonsense. After the long abstinence of the Middle Ages, the hunger for knowledge would be omnivorous.

This influx of manuscripts enabled Cosimo de' Medici to add still further to his great library, which at its height was said to have included more than 10,000 manuscripts of Ancient Greek, Latin and Hebrew texts. For once, he was not following in his father Giovanni di Bicci's footsteps: his father had owned just three books, all of them devoted to medieval theology. In his retirement Giovanni had discovered the pleasure of commissioning public works – this was how a wealthy citizen of Florence was traditionally expected to honour his city; it was almost considered a civic duty. Cosimo would now begin following his father's example, but on a scale that none could have imagined.

9

Art Reborn: The Egg Dome
and the Human Statue

THE NEW HUMANISM that arose from the rediscovery of ancient knowledge and literature would in turn give rise to the Renaissance, which began as a 'rebirth' but would soon evolve an originality of its own. There is one crucial aspect that links this long and gradual process, which would come to full flowering as the fifteenth century progressed. This aspect is knowledge – the early humanists rediscovered it, and the Renaissance artists saw themselves as extending it. The most characteristic and original expression of the Renaissance would be its art, yet crucially its artists saw this activity as a form of learning; and here at least, the passage from humanism to the Renaissance is all but seamless.

The Renaissance artists would paint images of a visibly different humanity from that depicted in the religious paintings of their medieval predecessors. This was achieved by shedding previous stylisation and formalism, and although much of the medieval religious symbolism would be retained, this would increasingly be tempered by the artist imbuing his figures with an element of psychological realism. Human beings would be depicted with all the verisimilitude of a classical statue, usually placed in a recognisable landscape. Although the subjects remained for the most part religious (saints, the Madonna, biblical scenes and so forth), these holy figures were seen less as transcendental or metaphysical figures and more as they might have lived in the reality of their human lifetime. Art would become a form of learning about what a human being was, of understanding the purely human condition; this new art would seek to teach man about himself, and his world, in an almost scientific manner –

indeed it would, in many ways, aspire to be a science. As we shall see, later Renaissance artists, such as Leonardo da Vinci, would even use their art to depict the secrets of nature, and of human nature — drawing the intricacies of flowing water, human anatomy, as well as imagined or invented complex mechanical objects. It is important to remember that this aspect of art as a form of knowledge was always an integral part of the new enterprise; from the outset, Renaissance artists saw themselves as discovering new truths — about art, about technique, about humanity and the world.

The first manifestations of this new artistic movement would be seen in fifteenth-century Italy, all but exclusively in Florence. Yet why did it originate here — why not Naples or Venice, Milan or Rome? All these other cities had sufficient wealth and elements of sophistication, as well as vivifying contacts with international trade, yet each had in its own way a debilitating factor that hampered the innovation, independence and breadth of outlook required to instigate such a major transformation as the Renaissance. Naples and Milan were subject to autocratic rulers; Rome remained for the most part a backward city, liable to the vagaries of different popes; whilst Venice was ruled by a stable patriciate. Florence, on the other hand, saw itself as a quasi-democratic republic, yet its arcane democratic process was unstable as well as being liable to corruption, and it may well have been this political instability that proved so conducive to innovation. The city also had a long tradition of civic patronage: successful merchants were expected to contribute to the glory of the city almost as a patriotic obligation. Partly as a result of all this, Florence had a tradition of artistic excellence going back generations — in the fourteenth century, Dante, Petrarch and Boccaccio all had close links with Florence — and it still saw itself as a city of art, producing as well as attracting painters and artists who required patronage. This became a self-perpetuating process that would encourage the creative spark of rivalry and innovation, whilst in conjunction with this there was a flourishing intellectual tradition whose interest in ancient manuscripts nurtured early humanistic ideas, resulting in an intellectual cross-fertilisation whereby artists and poets mingled with the new philosophical humanists and scholars. All these factors, rather than any one particular reason, probably accounted for Florence's unique role in the founding of the Renaissance

– and unique in furthering this role would be the Medici. The vast yet discriminating patronage of the Medici family, particularly Cosimo, would play a formative part. The Florentine Renaissance would certainly have happened without the Medici, and the Medici would be just one Florentine family amongst several who contributed to this initial flowering – yet their distinctive and enlightened contribution, their particular encouragement of many of the main Renaissance artists, would leave its indelible mark. There would be an element of the Florentine Renaissance that was characteristically Medicean, and for better or worse it would arise from their role as godfathers, through several generations, of both the city and its cultural life.

The Medici were to be involved in the development of this new art from the very outset. In a telling coincidence, Giovanni di Bicci's first participation in artistic patronage would result in what many consider to be the first great Renaissance work of art – the bronze doors for the Baptistery of San Giovanni. The commissioning of this work was inspired by an event that had taken place in recent Florentine history. In 1401 there had been an outbreak of plague in the city, causing widespread fear and consternation. Fortunately this outbreak abated almost as quickly as it had first appeared, yet memories had been stirred of the Black Death, which had struck so devastatingly just over half a century previously. As a thanksgiving to God for protecting the city from another Black Death, the Florentine authorities decided to provide some magnificent new bronze doors for the twelfth-century Baptistery of San Giovanni. This stood in the piazza in front of the Cathedral of Santa Maria del Fiore, and held a particular place in the heart of all Florentines, for the Baptistery was the location where every child born in Florence was baptised.

Artists were invited to submit models of the doors for a competition, and a committee was set up to judge the winner. Giovanni di Bicci served on this committee, and it may well been his earliest taste of civic office, providing the shrewd middle-aged banker with his first experience of the world of art and patronage. The decision that the committee finally arrived at was a controversial one: the winning design was judged to have been provided by an unknown illegitimate twenty-four-year-old goldsmith called Lorenzo Ghiberti.

It would take Ghiberti more than twenty years before he was finally satisfied with the bronze doors he produced; and in order to achieve this, he would have to transform the art of bronze-casting, introducing both new methods and new apparatus. This was almost as much a feat of technology as it was a work of art. Ghiberti's doors contained a series of biblical scenes cast in relief, depicting classically draped figures who were remarkably lifelike, enacting dramatic scenes, often against striking architectural backgrounds, such as an imposing Ancient Roman arch or Noah's Ark depicted as a pyramid. These backgrounds, and the drapery in which many of the figures were clothed, reflected Ghiberti's deep interest in the formerly ignored ancient ruins that were now being noticed as if for the first time, as well as his interest in the newly discovered classical learning (his depiction of Noah's Ark as a pyramid comes from the third-century Greek theologian Origen, a description that was ignored throughout the medieval era).

Ghiberti's Baptistery doors were received with great acclaim, and are now regarded as one of the formative works of early Renaissance art. Such was their success that Ghiberti was commissioned to design another set of doors for the eastern entrance to the Baptistery, and these would take him more than thirty years to complete, finishing in 1452 – though this was not entirely due to his perfectionism. During this period Ghiberti also accepted many commissions for other work: the Baptistery doors had made him famous, and as a result he would become one of the richest artists in the city. His later *catasto* tax returns show that he owned a farm outside Florence, as well as a vineyard and even a flock of sheep. His self-portrait, which he included unobtrusively in the east doors, depicts an amiable, balding man. He would take so long over these second Baptistery doors that they would only be installed in the year following his death. It was said that when the young Michelangelo first saw these doors years later, he was so overwhelmed by their beauty that he declared 'they could be the gates of Paradise'.

Yet not all the artists of Florence were so impressed. The man who narrowly lost out to Ghiberti in 1402 had been so angry at his rejection that he had packed up and gone to live in Rome. This was the artist Filippo Brunelleschi, who had been born in Florence in 1377 and was renowned as an extremely difficult character: proud, easy to take offence, secretive and possessed of a volatile temper. One of his favoured habits was sending scurrilous and insulting anonymous verses to people he felt had somehow slighted him.

Brunelleschi felt so humiliated over his defeat by Ghiberti in the competition for the Baptistery doors that he decided to abandon fine art and become an architect; this time, he promised himself, no one would better him. He travelled to Rome with the precocious sixteen-year-old artist Donatello, who was possessed of an equally inflammable temperament, and together the two of them searched and argued their way through the ruins of Ancient Rome, unearthing statues and studying pediments. Extraordinarily, Brunelleschi never confided in Donatello that he was in fact studying to become an architect, though in the course of these explorations he would come to understand one of the greatest secrets of architectural history.

Amongst the few remaining intact classical buildings in Rome was the Pantheon, with its miraculous 142-foot-wide dome, which had been built for the Emperor Hadrian at the height of Rome's imperial grandeur. The secret of how its dome had been constructed had long been lost, and for 1,300 years this had remained the widest dome ever erected. Brunelleschi became intrigued, and somehow contrived to climb up onto the roof of the Pantheon, where he removed some of the dome's outer stones and discovered that it had an inner dome. This inner vaulting consisted of blocks of stone that dovetailed into one another, so that they became virtually self-supporting; at the same time, the connections between the inner and outer dome were constructed in such a way that they actually supported each other.

When Brunelleschi returned to Florence around 1417, he quickly established a name for himself as one of the city's leading architects. As we have seen, in 1419 Giovanni di Bicci headed the committee that commissioned Brunelleschi to build the city's foundling hospital, named in quaint euphemistic fashion Ospedale degli Innocenti. This would be Brunelleschi's first major work, and its clean classical façade would mark a distinct contrast to the surrounding medieval buildings, incorporating as it did such rediscovered technical details as graceful supporting pillars. In the course of this work, the dry ageing banker and his temperamental architect unexpectedly formed a deep bond of friendship. From the outset, Brunelleschi had expressed very definite ideas about the type of building he wished to erect; while Giovanni for his part felt very uncertain in the novel role of patron, and took to consulting his humanist-educated son Cosimo. It required little encouragement for Cosimo to become enthusiastic about the project, and his explanation of Brunelleschi's innovative aims soon filled Giovanni with admiration for his architect, while Cosimo's informed understanding of Brunelleschi's intentions meant that soon he too became a friend of Brunelleschi. The two men now managed to persuade Giovanni to branch out in his role as patron, and as a result he commissioned Brunelleschi to restore and enlarge San Lorenzo, the church of the Medici clan. Brunelleschi would eventually finish the sacristy of San Lorenzo just in time for Giovanni's burial here in 1429 – although by this stage he had become involved in a far greater project, the one for which he will always be remembered.

The Cathedral of Santa Maria del Fiore had been started as long ago as 1296, when Florence's first banking boom and its ascendancy as a centre of the wool trade had made it one of the richest cities in Europe. Filled with civic pride, the inhabitants of Florence had come to see their city as the embodiment of a new Rome. To celebrate this self-acclaimed eminence, it had been decided that the new cathedral should be one of the largest in all Christendom, a match for the great Gothic cathedrals of northern Europe, and the Byzantine Santa Sophia in Constantinople with its famous dome.

But in rapid succession Florence had been hit by the bankruptcy of the Peruzzi, Bardi and Acciaiuoli banks, followed by the Black Death, with the result that just half a century after building had begun, the new cathedral remained little more than an abandoned building site. The unfinished façade enclosed a patch of waste ground exposed to all weathers, making it look more like a ruin than a construction project, while the eastern foundations had remained exposed for so many years that the street running beside the proposed cathedral had become known as Lungo di Fondamenti ('Along the Foundations').

Yet prosperity had eventually returned: the European wool trade had begun to flourish again, and the second generation of Florentine banks had asserted their pre-eminence, with none throughout Europe able to match the Medici Bank. Once more work had started again on the Cathedral of Santa Maria del Fiore, and by 1418 it was ready for the construction of its great crowning dome. This brought to light a crucial problem, for according to the original model of the cathedral the dome would need to have a span of 138 feet, wider than any but the Pantheon in Rome. This dome had been intended to represent the pride and achievement of the great city of Florence, but unfortunately the ambition of its citizens had far outstripped the achievement of any contemporary architect – with the result that instead of representing the city's pride and achievement, the impossible dome was now exposing Florence as a laughing stock.

The question remained as to how such an enormous structure could be erected without the walls of the cathedral buckling beneath the insupportable weight. At anxious meetings of the Signoria and the relevant committees, all manner of ingenious ideas were put forward. Perhaps the dome could be constructed out of a lightweight material, such as pumice stone; but then it was discovered that there simply was not enough wood available to build sufficient scaffolding. A suggested solution to this problem was that the entire inside of the cathedral should be filled with earth, so that the dome could be constructed with its stones supported from beneath. But there then remained the question of how all the earth was to be cleared from inside the completed cathedral. A proposal was made that it should be liberally mixed with small coins, which would encourage the poor, and small boys, to carry it out for free! The committee despaired, and as a final resort a prize competition was announced.

Brunelleschi entered the contest, proposing an egg-shaped dome supported by stone ribs, and out of the eleven submitted entries his was judged to be the best. But before awarding him the project, the judges wanted to be sure he was able to complete the task, and demanded to know exactly how he planned to construct his dome. Brunelleschi adamantly refused to reveal his secret, and in answer to the committee's persisting demands he proposed a question of his own: producing an egg from his pocket, he asked the committee if any of them could tell him how to make it stand on its end. When no one could answer this, Brunelleschi banged the upright egg sharply on the table so that it cracked open, but remained upright. The committee immediately protested that any of them could have done this, but Brunelleschi replied: 'Yes, and you would say just the same if I told you how I intended to build the dome.'

The committee remained wary. Eventually they awarded him the project, but in order to safeguard themselves they insisted on one condition – Brunelleschi would have to take on a partner to assist him in this project. The partner whom the committee chose was Ghiberti, and when Brunelleschi heard that he would be expected to work alongside his great rival, he was beside himself with rage, so much so that the committee was forced to call the palace guard to have him forcibly removed and thrown out into the piazza. Yet in the end, by sheer persistence and obstinacy, Brunelleschi got his way. Even so, he would remain as suspicious as ever: from now on he would jealously guard the secrets of his construction methods, labelling his plans with cryptic symbols, using his own cipher of Arabic numerals for the calculations. Not only were his methods secret, but many of them had never been tried before; the risk was enormous, and even Brunelleschi himself was not sure they would work. He decided to build the dome without erecting any supporting scaffolding, devising instead a method by which its arching stones supported themselves during its construction. The secret of his method was adapted from the Pantheon in Rome: he built two domes, one within the other, each in its own way supporting the other, with the bricks of the inner dome laid in an interlocking self-supporting herringbone pattern. Yet these techniques were much more than mere copies; the Romans may have left their dome, but they had left no instructions telling how they had *built* it. This meant that when it came to the actual details of construction, Brunelleschi was forced to resort to a blend of historical detective work, inspired guesses and ingenious invention. Here was learning reborn, yet at the same time adapted. The result was a superb work of art, one of the masterpieces of the early Renaissance. It was also a supreme achievement of engineering: in all, the dome required four million bricks, weighing around 1,500 tons, and besides inventing a crane to lift them, Brunelleschi later conceived of a novel hoist that proved even more efficient. Once again art had required science; at the very outset of the Renaissance these two were inseparable, advances in one proving impossible without advances in the other.

The building of the dome of Santa Maria del Fiore would take Brunelleschi more than fifteen years, at last being completed in 1436. This spectacular new feature would transform the skyline of Florence; yet at the same time the city was also being transformed at street level. Whilst

Fig 5 Brunelleschi's dome, Santa Maria del Fiore

Brunelleschi worked on the dome, he continued working for Cosimo on the Medici Chapel in the church of San Lorenzo, and completed many other projects in the city. Now that his father Giovanni was dead, Cosimo de' Medici felt free to begin pouring money into a number of building schemes, and in the midst of medieval Florence a new Renaissance city was beginning to appear. The architects chosen by Cosimo – such as Brunelleschi, Donatello and Michelozzo – had all studied the ruins of

Ancient Rome, and now proceeded to construct their own versions of its classical style in Florence.

The new art may have required science, but it also required money, and this was largely provided by Cosimo, who according to one admiring historian 'appeared determined to transform medieval Florence into an entirely new Renaissance city'. This was hardly an exaggeration, for Cosimo funded the construction, or renovation, of buildings ranging from palaces to libraries, churches to monasteries. When his grandson Lorenzo the Magnificent examined the books many years later he was flabbergasted at the amounts that Cosimo had sunk into these schemes; the accounts would reveal that between 1434 and 1471 a staggering 663,755 gold florins had been spent. (Cosimo died in 1464, but the legacies and unfinished projects went on.) Such a sum is difficult to put into context; suffice to say that just over a century beforehand the entire assets of the great Peruzzi Bank at its height, accumulated in branches all over western Europe and ranging beyond to Cyprus and Beirut, were the equivalent of 103,000 gold florins.

Yet such munificence was always built on a foundation of solid banking practice. An examination of the Medici Bank records shows that while it made use of the most efficient financial instruments available, it was in no way innovative in its practices; it was if anything highly conservative compared with other similar institutions. Neither Giovanni di Bicci nor Cosimo de' Medici introduced any novel methods or ways of doing business, their practice being based entirely on the efficient and prudent use of proven methods pioneered by others. This should always be borne in mind, for it was only this, and the Medici political organisation, that made all Cosimo's other activities possible. No matter what he was doing, he was always first and foremost, every day, a cautious and highly astute banker. Indeed, the only persistently creative element in his accounts appears to have been with regard to his tax returns; but then this too had long been an established Italian banking tradition.

Cosimo may have been conservative in his banking practice, and may have consciously conducted himself in a modest and retiring fashion, yet surprisingly he was capable of tolerating the most extravagant behaviour amongst his protégés. This is perhaps epitomised by an incident involving the touchy Donatello, who was probably his favourite. One day, on the recommendation of Cosimo, a Genoese merchant commissioned Donatello to produce a life-sized bronze head; but when Donatello had finished, the merchant refused to pay for it, claiming that Donatello was charging him too much. Cosimo was called in to mediate, and ordered the head to be carried to the roof of his palazzo, where it was placed on the parapet, so that it could be seen in the best light. Yet still the Genoese merchant complained that he was being asked to pay too much, pointing out that Donatello had only taken a month to complete the commission and was charging more than fifteen florins. Upon hearing these words Donatello became incensed, declaring that he was an artist, not a labourer who was paid by the hour. Before anyone could restrain him, Donatello leaped forward and pushed the bronze head over the parapet, whereupon it crashed down into the street below, shattering into fragments. The merchant was immediately smitten with remorse at what he had caused to happen, and promised to pay double if Donatello would make him another head; but despite the merchant's promises and Cosimo's pleadings, Donatello remained adamant, refusing point blank to produce anything for the merchant, even though he was a friend of Cosimo.

Surprisingly, Cosimo did not censure such behaviour. He appears to have been one of the first patrons to recognise the new kind of artist being produced by the Renaissance, insisting: 'One must treat these people of extraordinary genius as if they were celestial spirits, not as if they are beasts of burden.' The effect of humanism had been to encourage a new emphasis on individuality; the personality was becoming recognised as an integral part of what a human being was – not just the prerogative of rulers. Donatello was very much a case in point; his complex personality consisted of conflicting elements, which would inform his art in a manner hitherto unseen. Yet paradoxically, his character retained a distinctly medieval otherworldliness, and he cared so little about his personal appearance that in the end Cosimo decided it was time he smartened up. To encourage Donatello out of his scruffy ways, Cosimo gave him a set of fine red clothes, complete with a new cloak; Donatello wore his smart red outfit for a few days, but soon reverted to his habitual working-man's clothes, and Cosimo gave up.

Despite Donatello's prickly pride, he in fact cared little for money;

he would place what he earned in a basket in his studio, telling his assistants that they could help themselves without asking, whenever they needed some ready cash. Yet for such trust, he demanded absolute loyalty. When one of his assistants ran away, Donatello is said to have chased him as far as Ferrara with the intention of murdering him. Though there is probably more to this story than meets the eye: Donatello was homosexual, and many of his violent outbursts certainly resulted from passionate entanglements. His first appearance in the records is as a fifteen-year-old involved in a fight with a German, and according to this report Donatello's opponent ended up being hit over the head with a heavy piece of wood, causing profuse bleeding. It was a year later that Donatello set off for Rome with Brunelleschi, and this would mark the beginning of a lifelong friendship, interspersed with stormy interludes – Donatello would receive more than his fair share of insulting poems, but he evidently soon forgot them.

Donatello made no secret of his homosexuality, and his behaviour was tolerated by his friends; certainly Cosimo is known to have played his part in patching up at least one lovers' quarrel between Donatello and one of his young assistants. Attitudes to homosexuality in Florence appear to have been ambiguous. The passionate young Italian male found himself in a difficult situation, with girls marrying much younger than men and a high premium being placed on their virginity. As a result, any young blood who attempted to interfere with this was liable to find himself in serious trouble, not to say mortal danger, from the offended family; deflowering a virgin meant devaluing a considerable family asset, to say nothing of dishonouring the family and any prospective groom.

All this meant that sodomy amongst young men was covertly tolerated, despite the frequency of edicts expressly forbidding this practice (1415, 1418, 1432). In fact, homosexuality was seldom prosecuted, and its practice was so rife in Florence in the fourteenth century that the German slang term for a 'bugger' was *Florenzer*. When Florence lost a war against Lucca in 1432, the more diehard members of the Florentine military blamed their defeat on the fact that so many of the conscripts were homosexuals. The authorities were deeply worried by this and decided that something had to be done about it; yet another decree was issued banning all kinds of homosexual behaviour, but this time they also decided to take more positive action. A number of licensed bordellos were opened around

Fig 6 David with Goliath's Head by Donatello

the Mercato Vecchio (Old Market), and the prostitutes who worked from them were known as *meretrici* – meaning 'to merit paying', the source of our word 'meretricious'. As was the custom elsewhere in Italy, all *meretrici* were required to wear distinctive gloves, high-heeled shoes and little tinkling bells in their hair; they were also instructed 'to keep out of respectable churches'. The introduction of *meretrici* was to prove highly popular in Florence, and would remain so for years to come – within 130 years prostitutes numbered one in every 300 of the population.

However, none of this was to influence Donatello, whose masterpiece would prove to be one of the most overtly homosexual artworks of its era. This was the bronze life-sized *David* that he produced for Cosimo, which was placed on a pillar in the inner courtyard of the Palazzo Medici and would become one of the most treasured of all the works commissioned by the Medici. Despite this fact, it has been argued that this was not originally created for the Medici, yet merely bought by them, as there is no record of it being commissioned; but the evidence against this view is to be found in the laurel wreath that adorns the hat on David's head and the larger laurel wreath that encircles the base of the statue. The saint to whom the Medici church was dedicated, and the patron saint of the Medici family, was San Lorenzo; this is echoed in the Italian for laurel, which is *lauro*.

This statue is an unabashed masterpiece of homoerotic sexuality; and its sensuous nudity is only emphasised by the young David's calf-length ornamented leather boots, large floppy 'country-style' hat and the long curly tresses that fall down over his shoulders. His open-toed boot rests casually on the helmeted severed head of the slain giant Goliath, but in such a way that the exaggerated feathered wing of Goliath's helmet softly caresses his inner thigh. The specially darkened bronze adds highlights to the soft smoothness of the flesh, giving it a sensuality that ensures this is no idealised Renaissance figure, or emblematic ancient hero, at which we gaze in awe; on the contrary, this is a figure that beguiles the eye, all but enticing the spectator to feel its radiant surface. Yet such is the power of its beauty that somehow it transcends its flagrant homoeroticism: this is much more than an object of desire, it is an aesthetic masterpiece.

Once again, there was a major scientific aspect to this work of art. It was the first free-standing bronze sculpture to be produced in over a millennium, and as such represented the rediscovery of a lost knowledge; its casting alone was a huge technical achievement. Previously statues had been created for niches in buildings, or as architectural embellishments, rather than as complete objects in themselves; and the fact that this sculpture is to be seen in the round also required further scientific understanding. Donatello's *David* is a work of great anatomical precision, requiring more than a passing knowledge of this subject. The adolescent podginess softening the line of the rib bones, the slightly protuberant stomach, the swivel of the hips and the lined skin on the forefinger clutching the sword all indicate an eye for physiological detail. Yet at the same time there is no denying that this is a statue of a particular human body, a particular individual. The sensuality of its hand-on-hip pose may appear to outrage sexual orthodoxy even now, but it is not an exaggeration; anatomically and psychologically it is masterful – art and science combined here too.

Yet despite all this, Donatello's *David* remains something of a mystery. David was emblematic for the Republic of Florence: the hero who slew the Goliath of oppression was also seen as the embodiment of a republic free from autocratic rule. This would explain why it was originally commissioned, just as Donatello's homosexuality may explain why the commission was fulfilled in this particular way. Yet was Donatello really expected to produce such a statue? There would certainly have been preliminary sketches and models – which would have been seen by Cosimo, so he must have known what was coming; and why did the finished work prove so acceptable that it was given the place of honour in the middle of the courtyard of the Palazzo Medici? There is no record of it having caused any controversy when it was first erected; indeed, the very opposite was the case – the Medici family, and Cosimo in particular, appear to have taken it to heart, despite the fact that this was not a slightly inappropriate statue embodying republican Florence, it was *wholly* inappropriate.

Yet the key to this statue's mystery may well lie in its very inappropriateness; its supreme beauty, which transcends any particular sexuality to an almost hermaphroditic degree, may well contain esoteric meaning. The hermaphrodite was a compelling figure in classical mythology – a combination of Hermes and Aphrodite – who also played a central role in alchemy and hermeticism, both of which underwent a revival during the Renaissance, along with other such esoteric 'sciences' as astrology, magic and geomancy. These had all thrived in Constantinople, and arrived in western Europe with the influx of manuscripts and adepts that preceded the fall of the Byzantine Empire, with the result that the Renaissance saw a rebirth of rational *and* irrational knowledge. (Indicative of this ambivalence is the fact that before Ficino could finish his translations of Plato, he would be diverted to translate the *Corpus Hermeticum* by the legendary Greek alchemist Trismegistos.) It could well be that Donatello's *David* was intended to represent some kind of summation of knowledge, or of completed beauty, whose allusions now escape us; its combination of male and female sexuality would not be out of place in a Platonic ideal of human perfection.

10

'Father of the Country'

W E KNOW THAT Cosimo de' Medici was an instinctively cautious man in his personal, political and professional life – yet why was he so profligate in his patronage? There are several reasons for this, each an integral part of his complex character. First of all he felt guilt, for although the Church tended to turn a blind eye, Christianity still explicity forbade usury: 'If you lend money . . . you shall not extract interest' (Exodus 22:25), and many other references make this all too plain. Cosimo was also mindful of Christ's pronouncement: 'It is easier for a camel to go through the eye of a needle, than for a rich man to enter into the Kingdom of God' (Matthew 19:24). Throughout his life Cosimo remained a devout Christian, insisting that the ledgers of the Medici Bank, like those of all other banks of the period, should be headed with the inscription: 'Col Nome di Dio e di Bona Ventura' (in the context, this has frequently been translated as 'In the name of God and Profit', the latter being what 'good fortune' means for a banker). By middle age this conflict between Cosimo's faith and his worldly activities had begun to trouble his conscience; and when he was in his early forties he had a private audience with Pope Eugenius IV, during his residence in Florence. The pope suggested that to salve his conscience he could fund the rebuilding of the monastery of San Marco, and Cosimo immediately set Michelozzo to work on this project, one on which he would eventually spend more than 30,000 florins. This was a huge amount, but Cosimo seems to have taken this project very much to heart; he even retained his own cell in San Marco, where he would retire for periods of meditation. During these periods he began holding theological discussions with the prior, Antonio Pierozzi, a small intense man of austere and formidable character, whose exceptional spiritual qualities would cause him to be canonised after his death.

Something in Pierozzi's character appealed deeply to Cosimo, and it was probably the saintly prior who convinced him to seek full forgiveness for his sins. In the case of usury, this could only be done by disbursing himself of all that he had gained through such practice. This would certainly account for the sheer extravagance of Cosimo's patronage – though a careful study of the *libro segreto* reveals that even the colossal 660,000 florins he is known to have spent did not account for all he had gained. It has been estimated that Cosimo inherited somewhere in the region of 100,000 florins from his father Giovanni di Bicci, yet despite his vast charitable spending he is thought to have left more than 200,000 florins.

There is no denying that Cosimo's motives for his charitable projects were not entirely spiritual. They certainly furthered his political aims, as well as raising his standing in Florence, and that of the Medici Bank far beyond it. Cosimo is known to have rebuilt the residential college for Florentine students in Paris, and to have refurbished the Italian church of Santo Spirito in Jerusalem. Yet he remained a political realist, as we know from his contemporary Vespasiano, who records him saying: 'I know the ways of Florence, within fifty years we Medici will have been exiled, but my buildings will remain.' He wished to immortalise himself in the works that resulted from his patronage. This may well explain why he usually chose to patronise publicly visible projects; when it came to more private and less visible patronage, such as painting, he preferred to leave this to his sons Piero and Giovanni.

Cosimo may have had little faith in the permanence of Medici power after he was gone, but he made sure that the family remained in control of Florence as long as he was alive, and any potential political opponents were quickly warned off. Many fortunes were made during Cosimo's 'reign', and money meant power in Florence; in this the city lived up to its republican ideal, at least in part – and certainly more than any other major city in Italy (or indeed Europe). In Florence, power traditionally lay in the hands of the business class; the landowning aristocracy was specifically eliminated from the democratic process, they could have their titles instead of the vote – though some managed to circumvent this ban by becoming members of a trade guild.

When Cosimo noticed that any family was accumulating sufficient wealth to become a possible focus of opposition, he was not slow to issue a covert warning. But despite its underhand nature, the advice would be quite straightforward: the head of the family should disperse his capital by purchasing country estates, and he would then be ennobled; if not, he was liable to face a ruinous tax assessment by the inspectors, who were all stalwarts of the Medici party.

Cosimo's power was everywhere; as a foreign envoy to the city remarked: 'It is Cosimo who does everything . . . Without him nothing is done.' Yet his power was also elusive; he was not the government, merely the power behind it, and such power was difficult to oppose or eliminate. In the words of the renowned twentieth-century Renaissance historian J. R. Hale: 'given the city scale of most Italian statecraft, it is not without reason that [Cosimo] has been compared to the "boss" of Chicago or Dallas ward politics or the "padre" of a power zone of the Mafia'. This is fair comment – a number of bloody deeds were done in his name, if not necessarily on his direct orders, in back-streets at night – yet it is difficult to characterise as a tyranny a government that relied on such widespread public acquiescence. The people of Florence evidently felt that they needed their godfather; even if they did not necessarily want him, they understood that the alternatives were worse.

This may have accounted for the internal politics of Florence, but its external politics was a different matter. Here Cosimo was very much the visible moving force, and wished everyone outside Florence to know this. There is no doubt that he was an extraordinarily astute statesman, constantly working for the good of Florence – and its citizens, ruled as well as ruling. Cosimo had a vision that extended far beyond local politics, and this was largely due to his position as a banker. If the Medici Bank was to thrive, or even survive, it was necessary to keep a very close watch on the political scene; and here his international network of branches and agents served him well, supplying a constant flow of intelligence. By the 1450s the Medici Bank had established branches over much of western Europe – from London to Naples, Cologne to Ancona. The only countries that remained mostly beyond the Medici reach were Spain (which jealously monopolised its trade with the New World), Austria and southern

Germany (the province of the great German financial family, the Fuggers of Augsburg) and the Baltic (monopolised by the Hanseatic League).

Although Cosimo may have sinned as a godfather of the Renaissance, he was undeniably amongst the saints when it came to the major players on the Italian scene. Florence's main adversary was the powerful and intermittently rich city of Milan, whose shifting territorial border seldom lay much more than fifty miles to the north. Milan had been ruled since 1412 by Duke Filippo Maria Visconti, the degenerate scion of an illustrious family, who lived as a recluse in his impregnable fortress in Milan, assuming the proportions of a grim legend, even amongst his own people. Immensely fat and fearsomely ugly, he rarely appeared in public; he refused to attend public ceremonies, even those involving a visiting emperor or royalty, owing to his touchiness about his appearance. Having succeeded to the dukedom on the assassination of his older brother, he remained paranoid about plots to kill him, sleeping in heavily armed bedchambers, and switching beds three times a night to elude possible assassins. He was also ludicrously superstitious: his terror of thunder drove him to construct a special double-doored soundproofed chamber in the midst of his castle, so that he could not hear this frightful omen.

When Filippo Maria had suddenly ascended to the dukedom at the age of twenty, he had found the coffers all but empty; in order to remedy this he married Beatrice, the forty-year-old widow of one of his *condottieri*, who brought a dowry of 40,000 florins. Marital relations between the reclusive, overweight Filippo and the unexpectedly cultured, former mercenary general's wife proved difficult from the outset, and after a few years paranoia took over. Beatrice was arrested and put on trial for infidelity with a teenage pageboy, whose only transgression had been to entertain his mistress, in the company of her maids of honour, with his lute playing. All, including the maids of honour, were tortured until they confessed Beatrice's infidelity, and were then executed, while all evidence relating to their 'trial' was stricken from the records. Later, a second, politically expedient marriage was arranged with the young Maria of Savoy, thus protecting Milan against attack from the north. But when the couple retired to their wedding bed, Filippo heard a dog howling in the night, and as a result of this dreadful omen refused to have his wife under the same roof as himself – a decision that almost certainly saved her life. However, this meant that there was no direct Visconti heir to the dukedom, though Filippo did produce an illegitimate daughter called Bianca.

With such a figure as his immediate neighbour, Cosimo de' Medici was forced to exercise his considerable diplomatic skills to the full. Despite living locked in his castle, Filippo Maria Visconti had dreams of making Milan the supreme power in northern Italy, and his scheming to this end exhibited all the skill of the convinced paranoid. It would be almost impossible to guess his next move, which might well be prompted by his latest consultation with his astrologer. Whim was another factor to keep his enemies guessing, and proved particularly effective in dealing with the powerful *condottieri* whom he employed to fight his wars. When payment was withheld, they would often fight on – rather than withdraw and have another *condottiere* move in and pick up their pay. Visconti knew how to play on even the slightest fears and suspicions of others.

Cosimo managed to achieve a measure of equilibrium in northern Italy by maintaining Florence's traditional alliance with Venice. Even so, Milan remained a continuous threat, with Duke Filippo Maria encouraged by the exiled Rinaldo degli Albizzi, who had sworn revenge on Cosimo. Milanese armies invaded Florentine territory in 1437, and again in 1438; both times they were successfully repulsed, but not without strains beginning to show on the international scene. In order to combat Milan's mercenary troops, Cosimo hired his new friend, the great mercenary general Francesco Sforza, ordering him to drive the Milanese forces from Florentine territory, and then take Lucca, a move that he knew would be popular in Florence. Sforza advanced, forcing the Milanese troops to retreat to Lucca, but was unwilling to press home his advantage by actually attacking the city and the Milanese forces. He had no wish to offend Duke Filippo Maria, as he still had hopes of marrying the Duke's illegitimate daughter Bianca. At the same time Venice was refusing to support Florence in an attack on Lucca, being reluctant to see any increase in Florentine territory. Cosimo himself travelled to Venice in 1438 in an attempt to persuade his allies to join him, but Venice remained obdurately neutral; Cosimo now realised that he could never fully rely on Venice.

In 1440, Milanese mercenaries led by Rinaldo degli Albizzi again marched into Florentine territory, but were again repulsed, causing Rinaldo to give up in disgust and set out on a prolonged pilgrimage to the Holy Land. Meanwhile Sforza was rewarded for his covert loyalty to Milan, and Duke Filippo Maria allowed him to marry Bianca, even making vague promises about naming Sforza as his heir.

Six years later, in 1447, Filippo Maria of Milan died. He had nominated no successor, and claims to the dukedom of Milan came in from all sides. Sforza's claim was ignored, as King Alfonso of Naples and the French Duke of Orleans both pressed their separate claims; meanwhile the people of Milan declared their city state a republic, on the Florentine model. After three years of international diplomatic intrigue and squabbling, Sforza simply moved in with his army and declared himself Duke of Milan. Cosimo had backed the right man; Florence's old enemy had now become its ally.

But Sforza's move had dangerous consequences. Venice immediately broke off relations with Florence and allied itself with the Kingdom of Naples, which still laid claim to the dukedom of Milan. Florentine citizens were expelled from Venice and Naples, and the Medici Bank was forced to close its branches in these cities, at considerable cost: everyone reneged on their debts to the enemy. In compensation, Sforza invited Cosimo to open a branch of the Medici Bank in Milan, offering him a palace for its premises. Such would be Sforza's reliance on the Medici Bank that this palace virtually became the dukedom's ministry of finance; once again, Cosimo's luck had held.

A precarious peace now held in Italy, with Naples and Venice appearing to be willing to bide their time; to Cosimo's relief, this meant that trade could continue. However, although the alliance with Milan may have been good for Florence's merchants and external trade, it was not welcomed by the majority of the populace. Many had fought in the wars against Milan, and found this alliance with their old enemy difficult to stomach. Meanwhile aggrieved exiles returning from Naples and Venice spread rumours that Cosimo was supporting Sforza only because the mercenary general owed him a fortune, which he wanted to get back through the coffers of Milan.

These changes in the Italian political scene soon began to have implications further afield. Feeling under threat, Venice appealed to the Holy Roman Emperor Frederick III to dismantle the alliance between Florence and Milan, which threatened the whole of northern Italy. In response to this threat, Cosimo decided that his only option was to appeal for support from the Emperor Frederick III's enemy, King Charles VII of France. He knew that this appeal would have to be handled with extreme care, for France had long had territorial ambitions in Italy, and a full-scale French invasion had to be avoided at all costs. Initially Cosimo thought of travelling north to meet Charles VII himself, but he recognised that the situation was too precarious at home for him to leave Florence on a long mission to France. Instead he chose as his ambassador his humanist friend Agnolo Acciaiuoli, a member of one of the old Florentine families that had remained loyal to the Medici; Acciaiuoli himself had even been banished by Rinaldo degli Albizzi during Cosimo's exile. He was also an extremely gifted orator, and had spent many happy hours with Cosimo reading the Roman author and rhetorician Cicero. Perhaps compensating for his ineptitude as a public speaker, Cosimo greatly admired Cicero's speeches, which defended the republican virtues of Ancient Rome and stressed civic duty as one of the necessary requirements of the good life.

In 1451 Acciaiuoli was despatched to France, where his oratory duly charmed Charles VII, who promised to recognise the new Milan–Florence alliance for the next two years. Deprived of trade with Venice, Florence had now turned to France, and Charles VII's assurance meant that the increasing trade between the two states could continue, for the time being. But Acciaiuoli had been forced to make one minor concession: Milan and Florence agreed to stand aside if French claims to the kingdom of Naples were pursued. This meant that René of Anjou, the French claimant, was now free to move south to Naples, crossing Florentine Tuscany unhindered.

Cosimo remained wary of French intervention in Italy, but he was presented with an unexpected opportunity to counteract this. In 1452 the Holy Roman Emperor Frederick III passed through Florence on his way back from the formality of his coronation by the pope. Cosimo ordered that the emperor and his entourage of 1,500 Austrian knights should be housed and entertained at the city's expense, while the Medici Bank was told to cover all outstanding debts for the quickly depleted city excheq-uer. The cost proved enormous, but it bought the lasting goodwill of the emperor. The citizens of Florence, on the other hand, were less impressed, and there were increased mutterings against the Medici. The cost of supporting Sforza in Milan was proving a major drain on the city finances; his large mercenary army was no longer fighting, but still had to be paid – and now the populace of Florence was subsidising drinking bouts by thousands of loutish Austrian knights. What next would the Medici expect of them?

Then disaster struck: King Alfonso of Naples, outraged that Florence had recognised French claims to his throne, despatched an army under his illegitimate son Ferrante to march on the Florentine Republic. News soon reached Florence that Ferrante and his troops had crossed the southern border and were advancing through the countryside south of the village of Rencine. The city was in turmoil; this was all the fault of the Medici. Cosimo was horrified, but maintained a brave face. At one point a panic-stricken merchant burst into his study in the Palazzo Medici, crying out: 'Rencine has fallen!' Cosimo looked up calmly from his desk and asked with a puzzled frown: 'Rencine? Where is this Rencine?' It was as if he considered it a matter of little importance.

Cosimo assured those around him that there was no need for alarm, but it was not long before his nerve broke. As the panic-stricken citizens of Florence clamoured outside the Palazzo Medici, demanding to know what was to become of them, Cosimo crept upstairs to his bedchamber. At sixty-four years old, it was suddenly all too much for him. Some reports claim that he feigned illness, others that he actually fell ill with worry; in all likelihood, he suffered a minor nervous collapse. The arch controller was unable to face the prospect of having lost control; this time he stood to lose everything, and there was nothing he could do about it.

At this moment, the news reached Florence that René of Anjou and his formidable French army had crossed the border and were heading south to attack the Neapolitans. As if by a miracle, Florence had been saved. Cosimo retired to his country villa at Cafaggiolo in the mountains to recover, and gradually regained his old composure. Yet now there was another threat to be faced. In 1453 Charles VII's two-year guarantee of support ran out, which meant that the Venetians could attack at any moment. But once again Florence's luck held, as news reached Europe of a crippling blow to Venice: Constantinople had fallen to the Ottoman Turks. This was a disaster for Venetian trade, and its far-flung Greek and Adriatic possessions now stood at the mercy of the Turks. Yet it was soon realised that this was more than just a catastrophe for Venice; the whole of Italy now came under threat from the Turks. In 1454, Venice united with Florence, Milan and the pope in a Holy League against the Turkish infidel; this was soon joined by Naples, and a period of peace now emerged in Italy.

Cosimo de' Medici firmly believed: 'Trade brings all mankind together, and casts glory on those who venture into it.' This was the crucial difference between him and his rivals on the Italian and European scene. Kings, dukes, princes, emperors and popes had the traditional agenda of power and territorial ambition. With the exception of Venice (also significantly a republic), trade was not their prime concern; such things were a matter for merchants and bankers. Cosimo was not interested in senseless conflict; in this, he was very much a modern ruler. Instead he was interested in money, which he saw as his power base; and here his interest was at least in part also that of the citizens of Florence. Yet his pursuit of prosperity, both for himself and Florence, was to prove as risky as any king's pursuit of glory and conquest. In foreign policy, Cosimo had been perceptive enough to back Sforza, a choice that had echoed his father's risky backing of Baldassare Cossa. But Baldassare had become pope and had entrusted the Medici with the lucrative papal account; Sforza, on the other hand, had merely become Duke of Milan, a cornerstone in Cosimo's policy to achieve peace, but a constant drain on Medici finances. The Medici Bank's main source of income remained its revenue derived from the papal Curia: the link with Rome remained as vital as the link with Milan.

Yet Cosimo had been forced to take a big risk here. Years before Sforza took over in Milan, he had begun carving his own private state out of land in the Romagna, which consisted of a number of quasi-autonomous small city states, though it officially belonged to the Papal States. This made Sforza no friend of Pope Eugenius IV, who had been less than happy when he learned of Cosimo's meeting and consequent friendship with Sforza. As a result, the Medici Bank lost the account handling the papal revenues in the last years of Eugenius IV's papacy. But although it had forfeited the Court of Rome branch, it still retained its other Rome branch, which continued to transact a very lucrative business holding large deposits in the pope's personal account, as well as those of many of his cardinals.

Cosimo had foreseen this development, and as ever he had taken precautions. Aware that the ageing Eugenius IV would not live much longer, he had long ago begun quietly cultivating a friendship with Tommaso Parentucelli, his most likely successor.

Parentucelli was the son of a poor physician from remote northern Tuscany, and as a young man he had been forced to abandon his studies at the University of Bologna due to lack of funds. Around 1420 he had arrived in Florence, where he had been employed by Rinaldo degli Albizzi and Palla Strozzi as a tutor for their children. During this time he had embraced humanism and joined Cosimo's circle. He soon shared Cosimo's love of books and played a major role in helping Cosimo set up his library, which was open to all and even loaned rare manuscripts to impecunious scholars such as Parentucelli. For his part, Parentucelli read every book and manuscript he could lay his hands on, so that within a few years it was being said of him that 'anything he does not know lies beyond the limits of human knowledge'. He soon attracted the attention of Eugenius IV, who appointed him Bishop of Bologna, and Cosimo now loaned Parentucelli large sums of money so that he could seek out and purchase rare manuscripts for the Church. The two of them would meet up again when Parentucelli attended the Ecumenical Council in Florence in 1439. Here his deep learning impressed the Byzantine delegates, and he managed to play a leading role in persuading the Armenians, Ethiopians and Jacobites to forget their differences with Constantinople and join in the ecumenical aims of the Council.

When Eugenius IV finally died in 1447, Parentucelli succeeded him as Pope Nicholas V, and Cosimo's position as the papal banker was once again assured. Yet their friendship was much more than a monetary matter. Nicholas V would go on to consult Cosimo about the founding of the Vatican Library, which he modelled directly on the Medici Library. Likewise the pope's wish for peace in Italy 'without using arms other than those of Christ' coincided with Cosimo's more secular wish for peace and prosperity; meanwhile it was Nicholas V who introduced Cosimo to his Sienese friend Aeneas Piccolomini, who would become Pope Pius II eleven years later in 1458.

Where Nicholas V had been the first pope who was also a humanist, Pius II would take things one step further and become the first humanist who was also a pope. Yet it was more than his overriding belief in humanism that made Piccolomini an unlikely choice as pope. He was well over forty before he had even taken holy orders, by which time he had established a deserved reputation as both a highly accomplished Latinist and an equally accomplished womaniser. His erotic *The Tale of Two Lovers*, and his sparkling Latin verse, had early brought Piccolomini to the attention of the Holy Roman Emperor Frederick III, who had appointed him his poet laureate. Piccolomini appears to have taken holy orders purely out of ambition, for they made little difference to his behaviour. Though he did now turn his wide humanist learning to a few more serious works, such as his ground-breaking geographical history entitled *On Asia* – which would later inspire Christopher Columbus to seek a westward passage to Cathay (China).

At the age of fifty-three Piccolomini eventually achieved his ambition and became Pope Pius II. Yet to Cosimo's dismay, the new pope gave the papal account to a banker from his home town of Siena, though he did retain his personal account with the Rome branch of the Medici Bank. Cosimo immediately launched a charm offensive to persuade Pius II to reconsider his decision, and when the new pope passed through Florence soon after his appointment, a suitably lavish show was laid on. This featured knights jousting by torchlight in the Piazza della Signoria, and a pageant whose cast included Cosimo's nine-year-old grandson (the future Lorenzo the Magnificent). Behind closed doors sumptuous banquets were laid on, where the honoured guests were served the finest wines and partnered by Florence's most beautiful courtesans.

By now Cosimo was becoming an old man and had begun suffering from bouts of gout and arthritis. As a result, when he was presented to the pope he was unable to greet him properly: he could neither rise, nor could he kneel at his feet. Cosimo made a joke of this, and they both laughed, though his attempt to win the coveted papal account proved unsuccessful. Yet once again Cosimo had taken precautions, and by the time Pius II died five years later he had already ingratiated himself with the future Pope Paul II, with the result that the papal account returned once more to the Medici Bank.

Towards the end of his life, Cosimo took to spending more time amidst the clear mountain air of his estates in the Mugello valley. He would rise early to prune his vines or supervise the collection and pressing of the olive harvest; only later would he attend to the messages brought on horseback from the city. In the evenings he would discuss Plato with Ficino, whose cottage was nearby; and occasionally there would still be meetings of the so-called Platonic Academy, which Cosimo had founded for the discussion of the philosopher and his work. In winter, these meetings occurred on a regular basis at the Palazzo Medici, with many of Cosimo's humanist friends in attendance, whilst on summer evenings they would sometimes take place in the garden beneath the towers of his country villa at Cafaggiolo. (Recent scholarship has questioned the entire existence of the Platonic Academy, but it seems clear that members of the humanist circle in Florence did meet fairly regularly on a semi-formal basis to discuss ancient philosophy, and that these meetings are what came to be known as the Platonic Academy.)

Cosimo had always been a withdrawn man, while his urbanity and his self-composure earned him a reputation for inscrutability. Yet in old age the constant pain of his arthritis, his gout and his bladder problems made him by turns sorrowful and sardonic, though this caustic manner retained its humorous edge. When his saintly old friend Pierozzi, now Archbishop of Florence, tried to persuade him to ban all priests from gambling, Cosimo replied: 'First things first. Shouldn't we start by banning them from using loaded dice.'

Previously, according to Ficino: 'He was as avaricious of time as Midas was of gold.' Now he would spend hours on end sitting silently in his chair, and when his wife Contessina nagged him, asking him what he was doing, he would reply: 'When we are going to the country, you spend weeks preparing for the move. Allow me a little time preparing my own move to the country from which I will not return.'

Yet he still busied himself deeply in the affairs of Florence, refusing to pass on the reins of power to his sons, who had proved a disappointment to him. His eldest son Piero had been sickly from childhood; he was now approaching fifty and suffered badly from the family affliction of gout, whilst his heavy-lidded eyes made him appear permanently sleepy. His younger brother Giovanni was Cosimo's favourite, although he believed in enjoying himself too much; he may have inherited a measure of his father's intelligence, but he was obese and never took any exercise. Piero helped look after the bank, which he managed competently enough, and

Giovanni was sent on the occasional diplomatic mission, where his wit and charm saw things through. But Giovanni could lapse into grumpiness: he too suffered from the family gout. The Milanese ambassador recorded one memorable occasion when he called at the Palazzo Medici to find the elderly Cosimo lying in the master bed, with his middle-aged sons lying on either side of him: all three were suffering from gout, each as disgruntled as the others.

Cosimo felt unable to rely on his sons, even on the occasion when he himself had broken under the strain of Ferrante's Neapolitan invasion. Some years later, when Ferrante had succeeded to the throne of Naples and once more threatened war, Cosimo used guile. The seeds of the Renaissance had by now spread to Naples, where Ferrante had received a humanist education and still retained a deep interest in ancient learning. Cosimo heard that Ferrante had set his heart on possessing an invaluable, extremely rare work by the first-century BC Roman historian Livy, of which only a very few original manuscripts remained. In order to defuse the crisis that had blown up between Naples and Florence, Cosimo sent Ferrante the priceless Livy manuscript of this work which he had in his collection. Ferrante was overjoyed, and at the same time flattered to be recognised as a great scholar. Cosimo knew how to do such things, but he was now worried about what would happen when he died and one of his sons took over. Many had scores to settle with the Medici, and he had forebodings: 'I know that at my death my sons will be involved in more trouble than the sons of any citizen of Florence who has died for many years.'

Then in 1463 Giovanni died of a heart attack. Cosimo was devastated, even more so because he felt sure that Piero too could not live that much longer. As the servants carried him on his litter through the halls of the Palazzo Medici, Cosimo would be heard to remark: 'Too large a house for so small a family.' Left on his own, he would now lie in his bed with his eyes closed, and when Contessina scolded him he would remark sardonically: 'Where I am going it will be dark. I want to get used to it.'

He knew that he would soon die, and searched in philosophy for a meaning to his life. No more Cicero and civic duty; now he sought to understand Plato and the *summum bonum* (the supreme good). During his last days he called Piero and Contessina to his bedside, and according to Piero he explained that he wanted no pomp or ceremony at his funeral.

In 1464, at the age of seventy-four, Cosimo de' Medici finally died whilst listening to Ficino read Plato. His funeral was a simple affair, but all of Florence silently thronged the streets around the Medici church of San Lorenzo as his coffin was laid to rest. The Signoria ordered that on his tombstone should be carved the words *Pater Patriae* (Father of the Country).

II

Piero the Gouty

PIERO DI COSIMO de' Medici – or Piero the Gouty as he came to be called – would rule Florence for just five years. This period is often overlooked as a brief interlude between the prudent rule of Cosimo and the more flamboyant era of Lorenzo the Magnificent. It was much more than that.

When Cosimo died in 1464, the 'succession' passed to Piero; Cosimo's 'rule' had been a fact, but not a publicly acknowledged one (both the preceding sets of inverted commas are apt here, indicatively). With Piero, the Medici ascendancy becomes for the first time an accepted fact; he is understood as the ruler of Florence, and this has come about as a result of a family succession: no democratic process was involved. And what was tacitly acknowledged at the beginning of Piero's five-year reign would have become a consolidated fact by the end of it, when his son Lorenzo succeeded (no question of inverted commas here). The sea change was subtle but fundamental: Lorenzo the Magnificent would walk the streets of the city as its acknowledged leader; Cosimo would never have done this. His son Piero undemonstratively accepted the fact of his leadership; Lorenzo would see it as his right, and revel in it.

Despite Piero's debilitating illness, he was much more striking in appearance than his father; the busts and portraits show a sternly hand-some man, a rarity in the Medici family. There were hidden depths to Piero, which Cosimo probably never realised. Even so, he had arranged for Piero to marry an exceptional woman: Lucrezia Tornabuoni, the daughter of the Medici Bank's long-term manager in Rome. Lucrezia was a forceful, spirited and intelligent woman, who was both a good mother and a woman of deep spirituality. She would play a leading role in Piero's dispensation of patronage and personally befriend several artists; she would also write poetry of some distinction, though this is little read today on account of its almost exclusively religious content. And as we shall see, her formative influence on her eldest son Lorenzo would be striking.

There is no denying that Piero's gout affected his character. He could at times display an appealing social grace that his father lacked, but during his increasingly frequent bouts of pain he could be cold, distant, or irritable. Even the teenage Lorenzo could not help noticing how his father sometimes inadvertently alienated people, for Italian relationships, then as now, thrived on warmth – its lack could often upset people.

So what precisely was this 'gout', which so affected the Medici family and all but crippled Piero? There is no doubt that Piero's affliction was inherited from Cosimo, and Giovanni di Bicci's somewhat crabbed appearance suggests that it may well have afflicted Piero's grandfather too. There is also no doubting that Piero's disease would have been exacerbated by the diet prevalent amongst well-to-do Italians of the period. The higher social classes tended to eat an excessive amount of meat – out of enjoyment, for hearty nourishment, and as a show of their distinction, for meat was expensive. At the time it was habitually served with rich and pungent sauces to mask the taste of the meat, which quickly became tainted in the heat, in the centuries before refrigeration. Florentines in particular also favoured kidney and liver dishes. Vegetables were for the most part considered peasant food and eaten sparingly. But the real damage was done during winter, for this was the season of root vegetables, which were regarded as animal fodder. It was all right for the *popolo minuto* to feed themselves on such fare; refined people simply did not contemplate eating such things. As a result, vitamin and mineral deficiencies were prevalent amongst the upper classes, especially in the winter months.

Not surprisingly, Piero's gout got worse on such a diet, but it seems unlikely that it was caused by it. Medically, we now know that his gout and arthritis resulted from retention of uric acid; this would have caused kidney disease, and in consequence his facial complexion was probably a deep yellow. The retention of uric acid would also have resulted in crystalline desposits, causing painful and swollen joints, so it was hardly surprising that for large parts of his later life Piero was carried about in a litter.

Eyewitnesses report that on occasion he would become almost completely paralysed, to the extent that he could sometimes move only his tongue, in order to speak. Yet this invalid would prove an able leader: such mistakes as he made were not caused by a mind clouded with the pain of illness. His self-control and will-power must have been almost equal that of his father's.

For several years before Cosimo's death, a number of leading citizens in Florence had gradually grown discontented with his rule. The usual jealousies and resentments built up, increasing the ranks of the quietly disaffected. Amongst these was Cosimo's old humanist friend Agnolo Acciaiuoli, who turned against him and regarded Piero as totally inadequate to take over the reins of power. Acciaiuoli had come to see Cosimo as a coward in his old age; in his eyes, Cosimo had begun to 'avoid taking any decisions which might require him to be forceful'. As is often the case, there was an element of truth in this; several wealthy citizens of Florence had heavily overdrawn accounts at the Medici Bank, but Cosimo refrained from pressing them to pay off their debts. As a result, the accounts as a whole were not in a particularly healthy state when he died.

Another man who had quietly turned against Cosimo was his trusted adviser Diotisalvi Neroni, another member of a long-established Florentine family, who had accumulated considerable wealth. He was now ambitious to turn this wealth into power, and was exasperated at being balked by the Medici succession. He also shared Acciaiuoli's disdain for Piero.

When Piero took over the running of the Medici Bank from Cosimo, he felt it only prudent to ask his father's old friend Neroni to investigate the books and advise him on the bank's financial situation. Neroni decided to frighten Piero by exaggerating the parlous state of the Medici accounts. At this time, many Florentine merchant traders were severely over-stretched owing to developments in the eastern Mediterranean: the Turks and the Venetians had been at war since 1463, and this was playing havoc with the silk and spice trades from the Near East. As a result of Neroni's exaggerated concerns, Piero decided upon an immediate retrenchment in the bank's affairs: major debts were to be called in at all over-stretched offices of the bank – including those in London, Bruges and at home in Florence.

The result was regretful, and though it was not in itself calamitous, in retrospect it can be seen as the first significant decline from the high point in the bank's affairs established by Cosimo. For instance, it now became clear at the London branch that the debts owed by King Edward IV were unlikely to be paid. Such 'clarifications' at London, and similar ones at Bruges, hinted that the Medici fortunes in northern Europe were unlikely to continue prospering.

The situation in Florence became more immediately serious, at least in political terms, when Piero called in a number of debts at the local branch of the Medici Bank and many of the over-stretched merchants found themselves faced with bankruptcy. Opinion amongst the merchant class began to swing against the Medici, and the leader of this growing faction soon emerged as Luca Pitti, the head of an ancient banking family that had undergone a resurgence of commercial success over the previous decades.

Pitti had become renowned for his ostentatious spending, which was frequently used for purposes of self-aggrandisement. Many of the more extravagant features of Florence's welcome for Pope Pius II had been his doing, with Cosimo only reluctantly agreeing to such unnecessary waste (as he saw it). Pitti had wished to demonstrate his role as a prime mover in the city, as well as gain a certain international recognition for himself. For several years he had also been building a vast palace for himself on the hill on the south bank of the Arno, completely dominating the district of the city known as the Oltrarno ('across the Arno'). Cosimo had been willing to let Pitti flourish under the illusion that he was on the way to becoming the main political power in Florence. But partly owing to Cosimo's later unwillingness to face upsetting long-term problems, and partly through the surreptitious growth of the Pitti family's actual power, Luca Pitti was by this stage undeniably emerging as a very visible and flamboyant power to be reckoned with.

Florentine opinion now began dividing between the Party of the Hill (the Pitti faction, centred on its palazzo) and the Party of the Plain (the Medici faction, centred on its more modest palazzo on the flat ground to the north of the city centre). Acciaiuoli, and more covertly Neroni, sided with the Party of the Hill. They were joined by Niccolò Soderini, the idealistic son of another ancient Florentine family, who was also a highly gifted orator. Soderini now became the mouthpiece for the Party of the Hill, drumming up popular support for the cause by urging the

abolition of the corrupt voting system by which the Medici maintained
their power. Feeling that the time was ripe, the impetuous Pitti privately
called for immediate action against the Medici, urging that with popular
support, as well as the backing of the merchants, the Medici government
could easily be overthrown by an armed insurrection. Piero could be
captured and murdered, all the other leading members of the Medici
faction could be exiled, and the city would be rid of the family for ever.
Pitti was well aware that the Medici faction could summon military support
from Sforza in Milan, but he had already ascertained that in an armed
conflict the Party of the Hill could rely on the superior backing of Venice,
Ferrara and the new Pope Paul II, who was also a Venetian.

Yet Soderini was opposed to this, and managed to persuade the other
conspirators against armed force. His idealism won the day further afield,
and the call to 'liberty and equality' that Soderini urged was soon taken
up by the populace. As a result of mounting public pressure, the system
by which the Signoria was nominated by the guilds (so easily controlled
by the Medici) was replaced by more democratic election by lot (which
had been the city's historical method), and Soderini was elected *gonfaloniere*
on a tide of popular support.

However, the merchants quickly saw which way the wind was blowing; the populace were now demanding sweeping changes to the way the
city was run, and there was no telling where this would end. Ironically,
the political corruption of government by the ruling factions had led to
stability, and the merchants now saw power slipping from their hands.
Popular rule would only result in turbulence; trade would suffer, and the
city might be ruined. When Gonfaloniere Soderini began placing his idealistic proposals before the city councils (which remained in older, less popular hands), he found himself blocked at every turn. During his period as
gonfaloniere, he and his sympathetic Signoria achieved nothing; popular feeling turned against them, and when they left office someone pinned a notice
to the door of the Palazzo della Signoria proclaiming: 'The nine donkeys
have gone.'

To Soderini's disgust, Piero de' Medici had not been swept away on
a tide of popular democratic reform, and now that the merchants were
backing the old system he appeared more powerful than ever. Soderini
decided to throw in his lot with Pitti and his co-conspirators Acciaiuoli

and Neroni; the time for idealism was past, and more drastic measures were now required. The conspirators sent undercover messages to Ferrara and Venice, with the aim of coordinating their efforts, but soon events began to take on a momentum of their own.

In March 1466 news reached Florence that the great former *condottiere* and friend of Cosimo de' Medici, Francesco Sforza, had died. He was succeeded as Duke of Milan by Galeazzo Maria Sforza, his twenty-two-year-old son. Galeazzo was an exotic character, who was already rumoured to be showing signs of dangerous mental instability. Unsavoury stories now began to circulate of noblemen's wives being raped in the banqueting halls of his castle, and below in the dungeons he was said to conduct personally the torture of his enemies, on occasion tearing them limb from limb with his own hands.

Piero de' Medici realised the precariousness of his situation and decided to take a diplomatic gamble. In April he despatched his seventeen-year-old son Lorenzo on a visit to Naples, in the hope that he could win round Ferrante to the Medici cause. Several weeks later Lorenzo returned, having charmed Ferrante with his youthful intellect and panache, making a firm friend of the monarch.

Then in the midst of the summer heat of August, Piero was struck down with a severe attack of gout. Virtually paralysed, he was carried on a litter to recover in the cooler air of his villa at Careggi, in the countryside a couple of miles north of the city walls. But by now the conspirators had already made their move. Whilst Piero lay incapacitated at Careggi, news reached him that the Duke of Ferrara had despatched an army across the mountains into Florentine territory, with orders to capture Piero, together with his son Lorenzo, and murder them both. Worse still, the Venetians were also preparing to send an army, under their leading *condottiere* Bartolommeo Colleoni (a running together of *cuore leone*, meaning 'lion heart'). Colleoni had inherited the mantle of the late Francesco Sforza, and was now regarded as the most fearsome military leader in Italy.

Despite Piero's agonising debility, he reacted swiftly, ordering that he be carried back to Florence at once. Lorenzo rode on ahead, and as he approached the city some peasants in the fields called out to him that armed men were preparing an ambush just before the city gates. Lorenzo galloped back, warned his father, and they took a track across the countryside, arriving at another of the city gates. Once back at the Palazzo Medici, Piero set about rallying his supporters to the cause. Then unexpected news arrived that Galeazzo Sforza had despatched 1,500 armed horsemen from Milan to engage the forces sent by the Duke of Ferrara.

Piero's sudden return to the Palazzo Medici had caught the conspirators by surprise. Acciaiuoli, Soderini and Neroni rode off to gather their men, leaving Pitti at his half-built and indefensible palazzo. As time passed, Pitti became increasingly fearful that they had abandoned him, and eventually he lost his nerve. Leaping on his horse, he rode as speedily as he could over the Ponte Vecchio across the Arno, through the city centre to the Palazzo Medici. Here he sought an immediate audience with Piero. Accounts of this meeting vary: according to one, Pitti emotionally begged Piero to forgive him, swearing that from now on he would 'support him to the death'. It is unclear whether Piero knew at this stage how deeply Pitti was implicated in the actual plot to kill him; at any rate, it is known that he magnanimously pardoned Pitti. One report goes so far as to claim that Piero even agreed to Pitti's suggestion that in order to heal the divisions in the city, Piero should marry his son Lorenzo to one of Pitti's daughters.

By now Piero had assembled his armed guard and despatched a message to Galeazzo Sforza to ride with his cavalry poste-haste to Florence. Meanwhile Soderini sent word to the Duke of Ferrara's army to march for Florence at once; he then made for the Palazzo della Signoria with the aim of browbeating the Signoria into arresting Piero. Confusion and panic spread through the city, but did not culminate in the widespread popular uprising that Pitti had been expected to encourage. As a result, no one was sent to arrest Piero, while the armed bands supporting the conspirators lost heart and began melting away through the back-streets. The Duke of Ferrara's army soon learned of this and realised they had been misled about the situation in Florence. The populace would not rise up to welcome them as liberators, as Soderini had promised, so they decided to return home. Colleoni's army had not yet even left Venice, when news of this reached them.

The conspiracy had failed, and Piero ordered the Medici political machine into action to restore stability. A pro-Medici Signoria was elected, the *vacca* tolled over the city and those eligible to vote made their way to the Piazza della Signoria. Here 3,000 soldiers were assembled: a combination of the entire city guard and armed Medici supporters, complete with the young Lorenzo in full armour riding up and down the lines. The assembled citizens had been badly frightened by talk of civil war and invasion by foreign armies; they accepted the call for a Balìa, which quickly agreed on a return to the old method of appointing the members of the Signoria by the guilds, rather than the more democratic election by lot, which had led to Soderini becoming *gonfaloniere*. Any such democratic reform would be shelved for twenty years, until the city government was firmly established on a more stable footing. All were well aware of what had happened: the Medici rule had been reinstated and publicly confirmed, possibly for decades to come. Whether they wanted it or not, the citizens of Florence were now forced to accept this as a fact; and as far as it is possible to tell, such acceptance was not entirely grudging – this was the price to be paid for stability.

The leading conspirators Acciaiuoli, Neroni and Soderini were sentenced to death, but Piero intervened and the sentences were all commuted to exile. This was intended as a gesture to heal divisions within the city, but sending the conspirators into exile would prove a costly mistake. Soderini and Neroni travelled straight to Venice, whose rulers were growing ever more worried at the continuing alliance between Florence and Milan. The Doge of Venice and his council were soon persuaded of the necessity to act against Florence, and in May 1467 Colleoni was despatched to attack the city. At sixty-seven, the fearsome Colleoni was beginning to show his age; but he had learned his trade with Sforza himself, and he now commanded a huge army of 8,000 horsemen, together with 6,000 foot soldiers.

As ever, Piero acted swiftly on hearing this news, sending messages to Ferrante of Naples and Galeazzo of Milan, calling upon them to send as much support as they could muster. At the same time he appointed the mercenary general Federigo da Montefeltro as commander of the Florentine force (see colour plates); the forty-five-year-old Montefeltro, who was lord of the small city state of Urbino on the southern approaches to the Romagna, had a reputation second only to that of Colleoni as a military commander; he too had learned his trade under Sforza, and had even married his daughter Battista.

As the two armies began to manoeuvre amongst the hills and valleys of the Romagna, each warily tried to push the other into making a false move; Montefeltro was in fact attempting to avoid action, while he waited for the troops from Milan and Naples to arrive. His delaying tactics worked, and Montefeltro's army was soon joined by Neapolitan forces under the Duke of Calabria, and by a strong Milanese contingent led by Galeazzo himself.

Moving swiftly into action, Montefeltro managed to corner Colleoni and his forces in an unfavourable position; but before he could strike, Galeazzo inexplicably decided to allow the enemy forces to escape. When the Signoria in Florence sent a message demanding to know what had happened, Montefeltro remonstrated that Galeazzo had whimsically decided that no Sforza should take orders from one of his father's former junior officers. Diplomatically, the Signoria invited Galeazzo to Florence to give a first-hand report on the military situation, as well as his advice on how the Florentine forces should proceed. No longer hampered by the unreliable young Duke of Milan, Montefeltro managed to corner the Venetian army as it retreated towards Imola; Colleoni was finally forced to stand his ground, and battle was engaged. Montefeltro's forces quickly proved superior, but darkness fell and they were compelled to fight by the light of flares. In the confusion, Colleone ordered his men to retreat. Montefeltro declared a victory for the Florentine forces, but in reality the result had been inconclusive, as Colleoni returned to Venice with his army largely intact. Despite this, the Venetians were in no mood to continue with a long war, and one year later a peace treaty was signed between the two cities. Piero had managed to secure the old alliance; stability had been restored, both internally and externally, and he was now firmly established as ruler of the city.

Piero would also be responsible for the commercial coup that secured continuing profits for the Medici Bank (thus, in effect, masking the gradual decline of its banking activities throughout Europe). Some years previously his father Cosimo had involved the Medici Bank in the alum trade, which was operated under a papal monopoly. Alum was the mineral salt, resulting from volcanic deposits, that was used to fix vivid dyes on cloth; it was essential to the textile industry in Florence, and as far afield as the Low Countries and London. For many years Europe's principal supply of high-grade alum had been from mines in Asia Minor, just outside Smyrna (now Izmir), and these had been controlled by the Genoese until they fell into the hands of the Ottoman Turks in 1455. Out of necessity, the alum trade continued; yet according to a contemporary estimate, the Turkish sultan 'draws yearly from the Christians more than 300,000 pieces of gold'. This meant that the Europeans were virtually financing the war which the Turks were now waging against them in the Balkans and the eastern Mediterranean. Fortunately this ruinous anomaly came to an end in 1462, with the discovery of 'seven hills of alum' in the Papal State at Tolfa, just a few miles from the west coast of Italy near Civitavecchia.

The papal authorities immediately took possession of this valuable mineral resource, establishing a monopoly by announcing that from now on anyone who imported Turkish alum would be excommunicated. Indeed, so keen was the pope to protect this valuable source of income that he soon went one step further: henceforth, all indulgences sold for the pardoning of sins specifically mentioned that they were invalid for anyone who even used imported Turkish alum. However, this posed a doctrinal problem, for monopoly trading (like usury) was specifically forbidden by Church law. Fortunately the expert theologians at the papal court soon managed to find a loophole in the law. As the alum mines were depriving the infidel Turks of income, they were technically being used to further the cause of Christianity; this end fully justified the apparently illegal means, and in this particular case monopoly trading was therefore not a sin.

As the papal banker, the Medici Bank was ideally placed to move into the alum business; it also had an established network of sales outlets, in the form of its Europe-wide branches. Thus by 1464 the Medici Bank was handling almost half the alum mined at Tolfa. This must have involved a considerable operation, for it is known that by 1471 the annual extraction of alum at Tolfa amounted to around 70,000 cantaras (the cantar was the ancient pan-Mediterranean cubic measure, equivalent to a drinking pot or tankard), a figure equal to approximately 3,444 tons.

Cosimo had been too ill to supervise this business, which was inaugurated in the year of his death; instead it was handled by Piero's father-in-law Giovanni Tornabuoni, the long-serving manager of the Rome branch. After Cosimo's death, Tornabuoni began complaining to Piero that there was barely any profit to be made in the alum market. The overall monopoly was being handled so incompetently by the papal authorities that the market was frequently flooded, causing the price to collapse before more expensively purchased alum could reach its destination. He advised Piero either to quit the alum trade altogether or to attempt to secure sole trading rights from the papal authorities, which would enable a Medici monopoly, allowing the sale price to be fixed at a suitable level. But in 1465 the war between Florence and Venice resulted in the Venetian Pope Paul II withdrawing the papal account from the Medici Bank and transferring it to one of his relatives.

This left the Medici Bank in a quandary: remaining in the alum business at all would be difficult under Paul II, let alone seeking to secure a monopoly. Once again, Piero took a gamble on his son, and in March 1466 despatched the seventeen-year-old Lorenzo to Rome, relying not only on his youthful ability to charm, but more surprisingly on his business judgement. Piero wrote from Florence to Lorenzo on his arrival in Rome that he should 'settle this and other matters as you think best'. Lorenzo had already been heavily briefed by Piero on what to say: only the Medici Bank could afford to equip galleys carrying alum on the long voyages to London and the Low Countries. The dangers presented by shipwreck and piracy meant that any lesser agent might soon be ruined, whereas the Medici Bank could afford to cover such losses. The combination of Lorenzo's social graces and Piero's cogent arguments won the day, and on 1 April 1466 the Medici Bank was awarded the alum monopoly. Writing to Piero next day, Tornabuoni happily assured him that from now on the bank would be able to secure double the previous price of alum on the London and Bruges markets. The Medici Bank was guaranteed a vast income for many years to come.

Estimates vary as to precisely how vast this income was. It is known that the papal authorities were paid a royalty of just under two florins for each *cantar* that passed out of the court warehouses at Civitavecchia; likewise, it is known that the Medici Bank in Bruges usually received between three and four florins per *cantar*. Even allowing for shipping costs, this meant that the bank probably received a minumum of around 70,000 florins per year – a colossal sum when one considers that the profit of the entire Medici Bank in the twenty-three years until 1420 was 152,000 florins.

Piero the Gouty would also maintain another great Medici tradition:

that of patronage. While Cosimo had been interested in leaving a permanent Medici legacy in the form of buildings, he had largely delegated the commissioning of paintings to his sons Giovanni and Piero, a decision which not only shows their interest in painting, but also implies a developed knowledge. While his father was alive, and even during the hectic five years of his own rule, Piero would regularly commission works by a number of painters. He continued to support his father's favourite, Donatello, and when Donatello died in 1466, he went so far as to honour the artist's wish to be buried in the church of San Lorenzo close to Cosimo – a gesture that is indicative of the deep empathy which the Medici developed with the artists who worked for them. The Medici were among the first to understand, and publicly acknowledge, that artists were more than craftsmen; at the same time, the artists themselves were developing a personal assurance that went hand in hand with the emergence of humanism. They were beginning to believe in themselves, in their unique vision of the world; indeed, it is from this period that we can date the concept of the artist as 'genius', and all that entails. Here we see the artist exhibiting exceptional talent, exceptional behaviour, exceptional self-assurance – and, paradoxically, as a result of all this, exceptional psychological torment.

Typical of this new social type was the artist Fra Filippo Lippi, who would be taken on by Cosimo, would work for Piero, and become a friend of the young Lorenzo. Lippi was born the son of a butcher in Florence around 1406. Orphaned at an early age, he was brought up by an impoverished aunt, but would frequently run off to live a barefoot gutter life amongst the street urchins, a period that would form a crucial aspect of his character. When he was fifteen his exasperated aunt placed him in the monastery of Santa Maria del Carmine in the Oltrarno, where he would take his vows as a Carmelite monk (hence his title 'Fra', short for *frater* or 'brother'). Life in the monastery may have had little effect upon the unruly Lippi, but it would introduce him to the other formative element in his character.

In 1426 the twenty-five-year-old Renaissance pioneer Masaccio was hired by the monastery of Santa Maria del Carmine to paint a series of frescos on the walls of the Brancacci Chapel. Masaccio was one of the first to discover a new lifelike method of painting, which gave the figures in his frescos a verisimilitude and dramatic force never seen before. Fra Lippi was intrigued, and would spend many hours watching the young

Masaccio at work. When Masaccio discovered that Lippi had a natural talent for drawing, he began showing the young friar the secrets of his painting: the use of light and perspective, the understanding of anatomy and the depiction of emotion.

Masaccio would die two years later, in 1428, but his new expressive technique would achieve full maturity in the artistry of Lippi, who soon abandoned the monastery and travelled to Padua with the aim of becoming a painter. None of his early paintings from this period survives, yet his originality must have been evident from the beginning because the effect of his style is distinctly recognisable in other Paduan painters of this time: a new spirit was moving through the world of painting.

Possibly as a result of a brawl over a woman, Lippi left Padua under a cloud and travelled south along the coast to Ancona. Here he went sailing one day, but was blown out to sea and taken captive by a galley of Moorish corsairs, who carried him off to North Africa as a slave. After he had been in captivity for eighteen months, he drew a portrait of the local caliph on his prison wall; because of the Muslim ban on figurative representation, the caliph had never seen a picture of himself before and was so enamoured that he gave Lippi his freedom. Perhaps inevitably doubt has been cast on this story, whose only source was the unreliable Lippi himself, yet there is no denying that around this time he turned up in Naples, where he combined working as a court painter with low life in the bordellos. Either now or some time later, he was briefly imprisoned and suffered a public flogging for fraud; at any rate he certainly left Naples and returned home to Florence in 1437.

Here he managed to secure a commission from the nuns of Sant' Ambrogio to paint an altarpiece, which proved of such exceptional quality that it brought him to the attention of Cosimo de' Medici. Even today, this excellence in his work remains immediately recognisable. His faces stand out from their background, very much as if they are in relief. It is said that Lippi learned this technique from studying reliefs by Donatello, and its effect, together with the expressive individuality of his faces, must have made his paintings sensational when they first appeared. There is the distinct feeling that each madonna was a woman he knew, and even the fat-faced child in her arms was always a recognisably individual infant, rather than a spiritualised type (see colour plates).

Largely owing to the way painters were employed at this time, Lippi's commissions were almost exclusively religious. Perhaps inevitably, in the light of his character, they are not imbued with a deep spirituality, but they do possess a compelling actuality. His Annunciations, his madonnas, and his altarpieces all depict very real scenes, while the spirituality of those taking part is not solemn or exaggerated – we simply read their attitude, or expressiveness, from the natural cast of their faces, much as we would in real life. And his later delicacy of line and colour is reminiscent of that presence detected in the painters of Padua: with a start of recognition, we see a ghostly prefiguring of Botticelli in all his glory of line and colour.

Lippi's luminous talent, and this alone, would appear to account for Cosimo de' Medici's unending patience when dealing with this recalcitrant artist, for Lippi's patrons were rewarded with continual ingratitude – one of the few constant elements in his character. With Lippi, the godfatherly qualities of the Medici had to be exercised to the full; Cosimo, and later Piero, soon learned to withhold payment for commissions until completion, though at times even this would provide insufficient incentive. As a last resort, Lippi was given a studio in the Palazzo Medici, and here he was confined – meals and painting materials were provided, but otherwise the door remained locked – until the commissioned painting was produced. At such times Lippi was even forced to sleep in this studio; we know this, because on one occasion he managed to escape from it by tearing up the bed sheets, knotting them together and lowering himself down into the street. He then disappeared for several days, while Cosimo sent servants to seek him out in the bordellos around the Mercato Vecchio (the modern Piazza della Repubblica) and the drinking dens in the slums at the edge of the Santa Croce district (along the marshy northern bank of the Arno to the east of the city centre). Yet Lippi must have played his part in bringing Cosimo to that sympathetic understanding that he would show towards the artists he employed, for after this incident he 'resolved in future to try to keep a hold on him by affection and kindness and to allow him to come and go as he pleased'.

Perhaps as part of this enlightened strategy, in 1446 Cosimo encouraged Lippi to leave the fleshpots of Florence and work in the countryside at Prato, beneath the mountains ten miles to the north-west. On Cosimo's recommendation, Lippi was given a commission by the rector of St Stephen's church, who happened to be Cosimo's illegitimate son Carlo: Lippi would insert a portrait of him in one of his frescos.

Soon afterwards, Lippi was commissioned to paint an altarpiece for the nuns at Santa Margherita in Prato. Here he managed to persuade the abbess to allow him to use a nineteen-year-old nun called Lucrezia Buti as a model for the Madonna. Within a few months Lucrezia became pregnant, and the two of them ran off together. As both of them were in holy orders, this caused such a serious scandal that the Church authorities ended up taking the case to the pope.

This time it would take all of Cosimo's influence to sort matters out. In 1458 the renowned humanist and erotic story-teller Piccolomini became Pope Pius II, and when he was welcomed to Florence on his festive visit, Cosimo persuaded him to look into the case of Lippi and Buti. As a result they were both released from their vows by special dispensation of the pope, which enabled them to get married and set up home with their young son (who would grow up to become the distinguished Renaissance painter Filippino Lippi). Yet Lippi senior would soon abandon his wife and son, embarking on a series of increasingly superb religious masterpieces and increasingly unforgivable escapades, on one occasion ending up on a charge of embezzlement from his assistant which resulted in him being 'tortured on the rack till his bowels gave way'. At sixty-three he finally died in Spoleto on 8 October 1469; poisoned, it is said, by the outraged relatives of a young girl whom he had seduced.

Amazingly, Lippi was buried in the cathedral at Spoleto, almost certainly at the instigation of the Medici family. This would be one of the last acts of Piero the Gouty, who died just two months later – of the disease by which he is now known. To the end, he followed his father in being an unobtrusive, yet for the most part wise and decisive ruler. During the last months of his life when he was confined to his bed in the Palazzo Medici, he learned that certain young unruly elements in his party had begun taking advantage of the Medici ascendancy – 'as if God and fortune had given them the city for a prey', as Machiavelli put it. Members of other families were being waylaid at night, and sometimes even robbed in broad daylight, when they passed through the busy district around the San Lorenzo church (traditionally recognised as Medici territory). Despite Piero's agonising condition, he summoned the ringleaders to his bedside, where they were warned that if the streets of Florence remained unsafe for certain families, he would be forced to invite back the exiled heads of these families, so that they could protect their kith and kin. The bluff worked, and once again the streets of Florence became safe for all. Piero's legacy was the restoration of peace, both within Florence and amongst the surrounding states.

Part 3

The Prince and the Prophet of Doom

12

The Renaissance Prince

TWO DAYS AFTER the death of Piero de' Medici in December 1469, a delegation of leading Florentine citizens called at the Palazzo Medici to see his son Lorenzo. They were led by Tommaso Soderini, who had remained loyal to the Medici throughout his brother Niccolò's revolt and exile. First the delegation offered Lorenzo their condolences on the death of his father; then, as Lorenzo wrote in his *Ricordi* (a brief record of the Medici family): 'Although I was very young, being just twenty years of age, they encouraged me to take upon myself the care of the city and the state, as my father and grandfather had done.' Thus, the Medici succession was now openly acknowledged. Lorenzo goes on: 'This proposal was naturally against my youthful instincts. Feeling that the burden and danger might be too much for me, I consented to it unwillingly.' This is of course false modesty (a rare instance in Lorenzo's case); he had been groomed for leadership from an early age, a fact of which he had long been aware. Yet his bashfulness was not total hypocrisy, for he knew that the people of Florence still wished to see themselves as citizens of a republic. This was part of their proud patriotic heritage, which distinguished them from the other states in Italy.

This essentially unresolved issue between actual and constitutional power would remain acceptable, but only for as long as all consented to the charade. In his *Ricordi*, Lorenzo goes on to explain the real reason why he was willing to 'take care' of the city: 'I did so in order to protect our friends and property, since it fares ill in Florence with anyone who is rich but does not have any control over the government.' The situation was unavoidable: the Medici were recognised as leaders, but not accorded the title – yet they had to take on the role, in order to survive. The historian Francesco Guicciardini, who was a child in Florence at the time of Lorenzo, would aptly characterise the contradictions of Lorenzo's rule as 'that of a benevolent tyrant in a constitutional republic'.

Lorenzo de' Medici was born in 1449, and his life reached back to the great founding years of Medici power: as a young child he had been his grandfather Cosimo's favourite. One day, when the aged Cosimo was meeting an important delegation from Lucca, his grandson had happened to wander into the room carrying a stick. Lorenzo asked his grandfather if he could carve the stick into a flute, and Cosimo at once set to work, whittling away the wood. After the child had left, happily bearing his new flute, the delegates from Lucca remonstrated with Cosimo for interrupting an important meeting. Undaunted, he replied: 'Aren't you too fathers or grandfathers? You are lucky the boy didn't ask me to play a few tunes on his new flute. For if he had, I would certainly have gone on and done so.'

A major influence on Lorenzo was undoubtedly that of his mother Lucrezia (née Tornabuoni); her powerful and profoundly artistic personality would introduce – by nature and nurture – a creative side into the Medici inheritance that had not previously been evident. Related to this was another formative aspect in Lorenzo's upbringing. Hitherto, the powerful families in Florence had existed largely as clans; and this was reflected in not only how they lived, but where they lived. Extended, almost tribal families would live together in the family palazzo, with one leader presiding over a largely communal existence; loyalty, and to a large extent individuality, would be subsumed into a clan identity. This would also be true of the family clans that did not live in palazzi: these would be gathered together in neighbouring houses.

Yet something different was beginning to emerge in the new palazzi which the leading families of Florence were now building for themselves. These palazzi were still large: the one being constructed by the Pitti family was larger than the palaces of many rulers in Europe. But with the emergence of a new humanist individuality, the family clans began to separate out into individual nuclear families – a development that was reflected in the interior design of these new palazzi, and in the way they were occupied. The Palazzo Medici was built for one family and their dependants, not for the whole clan; whereas the Palazzo Bardi, in which they had previously lived, stood on an entire street of Bardi properties, whose doors would be open to all other members of the clan. At the Palazzo Medici, by contrast, the family in residence could withdraw from public life and enjoy a private life that was their own: in such a way, a separation between public and domestic life began to evolve.

This loosening of the clan bond led to a tightening of the bonds within the family – parents became closer to their children, and their grandchildren. Witness Cosimo's words to the delegation from Lucca: 'Aren't you too fathers or grandfathers?' He considered playing with Lorenzo almost as important as meeting a foreign delegation, whilst tellingly the members of the delegation from Lucca, where the ideas of the Renaissance had not yet fully taken hold, simply did not understand what he was talking about.

It is significant that the Medici moved into their new palazzo on the Via Larga just five years before Lorenzo was born. In his case, this would result in an unusually close relationship with his mother; and as we shall see, he also developed a particularly close relationship with his attractive younger brother Giuliano. Piero's relationship to his eldest son also seems to have been closer and more sophisticated than the paternal relationships of the previous generations. Giovanni di Bicci's influence over his son Cosimo, for instance, had been almost total; again and again, Cosimo's principal decisions had been identical to those his father would have taken. Only later, after Giovanni's death, had Cosimo managed to emerge from his father's psychological shadow and begun to blossom as an individual character. In Cosimo's relationships with his sons, on the other hand, the heavy patriarchal influence had been tempered by closeness: when suffering from gout, they all took to bed together. The sons were also given responsibility, being delegated with the important and costly business of commissioning painters. This trust came to fruition in Piero's unobtrusive but able rule: more than once his decision saved the day, yet he was capable of entrusting his young son Lorenzo with missions of almost equal decisiveness. Piero's relationship to his son would be especially close and understanding, the like of which had not previously been seen in the Medici family.

When grandfather Cosimo died and Piero the Gouty took over the reins of power, Lorenzo de' Medici was just fifteen years old. Piero must have known that he had not long to live, for Lorenzo was not only prepared for leadership, but in many respects became the public face of his father's rule. This is no exaggeration, for at the age of fifteen Lorenzo was already being despatched on missions in the place of his incapacitated father, as the representative of the Republic of Florence. His first mission was to Milan for the wedding of the son of Ferrante, King of Naples, to the daughter of Galeazzo, Duke of Milan. 'Remember to be civil and alert,' Piero wrote to his teenage son. 'Act as a man, not as a boy. Show sense, industry, and manly endeavour, so that you may be employed in more important things.' Piero's trust in his youthful son proved well founded, and soon Lorenzo was being entrusted with missions to Bologna, Ferrara and Venice. He would be just seventeen, but already possessed of some diplomatic experience, by the time he was sent to Rome to see Pope Paul II in 1466, with the delicate task of securing the alum monopoly for the Medici Bank.

Yet it was at this time that Piero made his one great, and possibly unavoidable, mistake over his son. Whilst Lorenzo was in Rome he was expected to undertake a crash course in running the bank from his uncle, the able manager of the Rome branch, Giovanni Tornabuoni. However, owing to circumstances, this course lasted just a few weeks: Lorenzo had neither the time nor the inclination to learn about banking. His person-ality, his artistic intellect, his flamboyant character were completely unsuited to the meticulous and for the most part cautious business of running the family bank. This would later prove to be a severe flaw, but for the time being it was a mere shortcoming, one that could easily be overcome by expert advice from the trusted managers who oversaw the day-to-day running of each branch of the Medici Bank.

Even at this age, all the evidence points to Lorenzo being more than just talented. In the family tradition, he had received the finest humanist education available; no prince in Europe could have been so well tutored in the new learning. First he had been instructed by the skilled Latinist Gentile Becchi (later Bishop of Arezzo), from whom he had learned to love the poetry of Ovid, together with the rhetoric and civic values of Cicero. Later, he had learned Greek from Cosimo's protégé Marsilio Ficino, whose infectious enthusiasm had instilled in Lorenzo a deep love of Plato's idealist philosophy. Ficino had enjoyed teaching Lorenzo, remarking upon his 'naturally joyful nature'. By his early teens, Lorenzo had been allowed to attend the meetings known as the Platonic Academy, which had been instigated by Cosimo. Here he had witnessed, and soon begun to take part in, intellectual debate of the highest order; he would have heard Bracciolini and other members of Cosimo's humanist circle discussing the emergent discoveries of Greek philosophy, Latin rhetoric, the latest ideas of art and science. He would also have heard the likes of Joannes Argyropoulos, the leading Byzantine scholar, who had first met Cosimo at the Ecumenical Council of Florence, and had later settled in Italy to play a leading role in the revival of Greek learning. It would all have appeared so fresh, so new — even though much of it had lain dormant for more than a thousand years. Lorenzo was very much a product of the Florentine intellectual tradition, on which he in turn would be such an influence.

Yet Lorenzo's education had extended to more than intellectual learning. He enjoyed hunting — on horseback and with falcons — as well as the boisterous rough-house of that early 'no rules' ball game, played between packs of boys, that was the precursor of modern football. He was strong, intelligent, energetic: a natural leader. Out riding, he enjoyed leading the group in facetious bawdy songs, which he often wittily embellished on the spur of the moment. All this is more than just the understandable hyperbole that so often accrues to the youth of a great figure: at the very age when he was first being entrusted with diplomatic missions by his father, Lorenzo was also beginning to produce his first original poetry. This he wrote in Tuscan dialect, rather than the more formal Latin preferred by many. At seventeen, his linguistic ability was such that he could confidently assert: 'Tuscan can faithfully express just as many subjects and feelings as Latin.' This was the Florentine dialect that Dante had been the first great poet to champion, the idiom that was in the process of becoming the Italian language, and several of the poems produced by Lorenzo de' Medici in his maturity would be of sufficient calibre to enter the canon of early Italian poetry.

There is no doubt that from the outset Lorenzo de' Medici was impressive, though curiously we know from his many portraits that his physical appearance was distinctly unimpressive (see page 2 and front cover). In this, he was very much a Medici. His sallow features were undeniably ugly, framed

by lank centre-parted hair that fell to his shoulders; below his beetled brow
his eyes were heavy-lidded, like his father's. He had an over-emphatic chin
with a protruding lower lip, while his nose was broad and squashed, so
much so that he literally had no sense of smell – though this may have
accounted for the precision with which he used his other senses, in aesthetic
judgement and in his poetry. His movements were clumsy, his figure tall
and powerfully built, but ungainly; only his hands were long and delicate.
According to Guicciardini: 'his voice and pronunciation [were] harsh and
unpleasing, because he spoke through his nose. But the fact remains that
he was attractive to women.' The man himself appears to have been the
antithesis of his physical appearance.

These contrasting elements echo throughout descriptions of his character. According to Machiavelli: 'to see him at one time in his grave
moments and at another in his gay, was to see in him two personalities
joined as it were with invisible bonds'. The enigma of Lorenzo's character appears to have struck many perceptive observers. His friend, the poet
Angelo Poliziano, describes a day spent in his company: 'Yesterday we all
rode out of Florence, singing happily. Occasionally we broke off to talk
seriously of holy things, to remind ourselves that it was Lent.' They stop
to drink; Poliziano remarks on the 'brilliance' with which Lorenzo enlivens
the whole company. That evening they sit reading the philosophy of St
Augustine, 'then the reading resolved itself into music' and dancing. First
thing next morning, he observes Lorenzo setting off for Mass. Thus did
twenty-four hours in Lorenzo's company pass.

It all seems too much: yet the frantic pace, and the frantic switches
of mood, would continue. The privileged youth of Florence of this period
lived a golden life; a friend describes a delightful episode, in a letter to
Lorenzo, who happened to be away: 'The entire city is covered in snow –
a nuisance for some, because they are forced to stay indoors, but a source
of joy for us.' At two in the morning, bearing flares, playing trumpets and
flutes, a group of them sets off to serenade the girl to whom one of them
is betrothed. They start throwing snowballs up to her balcony. 'What a
triumph, when one of us succeeded in raining snow over her face, which
was as white as snow itself! . . . And Marietta, as skilled as she was beautiful, began pelting snow down upon us, while the trumpets tooted and
the others cheered in the night.'

Such a scene remains as vivid now as it must have been then. In referring to this event, the Medici biographer G. F. Young points out the appositeness of Lorenzo's poem:

> *Quant'è bella giovinezza*
> *Che si fugge tuttavia.*
> *Chi vuol esser lieto, sia*
> *Di doman non c'è certezza.*

(How youth is beautiful
Yet also so ephemeral.
Waste not time on sorrow
For there's no certain tomorrow.)

But this is poetry of reflection: reflecting on such scenes, and reflecting too Lorenzo's character. If there was an 'invisible bond' between Lorenzo's 'two personalities', it may well have lain in this very double-sided element: participation and reflection.

Like his grandfather, Lorenzo developed a profound love of Plato's philosophy, according to which the world was a mere dream, though this dream was constructed from perfect abstract ideas. The beauty of this appealed to Lorenzo, inspiring his creativity; yet Ficino remarked perceptively that Lorenzo did not believe in Plato, he used him — though it is possible that Lorenzo used Plato for more than creative purposes. Behind all the display, the bouts of glorious but ephemeral energy, there lay a certain detachment, a hint of almost philosophic contemplation, which may well have informed the deeper elements of Lorenzo's character, the devil-may-care confidence, the occasional acts of selfless bravery.

Where Lorenzo was concerned, Piero was determined to leave nothing to chance, and during the last two years of his life he set about arranging a good marriage for his eldest son. The leading families of Florence invariably cemented their alliances with marriages, and Piero had even promised Luca Pitti that he would marry Lorenzo to one of his daughters, as a gesture to unite the city. Though this was quietly shelved, for two reasons: Piero had later learned of Pitti's insistence on his murder, and also, following the failed coup and Pitti's abject cowardice, this once-powerful figure was now regarded with derision and contempt by the citizens of Florence.

Piero was a realist, and broke his promise, but he also broke with the old Florentine tradition of marrying his son into a leading local family; controversially, he decided to look further afield for a suitable wife for his son and heir. However, he was too ill to travel himself, so the reconnaissance work would be done by his wife Lucrezia. On the pretext of visiting her brother Giovanni Tornabuoni, Lucrezia was despatched to Rome, from where she sent a report on the sixteen-year-old Clarice Orsini, the girl whom Piero had in mind for Lorenzo: 'She is fairly tall and fair-skinned. She is gentle in manner without the sophistication of a Florentine, but she should be easy to train . . . Her face is on the round side, but pleasant enough . . . I could not judge her breasts, for the Romans keep theirs covered, but they appeared to be well formed . . . She appears above average, but cannot be compared to our daughters.' Such were the blood-stock reports that preceded arranged marriages, though Lucrezia did add: 'If Lorenzo approves, he will inform you.'

Despite this, it appears that Lorenzo had little choice in the matter; Piero had his own agenda, and in choosing a Roman wife for his son and heir he was quite willing to court unpopularity in Florence. Rome was considered very provincial, and the Florentines regarded themselves as the new Romans, the inheritors of the mantle of Ancient Rome; while marrying into a Roman family suggested that no Florentine family was good enough. Yet there was no denying that the Orsinis were an old and distinguished Roman family; their family seat was the most magnificent castle in central Italy, on the shores of Lake Bracciano twenty miles north-west of Rome, and they also had large estates on the outskirts of Naples. But most of all, they maintained their own sizeable private army. Piero had learned his lesson from the recent revolt led by Luca Pitti, and was determined that from now on when the Medici required armed backing they would not have to depend on the support of others; they would be a force to be reckoned with in their own right.

Yet this was not all, for Piero was almost certainly carrying on a secret Medici agenda passed down to him by Cosimo; in marrying an Orsini, the Medici were for the first time marrying above their class, into one of the leading aristocratic Italian families. The Medici may have been the papal bankers, but the Orsini had power within the Church itself; Orsini were regularly appointed cardinals, and one had even been a pope. By marrying Lorenzo into the Orsini family, Piero was undoubtedly looking to the future.

As expected, Florence did not take kindly to a Roman bride being selected for Lorenzo, and to overcome this Piero decided to mount a festival for the people of Florence, to celebrate his son's betrothal. Or so it would appear; in fact, by this stage Piero was too ill to organise such an event, and instead Lorenzo himself took charge. And it was now that he began to emerge in his authentic colours, for the result was a truly spectacular tournament, which was staged in the traditional arena of the Piazza Santa Croce in March 1469.

We have to imagine the expanse of the stone-slabbed square covered with sand (to prevent the horses' hooves from slipping). One side of the square was lined with a specially erected stand, draped with vivid awnings, where the leading families of Florence were seated. The colourful crowds were crammed beneath the buildings on the other three sides of the square, with others craning from the windows and balconies with their draped pennants, and yet others perched high on the rooftops beneath the clear blue sky. The line of liveried heralds played a fanfare as the eighteen competing knights appeared on horseback, each led into the arena by a pageboy in coloured tunic. One by one the knights filed past the stand, dipping their lances before the throne of the 'Queen of the Tournament'; this was Lucrezia Donati, the young wife of a leading citizen, who was popularly acclaimed as the most beautiful woman in the city. The dazzling armour and plumed helmets of the knights shimmered in the sunlight as they rode to their stations, raising their heraldic shields to the cheering crowds. But none appeared more superb than Lorenzo on his white charger bedecked with red and white velvet, a white silk cloak lined with scarlet flowing from his shoulders, his Medici shield studded with a glinting diamond. Then the jousts began, each with one knight riding against another until the winner unseated his rival. The roar of the crowd rose as the horses' hooves thudded over the sanded stone and the two competing knights rode towards one another . . .

> Achilles' rage their lances' clash inspires,
> Their sparkling armour rivals Etna's fires.

The actual details of the tournament were recorded by Lorenzo's friend, the poet Luigi Pulci, in his poem *The Joust of Lorenzo de' Medici*, which would become one of the best-known ballads of the period. Yet despite the bravado and excitement, it was mainly show; no one was meant to get hurt, least of all Lorenzo. However, accidents did sometimes happen, for during an earlier tournament the great *condottiere* Montefeltro, Lord of Urbino, had accidentally lost an eye. But on this occasion there were to be no accidents; and there was no doubt about who was going to win, yet as Lorenzo graciously conceded: 'I was given the first prize, even though I was not well versed in the use of weapons or skilled in how to inflict blows on my opponent.' The event was a huge success, and the citizens of Florence went away happy – a lesson that Lorenzo would take to heart. It hardly seemed to matter that afterwards the whole thing was found to have cost the equivalent of more than 8,000 florins – 2,000 florins more than Clarice's promised dowry!

Four months later Clarice Orsini arrived in Florence for her wedding, and rode to the church on Lorenzo's white charger – the one on which he had won the tournament, a gift from the King of Naples. The ceremony was followed by three days of banquets at the Palazzo Medici; in the courtyard and the gardens, tables of wild boar and suckling pig were laid out beneath the colourful canopies, minstrels played from the balconies, and the guests danced on a raised stage beneath the entwined arms of the Orsini and Medici families. By the end, more than 300 barrels of the finest Tuscan wine had been emptied.

Once again, everyone went home happy – with the possible exception of the bride and groom, for it soon became evident that Lorenzo and Clarice were an ill-matched couple. Lorenzo would have been a difficult man to live with at the best of times, his charismatic ugliness proving an almost animal attraction to some women, though to be fair he did not make as much use of this as he might have done. He seemed to expend more energy on writing amorous sonnets of a strictly platonic nature, in the long-established Italian tradition; every poet was expected to have his 'love' – just as Dante had his Beatrice, and Petrarch had his Laura. Such relationships were often not even personal ones, remaining strictly a matter of poetry; in this way, Lorenzo wrote love poems to Lucrezia Donati, the 'Queen of the Tournament', and would continue to write sonnets to her successors as the Beauty of Florence.

For her part, Clarice proved to be a somewhat frumpy young woman of pedestrian intelligence, but convinced of her own superiority. The sophisticated merry-go-round of Florentine society bewildered her, and she defensively looked down upon it. Her attitude to Lorenzo would sometimes become similarly disapproving, though for the most part this remained muted. The fact is that both of them seem to have made a considerable effort to keep up the appearance of a normal Italian marriage of the period; and as was often the case, the appearance soon became much of the reality – Lorenzo and Clarice would eventually have no fewer than ten children (three of whom died in childhood). They were often apart, but their letters to one another reveal a neutral chattiness; she writes: 'If you have any news which is not a state secret, do write and tell me. It would give us all here great pleasure.' Though she frequently nagged Lorenzo about his friends, who considered her dull and were inclined to slight her when he was not around.

Within months of the church bells of San Lorenzo ringing out to celebrate the wedding of Lorenzo, they were tolling for the death of his father Piero, and the twenty-year-old Lorenzo then assumed the role for which he had been groomed. Like his father before him, he began by totting up the accounts and 'found that we possessed 237,988 scudi' (at the time probably around 200,000 florins). His father's short period in charge had not diminished the family fortune; and the overall profits of the Medici Bank would have appeared similarly healthy, buoyed up as they were by the alum monopoly.

Yet trouble was not long in coming, and in the spring of 1470 alarming news reached Florence. One of the conspirators who had been banished by Piero the Gouty along with Neroni and Acciaiuoli, a vindictive and unscrupulous man named Bernardo Nardi, had launched an invasion. Leading a column of armed men, he had marched into Prato, just ten miles down the road, where he was said to be waiting for military backup led by Neroni, before marching on Florence itself. The Signoria immediately summoned the city's militia, which was ordered to march post-haste for Prato.

Fortunately this event would peter out into an anticlimax, for by the time the Florentine soldiers arrived at Prato, they found that the revolt was over. The local mayor Cesare Petrucci had summoned the Prato militia, captured Nardi and his rebels, and publicly hanged all the ringleaders. Lorenzo was particularly pleased by Petrucci's swift action; not only had it saved Florence, but it had also shown that the population in the countryside was firmly behind Medici rule. In keeping with the policy instigated by his grandfather Cosimo on his return from exile, Lorenzo earmarked the country mayor for future promotion. Such men often proved even more loyal than long-term members of the Medici faction, and Petrucci would prove no exception. (He would eventually become *gonfaloniere*, and as such it was his timely action during the Pazzi conspiracy that would save the day for the Medici.)

Several months after the events in Prato, the well-ordered Medici political machine encountered unexpected opposition within the city. The standing council refused to appoint the Medici recommendations, put forward by Tommaso Soderini, for the committee that oversaw the voting for members of the Signoria. This resulted in a return to more democratic election by lot, ironically the very system that had led to Soderini's brother, the conspirator Niccolò Soderini, being elected as *gonfaloniere*. Lorenzo bided his time, waiting till the balance again fell in the Medici favour, before installing a system that left the Medici even more firmly in control. He justified his action by insisting that Florence needed a 'constant government' when dealing with its enemies. From this time on, all major councils – whether of war, finance or public order – would retain a functional Medici majority.

Lorenzo was now free to consolidate Florence's foreign policy, and in 1471 the touchy Galeazzo, Duke of Milan, was invited on a state visit to Florence, along with his wife Bona, a member of the House of Savoy. (The Sforzas had continued the Visconti tradition of marrying a Savoy, thus protecting Milan's northern alpine frontier.) Galeazzo's visit was another occasion for pageants and celebrations, enjoyed by the public and much appreciated by the distinguished visitor – who brought with him a 2,000-strong retinue of brocaded knights, liveried soldiery, falconers and even 500 hunting hounds. Florence was impressed, but nonetheless its citizens, and especially its leader, took delight in quietly displaying its cultural supremacy. Galeazzo's stay in the Palazzo Medici, with its superb paintings and sculptures, so inspired the visiting duke that on his return to

Milan he too began commissioning artists and architects to adorn his city.

Galeazzo's father Francesco, the burly ex-*condottiere*, had been urged by Cosimo de' Medici to commission buildings and statues; this early Renaissance period in Milan had also been assisted by Pigello Portinari, the important local manager of the Medici Bank, which did so much to support Francesco Sforza. Yet in many ways Milan still lagged behind Florence in such cultural matters. Indicative of this was the cathedral that was being built in the city, which was unmistakably Gothic – a great medieval building, complete with spires and flying buttresses, which could have been built in France or Germany in previous centuries. Even so, the full flowering of the artistic Renaissance in Florence, assisted so strongly by Medici money, was now beginning to spread to its neighbouring Italian states.

Despite this, the relationship between these states did not improve: Italian politics remained as difficult and devious as ever, and the most insignificant act could provoke a diplomatic contretemps. Lorenzo's lavish public display for Galeazzo, Duke of Milan, was regarded with jealousy by Ferrante, King of Naples, who, after all, had sent a magnificent white charger for Lorenzo's wedding – the young ruler of Florence was meant to be *his* friend.

In 1471 Pope Paul II died, and was succeeded by Pope Sixtus IV; the sophisticated Sienese humanist had been succeeded by an altogether more difficult and determined character. Sixtus IV had been born on the Ligurian coast near Genoa; entering into a Franciscan monastery in his youth, he had shown a precocious, if hard-headed, intellect. This, allied to piety and ambition, had enabled his rapid rise in the Church; by the age of fifty-seven, when he was elected pope, he presented a formidable figure. A tall, stocky man with a huge head, a flattened nose and no teeth, he was determined to recuperate the political power of the papacy. His first aim was to gain control of the central Italian Papal States, many of which were now independent in all but name.

In 1471, Lorenzo de' Medici headed the Florentine delegation to Rome to congratulate the new pope on his succession; and to all appearances, Sixtus IV was deeply impressed by his important young visitor. He agreed to continue the papal account with the Medici Bank, but was unwilling to make Lorenzo's younger brother Giuliano a cardinal; despite their marriage into the Orsini family, the Medici were not yet able to make their way into the hierarchy of the Church. (Unbeknown to Lorenzo, Sixtus IV already had plans to appoint no fewer than six of his nephews as cardinals.) As a consolation, the pope presented Lorenzo with an Ancient Roman marble bust of the Emperor Augustus. This time it was Galeazzo, Duke of Milan, who was jealous, and this news was accompanied by reports of a sinister development concerning the ruler of Florence's main ally. Word from Accerrito Portinari, who had suceded his brother Pigello as manager of the Medici Bank in Milan, suggested that Galeazzo was now becoming dangerously deranged. His increasingly exotic behaviour had recently included bricking up his astrologer (a priest) in a cell with a glass of wine and a chicken leg, after he had predicted that Galeazzo would reign for fewer than eleven years.

Yet there was little time for Lorenzo to ponder this ominous development, for he was now faced with a full-blown crisis. Further deposits of alum had recently been discovered outside Volterra, a town in southern Tuscany under Florentine rule; and the authorities of Volterra granted the mining concession to a company with three Medici supporters as major stockholders. Yet it soon became clear that the alum mine contained much larger deposits than had previously been thought, whereupon the Volterra authorities decided to withdraw the mining concession and place it in the hands of their own citizens. The move was countermanded by the authorities in Florence, but when news of this reached Volterra, a riot broke out and several Florentines were killed. One of the Medici stockholders was thrown from a window, and the local mayor, appointed by Florence, escaped only by barricading himself in his palazzo.

Against the advice of Tommaso Soderini and the Signoria in Florence, Lorenzo decided that a show of force was necessary; if Volterra broke from Florentine rule, other Tuscan cities might easily follow. The *condottiere* Montefeltro, Lord of Urbino, was hired to march with his mercenary army on Volterra, which immediately sent out vain appeals for help to Venice and Naples. After a four-week siege, the city surrendered and the gates were opened; but at this stage Montefeltro lost control of his mercenaries, who went on the rampage, murdering, looting and raping. When news of this reached Florence, Lorenzo was horrified and set out at once for Volterra; in an attempt to make amends, Lorenzo himself rode amongst the population, handing out money to the distressed citizens. He was genuinely repentant – but it had been his decision to send in the troops. He may have been groomed for the leadership from an early age, but he had yet to acquire the practical expertise of his grandfather or his father, who would certainly have attempted to defuse the situation first, resorting to violence only as a last measure.

13

Murder in the Cathedral

O N THE DAY after Christmas 1476, as Galeazzo, Duke of Milan, entered church, he was stabbed by three noblemen. The population rallied to the support of his wife Bona of Savoy, but ongoing intrigues amongst Galeazzo's surviving brothers rendered the situation highly unstable; Florence's main ally was in disarray and could not be relied upon. Meanwhile Sixtus IV had launched his campaign to secure the papal territories in the Romagna. This was the man of whom it was said that he 'elevated nepotism into a political principle'; in need of a trustworthy army, he arranged for one of his nephews to marry the oldest daughter of Montefeltro, Lord of Urbino, who was rewarded by being promoted to ducal status. It was understood that from now on the new Duke of Urbino would use his mercenary army in the service of the pope, rather than Florence. At the same time, Sixtus IV embarked on his programme of appointing his relatives as cardinals; with little thought for the feelings of Lorenzo de' Medici or the citizens of Florence, he made his degenerate twenty-five-year-old nephew Piero Riario a cardinal and appointed him Archbishop of Florence. The new archbishop's quaint habit of presenting his mistresses with gold chamberpots was soon the talk of the city, though alas for the gossips, within three years he had dissipated himself into an early grave.

More serious were the machinations involving Archbishop Riario's brother Girolamo, who was strongly suspected of being the pope's son rather than his nephew. As part of his campaign to extend papal power, Sixtus IV sought to buy the city state of Imola and install Girolamo Riario as its lord. This city belonged at the time to Milan, and its owners demanded the equivalent of 40,000 florins, whereupon Sixtus IV approached Tornabuoni at the Medici Bank in Rome for a loan to cover this sum. Tornabuoni contacted Lorenzo, who was hesitant, with good reason: not only did Sixtus IV already owe 10,000 florins on his personal account, but Imola was strategically important to Florence, commanding its trade route over the mountains to the Adriatic. On the other hand, Lorenzo had no wish to offend the pope, so he decided to play for time, and hedged. Unused to being thwarted, Sixtus IV flew into a rage and withdrew the papal account from the Medici Bank; instead, in what may well have been a prearranged move, he turned to the Medici's main rivals, the Pazzi Bank. Francesco de' Pazzi, their manager in Rome, readily agreed to the pope's request for a loan.

The Pazzi were of a distinguished Florentine lineage, and had been one of the city's leading families for almost 500 years. An early member of the family had returned from the First Crusade in the eleventh century with several flints chipped from the Holy Sepulchre in Jerusalem, and these had been housed in the church of Sant'Apostoli, becoming Florence's most revered holy relics. The Pazzi had formerly been of aristocratic rank, which they had set aside only to enter the bankers' guild in the fourteenth century. The bank they had established soon thrived, to the point where it was the only bank in Florence which could be considered as remotely rivalling the Medici Bank. They had commissioned Brunelleschi to design a family palazzo, and the *catasto* tax returns show that by 1457 the Pazzi had become the second-wealthiest family in Florence. Piero de' Medici had taken note of this, and had arranged for Lorenzo's favourite older sister Bianca to marry Guglielmo de' Pazzi, the younger brother of Francesco. This had united the two families so that they now maintained only a friendly rivalry; Guglielmo had become a close friend of Lorenzo, spending time in his house and going hunting with him.

Francesco de' Pazzi, on the other hand, harboured a bitter grudge against the Medici. An arrogant and pretentious man, he resented the airs put on by the Medici, as well as their power and their money; but now he had succeeded in delivering a serious blow to the Medici wealth, by securing the papal account. In his view, it was only Medici money that had managed to balk the Pazzi from political power in Florence. Now was the time to strike, before the Medici could recover.

Francesco de' Pazzi was well aware that the Medici had several power-ful enemies, who would be willing to assist in any move against them. To begin with he approached the coarse and aggressive Girolamo Riario, the new Lord of Imola, who had already shown signs of wishing to extend his power; and Riario agreed that he would be only too pleased to see Lorenzo de' Medici assassinated. Next Francesco de' Pazzi approached Francesco Salviati, a bitter opponent of Lorenzo who had been appointed Archbishop of Pisa by Sixtus IV. Salviati had been aptly described by Lorenzo's friend, the poet Angelo Poliziano, as 'an ignoramus, contemp-tuous of both human and divine law, steeped in crime and disgrace of all kinds'. Lorenzo had opposed Salviati's appointment in Pisa, and for three years had refused him permission to cross Florentine territory to take up his post, thus depriving him of the vast financial benefits that accrued to his office. Archbishop Salviati enthusiastically agreed to take a leading role in the plot.

Next Francesco de' Pazzi hired the *condottiere* Gian Battista da Montesecco, who was given orders to station his troops at Imola and other strategic points along the mountainous eastern border of the Florentine Republic. They were to wait until the conspirators struck, and then march upon Florence. There would be confusion after the downfall of Lorenzo, but the people would be only too pleased to see the end of the Medici tyranny and would rise up in support of the conspirators; there would be no opposition to his troops, who would not be required to shed any blood. Pazzi and Montesecco both knew that Florence could no longer rely on the supreme skills of Montefeltro, now happily Duke of Urbino.

The conspirators travelled to Rome, where Sixtus IV gave them his blessing, characterising Lorenzo as 'evil and contemptible trash, who shows no respect'. Then, adopting a hypocritically pious air, he warned the conspirators that there should be no bloodshed, for the pope could not possibly sanction the taking of human life. But the conspirators knew that they could not accomplish their aim without bloodshed, so according to Montesecco, who was present at the meeting, they continued to press the pope, eventually demanding: 'Holy Father, are you content that we steer this ship? And that we steer it well?' Finally he nodded. 'I am content.' Montesecco, as well as the other conspirators, was in no doubt that the pope was fully aware of the deed to which he was giving his assent.

Francesco de' Pazzi travelled to Florence with his plan to murder Lorenzo de' Medici, together with his brother Giuliano, his only likely successor. Pazzi now sought the support of the fifty-seven-year-old head of his family, Messer Jacopo de' Pazzi (the title *messer*, or 'master', was the equivalent of 'sir'), a distinguished banker and silk merchant, who had spent several years abroad, mainly in France; on his return he had even served a term as *gonfaloniere*, and had been knighted by the Signoria for his services to the city. In the words of Salviati, Archbishop of Pisa: 'When we have him in our side, the deed is as good as done.' Yet as soon as Francesco de' Pazzi and the *condottiere* Montesecco revealed to Jacopo de' Pazzi the details of the conspiracy, his manner turned 'as cold as ice'; he insisted that it would never work. Montesecco then revealed the details of the conspirators' conversation with the pope, and on hearing this Jacopo was finally persuaded, agreeing to back the conspiracy.

After several delays, the conspirators finalised their plot, spreading the word amongst trusted friends who could be relied upon to take part. Two priests (one an embittered citizen of Volterra) were chosen to stab Lorenzo. An aristocratic ne'er-do-well named Bernardo Bandini (sometimes known as Baroncelli), who had money invested in the Pazzi Bank, was brought in to stab Giuliano, with the assistance of Francesco de' Bardi himself. They would strike when Lorenzo and his brother were attending Mass at the cathedral, and the signal for the assassination would be the raising of the Host by the priest. It would take place on the fifth Sunday after Easter, 26 April, though in later years a myth grew up that this was in fact Easter Sunday, a story encouraged by the Medici to make the deed appear even more infamous, for taking place on the holiest day of the Christian calendar.

Lorenzo's brother Giuliano would in the event be assassinated, but otherwise the plot would fail, with many of the conspirators meeting a gruesome fate, though none more so than Messer Jacopo de' Pazzi. When news reached him in the Palazzo Pazzi that the plot had failed, he is said to have succumbed to a paroxysm of anguished despair; after he had recovered, he fled the city on horseback, accompanied by a number of armed retainers. Lorenzo sent bands of armed men in pursuit to search for him, as news of what had happened in Florence spread through the countryside. Several of Jacopo's men were killed in a violent clash, but Jacopo himself managed to flee into the mountains, ending up at the remote hamlet of Castagno di San Godenzo. Here he was recognised by some peasants, who managed to capture him and hand him over to the pursuing Medici men; they then brought him back to Florence, where he was cast into a dungeon in the Bargello and tortured.

Next day, more dead than alive, Jacopo de' Pazzi was dragged down the street to the Palazzo della Signoria and hauled upstairs; here he was humiliatingly stripped to his underwear and bundled out of a north window with a rope around his neck, where his writhing body swung beside those of the other four conspirators. When the hanged men were finally cut down, Jacopo's corpse was taken to be buried at Santa Croce, the Pazzi family church. But worse indignities were to come for Messer Jacopo de' Pazzi. During the following days Florence and the surrounding countryside were inundated with a succession of heavy rainstorms that washed away most of the cereal harvest; this misfortune was blamed on the Pazzi, and an angry crowd threatened to break open the tomb of Jacopo de' Pazzi, so the friars exhumed his body, which was then buried in unconsecrated ground outside the city near the public gallows. But two days later, according to Machiavelli, a 'great throng of boys' dug up his body, and his cadaver was then 'pulled by the noose with which he was hanged, and he was dragged naked through the whole city'. The leaders of the mob preceded him, crying out: 'Make way for the great knight!' When they arrived at the Palazzo Pazzi, his remains were subjected to further mockery; the cadaver's rotting head was rapped against the door like a knocker, to cries of: 'Open up! The great knight is here!'

Finally, with a rousing cheer, the stinking remains were thrown into the Arno from the bridge at Rubinconte, upstream of the city centre. Crowds rushed to the embankment to watch as the cadaver floated downstream past the Ponte Vecchio, through the city. Yet even this was not the end, for the decaying corpse floated on down the river, where it was washed up onto a mud bank, and here it was discovered by a group of urchins, who began parading the skeletal remains. Next they tied a rope around the skeleton's neck and enacted a mock hanging, hauling the body up over the branch of a willow tree; then they beat the tatty hanging remains with sticks until the bones fell apart, before finally throwing them back into the river.

According to Machiavelli, this was 'an extraordinary instance of the fury of the people'. Poliziano, who also describes these events, merely states that the mob were 'driven by the Furies'. But what was the real reason for the extreme feelings that surfaced here? This grotesque sequence of events seems indicative of the seething tensions that lay beneath the surface of everyday life in Florence. Here was an occurrence in which eventually more than just a 'throng of boys' could legitimately vent their pent-up anger; on this occasion the despised 'snivellers' were able to get away with expressing their deepest feelings for their would-be rulers. These macabre scenes were the occasion for much jeering, vicious ridicule and execration; notably absent from all accounts are any mention of cheers for the Medici, cries of *'Palle! Palle!'* or shouts of approval for the proud victors. This perhaps is the key to such savagery, rather than any 'extraordinary . . . fury of the people' or their being 'driven by the Furies'. When overt wealth existed cheek by jowl with the perpetual poverty of the *popolo minuto* within the confines of a walled city, such an explosion becomes understandable. Rather than coming as an inexplicable surprise, it is more likely that the fate of Jacopo de' Pazzi's corpse gives a rare insight into the fraught social reality over which the Medici godfathers ruled.

When news of the failed conspiracy reached Rome, Pope Sixtus IV is said to have become apoplectic with rage; the hanging of one of his archbishops in full ceremonial robes was deemed nothing less than a sacrilege, for this was a direct insult to the Church! The fact that there had been a conspiracy, in which he had been one of the prime movers, was quickly forgotten. Sixtus IV issued a papal bull excommunicating Lorenzo de' Medici, together with all the citizens of the Florentine Republic. Encouraged by the pope's wrath, his hot-headed 'nephew' Girolamo Riario, Lord of Imola (who had decided against joining his fellow conspirators in Florence), marched on the Florentine Embassy; backed by 300 soldiers of the papal guard, he arrested the Florentine ambassador. Sixtus IV now despatched a papal delegation to Florence, ordering the citizens to hand over Lorenzo de' Medici so that he could be tried for sacrilege, blasphemy, insulting the Church, murdering the Archbishop of Pisa and a list of other misdemeanours. Lorenzo was declared 'culpable, sacrilegious, excommunicated, anathematised, infamous, unworthy of all trust and spiritually disqualified from making a will'. At the same time, the *gonfaloniere* and Signoria of Florence were condemned in similar overheated terms 'to have all their property confiscated by the Church, their houses levelled to the ground, their every dwelling place rendered unfit for habitation of any kind. May everlasting ruin accompany their eternal disgrace.' In a separate, less publicised edict, the pope ordered the seizing of all Medici assets in Rome, including the Medici Bank, with all debts to this bank being declared null and void (thus at a stroke saving himself 10,000 florins).

The citizens of Florence greeted news of the papal bull of excommunication with wary scorn, and made it clear that they had no intention of handing over Lorenzo de' Medici to the pope. The bishops of Tuscany were also none too pleased to discover themselves excommunicated en masse, and summoned a congregation in the cathedral at Florence, which was attended by all leading citizens. Here they defiantly announced that the Signoria had been justified in their defence of the republic against the conspirators, and afterwards issued a decree of their own excommunicating the pope. This they had printed on the first printing press in Florence, which had been established just a year previously, and the decree was then distributed around Tuscany, with the result that many more read of this excommunication than of the one issued by the pope himself.

But then came more serious news: in his fury, Sixtus IV had declared war on Florence, and had now drawn in King Ferrante of Naples as his ally: Florence soon found that it was standing virtually alone. The Orsini set about rallying the family army, but this was little more than a gesture, while Milan was still involved in its own internal power struggle and sent only a token force. Venice was keen to protect northern Italy, but considered Florence a lost cause: it too despatched only a token force. As a last resort, Lorenzo managed to secure the Duke of Ferrara, and his small mercenary army, to lead the Florentine forces.

The pope summoned the papal forces under their new commander Montefeltro, Duke of Urbino, now recognised as the supreme military commander in all Italy; and these were joined by a large army from Naples under the Duke of Calabria, son of King Ferrante. While the Duke of Urbino stood by with reinforcements, the Duke of Calabria advanced into Florentine territory. In reply, the Duke of Ferrara executed a series of tactical responses – according to his despatches to Florence, he was 'outmanoeuvring' the enemy; in practice, however, this merely involved a series of retreats. The worried Signoria in Florence despatched messages remonstrating with their commander, demanding what he was being paid for if he refused to fight. Meanwhile the Duke of Calabria continued his advance, eventually reaching the town of Colle, thirty miles south of Florence, where he met with unexpectedly stout resistance from the local citizens, who refused to surrender their town. Finally, after a siege lasting two months, Colle fell to the Neapolitan army; but already it was November and the cold weather had begun to set in, so the Neapolitan army retired to winter quarters in Siena. On learning this news, the Duke of Ferrara retreated to Ferrara, and his Milanese troops decided that they too would return home.

By now civil order was beginning to break down all over Tuscany. Bands of armed brigands, passing themselves off as advanced scouting parties for the enemy, had begun descending from the mountains and terrorising the countryside. In Florence itself, the people were frightened and angry; food stocks from the countryside were running low, and they were being taxed to the limit to pay for the war, yet no one was defending them. To make matters worse, there had been a recent economic downturn in the wool trade, which had affected everyone, from the traders to the *ciompi*; with new taxes to pay for the war, many traders were now facing ruin, while the laid-off *ciompi* and their families faced destitution. Then panic set in as news spread that cases of bubonic plague had been reported in the Santa Croce district. And still the war dragged on and on.

At the end of 1479 Lorenzo de' Medici took stock of the situation: he concluded that the citizens of Florence were being made to suffer largely on his behalf, for the enemy was really only interested in the overthrow and destruction of the Medici. In December, he decided to take a desperate gamble: having ensured that the loyal Tommaso Soderini was elected *gonfaloniere*, Lorenzo slipped out of the city and rode for the port of Pisa. On the way, he stopped to write a letter to the Signoria, in which he explained:

> I have decided, with your approval [*sic*], to set sail for Naples at once. I am convinced that the action of our enemies is mainly directed by hatred against me, and that by giving myself up to

them I may be able to restore peace to our city . . . Because it has been chosen that I have greater honour and responsibility than other private citizens, I feel more bound to serve our country, even if it means risking my life . . . I desire that by my life or my death, my fate or my fortune, I may contribute to the welfare of our city.

According to a contemporary report, by the time Lorenzo's letter had been read through, many members of the Signoria were in tears, and there is little reason to suspect that this was an exaggeration.

However, it has been suggested that Lorenzo over-dramatised the situation: he had already been secretly in touch with Ferrante, King of Naples, who had in fact sent a galley to Pisa to collect him. On the other hand, others have pointed out that Ferrante was notoriously unpredictable in temperament, and it might well have been to his advantage to have Lorenzo assassinated aboard ship, or confined permanently to the dungeons on his arrival at Naples. Yet neither event happened, and as soon as Lorenzo set foot on the quayside at Naples he was embraced by Ferrante's son Federigo. Lorenzo's valiant mission appealed to Ferrante, and its sheer drama was appreciated far further afield; amongst Italy's recent history of devious and untrustworthy leaders, here at last was a hero.

There is no doubting that Lorenzo was in real danger, for Ferrante was volatile and vicious; it was said of him: 'No one could tell whether he would be furious or amused.' In the event, Ferrante welcomed Lorenzo, but refused to be hustled into any decisions; an accord with Florence meant a rupture with Sixtus IV, who had already made one of Ferrante's sons a cardinal – a rare appointment indeed for anyone outside the family. Lorenzo lodged in the quarters of the Medici Bank, and went to call upon King Ferrante. The result was a courteous stalemate. Beneath the diplomatic niceties, a game of cat-and-mouse began; Ferrante insisted that Lorenzo could not leave, explaining that he wished to have more time to enjoy Lorenzo's inspiring company.

Lorenzo must have sensed that Ferrante would prevaricate, and came prepared. He launched a charm offensive on the people of Naples and their king, and began distributing largesse in the most extravagant fashion. The hundred galley slaves who had rowed his flotilla from Pisa to

Naples all had their freedom purchased by Lorenzo, who also gave them each ten florins and a new set of clothes to replace their wretched rags. He started dispensing dowry money amongst the poor, so that their daughters could make good marriages, gave lavishly to charities, and sponsored festivals. One of the officials who 'looked after' him reported that by day he appeared 'composed, confident and gracious'; but at night Lorenzo frequently descended into grim despair. The poetry he wrote would often reflect this juxtaposition of light and darkness in his character:

> Orange blossom seen at dawn is bright,
> Yet seen at dusk it holds the first of night.

As the months passed, Lorenzo continued with his lavish spending – a strategy that was surely compensation for his nightly anxieties, as much as a matter of policy. Yet where did all the money come from? The Medici Bank had suffered badly from the recent economic downturn in Italy and throughout Europe; restrictions in the English wool trade had plunged the London branch even further into debt. The Bruges branch was also heavily in debt, a situation that was exacerbated by the recklessness of the local manager Tommaso Portinari (brother of the Milan manager). In contravention of his contract, Portinari had invested considerable sums in various maritime ventures, including a large but disastrous Portuguese trading expedition to Guinea on the west African coast. Portinari had also paid 8,000 florins for the purchase and refurbishment of the Hotel Bladelin as the Medici Bank's new premises (even today, this remains one of Bruges's more substantial historical buildings). Examining the figures in war-torn Florence during 1479, Lorenzo had discovered that between them the London and Bruges branches owed the colossal sum of 70,000 florins, which led him to comment sarcastically: 'These are the great profits which are accruing to us through the management of Tommaso Portinari.' In slight mitigation of Portinari, the stories of Lorenzo's earlier pageants and extravagances in Florence must surely have had their effect; if the Medici could afford such munificence at home, surely their premises abroad should reflect this wealth. And now Lorenzo was in Naples, once again spending as if his life depended upon it (which for once had more than an element of truth). The question of how and where Lorenzo obtained this money is crucial to any assessment of his financial probity.

The Florentine authorities certainly knew that he was spending heavily and made money available to him: 'I herewith send you the mandate,' the clerk to the Signoria wrote to him, 'and the letter of credit you asked for.' Before leaving Florence, Lorenzo had raised 60,000 florins by mortgaging the castle-villa of Cafaggiolo and his estates in the Mugello. Was this for use in Naples, or to cover the bank's debts? Many commentators have asserted that now, and at other times, Lorenzo embezzled large amounts from the Florence exchequer. The separation between the financial dealings of Florence and those of the Medici had already become blurred during Cosimo's time — mostly to Florence's advantage. Did Lorenzo consider that it was time the Medici benefited from this arrangement? One surviving document shows that at some time during his reign Lorenzo diverted 74,948 florins to his account 'without the sanction of any law and without authority'. It is impossible to tell what this was for — a later generation of the Medici destroyed all relevant documents relating to these years. However, the historical expert on Medici financial affairs, Raymond de Roover, asserts quite plainly: 'It is likely, therefore, that bankruptcy after the Pazzi conspiracy was averted only by dipping into the public treasury.' It would appear just as likely that Lorenzo considered this was to the advantage of both the Medici and Florence; and pragmatism, if not morality, would seem to support this view.

The longer Lorenzo was detained in Naples, the more it became clear that Ferrante was having difficulties of his own. The Turkish fleet was becoming an increasingly menacing presence along the coasts of southern Italy; and the King of France had ominously reasserted his claim to the throne of Naples. Ferrante finally agreed to a peace treaty with Florence. Sixtus IV was infuriated, but having little alternative, he decided to sign up to this treaty; he would bide his time.

Lorenzo returned to Florence a hero, and once again took advantage of this opportunity to strengthen his hold on the government. A new council of seventy men was created, which would hold office for five years, and the election of members was duly organised by the Medici party; this council even had powers to overrule the Signoria. An element of more permanent political stability had been created in Florence, and to cement this Lorenzo began acting less impetuously and more in the stealthy manner of his grandfather. The loyal Tommaso Soderini was used as Lorenzo's roving ambassador, representing him at various foreign court functions, to avoid the possibility of him building up a political power base within the city he had presided over during Lorenzo's absence.

In 1480 the Turkish sultan Mehmet the Conqueror landed troops in southern Italy and occupied the port of Otranto. Mehmet had already overrun the whole of Greece and occupied most of the Balkans; Italy appeared to be the next step in the extension of the Ottoman Empire. Sixtus IV issued a desperate appeal for all to rally in the defence of Christendom, an appeal that was quickly answered by the Italian states, including Florence. The pope decided that he was willing to forget his differences with Lorenzo: there was no point in further scheming under such circumstances. Then, just as suddenly as they had arrived, within a year the Turks withdrew; Mehmet had died, and a new sultan had taken over: there would be peace for the time being. Equally surprisingly, the pan-Italian peace also held through the following years. During this period Lorenzo would play an increasingly influential diplomatic role; although still only in his early thirties, his actions in defence of Florence and his attempts to maintain peace meant that he was now respected as a states-man throughout Italy. When difficulties arose, his advice would prove crucial, and as a result he became known as 'the needle of the Italian compass'; he was the one who could be relied upon to point the way forward. Apart from a couple of lesser outbreaks of hostility, Italy would remain at peace for the rest of Lorenzo de' Medici's life.

14

Plato in the Piazzas

NOW CAME THE period when Lorenzo de' Medici's patronage would flourish as never before, when he would fulfil the expectations of the name by which he is known to history: Lorenzo the Magnificent (in Italian *il magnifico*, an epithet which significantly he seems to have attracted as a child). Even if this magnificence could sometimes degenerate into arrogance or pure show, there is no doubt that it informed the full range of his being – from his personality to his politics, from his patronage to his poetry. Although this quality was not necessarily good in itself (indeed, it was more of an amoral force), it could be said that in Lorenzo it resembled the Platonic idea of Good, of which he wrote:

> Each art, each science, every daily act
> and choice goes back, it seems, to that same good
> as every stream flows back into the sea.

Lorenzo was a more-than-accomplished poet, but he had the grace to recognise a greater one in Poliziano, whom he would support for much of his life.

Angelo Poliziano (often known as Politian) was born five years after Lorenzo in 1454 at Montepulciano, in the wine-growing region in the south-east of Tuscany. His father was a talented lawyer and a loyal local supporter of the Medici, who were not always so popular in the countryside; indeed, this affiliation would result in his murder during the failed Pitti-led uprising against Piero the Gouty in 1466. Not long after this

Poliziano was sent to Florence, where he was educated in the finest humanist tradition, possibly at Medici expense. He quickly showed exceptional talent; by the age of nineteen he was fluent in both Greek and Latin, and it was his ability to compose epigrams in Greek that first brought him to the attention of Lorenzo. Poliziano appears to have moved into the Palazzo Medici as early as 1473, where he made full use of the Medici Library, which Cosimo had established and Piero had extended. Two years later, Lorenzo employed Poliziano as tutor to his three-year-old son Piero, a task that Poliziano clearly relished.

Poliziano and Lorenzo soon became very close, sharing a ready wit, lively intelligence and a sheer zest for life. For Lorenzo, Poliziano was the one who made him forget his political cares, who reminded him of his intellectual brilliance, who could talk to his heart; for his part, Poliziano simply worshipped Lorenzo. The word is not too strong: his actions constantly betray it, and he says as much himself in his letters to Lorenzo and his mother, the exceptional Lucrezia, who became Poliziano's confidante. A fresco from this period by Ghirlandaio depicts Poliziano in profile, with his charge the young Piero at his side, turning his cherubic face with its pageboy cut to look at the painter. Poliziano, with his flowing shoulder-length

Fig 7 Angelo Poliziano
and Piero de' Medici

dark hair and darkly handsome face, gazes heavenwards with a soulful expression, though this would appear uncharacteristic, judging from all we know of him. Yet even here his features hint at the passionate temper and quick wit that he deployed in real life; the fact that he took minor holy orders also appears something of an anomaly, although possibly he was appointed to the benefice of San Paolo at Lorenzo's wish, in order to provide him with an independent income.

There is no doubting that Poliziano's learning was more than just the show of brilliance that some accord it; he conversed fluently in Greek with Argyropoulos and contested Plato's philosophy with Ficino. His earlier poetry was written in superb classical Latin, and he wrote masterly Greek epigrams, though later Lorenzo persuaded Poliziano to follow him in writing poetry in Tuscan. As a result, Poliziano began composing *The Joust of Giuliano de' Medici*, a companion piece to Pulci's *The Joust of Lorenzo de' Medici*. This described the love felt for Lorenzo's younger brother Giuliano de' Medici by the seventeen-year-old Simonetta Vespucci, who had now succeeded to the title of Florence's most beautiful woman:

> For Giuliano many a maid her love confessed
> But none could melt the ice within his breast.

This was intended as a private joke amongst Lorenzo's circle; Giuliano was good-looking and liked to think of himself as a heartless womaniser, whereas in fact he was constantly falling in love, which was not always requited, leaving him heartbroken. Poliziano's epic would be his first masterpiece in Italian, though it remained incomplete. In the midst of Book 2, stanza 46, the 'Joust' was abruptly abandoned. Poliziano was so overcome with grief when Giuliano was assassinated in the Pazzi conspiracy that he could not write another word of the poem.

On Sunday 26 April 1478, Poliziano was standing beside Lorenzo when the two priests attempted to stab him; according to his own report, he played a heroic part in the saving of Lorenzo's life, though this seems unlikely, as he was known to be something of a coward. Later that day, he witnessed the events in the Piazza della Signoria, when Salviati in his archbishop's robes was flung from the window of the palazzo with a rope around his neck. It is to the eye of the poet that we owe the gruesome detail of Salviati desperately trying to bite into the naked body beside him as he swayed on the end of the rope.

The following year, when Florence was threatened by the Neapolitan army to the south and by plague within, Lorenzo despatched his wife and family, together with Poliziano, to Pistoia, twenty miles to the north-west. Poliziano wrote regularly to '*Magnifice mi Domine*' ('My Magnificent Lord') describing the joys of the summer countryside. 'We want for nothing. Presents we refuse, save salad, figs and a few flasks of wine, some *becca-fichi* [small birds considered a tasty delicacy] or things of that sort.' Describing the generosity and kindness of the locals, he wrote quaintly: 'They would bring us water in their ears.' Yet in reality he was bored by the countryside and the lack of intellectual company; this became even more evident when they all moved to Cafaggiolo out in the Mugello for the winter, with Lorenzo still in Florence. Poliziano captured something of the Medici family atmosphere in a letter to Lorenzo:

> The rain is so heavy and so continuous that we cannot leave the house and have exchanged hunting for playing at ball, so that the children should have exercise. Our stakes are generally the soup, the sweet, or the meat; and he who loses goes without; often when one of my scholars loses he pays tribute to Sir Humid [a popular Italian euphemism for when a child cries]. I have no other news to give you. I remain in the house by the fireside in slippers and a greatcoat; were you to see me you would think I was melancholy personified.

Lorenzo's wife Clarice had taken to her bed, coughing her lungs out with the damp – in fact, the beginnings of the consumption from which she would die ten years later.

Poliziano was despondent, Clarice was resentful, and their dislike for each other increased with every grey, rain-soaked day. The end was not long in coming. Clarice was horrified to discover that the tutor was teaching her children Latin from pagan classical texts, and insisted that they must learn Latin by reading Christian texts such as the Psalms. Poliziano refused point blank to condemn his beloved charges to the pieties of their dull provincial mother, whereupon Clarice finally exploded and threw him out.

They both wrote hurriedly to Lorenzo, pleading their separate cases. 'I have endured a thousand insults,' complained Clarice. 'When you have heard my side, you will realise I am not in the wrong,' insisted Poliziano. Meanwhile, Lorenzo was back in Florence frantically attempting to rescue the crumbling finances of the Medici Bank, struggling to save the republic as the citizens despaired at the news of the advancing Neapolitan army. Even international crises do no preclude domestic ones.

But for this clash with Lorenzo's wife, Poliziano might well have been recalled to accompany Lorenzo, and give him heart, on his daring mission to King Ferrante in Naples a few months later. In the event, Poliziano left Tuscany in a huff and took up residence at the court of Cardinal Gonzaga at Mantua. After a year of grumpy exile, Poliziano was finally tempted back to Florence by Lorenzo. In an effort to heal the rift, Lorenzo arranged for Poliziano to be appointed professor of Greek and Latin at Florence University, and a canon of the cathedral, a well-paid sinecure, although he was no longer allowed to live at the Palazzo Medici. Later, Lorenzo hired him to tutor his chubby thirteen-year-old second son Giovanni, for whom Lorenzo had high hopes; already he had managed to persuade the new pope Innocent VIII to make Giovanni a cardinal, and now he needed a suitable education to equip him for high office. Young Giovanni was hardly a prepossessing figure, with his big Medici nose protruding from his round face, and his prominent Medici jaw leaving his mouth permanently open; even so, Poliziano quickly discovered that Giovanni had inherited much of his father's intelligence and determination. However, it should have been clear to Lorenzo that the worldly and witty Poliziano was hardly the right tutor for a coming man of the Church; and as we shall see, Poliziano's effect on Giovanni would in time have momentous consequences.

It was during these years that Poliziano would write much of his finest poetry in the Tuscan dialect, and as a result Tuscan would make further advances as the educated language of all Italy. The sophisticated tone and erudition of his poetry also did much to further a social concept that was now making itself felt throughout Italy – that of the *gentiluomo* (gentleman). Previously, the notion of a gentleman (and the more couth behaviour with which it was associated) had applied only to the courts of the nobility, and even here gentility was often in short supply. With the coming of the Renaissance, especially in Florence where the Medici were not of the noble blood, the idea of the gentleman began to spread. Gentle manners, gentle speech, gentle appearance, gently informed appreciation of the gentler arts – all these were now seen as open to the aspiration of a wider section of society.

A typical example is seen in Federigo da Montefeltro, the new Duke of Urbino (see colour plates). He had begun his career as a *condottiere*, used to commanding rough mercenary troops. But later in life he would transform the remote city of Urbino into a haven of Renaissance culture. Architecture, painting, even poetry and music, all these would flourish in what had previously been a provincial backwater. (It was here that Raphael would be born and grow up; this small mountain town would have the cultural atmosphere to nurture a genius of the High Renaissance.)

In Florence, artists, philosophers and poets had begun to transform their behaviour into that of a 'gentleman', and this would soon be echoed in other Italian cities (though for the time being, this would remain an exclusively Italian phenomenon). Now these cultured manners began spreading to merchants, civil servants, military officers and priests. Poliziano's witty, graceful and scholarly poetry would come to be seen as exemplary of the new, lightly worn sophistication and learning expected of a gentleman.

But what exactly was Poliziano's poetry about? His treatment of love, especially his love for Lorenzo, is largely Platonic, or pastoral, or even coy, in its enthusiasm; but then we come to his late masterwork of 1480, *Orpheus*. Amazingly, this five-act verse work was composed in a single day, for one of Lorenzo's famed carnivals laid on for the people of Florence. Poliziano's text was intended to be set to music and sung, thus making it the first libretto in the modern sense of the word. (*Libretto* means 'little book' in Italian; only in the following century would it come to mean the text to which music is set.) Poliziano's *Orpheus* also has the distinction of being the first secular drama in the Italian language. Yet it is the twists and turns of the plot that are most intriguing, and these are even more suggestive than usual in Poliziano's work. To begin with, he follows the legend: Orpheus and his lyre charm the wild animals, the trees, the very stones themselves, and finally even the vengeful gods of the Underworld succumb to his music. Here we see the epitome of culture overcoming barbarity; but as Orpheus ascends the path out of the Underworld, leading his beloved Eurydice, he cannot refrain from looking back at her, and thus he loses her. (Lorenzo de' Medici gave this a Platonic interpretation: Orpheus turns from spiritual love back to carnal love.) Yet now that Orpheus no longer has Eurydice, he lapses into carnal behaviour as never before; with every show of enthusiasm, he takes to seducing young men, declaiming:

> This to husbands I advise
> Flee all women, leave your wives.

Eventually Orpheus is set upon by drunken worshippers of Bacchus, who in their frenzy tear him limb from limb. Was this intended as Orpheus's just deserts for his pederastic diversions? Or was the whole thing simply intended as boisterous entertainment for the carnival crowd? One cannot help feeling that there may also have been a suggestive element intended for Lorenzo and his knowing humanist pals.

At the age of forty, Poliziano succumbed to a mortal fever; and a scurrilous story attached to his death casts a light (or shadow) over the character of a man who is otherwise largely surface appearance. We know the darkly handsome profile by Ghirlandaio, the bravado of Poliziano's claimed defence of his beloved Lorenzo in the cathedral, the embodiment of melancholy in his greatcoat and slippers slumped before the winter fire – but what really inspired him, what drove him? According to the story, Poliziano was said to have been reduced to his bed by some species of 'frenzied fever', requiring his friends to watch over him. Somehow eluding his friends, he managed to get up and rush out of the house. Eventually he was discovered in a street playing the lute beneath the window of a young Greek boy with whom he had fallen in love (and who, according to one version, was the actual cause of Poliziano's fever). Finally, his friends brought him back to bed, where he expired in a delirium of love.

Allowing for customary poetic exaggeration, this story would seem to confirm what much else about Poliziano's life and work more or less subtly suggests – the fact that he was homosexual. This raises the question of his love for Lorenzo, and of Lorenzo's feelings for Poliziano; risking widespread outrage, it is possible to suspect that their attachment may on occasion have been more than platonic. In the light of his sexuality, the ardent love expressed by Poliziano for Lorenzo takes on a less purely poetic aspect. There is of course nothing but suggestive evidence to support this suspicion. Apart, that is, from one disputed fact about Donatello's somewhat ambisexual *David*; according to this, the statue was not commissioned by Cosimo de' Medici at all, but was installed on its pedestal in the *cortile* of the Palazzo Medici much later by Lorenzo de' Medici. Was this portrayal of *David* meant as some kind of implied statement? This is not to deny the statue's mysterious undetected hermetic references; its very blatancy and its secrecy may have been intended to overlay each other – such cunning would have been appreciated by the more worldly members of Lorenzo's humanist circle.

This esotericism would certainly have appealed to the leading philosopher amongst Lorenzo's friends, Pico della Mirandola, the most precocious and spectacular of all the intellectual talents who gathered at the Palazzo Medici. Pico's achievements would appear to be almost completely contradictory: he would express the principle of humanism with more lucidity and understanding than any other, yet he would also muddy the intellectual waters by taking on board such dubious 'knowledge' as astrology, alchemy, numerology ('number magic') and all manner of esoteric hermeticism. His rallying cry of humanism appears in a work aptly entitled *On the Dignity of Man*, in which Adam is informed by God:

> You have been given no particular function. You may give your life whatever form you choose, do whatsoever you wish. All other things and creatures are constrained by My laws. But you have no limitations, and can act in accord with your own free will. You alone can choose the limits of your nature. You have been placed at the centre of the world more easily to observe what is in it. You have been made neither of heaven nor of earth, neither mortal nor immortal, so that with freedom of choice and honour you can make yourself into whatever you wish.

This rings as clear today as it must have done more than 500 years ago. The Renaissance would produce no original philosophy, as such; it was too busy absorbing classical thought, and freeing itself from the constrictions of scholastic Aristotelianism. Yet Pico's statement of the human condition as good as defines the aspirations and self-understanding of Renaissance humanism; and the man who wrote this was just as remarkable as his words.

Born in 1463, the younger son of a minor Italian prince, Pico studied philosophy at Padua, where he also learned Greek, Hebrew and Arabic. He then completed his education in Paris, which despite its reputation as a stronghold of the old Aristotelian ideas was still regarded as the intellectual capital of Europe. (In actuality, Padua was already quite the equal of Paris as a teaching university. As an intellectual centre, Florence arguably outstripped them both.)

After Paris, Pico returned to Italy, travelling to various university centres, including Perugia, Florence and Padua. In 1484 he settled in Florence, with the intention of studying Plato under Ficino. Pico was just twenty-one years old, yet he would quickly establish himself as the supreme star amongst the intellectuals of Florence University; and this is no exaggeration, as evidenced by the fact that he now knew more than twenty languages. At this time Poliziano was professor of Greek and Latin at the university, and it was probably he who introduced Pico to Lorenzo de' Medici.

In the words of Poliziano, Pico 'was a man, or rather a hero, on whom nature had lavished all the endowments both of body and mind'. Amazingly, this too would seem to be no exaggeration; judging from the portrait of Pico that still hangs in the Uffizi Gallery in Florence, he was almost impossibly beautiful. He had a long, straight, delicate nose, sensual lips, a high forehead and a head of wavy hair falling in curls about his shoulders. He seems to have been conversant with the entire range of human knowledge available to the Renaissance since the fall of Constantinople, from the Jewish Kabbala to Greek mathematics. His criticism of astrology would decisively influence Kepler's astronomy, while his skilful combination of Ciceronian rhetoric and Aristotelian logic in debate was said to be dazzling. Yet this cornucopia of erudition was not entirely for display purposes; the archaic and the spurious may appear to have been swallowed wholesale, along with more respectable forms of knowledge, but there was method in this manic learning. Pico adopted the philosophic idea of syncretism; he intended to take the finest elements from all branches of thought and belief, with the aim of synthesising them into a philosophy of universal truth. Such was the scale of Pico's ambition, though this was in fact a project whose time had not yet come. In the next century, the new science of Galileo and Descartes would undertake a remarkably similar task, aiming to unite all knowledge by the use of scientific method. Pico's project, on the other hand, would extend far beyond science.

With characteristic panache, in 1486 Pico produced his 900 theses drawn from Greek, Latin, Hebrew and Arabic sources, claiming them as the central text of a new universal knowledge and belief system. He challenged any scholar in Europe to come to Rome and debate with him the truth of these theses before a public audience. Sadly, before this great intellectual contest could take place, Pico's 900 theses were scrutinised by the papal authorities and thirteen of them were found to be heretical. Two of these are of particular interest. Firstly, 'Because no one's opinions are quite what he wills them to be, no one's beliefs are quite what he wills them to be.' In other words, our opinions and beliefs are formed by something more than what we consciously decide. This crucial self-insight – that we can never be entirely rational – had implications that would take

Fig 8
Pico della Mirandola

[181]

centuries to unravel. Secondly, 'When the soul acts, it can be certain of nothing but itself.' Despite the clutter of contradictory forms of knowledge, Pico's insights often see far beyond the Renaissance into the modern world to which it would give birth. He can be seen as groping towards a clearer picture of what we actually are. (This latter thesis is a recognisable precursor of Descartes's 'I think, therefore I am'.)

But some of Pico's other theses present a rather more murky picture. For example: 'No science affords better evidence of Christ's divinity than magic and Kabbalistic practices.' Pico might have thought he could argue his way out of such tight corners with the finest minds in Europe, but even he knew that papal pronouncements of heresy were another matter altogether. Questions in this sphere were not a matter for intellectual debate: heretics were liable to be burned at the stake.

To answer his critics in Rome, Pico composed a long treatise in Latin arguing his case. Lorenzo de' Medici loyally (and somewhat recklessly) allowed this to be dedicated to him in the warmest terms, before it was despatched to Pope Innocent VIII. But it was no use, the charge of heresy remained. Pico fled to France, but was eventually apprehended and escorted back to Rome. Fortunately, news of this reached Florence, with the result that Lorenzo intervened on Pico's behalf, and the pope permitted Pico to live in Florence pending further investigations.

There is no doubt that Pico and Lorenzo were very close; Lorenzo must have been a truly inspiring figure, in private as well as in public. Pico loved Lorenzo, though in a purely platonic sense; despite Pico's distinctly effeminate appearance, his sexual orientation was very normal – perhaps too much so. On more than one occasion during his travels, Pico was forced to leave town with an angry husband in pursuit. Indeed, his brief early visit to Florence came to an end when he attempted unsuccessfully to run off with the wife of a local tax inspector. It is unclear whether such activities had anything to do with his life being cut short in 1494 at the age of just thirty-one. By then Lorenzo de' Medici was dead, and Pico no longer had a protector; he is said to have been poisoned.

15

A Succession of Masters

ELEMENTS OF LORENZO'S personality are a recognisable evolution from that of his grandfather Cosimo through his father Piero, whilst it was from his mother Lucrezia that he inherited his artistic temperament and creativity. Such was his genetic inheritance – but this was only the beginning. Lorenzo grew up in the astonishing household of the Palazzo Medici, which was in the process of becoming one of the great intellectual centres of the Renaissance. During Lorenzo's life, no fewer than three of the outstanding artists of the Renaissance are thought to have spent at least a brief formative period of their early lives in the Palazzo Medici: Botticelli, Leonardo and Michelangelo.

Botticelli was born Alessandro Filipepi in 1444, and is said to have taken the name Botticelli (meaning 'little bottle') from his oldest brother, who had a pawnbroker's shop at the sign of Il Botticelli. His father was a tanner who lived and worked in the poor Ognissanti quarter, on the north bank of the Arno west of the city centre. Botticelli was a difficult child, who showed little interest in his education; his father apprenticed him to a goldsmith, but eventually recognised his embryo artistic talent and managed to place him under the tutelage of Fra Filippo Lippi. Here Botticelli would soon acquire Lippi's mastery of delicate line and colour, to such an extent that it would be several years before he finally outgrew Lippi's influence; despite this, the exceptional nature of his talent quickly became evident.

Soon after graduating from Lippi's studio, Botticelli was invited to live at the Palazzo Medici by Lucrezia, Piero the Gouty's wife. He would repay this by painting a delightful portrait of Lucrezia as the Madonna, with her two young children, Lorenzo and Giuliano, at her knee on either side of the infant Jesus. In this painting, Botticelli's original style is beginning to shine through the influence of Lippi and the sculptural effects he had learned from studying the works of Verrocchio.

Botticelli was taken on as a member of the family by Piero and Lucrezia; he would eat at table with them, along with Lorenzo (who was just five years younger than him) and the cherubic younger Giuliano, who would become his favourite. In summer, he would travel with the family out to Cafaggiolo; he would also listen intently at the meetings of the Platonic Academy which took place in the Medici residences. The Platonic ideas of Ficino and the classical mythology of Poliziano would introduce him to an entirely new world, which would fill the gap left by his inattentive schooldays.

Living with the Medici, Botticelli would also experience the excitement and terror of the political events that had the Palazzo Medici as their epicentre. After the attempted coup by Pitti and Soderini, when the seventeen-year-old Lorenzo saved Piero the Gouty from being ambushed, Botticelli would celebrate this event with his first full-scale masterpiece. This is *The Adoration of the Magi*, intended as a thanksgiving altarpiece for the church of Santa Maria Novella, in which Botticelli depicts several of the Medici family and their circle. To the left stands Lorenzo, the proud hero of the day, his hands resting on his propped sword, the head of one of his favoured white chargers peering over his right shoulder. Lorenzo's face is suitably idealised: this represents the Platonic hero, rather than the charismatic ugliness of reality. Poliziano leans on his other shoulder, squeezed next to the surprisingly plain figure of Pico della Mirandola. At the centre of the picture, worshipping the Virgin and Child, is the oldest of the three Wise Men, a posthumous portrait of Cosimo, 'Father of the Country'; to his right, one of the other Wise Men is Piero the Gouty; and at the far right of the painting stands the tall, bulky figure of Sandro Botticelli himself, swathed in a robe. His head is turned, looking out of the painting; he has an unexpectedly beefy face beneath his thick, curly red hair, but his heavy-lidded green eyes have a piercing stare.

It is difficult to distinguish Botticelli's character from the few stories that have come down to us, along with the overwhelming poetic presence of his paintings. He seems to have been intensely affected by the atmosphere of his surroundings; inside the powerful frame, behind that proud stare, there lurked a fragile temperament of extreme sensitivity, which appears to have been ill at ease with the outer man. He was said to have been clumsy and impulsive, and his behaviour was inconsistent, making him appear eccentric to some. But this was the man who lived outside his work; most who speak of him mention his almost complete absorption in his art, which could give him an abstracted air, characterised by some as an almost mystic dreaminess. Much of this would seem to fit the painter of the paintings we know – whether it is in any way the character of the actual màn we will probably never know.

Yet Botticelli was no otherworldly saint; such an existence would have been impossible in the Palazzo Medici of Lorenzo's time. There was always Poliziano's knowing wit, or Pico's arrogant brilliance, or yet another tale of Giuliano de' Medici's amorous antics. But like everyone else, Botticelli was in the end most drawn to Lorenzo, who certainly responded to him. However, with the Medici Bank in difficulty, Lorenzo could not always afford to pay him properly; money was needed for pageants and festivals to keep the citizens happy. Instead Lorenzo made sure that Botticelli was kept employed by those best able to afford his talents. As a result, he fulfilled commissions for Tommaso Soderini, the Tornabuoni family, the Vespucci family and even the Albizzi. It was now that he painted the first of the two transcendent paintings for which he will forever be remembered: *Primavera* (Allegory of Spring; see colour plates).

It was long thought that this was commissioned by Lorenzo the Magnificent himself, but in fact it was produced for a rich cousin called Lorenzo di Pierfrancesco de' Medici. Here Botticelli achieves a blend of Platonic ideas and classical mythology to depict a scene of buoyant lightness, colour and beauty. In the centre with her attendant figures stands Venus, the goddess of love; but this is a Platonic Venus, whose ideal love informs the workings of all Nature around her. To the right, the figure of Flora caught in the embrace of the West Wind is thought to have been based on Simonetta Vespucci, Giuliano de' Medici's 'great love', as celebrated by Poliziano. The year before this was painted she had died of consumption at the age of seventeen; the ghostly blue embrace of the West Wind swooping behind her, the startled backward glance of her face, and the sharply silhouetted leaves tumbling from her opened mouth take on a darker symbolism in the light of this knowledge.

Lorenzo may have enjoyed the company of artists and done his best to encourage them, but surprisingly his patronage of them was not as widespread as that of his father Piero. In fact, he preferred his collection of jewels to paintings, and this included several individual items worth 1,000 florins — by comparison, Botticelli usually received 100 florins for a painting, which even so was more than a year's wages for a skilled craftsman. Yet it would be a painter, Lorenzo's favourite, who produced the one artefact that perhaps mattered more than any other to Lorenzo. Botticelli, the poetic Platonist amongst painters, was Lorenzo's choice to paint the hanging Pazzi conspirators on the wall by the Palazzo della Signoria; and here surely was a reward for friendship and loyalty, rather than aptness of talent. Botticelli was ordered to depict in every lifelike detail the portraits of the men who would be publicly mocked, the men who had murdered the brother they had both grown up with, the brother they had both loved.

In 1481 Botticelli left to work in Rome for Pope Sixtus IV, on the recommendation of Lorenzo de' Medici, as part of the reconciliation process between Florence and Rome after the war. Lorenzo was now using Florentine art and artists for political purposes. Apart from impressing individuals (the pope, the Dukes of Milan and Urbino, and others), the artists concerned also helped promote an implicit message: Florence was the supreme centre of Renaissance culture — destroy it, and you are destroying Italian civilisation.

Botticelli worked in Rome for two years, painting frescos in the newly built Sistine Chapel (originally spelt Sixtine, for it was named after Sixtus IV). But Botticelli's major work for the pope consisted of several large biblical scenes; these appear less graceful, more awkward and more sombre-hued. This may well reflect the lack of freedom and ease that he felt in these commissions, as well as his feelings on his absence from the lightness and brilliance of Lorenzo's circle. On his return to Florence, Botticelli would quickly rediscover the lightness of his previous inspiration; once again he would be commissioned by Lorenzo's cousin Lorenzo di Pierfrancesco de' Medici, and in response he produced the second of his transcendent masterpieces, *The Birth of Venus*. This found its immediate inspiration in a verse from Poliziano:

She travels through sea where white waves surface,
A young virgin without a human face,
Towards the shore by lustful Zephyrs blown
Beneath blue sky on a shell she is borne.

Yet Botticelli's painting would become infused with much, much more than this simple classical scene. Where earlier Renaissance paintings had incorporated scientific discoveries (perspective, anatomy and so forth), *The Birth of Venus* embodies philosophy. The serene simplicity of Venus being washed ashore on her scallop-shell is in fact interwoven with all manner of highly complex Platonic allusions. Ficino and Poliziano once devoted an entire evening meeting of the Platonic Academy to elucidating different Platonic aspects of Botticelli's *The Birth of Venus*. Again, the main figure is said to have been a portrait of Simonetta Vespucci; this time she appears both more beautiful and more ethereal, a haunting evocation of the 'young virgin without a human face'. The legendary beauty that Giuliano and Lorenzo had loved in her life now becomes an otherworldly emblem of the Platonic love which created the world. This Venus has an idealised spiritual quality – part of the beautiful reality that is visible when we turn our gaze away from the shadows playing over the wall of the dark cave of mere worldly appearance.

The Birth of Venus confirmed a trend in art that was becoming ever more widespread. This picture was painted on canvas, and framed; it was not a fresco, such as might have appeared on the wall of a church. Paintings were now becoming valuable private possessions, rather than devotional treasures; and their contents would begin to reflect this. In the preceding centuries of the medieval era, the Church had been seen as the fount of knowledge, the sole spiritual source, its religion the inspiration of art. Now art was extending itself beyond its traditional confines; it was becoming secular, an embodiment of rediscovered learning and new scientific discoveries, a movable possession to be admired in the home, a celebration of philosophy or life rather than religion. Instead of stylised saints, these paintings were inhabited by portraits of recognisable human beings.

The second figure who may have spent time living at the Palazzo Medici in his youth was Leonardo da Vinci – though this remains disputed. What is not disputed is the decisive role that Lorenzo de' Medici played in Leonardo's early artistic career. Leonardo da Vinci was born in 1452, just outside the small country town of Vinci, in the hills above the Arno valley fifteen miles west of Florence. He was the first illegitimate son of a young peasant girl called Caterina and a twenty-three-year-old lawyer, Ser Piero da Vinci. ('Ser' was the honorary title accorded to accredited notaries, though it is far from certain that Piero da Vinci had actually qualified as such.) Piero da Vinci was already carving out a moderately successful career for himself as a state notary in Florence. The young Leonardo was brought up on the family estate in the countryside outside Vinci, probably by his grandmother; at twelve he moved to Florence, where he lived in his father's household as the only child. His father would not have another child until he married for the third time when Leonardo was twenty, and Ser Piero's first two childless wives appear to have doted on the young Leonardo as if he were their own. When they died in succession during his teenage years it must have been a source of deep personal pain, and this may have been responsible for a certain reserved self-possession that soon became evident in his character. Yet it was the continuum of unquestioning female love that lasted through his childhood, youth and into early manhood which affected him most. This gave him the utter self-belief which comes from being the centre of such a worshipping motherly world; and it may also have contributed to his homosexuality.

Leonardo was early apprenticed to the studio-school of Verrocchio, and here he soon established a reputation for his meticulous artistry. He also became known for his exceptional physical beauty, his self-confidence and his peacock dress sense; people soon knew who Leonardo was, and he wanted to make sure that they remembered this. By the age of twenty he had come to the notice of Lorenzo de' Medici, on account of his artistic talent rather than his fancy dressing. Even Lorenzo adhered to the Medici style laid down by his grandfather Cosimo: dress plainly and attract no attention to yourself. Only for pageants would Lorenzo dress up, though the magnificence of his appearance on these occasions suggests that his everyday wear marked a distinct repression.

From the outset, Lorenzo and Leonardo seem to have been wary of one another; whether Leonardo's homosexuality, and Lorenzo's possibly more covert bisexuality, had anything to do with this is difficult to say. What is clear is that Leonardo just did not fit in with Lorenzo de' Medici's circle. Having been brought up in the country, Leonardo had something of a yokel's accent; curious though it may seem, the beautiful young Leonardo struck Pico and Poliziano as a distinctly uncouth and ignorant young man; his education had been so poor that he did not even speak Latin. At Verrocchio's workshop Leonardo had already exhibited an almost pathological hunger for knowledge, though this was largely technical knowledge: how mechanical devices worked, how to build 'machines' for lifting, for pumping, for catapulting stones. None of these was like the theoretical science used by previous artists: the perspective lines they drew on the canvas prior to painting, the surface anatomical contours they learned from studying models.

Leonardo's precocious artistry was recognised by Lorenzo and his circle, but his intellectual precocity they simply dismissed as the hobby of a talented ignoramus. Plato had written above the gate to his Academy: 'Let no one enter here who knows not geometry'; Leonardo knew no geometry, no mathematics, and would not learn these for another ten years. Instead he taught himself by studying with his eyes, by examining things closely – by looking and looking and looking, and recording precisely what he saw.

In 1476 Leonardo was publicly denounced for practising sodomy. The charge appears to have been regarded very seriously, and he may well have spent a brief time in jail. The extreme punishment for homosexuality was being burned at the stake, but as we have seen, in practice attitudes were much more lax; for the most part, it was overlooked. So why was Leonardo singled out? The most likely explanation is that this denunciation was a covert attack on Lorenzo de' Medici and his circle; in the end the case was never brought to trial – almost certainly through Lorenzo de' Medici's intervention. However, Leonardo would have been stigmatised by this charge; already stigmatised by his illegitimacy (though not at home), he must have felt further alienated by this traumatic public event. He wanted to be known – but now he knew what they also knew about him and said about him behind his back.

Despite their personal lack of rapport, Lorenzo de' Medici's support for Leonardo was unwavering; indeed, it may have been during this period that Leonardo was invited to stay at the Palazzo Medici, in part for his own protection. Residence at the Palazzo Medici would also account for his friendship with Botticelli, whose painting he did not in fact like. It was probably Botticelli who first showed Leonardo da Vinci the Masaccios at the church of Santa Maria del Carmine. These works, by way of influencing Fra Filippo Lippi, had very much influenced Botticelli, and they would also have a profound affect on Leonardo. The living curves and shaded volume of Masaccio's figures were like a revelation to Leonardo; these were not simply depictions of human form, they appeared to exist on the canvas. Much of Leonardo's originality too would stem from this source, but he would develop in a completely different way from Botticelli. Where Botticelli embodied myth, Leonardo was more interested in the actual representation, and the psychology, of living figures in reality.

There is further evidence of Botticelli's firm friendship with Leonardo, and of Lorenzo de' Medici's close regard for him. When Lorenzo had wanted a mural of the Pazzi conspirators painted on the wall opposite the Palazzo della Signoria, he had turned to his beloved Botticelli — who might otherwise have seemed an unlikely choice for such a task. In 1479, when this mural needed altering (after Bandini had been brought back in chains from Constantinople and executed), Lorenzo would have turned once more to Botticelli, but for some reason he was unavailable. Botticelli almost certainly suggested Leonardo da Vinci to Lorenzo de' Medici, though Lorenzo would not have chosen Leonardo on this recommendation alone. Lorenzo prized this mural: it was also a very public statement on his behalf. Florence had many successful artists, several of whom had enjoyed Medici patronage for years, yet he chose the twenty-seven-year-old wayward Leonardo. There can be no doubting his regard for Leonardo the artist, or his willingness to have himself associated with him, even if their personal psychologies grated to a degree.

The enigmatic Leonardo now received, with Lorenzo's help, a major commission to paint *The Adoration of the Magi* for the Dominican friars at the church of San Donato at Scopeto, just outside the city. The contrast with Botticelli's reading of this subject could not be more extreme. In Botticelli's version, the well-dressed Medici figures assemble with some decorum before the Madonna and her Child. In Leonardo's version, the surrounding figures are overwhelmed and astonished at the sight of the miraculous divine presence, falling before him and gesticulating around him. In the background in contrast to this mêlée of figures, the clear lines of a classical building rise towards its unfinished higher floor with the exactitude of an architectural drawing. Leonardo was continuing with his self-education, drawing buildings, imaginary engineering projects, military machines, anatomical features. And this was the trouble: he was so interested in all these things that he soon lost interest in the project at hand. Despite years of intermittent work, along with the entreaties and then the threats of the Dominican friars, *The Adoration of the Magi* was never finished; this would be but the first of many such projects, which recurred throughout Leonardo's life.

Lorenzo de' Medici must have realised that Leonardo could not go on making enemies in Florence if he wished to survive as an artist. Taking a characteristic risk, he recommended Leonardo da Vinci to the new ruler of Milan, Lodovico Mauro Sforza, who had succeeded his brother Galeazzo Maria Sforza, after the latter's assassination. Lodovico Mauro Sforza was known as 'Il Muro' ('The Moor'), a pun on his middle name as well as a reference to his dark 'Moorish' appearance. He was another difficult Sforza — educated in the humanist tradition, he had developed a cultured taste; he was vain about his appearance (particularly his curly and coiffeured hair), but his absurdities of manner were tempered by an unmistakable Sforza robustness inherited from his *condottiere* father, Francesco Sforza. Lodovico was both headstrong and devious, by turns cowardly and brave: unreliable in foreign affairs, and unpredictable at home. Fortunately for Leonardo, Lodovico took an instant liking to him, and Leonardo responded to this.

Leonardo arrived in a booming Milan. This was the centre of a lucrative silk-making industry, commanding the rich Lombardy farmlands; the city was also famous for its millinery (which takes its name from Milan). But this prosperity was only beginning to absorb the full development of the Renaissance. The city in no way matched the cultural richness of Florence, or its cultural snobbery; the self-conscious young artist with the country accent immediately felt at home here.

Leonardo would remain in Milan for seventeen years; it was here that his full talent would blossom, and that he would find a measure of personal happiness. In 1490, he took on a ten-year-old boy called Giacomo Salai as his servant. On his second day of employment, Leonardo fitted him out in a set of new clothes and put aside the money to pay for these;

Giacomo immediately noted where he had concealed the money, and stole it. Leonardo was furious, but the boy refused to confess his guilt. Leonardo recorded that Giacomo was 'a thief, liar, pig-headed and a glutton'; he was also mischievous, but possessed a winning charm, and some years later Leonardo and Giacomo would become lovers. The untutored Giacomo would learn to put up with his master's long, enigmatic silences (which so often disconcerted his visitors), and Leonardo grew to tolerate his servant's persistent petty thieving. Giacomo Salai would remain with Leonardo for the rest of his master's life.

Leonardo was commissioned by the Duke of Milan to design a full-scale bronze statue of Francesco Sforza, the founder of the Sforza dynasty. The drawings and models Leonardo made for this great projected work of art would be amongst his most admired, and the task of casting the sixteen-foot-high bronze monument would tax his ingenuity to the utmost, although the project would never be completed. In 1495 Leonardo was also commissioned to paint a fresco of *The Last Supper* for the refectory of the Dominican friars at Santa Maria delle Grazie in Milan. This would prove to be the culmination of all his painterly knowledge, a work conveyed with such supreme authority that it appears both inevitable and timeless. Each of the saints grouped along the table on either side of the blessing figure of Christ has his own characteristic personality, which is imbued with both profundity and living emotion. The painting itself would take years to execute, but Leonardo would eventually bring it to completion in 1498. This time the flaw was in the preparation: the wall on which it was painted suffered from damp, and the pigments that Leonardo mixed using his own novel method were unsuitable. Within sixty years, according to an eyewitness, the fresco it was 'a mass of blurs': all that we know today of this masterpiece comes from copies by lesser artists.

In Milan, Leonardo would be left free to develop his ideas. Lodovico Sforza was intrigued and delighted by Leonardo's designs for 'battle machines', such as catapults, giant screws, armoured vehicles and battering rams. Leonardo also concocted schemes for draining tracts of countryside with networks of canals, and designs for ideal cities; he began dissecting human cadavers, recording the details of the inner human anatomy and organs. To entertain his master, he produced ice sculptures, designed firework displays and constructed mechanical monsters. Leonardo was, more than anything else, a sheer 'intellectual force'. Sforza housed him in an apartment within his large castle complex, for which Leonardo designed a central-heating system; he was also given a large painting studio, complete with apprentice artists and associates, though precisely what work he gave all these assistants remains a mystery. Where painting was concerned, Leonardo worked at his own excruciating pace, on his own. During the seventeen years that he was in Milan, he would complete just six paintings – though their quality was never less than sublime.

Yet even these were lucky to be finished. Leonardo would sit for days on end, musing over his ideas, sketching in his notebooks, making jottings in his secretive mirror writing. Here was the cornucopia of raw genius – his investigations covered everything from astronomy to the position of the child in the womb, from botany to facial expressions, from art to arsenals. The fact that there was a unifying idea behind these apparently disparate jottings is often overlooked; for Leonardo, this was all part of his scheme for the 'science of painting'. To him, the painter was the supreme scientist; he had the ability both to perceive the world in its every detail and to record its exact workings. Leonardo drew up a hugely ambitious plan which involved artists observing each and every detail in the world, perceiving its structure and its form, and recording this precisely as it was. Here art *becomes* science: as he remarks in one of his notebooks, 'my subjects require for their exposition experience rather than the words of others . . . I take [experience] as my mistress, and to her in all points make my appeal.' In Leonardo's ideas it is possible to see the scientific method in embryo, although it would be well over a century before Galileo advanced on these ideas, launching the era of modern science.

Leonardo's ambitious scheme for the 'science of painting' remained unrealised. It was of course unrealisable; and this is very much to the point in Leonardo's work. This is perhaps why he abandoned so many of his greatest projects: he had seen beyond what could possibly be done, he had exhausted his subject before he completed it. The subject thus held no further interest for him; there seemed no reason to finish it.

Leonardo liked Botticelli, even if he did not like his work (he does not say so directly, but he does on occasion speak of painting that is unmistakably Botticelli's, giving it as an example of how not to visualise a work of art). Yet when it came to the third member of the trio of supreme artists associated with the Palazzo Medici, Leonardo liked neither the man nor his art. Leonardo simply detested Michelangelo, and made no secret of it. He saw himself as a cool-headed scientist with no need for God; Michelangelo, on the other hand, was obsessed with God. Leonardo wished to record the precise and subtle nature of what he saw and understood, while Michelangelo sought to record humanity's spiritual struggle. To Leonardo, Michelangelo had a medieval mind; others have seen his work as the epitome of the Renaissance spirit – the embodiment of the human-ist ideal struggling and suffering in its attempt to realise itself.

Michelangelo Buonarotti was born in 1475, in the hilly countryside forty miles south of Florence at the small fortified town of Caprese (now Caprese Michelangelo, in his honour). His father was a Florentine, appointed as the local mayor by the state authorities. The Buonarotti family claimed descent from the Knights of Canossa, the eleventh-century rulers of Florence, but this was just family mythology and had no basis in fact; the family had been members of the gentry, but had fallen on hard times. Within six months of Michelangelo's birth, his father's spell as mayor was over and the family returned to Florence. As was often the case at the time, the young Michelangelo was farmed out to a country wet-nurse. For his first three years he lived at Settignano, a stone-cutters' village three miles up the Arno valley; years later, the great sculptor would claim: 'I absorbed with my mother's milk the sound of the hammers and chisels with which I make my statues.'

The young Michelangelo grew up in Florence, in genteel poverty at the family house in the Santa Croce district, on a respectable street but uncomfortably close to the riverside slums. His father maintained his social aloofness, and young Michelangelo was brought up in an atmosphere of stifling adherence to the 'old ways'. However, unlike almost all other artists, he did receive an education, at the school of Maestro Francesco da Urbino, where he learned grammar, rhetoric and Latin. This was no enlightened humanist school, and Michelangelo soon grew tired of copying out and learning by rote; instead he turned to drawing to pass the time, and decided he wanted to become an artist.

Buonarotti senior highly disapproved of his son's artistic endeavours: such activities were beneath a family of their standing. There were family rows, and according to Michelangelo he 'was often severely beaten'. But his grim stubbornness prevailed, and at the comparatively late age of thirteen he was packed off to the studio of Ghirlandaio; apprentices were usually taken on at ten, but despite lagging three years behind the others in tuition, Michelangelo's exceptional talent quickly became apparent to Ghirlandaio.

According to Vasari, in his renowned but not always reliable *Lives of the Artists*, in 1489 Lorenzo de' Medici decided to open a school for sculptors. He began making enquiries for suitable pupils, and Ghirlandaio immediately recommended the fourteen-year-old Michelangelo. Lorenzo's sculpture school was situated in a garden by the Piazza San Marco, just a few minutes' walk from the Palazzo Medici; here, in a pavilion, were stored the Medici family collection of Ancient Roman sculptures, which had been started by Cosimo on Donatello's recommendation. The school was run by Donatello's former pupil Bertoldo, a talented sculptor in bronze, who according to Vasari 'was so old that he could not work'. In summer the sculptures were moved out into the garden, where the pupils would sit in the shade copying them. In later life, Michelangelo would always claim that he was self-taught as an artist, and that his gift came from God alone, but the ageing Bertoldo probably taught him how to model figures in clay and wax. From early on, Michelangelo is said to have had a remarkable ability to carve stone so that it appeared as smooth as wax.

Michelangelo seems to have been a strange youth. As was often the case at the time, his character matured early; at fourteen he was mentally a young man, even if in many ways he remained gauche and shy. Though well mannered, he was awkward in company and appears to have had a phobia about the way he looked, despite his rugged and not unattractive appearance. This may well have been due to the first, perhaps unconscious, inklings of his homosexuality; he certainly had a forceful temperament, which he kept bottled up. As a result, he was often irritable and on occasion had a volatile temper; his nose had already been badly broken in a fight, and would remain flat for the rest of his life.

Michelangelo's legendary first encounter with Lorenzo de' Medici in the garden near San Marco would mark a turning point in the artist's life. Michelangelo was carefully carving, with hammer and chisel, the head of an old grinning satyr, using a Roman original as his model. He was so immersed in his task that he did not notice Lorenzo standing behind him, watching in awe at the precocious craftsmanship of the young pupil, whose work was going into far greater detail than the worn block of ancient marble before him. Michelangelo dug into his stone head, hollowing out the satyr's mouth. Delicately he chipped away to reveal its tongue, and finally the rows of individual teeth in the upper and lower jaws. Suddenly aware of someone behind him, Michelangelo spun round, and blushed. Lorenzo smiled, attempting to set him at his ease. He leaned forward examining the satyr's mouth, pointing out that it was not quite correct – no old satyr would still have all his teeth.

The young Michelangelo scowled, mortified at his mistake. As soon as Lorenzo moved on, the young sculptor immediately returned to work. He chipped off one of the satyr's teeth, digging into the gum to give it further authenticity, as if the tooth had fallen out. When Lorenzo came back, he was amused; but most of all he was amazed by what he had seen, and following this incident Michelangelo was invited to live and work in the Palazzo Medici. He was given his own room, and the equivalent of almost five florins a month (just over half the wage on which a fully fledged craftsman could support his entire family). In order to smooth matters at home, Michelangelo's father was even given a post in the customs administration office.

From now on, for the next four years, Michelangelo would dine at table with Lorenzo and his family – just as Botticelli, and perhaps Leonardo, had done before him. Amidst such surroundings he became a little more at ease with himself; and Lorenzo encouraged him to attend meetings of the Platonic Academy. Unlike Botticelli and Leonardo, Michelangelo would have had sufficient education to grasp at once the gist of what was going on. One can imagine him frowning in the corner as Pico, Poliziano and the others dazzled the company. Michelangelo was soon inspired by their Platonic philosophy, its breadth of abstract ideals giving a range to the narrow intensity of his religious faith. The poetry they declaimed demonstrated to him how it was possible to articulate feelings in words, feelings that in his case remained choked within him; he must have studied the actual poems too, for it was around this time that he began expressing himself in poetry. Although this talent would not mature for several years, his earliest efforts would prove to be much more than the amateurish efforts of a difficult teenager. In time, Michelangelo would write poetry that excelled even that of Lorenzo de' Medici – such that it became one of the great ornaments of the Italian language. His earliest extant fragments would hint at this talent:

> Burning, I remain in the shadow,
> As the setting sun retreats into its glow.
> The others have gone to their life of pleasure,
> I alone lie grieving, with the earth my measure.

Despite such literary promise, the fine arts would remain Michelangelo's main preoccupation, and these too initially received inspiration from the Platonic Academy. His early frieze *Battle of the Centaurs* was suggested by lines from Poliziano (adapted from Ovid) describing a legendary classical scene; according to the legend, a group of centaurs became so drunk at the wedding party of King Pirithous that they attempted to rape and carry off all the women. With youthful intensity, Michelangelo depicts a tangle of writhing, struggling naked bodies. It is a work of consummate artistry, influenced by Ghiberti's great bronze doors to the Baptistery, which the young Michelangelo had likened to the gates of paradise. Yet this is a hellish piece; and its chaotic but controlled composition probably owes more to the homoerotic fantasies of his overheated mind than to ancient myth. By contrast, his other early masterwork is a relief of classic stillness and beauty. *The Madonna of the Stairs* is clearly influenced by Donatello; the Madonna sits at the foot of the solid angular steps, suckling a realistically awkward, if somewhat muscular infant Christ, whilst in the background, higher up the steps, are the forms of playing children. But it is the drapes of the Madonna's voluminous dress that immediately draw the eye; here there is such exact lightness achieved in polished marble, such masterfully realised fluidity of form. There could be no mistaking that this was the birth of another superlative talent, first encouraged by the Medici; and as we shall see, Michelangelo would remain deeply involved with the Medici family until the end of his life.

16

The Tide Turns

IN THE LATE fifteenth century the world was entering a new age; and this is more than a commonplace of hindsight. The young men discussing Plato in the piazzas felt it; even the unlettered who stood in speechless awe before the new public works of art had an inkling. Brunelleschi's cathedral dome, Ghiberti's bronze doors, the vast palace slowly being erected by the Pitti family on the hill of the Oltrarno, the dazzling pageants laid on by Lorenzo the Magnificent – things could never be the same again. Florence was being transformed into a new city; yet something else was happening too. Beneath the thirst for new entertainments, new wonders and new ideas, there was a creeping bewilderment, as well as a creeping resentment, especially amongst the *popolo minuto*, who still traipsed back to the same slums when the tournaments and festivals were over.

England and the Low Countries had begun manufacturing their own cloth; as a result, they were exporting less wool and the Florentine cloth trade had undergone a slump. As ever, the *ciompi* had been the first to suffer, and as more men were laid off, more families began to be affected. There was increasing resentment against the new ways that Florence had begun to adopt; nothing was the same any more, all the old certainties were being eroded. In the midst of this slowly rising confusion, which was beginning to permeate all levels of society, only one man appeared to offer certainty, a priest called Savonarola.

Girolamo Savonarola had been born at Ferrara in 1452, the same year as Leonardo da Vinci; in all other respects, they were the antithesis of one another. Savonarola's grandfather was an eminent physician at the court of the Dukes of Ferrara, and his father appears to have held minor posts

at the same court, though without distinction. The young Savonarola was
an introspective child who seldom smiled; he was educated at home by
his grandfather, who as a physician had firmly advocated that alcohol,
when taken regularly and in sufficient quantity, induced health and a long
life. Unfortunately, his ideas on education were less enlightened; despite
the closeness of Ferrara to Florence, and the consequent Renaissance influence on its court, Savonarola's grandfather remained very much a believer
in the old medieval approach to learning, as well as the attitude to life
induced by the medieval belief in God. The gloomy, pale-faced youth with
the hooked nose would listen intently to his grandfather's tirades against
the evils of the modern world: man's sojourn on earth was but a preparation for the afterlife, and immorality resulted only in eternal damnation.
In between times, the young Savonarola strummed mournful tunes on his
lute and penned verses of depressive doggerel:

> Seeing the whole world cast into darkness,
> Utterly disappeared all virtue and goodness,
> Nowhere a shining flame,
> No one for his sins taking blame . . .

After his grandfather's death, Savonarola went on to study at the University
of Ferrara, and it was here that he first encountered the new humanist
ideas, which he studied but instinctively rejected. During this period he
became infatuated with a girl called Laodamia, the illegitimate daughter
of one of the distinguished Florentine Strozzi family, then exiled in Ferrara.
She lived in the house on the opposite side of the narrow street, and one
day when she was leaning out of an overhanging window, Savonarola leaned
from his own window and proposed to her. He was contemptuously turned
down: even an illegitimate Strozzi would never conceive of marrying a
mere Savonarola.

From this time on, Savonarola developed a nexus of increasing aver-
sion towards women, all sorts of finery, the upper classes and any form
of easy living. At the same time his attitude towards the new humanist
ideas hardened, and what he had previously despised he now grew to hate.
In the midst of the 1475 St George's Day celebrations at his home, the
twenty-three-year-old Savonarola crept out of the house and set off on

foot for Bologna, thirty miles down the road, where he entered the Dominican order and became a monk. In a belated explanation of his actions to his father, he wrote: 'I can no longer bear the wickedness of the people of Italy . . . As the instincts of the body are repugnant to reason, I must fight with all my strength to stop the Devil from leaping on my shoulders.'

In 1482, after living for seven years at various monasteries in northern Italy, Savonarola was posted to San Marco in Florence. This was the monastery that had been rebuilt at such huge cost by Cosimo de' Medici, who had maintained his own cell here for private meditation. At San Marco, Savonarola quickly established a reputation amongst the monks as a driven man of extreme asceticism and purity; he slept on a straw-filled pallet placed on a plain board, and refrained from taking part in the relaxed feast-day celebrations enjoyed by the other monks. When it was his turn to deliver the Sunday sermon to the public in the church of San Marco, nobody was impressed by the ugly little priest with strangely sensual lips who stuttered and mumbled his words. Yet it soon became evident that his awkward manner had nothing to do with shyness; beneath his heavy dark eyebrows, which joined above his large hooked nose, Savonarola's eyes burned with intensity. It was as if he was filled with a surging power that he was incapable of releasing. In his own later words, his sermons at this time were so ineffectual 'they couldn't even have frightened a chicken'.

Savonarola prayed and fasted, apparently begging God to reveal what it was that He wanted Savonarola to do in order to fulfil his wretched life on earth. Finally, in 1485 Savonarola experienced a revelation that inspired him 'to reveal the word of God as it spoke through him, to warn the world of the horrors that lay in store for the wicked'. By now he was serving at the small fortified town of San Gimignano, thirty miles southwest of Florence. He began delivering the Lenten sermons with the passionate eloquence of a man who had at last discovered his mission in life, castigating his congregation, warning them of the catastrophes that God was about to release upon the world. God's holy Church was holy no longer, for it had fallen into the ways of wickedness; from the lowest to the very highest, all had become sunk in iniquity; the Church would have to be scourged, and mightily purged, before it could return to the holiness and simplicity of true Christianity.

Word soon began to spread of this priest who preached like a man possessed, and within two years he was back at San Marco in Florence. Pico della Mirandola heard him speaking and was deeply impressed by the power and simple conviction with which Savonarola interpreted the biblical texts. Despite his great learning, Pico was undergoing a period of deep uncertainty; his '900 theses for the true religion' had been condemned by Rome, and he faced the prospect of being judged as a heretic. As a result of his growing self-doubt, what Pico heard at San Marco struck him with the full force of its certainty.

Savonarola's superiors were soon disconcerted with his new style of preaching, and decided that he would be better employed elsewhere. In 1487 he was posted to Bologna, as master of religious studies at the university; despite the occasional incoherence of his apocalyptic ideas, he had a deep knowledge and understanding of the Bible, the consequence of many hours of ceaseless study in his cell.

Back in Florence, Lorenzo de' Medici sought Pico's advice about his son Giovanni, the thirteen-year-old cardinal: what was to be done about the theological side of his education? Pico felt that the young Giovanni would benefit from being exposed to a good preacher, and recommended

Fig 9 Girolamo Savonarola

to Lorenzo that he use his influence to have Savonarola recalled to San Marco. This was just the kind of simple faith that the boy might appreciate.

The city of Florence had felt deeply honoured when Lorenzo's son was made a cardinal, and this had brought about a somewhat sentimental revival of religious interest amongst its citizens. Here was a jaded audience ripe for the hellfire message of Savonarola, and his sermons soon began attracting a large regular following. His fiery certainties seemed to strike a chord in all who heard him. The *popolo minuto* found comfort and reassurance: their poverty was like Christ's poverty, they would be amongst the chosen when the rich suffered eternal damnation. Many of those who had embraced the new humanist ideas also found themselves swayed. The uncertainties and pretensions inspired by these new ideas were stripped away to reveal a deeper, more ancient malaise, one that longed for the medieval certainties of the past. As a result of his education, Savonarola was fully acquainted with the new humanism, and knew how to turn its ideas against itself — each man alone was responsible for his own soul, and as Pico had said, 'You may give your life whatever form you choose'; yet what use were the philosophies of Plato and Aristotle, when they had caused their authors to suffer eternal damnation in Hell? The new humanist ideas had led only to senseless luxury and sensual pleasures; why, the poems written by the humanist poets were not even on Christian subjects, since they preferred the pagan myths to parables of righteousness. The painters were no better, and even when they did choose to paint religious subjects they included such garish colours and human details that 'they made the Virgin Mary look like a harlot'. (For reasons not too obscure, Savonarola was particularly keen on the iniquity of prostitutes, referring to them as 'lumps of meat with eyes'.) It did not take many such sermons to affect the fragile temperament of Botticelli; likewise, Poliziano soon recognised his own sins amongst Savonarola's diatribes, and he too began wondering about the fate of his immortal soul. The new humanism had swayed their lives and enlivened their art, but it had not yet had sufficient time to take root in their souls.

During the summer months of 1489 Savonarola delivered a series of lectures in the gardens of the San Marco monastery. These would have been almost within earshot of the gardens housing Lorenzo's school of sculpture, where Michelangelo was learning his art; and it must have been around this time that Michelangelo heard Savonarola preach, an experience that deeply impressed him. Even as an old man, he would claim that he could still hear Savonarola's strident tones and see his impassioned gestures as if it were yesterday. Yet curiously, Michelangelo was one of those least affected: his faith had always been strong, and he had seen his artistic and literary talents as an integral part of his spiritual life. His art and his poetry would continue to develop free from any constricting puritanical piety.

As Savonarola's audiences grew, so his message became bolder: 'If you wish to create good laws, first you must obey the laws of God, for all laws depend upon Eternal Law.' His sermons began to take on an increasingly political tone – he preached against the abuses of power, and how it corrupted those who wielded it. Soon he was denouncing the misuse ·of authority by the tyrants who ruled the cities of this earth; and his audience was quick to recognise the 'tyrant' who ruled their city. Without Lorenzo's name being mentioned, he soon became an increasing focus of resentment amongst the people.

At first Lorenzo decided to take a conciliatory approach, in the hope that Savonarola's ire would soon be tempered by life in civilised Florence. Pico assured Lorenzo that Savonarola's religious ideas were sound enough; he was at heart 'a good man'. Poliziano also recommended caution, suggesting that there was a certain truth in what Savonarola said; besides, he was popular with the people – he provided a suitable release for any pent-up feelings. Then Savonarola went further, likening the excesses of the modern 'tyrants' to those of Nebuchadnezzar and Nero; but still Lorenzo decided to bide his time. In 1491 Savonarola was appointed prior of San Marco, and that year the attendance at his first Lenten sermon was so large that he requested to give the remaining sermons in the larger venue of the cathedral. Ill-advisedly, Lorenzo allowed this request to be granted; Savonarola's sermons now began attracting vast crowds, and by word of mouth his latest castigation of the 'tyrants' spread throughout the entire city.

Although only in his early forties, Lorenzo was now beginning to succumb to the family illness: the gout and painfully swollen arthritic joints that had crippled his grandfather and killed his father. He too was suddenly reduced to being carried about on a litter, racked with pain; but the smooth government of the city continued as ever under its Medici appointees. Lorenzo remained in a quandary about what action to take over the troublesome priest who was beginning to question his authority; the undercover warnings that he sent to Savonarola by way of his supporters seemed to mean nothing, and went unheeded. He considered asking the pope to send Savonarola elsewhere, but the sixty-year-old Innocent VIII was also ill, the years of high living and depravity now beginning to take their toll.

News now began to reach Lorenzo that Savonarola was prophesying the death of the 'tyrant', and also the death of the pope. It was common gossip in Florence that Lorenzo was ill, and many also knew that Innocent VIII was not at all well; such knowledge only seemed to confirm the veracity of Savonarola's prophecies. If he could foresee the deaths of popes and rulers, what else could he see? Perhaps his terrifying apocalyptic visions were going to come true after all.

On 11 December 1491 Leonardo's second son Giovanni was sixteen. This marked his coming of age, and his official accession to the cardinalate to which he had been appointed three years previously. A great celebration was staged at the Palazzo Medici, but by now Lorenzo was too ill to attend; he was carried on his litter to an upper window, from where he watched briefly and unobtrusively as the banquet commenced below. Just over three months later, on 21 March 1492, he asked to be carried to the Medici villa at Careggi, where his grandfather Cosimo had died. Lorenzo was accompanied by his favourites Pico and Poliziano.

Two weeks after the ailing Lorenzo's arrival at Careggi, news from Florence reached the villa that two of the city's famous lions had mauled each other to death during a fight in their cage, an event that was taken by the citizens of Florence as a very bad omen. That night the new lantern placed atop the dome of the cathedral was struck by lightning, causing one of the marble balls supporting the lantern to be dislodged and roll down the dome, crashing to the pavement below and smashing into pieces. When news of this reached Lorenzo, he immediately demanded to know which side of the cathedral the ball had fallen, and was told that it had fallen on the north-west side. 'That is the side pointing to this house,' he told his attendants. 'This means that I shall die.' Even the great humanist, on his deathbed, was relapsing into the superstitions of a previous era.

Lorenzo summoned his eldest son Piero to his bedside, just as his great-grandfather Giovanni di Bicci and all subsequent heads of the family had done. Young Piero took after his uncle Giuliano, being unusually good-looking for a Medici; and now he was twenty-one, just four years younger than Giuliano when he had been assassinated. Unfortunately Piero had a tendency to arrogance and was more interested in hunting than in affairs of state. Lorenzo asked to be left alone with his son, then took his hand and began counselling him on the ways of the Medici: he was always to appear unassuming in public, remember the people of Florence as well as his own people . . . What had once been the earnest pleadings of his great-grandfather Giovanni di Bicci now had something of a hollow ring — such words had become a tradition rather than a testament.

According to Poliziano, it soon became clear that Lorenzo's illness was attacking him 'not only in all his veins, but also in his organs, his intestines, his bones, and even the very marrow of his bones'. As Lorenzo felt his life ebbing away, he took a momentous decision: privately, he sent word summoning Savonarola to his bedside. Whether he sent for the priest to give him absolution, or in a final attempt to heal the rift between them, so that he could bequeath his son a united city, is unclear; and descriptions of this fateful meeting vary greatly. The chastened Pico left a some-what mystical version of events, while the deeply upset Poliziano described a poetically emotional scene.

Despite the conflicting descriptions, it seems clear that Savonarola made three demands of Lorenzo. First, he asked if Lorenzo repented of his sins and adhered to the faith; whereupon Lorenzo replied that he did. Second, Savonarola demanded that he give up all his wealth, to which Lorenzo did not reply. Then Savonarola asked him 'to restore the liberty of the citizens of Florence'; once again Lorenzo said nothing, finally turn-ing his face away from Savonarola. The priest stood in silence for a while, then muttered an absolution and left.

A short time later on 8 April 1492 Lorenzo the Magnificent died.

According to legend, the entire city of Florence followed Lorenzo de' Medici to his grave, and this public display of grief confirmed in its unspoken way the succession of his son Piero. Others have suggested that this was indeed a legend, concocted by the Medici; instead, it is claimed that there was a conspicuous lack of public grief for Lorenzo, and in view of the troubled state of the city this seems more likely. Either way, Piero succeeded him as the uncrowned prince of Florence, for no one was in a position to stop this.

In Rome, the dying Innocent VIII voiced the fears of many: now that Lorenzo, 'the needle of the Italian compass', was gone, peace could not last long. Three months later Innocent VIII was succeeded as pope by Alexander VI, who gained office by the simple and effective (but highly expensive) method of bribing his opponents into supporting him. This involved no less than a mule train of gold and jewels, and is generally agreed to have been the first occasion on which someone actually bought the papacy outright. Alexander VI was a member of the Borgia family, which originated from Spain, and his papacy would introduce a new ruth-lessness and ambition to this office, as well as a new rogue element to the Italian political scene.

Piero de' Medici succeeded his father when he was twenty-one years old (just a year older than Lorenzo had been on his succession). Whoever succeeded Lorenzo the Magnificent was perhaps bound to suffer from comparison, though in fact Piero resembled his father in many ways. He was forceful and liked to enjoy himself; he also thought himself possessed of high artistic taste and considered himself something of a poet. Sadly, he was no poet; on the other hand, he did prove a great artistic encour-agement to the young Michelangelo, with whom he had been brought up.

To begin with, Piero was content to leave the everyday business of ruling Florence to his father's experienced chancellor Piero Dovizi da Bibiena, and the running of the bank to the ageing Giovanni Tornabuoni. The Medici Bank had been forced to close its London and Bruges branches in 1480, and for the bulk of Lorenzo's reign it had survived on a severely reduced basis – almost certainly aided by occasional moneys covertly diverted from the Florentine exchequer by Lorenzo. Likewise, the Florentine wool trade had remained in deep decline, its impoverished work-ers and small merchants being amongst the earliest to swell the congre-gation at Savonarola's sermons. Neither the Medici nor Florence could any longer afford the great popular pageants that had so endeared its citi-zens to Piero's father.

Despite this, Piero showed every sign of wishing to follow in Lorenzo's footsteps, though he also showed that he had no real understanding of his father's rule. He saw Lorenzo, and himself, as a dashing prince — favoured by fortune, a leading player on the Italian political scene, and worshipped by the populace. Yet he had none of his father's celebrated charm, and misjudged the basis of his power. The Medici family was the centre of a well-oiled political machine, which needed constant attention: rewards, important positions, gifts — all had to be regularly bestowed with tact and prudence. Without such things, the ever-shifting loyalties of Florentine politics were liable to turn treacherous. Piero also misjudged the balance of power that maintained peace on the larger Italian scene, and this conjunction of internal and external misjudgements would earn him the nickname 'the Unfortunate'. Yet it is doubtful whether even Piero's father could have overcome the series of unfortunate events that now took place.

Savonarola continued to preach his fiery sermons in Florence, telling his increasingly large and fearful congregations that in his visions he had seen 'a fiery cross hanging in the dark clouds above Florence'. He called upon all citizens to repent before it was too late, and railed against the unspeakable iniquities that now pervaded the Church at every level, including the very highest of the high. All knew what this meant, for the reputation of Roderigo Borgia had preceded his transformation to Pope Alexander VI. Savonarola's prophecy of the death of Lorenzo de' Medici and Innocent VIII had proved correct; and now he prophesied the death of a third 'tyrant', the seventy-year-old King Ferrante of Naples. According to Savonarola, this event would be followed by an apocalyptic invasion of Italy by a vast foreign army, which would stream down from the Alps to ravage the entire land like 'barber-surgeons with their choppers cutting off diseased and broken limbs'.

Piero de' Medici, meanwhile, was faced with the current reality of Italian politics, which also had its frightening aspects. In order to understand this situation, it is necessary to sketch in the wider picture. The ruler of Milan, Lodovico 'Il Moro' Sforza, was in fact only the regent, intended to rule Milan until the rightful heir Gian Galeazzo (son of the assassinated Galeazzo Maria Sforza) finally came of age. In order to cement relations between Milan and Naples, the young Gian Galeazzo had been married to Isabella, granddaughter of the ageing King Ferrante of Naples. But when Gian Galeazzo finally came of age, Lodovico Sforza refused to hand over the reins of power, on the grounds that Gian Galeazzo was incapable of ruling Milan and was 'little better than an idiot'. Although there was some truth in this assessment, Gian Galeazzo's wife Isabella thought otherwise, and appealed to her grandfather Ferrante of Naples to enforce the succession. Her father, Alfonso, Duke of Calabria, the heir to the throne of Naples, was particularly incensed and let it be known that he intended to march north, as he had done so successfully in the war following the failure of the Pazzi conspiracy.

Lodovico of Milan appealed to Florence for support, but Piero de' Medici prevaricated; his advisers were of two minds – Ferrante of Naples was also an ally of Florence. Lodovico then appealed to Venice and the pope: the peace of Italy was at stake, and only with their support could the balance of power be maintained. But they too prevaricated: no ruler wished to be seen supporting a usurper such as Lodovico Sforza – this could have had dangerous consequences in a land where there were frequently several claimants to any title. Lodovico 'Il Moro' Sforza quickly understood that he faced isolation – the whole of Italy could turn against him.

The Milan–Florence–Naples axis, which had been carefully main-tained by Lorenzo de' Medici and had kept the peace in Italy for so long, now lay in ruins. Worse still, Lodovico Sforza of Milan now took the drastic step of turning to an outside power for help. He appealed to Charles VIII of France for support, in return for which he would be will-ing to support Charles if ever he chose to exercise the dormant French claim to the throne of Naples.

Unbeknown to all the Italian powers, this was just the opportunity for which Charles VIII had been waiting. He was the only son of the 'Spider King' Louis XI, the eccentric monarch whose well-disguised capabilities had been responsible for consolidating France's position as the wealthiest and most powerful nation in Europe. Charles VIII had succeeded to the thone at the age of thirteen, but had not come of age and taken full power until 1491. The young king had an odd appearance: his posture was stooped and he walked with a curious swinging limp on his oversized feet (which, according to popular legend, each had six toes). His character was equally

Cosimo de' Medici

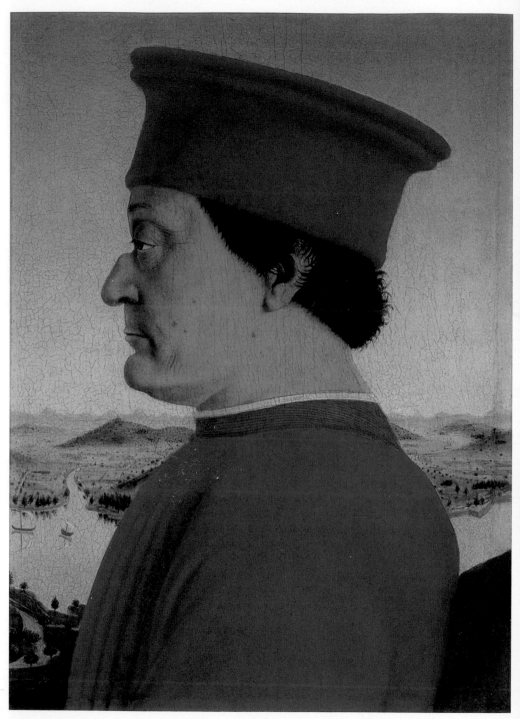

The *condottiere* Federico da Montefeltro, painted in profile to disguise the fact that his right eye and the right side of his face had been destroyed in a jousting accident

Madonna and Child by Fra Filippo Lippi

Detail from *La Primavera* (*Allegory of Spring*) by Botticelli

Pope Leo X with Cardinal Giulio de' Medici (the future Pope Clement VII) by Raphael

The Last Judgement by Michelangelo

Marie de' Medici by Rubens

Ferdinando II de' Medici

unusual: he had received virtually no education and remained astonishingly naive; however, his excessive lasciviousness and gluttony, as well as his habit of muttering to himself through his wispy red beard, made people uneasy in his presence. He had already exhibited increasing signs of megalomania, foreseeing himself as the ruler of a vast empire, and this lust for foreign power was fed by his advisers, who wished him out of the country so that they could pursue their own nefarious ends. It was suggested to Charles VIII that if France took its rightful control of Naples, it could then set about retaking Constantinople and Jerusalem, leaving it in control of the vastly profitable trade route to the Near East. Charles VIII listened eagerly, and was easily persuaded of this pan-Mediterranean role for France.

In January 1494 King Ferrante of Naples died, fulfilling Savonarola's prophecy concerning the third of the three 'tyrants'. Ferrante was succeeded by his son the Duke of Calabria, who became Alfonso II, whereupon Charles VIII of France immediately asserted his right to the throne of Naples, and made it clear that he was willing to use force in pursuit of this claim. If the French army were to cross the Alps, all Italy – with the exception of Milan – stood in danger as it moved south. Piero de' Medici announced that Florence would defend its territory against any invader, and would support Naples in repelling any foreign invasion of Italy. To many in Florence, who learned of these events with trepidation, it seemed that Savonarola's further prophecies were on the point of being fulfilled.

Yet not everyone was so easily worried: as ever, to celebrate the coming of spring, the leading families of Florence held a succession of festive balls in their palazzi. However, despite the surface gaiety of these cele-brations, all was far from well amongst the Medici faction; Piero's neglect of the Medici party machine meant that growing tensions remained unre-solved. Owing to the parlous state of the Medici Bank, the senior branch of the family headed by Piero was no longer the richest; the branch of the family headed by his cousins Giovanni and Lorenzo di Pierfrancesco de' Medici (who had commissioned Botticelli's *Birth of Venus*) had made a large fortune in the grain trade. As a result, Giovanni and Lorenzo had begun to resent the political power wielded by Piero, and these tensions came to a head in a trivial dispute at one of the spring balls. Piero de' Medici and Giovanni di Pierfrancesco de' Medici clashed over who should dance with a local beauty whom they both desired. As a result, Piero publicly slapped Giovanni in the face; Giovanni knew that he could not reply by challenging the ruler of Florence to a duel, and was thus forced to withdraw, with evident bitterness. The split in the Medici faction was now in the open.

Piero brooded on this difficult state of affairs. How would his father have acted? Lorenzo would certainly have taken decisive action, either by using his charm and making a generous gesture to heal the rift, or by striking at once to eliminate any threat. After dithering for a while, Piero chose the latter course, having Giovanni and Lorenzo di Pierfrancesco de' Medici arrested and imprisoned at Cafaggiolo, the Medici villa in the Mugello. They were detained on the apparently trumped-up charge of sending a secret message to Charles VIII of France. According to Piero, this message informed the King of France that although Piero de' Medici had said he would defend Florentine territory, there was a majority of others in the city who would not oppose any march on Naples.

In September 1494, Charles VIII led a vast French army across the Alps into Italy. Contemporary estimates of the size of this army vary between 30,000 and 60,000; it may well have contained at least 30,000 fighting men, and was probably accompanied by almost as many camp followers in the form of grooms, courtiers, musicians, jugglers, cooks, prostitutes and such. This was around twice the size of the previous largest army to cross the Alps and invade Italy, that of Hannibal in 218 BC, which is more reliably estimated to have contained 26,000 men. (The fact that this earlier estimate is more reliable is indicative of the state of organisation in the Roman era, and that of fifteenth-century France, which was still in the late medieval era.)

More ominous still, the army of Charles VIII contained hardened warriors used to taking part in the more bloody battles of northern Europe, which were a very different affair from the tactical 'manoeuvres' executed by the Italian city militia and their hired mercenaries, which passed for battles in Italy. The French army had at its vanguard the disciplined Swiss Guard, who were renowned for their ability to stand and break up any cavalry charge, whilst for Italian armies, a cavalry charge usually signalled the end of any battle, as all scattered for their lives. The French army was also equipped with formidable firepower in the form of mobile cannons, which fired iron cannonballs instead of stone ones; these could break up infantry charges in tight formation as well as inflict damage on city walls.

Lodovico Sforza welcomed Charles VIII to Milan. Charles VIII then passed on to Pavia, where he was received by the legitimate ruler of Milan, Gian Galeazzo and his wife Isabella, who pleaded with him not to attack her father Alfonso II of Naples. Charles VIII and his vast army continued on their inexorable march south, regardless. Lodovico of Milan was evidently disconcerted by Charles VIII's visit to Gian Galeazzo; within days, news spread that Gian Galeazzo had died from poisoning, while his wife and four children had been imprisoned by Lodovico, who had now officially proclaimed himself the rightful Duke of Milan. At the same time, Alfonso II of Naples marched rapidly north to confront the invaders. The two armies met on the coast at Rapallo, some 250 miles north of Neapolitan territory, and the result was a rout, with Alfonso II fleeing back to Naples with the remains of his army. Charles VIII's army advanced down the coast; the pope let it be known that the French army could have free passage through papal territory, and Venice declared itself neutral. Now only Florentine territory stood in the way. Charles VIII halted his army at the frontier of Florentine Tuscany, and a message was sent to Piero de' Medici demanding free passage through Tuscany to Naples.

The situation was delicate in the extreme. Piero had promised his support to Alfonso II of Naples, expecting other Italian states to follow suit, but now he found himself on his own. Should he renege on his promise and declare Florence neutral? After five days, still no message arrived at the headquarters of Charles VIII from Piero de' Medici, and in exasperation Charles ordered his troops to cross into Tuscany. The border castle at Fivizzano was overrun and all its garrison put to the sword; Charles VIII then ordered Florence to surrender.

The city was soon alive with rumour and counter-rumour. News now reached Florence that Giovanni and Lorenzo di Pierfrancesco de' Medici had escaped from Cafaggiolo and made their way to Charles VIII's headquarters. Here they had assured the French king that Piero de' Medici did not speak for all the citizens of Florence, most of whom wished to surrender. This evidence indicates that Piero's reason for arresting them was in reality more than a trumped-up charge, though by this stage such matters were of little importance. It soon became clear that what Giovanni and Lorenzo di Pierfrancesco de' Medici had claimed to Charles VIII was true:

they had many sympathisers in Florence who wished to surrender the city to the French. Leading citizens sought a scapegoat for the city's plight, and soon found one in Piero. Meanwhile Savonarola continued to preach his hellfire sermons from the pulpit of the cathedral; in his visions the fiery cross that he had seen hanging above Florence was now transformed into a fiery sword, which threatened fire and damnation for all who did not repent.

Piero at last decided to act; intent upon defending Florence and her Tuscan territories, he summoned the mercenaries at the city's disposal and despatched them north to defend the remaining border castles. Yet it soon became apparent to him that what little support he had in the city was draining away – even among his own branch of the family many were already openly speaking of surrender. It was now that Piero took the decision of his life. In emulation of his father, whose valiant one-man mission to Naples had saved Florence fifteen years previously, Piero set off alone to meet Charles VIII, pausing only to write an explanatory farewell letter to the Signoria.

But Piero was no Lorenzo the Magnificent, either in character or fortune; and Charles VIII was no impressionable Ferrante of Naples, who had been so readily moved by acts of heroism. Even at the time, Piero's solo mission was widely regarded as an act of desperation, rather than one of bravery. When he arrived at Charles VIII's headquarters at Sarzanello he did not receive a hero's welcome; on the contrary, Piero was greeted with contempt. Charles VIII immediately demanded the right to seize the port cities of Pisa and Livorno and occupy them for as long as his 'enterprise' required. Meanwhile Piero behaved abjectly, rather than adopting the vainglorious bravado of his father; to the secret astonishment and delight of Charles VIII, Piero agreed to all the French king's demands. Like Lorenzo, Piero's intention was to save his city, but he had no real understanding of the wider situation. Charles VIII desperately needed a defensive line to protect his army from becoming encircled in Italy, and to allow for his eventual march back to France. Despite Piero's much weaker forces, he had considerable bargaining power at his disposal; and had he shown strength of character, he might well have gained the respect of Charles VIII. They might even have been able to come to terms that would have been beneficial to them both; but this was not to be, and Piero's behaviour would cost him dearly.

After two weeks away, Piero returned to Florence on 8 November 1494. When he arrived at the Palazzo della Signoria to report on the outcome of his mission, he was astonished to find the door slammed in his face. The Signoria had now found someone to blame for their own indecision and helplessness; as a result, Piero's mission was regarded as an act of betrayal, and Piero himself was seen as a traitor. There was little justification for such accusations, which came from the very people who would have undermined his mission by surrendering at once; but Florence was a city in the grip of panic and hysteria – a scapegoat was needed, and Piero had presented himself for the role.

As Piero and his armed attendants waited uncertainly on their horses in the Piazza della Signoria, the Signoria ordered the *vacca* to be rung. The deep tones of the bell mooed from the tower over the city, summoning the citizens to the piazza; but events now began to take their own course. The congregating citizens in the piazza started jeering Piero and his men, then some began throwing stones and refuse at them; after a while Piero and his men rode off to the safety of the Palazzo Medici. In the distance they soon began to hear the roaring of the crowd from the direction of the Piazza della Signoria, where the members of the Signoria were publicly denouncing as traitors Piero de' Medici and his brother Giovanni.

The nineteen-year-old Cardinal Giovanni had returned from Rome to Florence as soon as he heard of Piero's mission to Charles VIII. Now he attempted to rally his brother, but to no avail. Piero appeared paralysed by despondency – the strain of his mission, and now his rejection by the people of Florence, had all been too much for him. Giovanni decided to take matters into his own hands, and together with an armed band of faithful Medici retainers he rode out into the streets, calling out the famous Medici rallying cry: '*Palle! Palle!*' But his cries met only with boos, together with answering cries of: '*Popolo e Libertà!*' Eventually the throng became so threatening that Cardinal Giovanni and his men were forced to retreat into the *cortile* of the Palazzo Medici, the great doors slamming closed behind them.

In the early hours of 9 November 1494, under cover of darkness, Piero de' Medici with his wife and two young children made their way through the deserted streets to the San Gallo gate, and departed the city for exile. Meanwhile Cardinal Giovanni and the last remaining loyal Medici retainers began moving through the rooms of the Palazzo Medici, collecting up as many valuables as they could carry. Disguised as a Dominican monk, Giovanni is then said to have taken these to the monastery of San Marco. This may appear a curious choice, for although this was traditionally a Medici stronghold (Cosimo had stored treasures here, before his exile), the prior of the monastery was now Savonarola. Yet some of the monks must have secretly remained loyal to the Medici, for several of the valuables rescued by Giovanni have come down to us via later Medici sources. Having rescued as much as he could, Giovanni too fled the city into exile, still disguised as a Dominican monk.

Next day, the Signoria formally banished Piero de' Medici and his family from Florence for ever, setting a reward of 4,000 florins on Piero's head, and 2,000 florins on that of Giovanni. Cosimo de' Medici had predicted: 'within fifty years we Medici will have been exiled'. This had come true in just over thirty years.

17

The Bonfire of the Vanities

PIERO DE' MEDICI, now known as Piero the Unfortunate, has been harshly judged by history; and his weakness of character is said to have been responsible for his failure as a leader. He is compared with his three Medici predecessors, who had ruled Florence for the previous sixty years, and is found wanting in both political acumen and personal judgement. This is unfair, for it discounts the good fortune that befell Cosimo *Pater Patriae*, Piero the Gouty and Lorenzo the Magnificent at opportune moments during their reigns, together with the resounding bad fortune that plagued Piero the Unfortunate. He may have had little of the exceptional character possessed in their different ways by Cosimo and Lorenzo, but this alone did not lead to his downfall. As if bad luck were not enough, Piero was also faced with two further major setbacks. The Medici Bank could provide him with no money to win over the people, or sufficient funds to oil the neglected Medici party machine; and most crucially, the political situation in Italy had become hopelessly destabilised by the intervention of Charles VIII. Given the nature of fifteenth-century Italian politics, the preceding period of stability had been the lucky exception; it was a miracle that it had lasted as long as it did. With the benefit of hindsight, we can now see that Lorenzo the Magnificent's much-vaunted diplomacy was in fact little more than a holding operation, for this peace was precarious at the best of times; allowing for even the most skilled diplomacy, it could not have withstood the intervention of France, which was in many ways a disaster waiting to happen. As for the situation in Florence itself — for better or worse, its citizens appear to have tired of Medici rule. The republican pride of the Florentines, a collusive collective myth for so long, now stirred into reality, provoked by the economic downturn and the provocative rantings of Savonarola.

The Medici had now been cut off from their power base in the city and forced into exile; but unlike Cosimo's exile sixty-one years previously, this had not been anticipated. No preparations had been made, and this exile showed little sign of being brief. As soon as Piero and his brother Cardinal Giovanni fled the city, the Medici party machine simply disintegrated, and the former leading family was soon openly held in contempt amongst all levels of society. Evidence of the extent of this is seen in the fact that when Giovanni and Lorenzo di Pierfrancesco de' Medici returned to the city from the French camp, they even went so far as to change their family name expediently and ingratiatingly from Medici to Popolano ('Men of the People'). All Medici emblems featuring the shield and *palle* were removed from their palazzi; and the palazzi of two men who had served as ministers under the Medici were burned to the ground. The Palazzo Medici on the Via Larga was soon penetrated by looters, but before it could be set on fire it was occupied by the city militia, despatched by the Signoria. The ransacking of treasures from the Palazzo Medici now took on a more official tone, as the Signoria appropriated the remnants of Lorenzo's great jewel collection, paintings, sculptures and other less portable valuables; Donatello's statue of *David* was removed from the *cortile* and placed on a column in the Piazza della Signoria. The *gonfaloniere* and the Signoria also appropriated the equivalent of 16,000 florins in cash from the local branch of the Medici Bank, which was already on the verge of bankruptcy and would barely survive this blow. However, at least some elements of the bank must have managed to survive elsewhere, or were resuscitated, for as we shall see, the Medici would not cease their banking activities completely until well over a century later.

All these Medici assets were seized in the name of the city, on the grounds that they had been gained at the expense of its citizens. As a final break with Medici rule, the Signoria rescinded the sentences of exile passed on the Pazzi and Soderini families, inviting them back to the city.

While these dramatic and chaotic events were taking place in Florence, the territories of the republic were also in disarray. Charles VIII marched

into Pisa, Florence's main link with the sea, and declared the city 'liberated from the tyranny of Florence', though in effect it now became occupied French territory. Although Piero de' Medici had already agreed to
this, but the Signoria had not dared to risk antagonising Charles VIII by
rescinding the agreement; despite this, the Signoria decided to despatch a
delegation of four ambassadors to Pisa to protest at the French occupation. Such was Savonarola's ascendancy in the post-Medici power vacuum
that he was chosen as one of the ambassdors for this important mission.

An unlikely practitioner of diplomacy at the best of times, Savonarola
was to excel himself in Pisa. To the consternation of the other members
of the Florentine delegation, Savonarola strode before the assembled court
of Charles VIII and launched into a messianic monologue. Even more
unexpectedly, he began by welcoming Charles VIII as an instrument of
God's will, sent to castigate the citizens of the corrupt Florentine Republic:
'Thou hast come as the Minister of God, an emblem of Divine Justice.
We welcome thy presence with joyous hearts and smiling faces.' Abruptly
changing his tone, Savonarola then proceeded to harangue Charles VIII,
informing him that although he was sent by God, Heaven was capable of
wreaking a terrible revenge even upon its own instrument, should the
French king choose to harm the city of Florence. Savonarola was behaving in precisely the opposite way to Piero de' Medici, and his attitude
could have had dire consequences; it would have cost Charles VIII nothing to put to death an insignificant and insubordinate prior. Many, including the pope, would indeed have welcomed this act. But as with the
humanists, Savonarola had the measure of his adversary. Charles VIII had
a medieval conception of the ever-present Will of God, and Savonarola
was well aware of his propensity to superstition. The figure who stood
before the mighty king in his plain sandals and worn robe spoke with the
conviction of a saint: he appeared to know God's Will, and even claimed
that God spoke through him. Here was one instrument of God warning
another of the divine responsibility of his role. Charles VIII was chastened, his surrounding courtiers and men-at-arms awed, as the unrepen-
tant priest turned on his heel and strode from the king's presence.

Savonarola's action on this occasion has been severely judged. To many
it was foolhardiness bordering on lunacy; but it is quite possible that
Savonarola believed what he said, despite his cunning manipulation of the

gullible French king. Others have seen it as an act of bravery – matching that of Lorenzo the Magnificent before Ferrante of Naples, the bravery so apparently lacking in his son Piero. Either way, Savonarola's behaviour before Charles VIII almost certainly saved Florence: both its citizens and its buildings. There is little doubt that Charles VIII would have sacked the city, probably loosing his soldiers on a rampage of rape and pillage; this would have served as an example to any others who might have considered opposing his march on Naples. The cultural treasures of historical Florence that we see today were to a large extent due to the patronage of the Medici; ironically, the saviour of many of these artefacts was their arch-enemy Savonarola.

Just eight days after the flight of Piero de' Medici, Charles VIII rode into Florence on 17 November 1494 clad in a crown and golden armour, beneath a canopy decorated with the fleur-de-lis. He was accompanied by his personal guard of twenty standard-bearing knights, and by an army of 20,000 men. The citizens watched in wonder and trepidation as the seemingly endless columns filed past – including the ranks of the grim Swiss Guards with their gleaming halberds, 4,000 Breton archers, 3,000 mounted lancers ('the flower of French chivalry'), the rows of cannons pulled by carthorses, and even kilted Scottish highlanders marching behind their wailing bagpipes. According to an eyewitness, the last were 'extraordinarily tall men from Scotland and other northern countries, and they looked more like wild beasts than men'.

The occupation of Florence would last for eleven days; Charles VIII occupied the few unransacked apartments in the Palazzo Medici, and his troops were billeted throughout the city. For the most part, the citizens of Florence were relieved at this peaceful occupation, and there were surprisingly few incidents – in all, only ten people were killed. A few days prior to the departure of the French, the Signoria were summoned by Charles VIII to the Palazzo Medici and handed a treaty to sign. This guaranteed the French army the right to take over any Florentine fortresses deemed necessary to protect their route, as well as confirming the occupation of the city of Pisa; these would be returned to Florence only when the French army withdrew. The city was also expected to pay 150,000 florins to finance the French army. The Signoria listened in stunned silence as the humiliating terms were read out. (The terms that Piero de' Medici was condemned for having endorsed so abjectly only included a *loan* of 200,000 florins.)

On 25 November, a herald read out the terms of the treaty to the assembled citizens of Florence in the Piazza della Signoria. Behind him stood the *gonfaloniere* and the Signoria, with Charles VIII seated beneath his canopy on a throne brought from the Palazzo Medici. But the Signoria had taken it upon themselves to make certain alterations to the treaty; to Charles VIII's astonishment he heard the herald read out that the city of Florence would pay to the French king just 120,000 florins. The king leaped to his feet, forcefully interrupting the herald – the correct sum of 150,000 must be written into the treaty at once, or he would order his men-at-arms to sound their trumpets, the signal for his soldiers to lay waste the city.

As it happened, the *gonfaloniere* was one Piero di Gino Capponi, who had been Florentine ambassador to France during the time of Lorenzo the Magnificent. While Capponi had been in France he had befriended Charles when he was no more than a gauche and backward child. Capponi regarded Charles VIII's demands as little more than insolence and personal ingratitude; in a fury, he now leaped to his feet, wrenched the treaty from the herald's grasp and began tearing it to shreds. The historian Guicciardini, who witnessed this scene as a young man, reports Capponi as 'quivering with uncontrollable rage'. He then turned to the king and exclaimed the words that would later become a proud Florentine proverb: 'If you sound your trumpets, we will ring our bells.' Charles VIII immediately realised that if all of Florence was summoned to arms by the bells, an unacceptable number of his soldiers were liable to be killed in the ensuing bloodbath. He attempted to joke his way out of the situation, making a childish pun that probably dated from the days when Capponi had been an uncle figure to him at the French court: 'Oh, Capponi, Capponi! You are indeed a fine capon' (i.e. chicken). Charles VIII then signalled his acceptance of the new sum inserted in the treaty.

Next day Charles VIII and the French army withdrew from Florence, merely refusing to acknowledge any bills that had been run up and removing 6,000 florins' worth of booty from the Palazzo Medici. The city heaved a collective sigh of relief.

Brave gestures were one thing, but it soon became clear that the *gonfaloniere* and his Signoria were no longer the effective rulers of Florence, for the collapse of the Medici political machine had left a structural void in the city administration. There was no one to advise on policy, and few functioning committees left to administer it; amidst this vacuum, it appeared that the citizens of Florence were taking their lead from a new quarter. Savonarola's sermons, delivered crucifix in hand from the pulpit of the cathedral, now became the order of the day, and his Sunday sermons were said to have been attended by up to 14,000 people, with the congregation spilling out of the cathedral and filling the entire surrounding piazza.

The situation in Florence had changed as never before. Now that Savonarola held sway, power was no longer a matter of politics, but of obedience to the dictates of the spirit; and a populace wearied of its obsessive materialism was only too eager to heed his cry: 'You must change your life!' Effectively, a bloodless revolution had taken place, and with the willing aid of the Signoria, Savonarola now set about establishing a more democratic government. This was loosely based on the Venetian model, which had proved highly stable – in contrast to the Florentine model, which ironically had achieved stable government only when it was corrupted, for the most part by the Medici. Previously, Florence's brief attempts at a broader democracy had proved hopelessly unmanageable, yet the government that was now installed by the Signoria, under the influence of Savonarola, is widely acknowledged as the most democratic Florence ever achieved. It quickly embarked on a programme of reforms: the tax system was overhauled, to make it fairer for the less wealthy members of society; the franchise was extended to anyone over the age of thirty who belonged to a family where a member had at one time served in the government; and a far-reaching political amnesty was granted, allowing many exiles to return home (this even included minor members of the Medici faction). Such a democracy was unique in Italy at the time, and might even have proved stable, but for two crucial factors. The new democratic Florence soon began to attract enemies, and Savonarola had an agenda that went far beyond democratic reform.

Savonarola's declared aim was to establish a 'City of God', which would instigate 'the purification of Italy' from all personal, political and clerical evils. The people of Florence had long harboured the belief that they were the chosen people of Italy, the citizens of the new Rome; and

Savonarola's calls stirred this deep folk-belief. He began preaching a new 'universal peace', calling upon citizens to give alms to the poor, and even urging the churches to donate their silver and gold. In an excess of joyous spiritual emotion, he declared: 'Oh Florence, I cannot tell you all that is in my heart, for you are not yet ready to bear it.' Bands of children dressed in white were sent out into the streets singing hymns, to collect for the poor; these 'blessed innocents' passing through the city were to be given all ornaments and jewellery, all fine clothes, mirrors, pagan books and idolatrous paintings. Standing in his pulpit, with his crucifix upraised to the heavens, Savonarola demanded that all things which were not 'necessities of life' be forsworn.

At the same time, tumultuous events were taking place elsewhere in Italy. After leaving Florence, the army of Charles VIII had continued on its march south to Naples, where Alfonso II waited grimly in his palace. Racked with foreboding and nightmares, he began suffering from hallucinations, imagining the very stones beneath his feet crying out with fear, until eventually he fled to Sicily, hiding in a monastery. Charles VIII and his army entered Naples without opposition on 22 February 1495, passing in triumphant procession through the streets of obsequiously cheering crowds. Three months later, seated on the throne and bearing the sword of Charlemagne, Charles VIII was duly crowned King of Naples. Everything was done to make him feel at home, and he soon found he was enjoying himself so much that he abandoned the idea of continuing on to claim the throne of Jerusalem. His pleasures were almost childish: court painters were hired to paint lascivious pictures of his succession of mistresses, and these pictures were then bound into a book, which the king would peruse before deciding upon his choice (or choices) for the day.

Yet not everyone in Italy had acquiesced to Charles VIII and his seemingly unstoppable army. On his march south, the French king had passed through the Papal States unopposed, but this did not signal the end of papal opposition. The bald and fat Borgia pope Alexander VI was already establishing himself as 'the Nero among popes'; however, although he was a Borgia in his depravities (he would even be suspected of incest with his daughter Lucrezia), he was also a Borgia in his ruthless determination. Using his position as leader of Christendom, Alexander VI called for a

Holy League to combat Charles VIII and drive him out of Italy. The Holy Roman Emperor Maximilian I pledged his support, Venice also joined, and Alfonso II, who had by now fled to his homeland Spain, persuaded the Spanish king to support the League. They were soon joined by Lodovico of Milan, who now sorely regretted having invited the French into Italy. Only Florence refused to join; Savonarola would hear nothing against Charles VIII, whom he still regarded as 'an instrument of God', and the Signoria, for its part, felt that under the circumstances Florence's treaty with Charles VIII was binding. This meant that the republic was now isolated in Italy, and thus dependent upon France for trade; but this was no great setback, for France was rich and its southern coast lay just 150 miles across the Gulf of Genoa from Tuscany.

In the summer of 1495 Charles VIII left Naples on the long march back to France; his vast army straggled over the hills, trailing long mule caravans of booty, followed by its motley bands of camp followers. Amongst these were carriers of a mysterious new disease, now known to be syphilis, which the French soldiers had caught in Naples. This had almost certainly been brought to Europe by sailors returning from the New World, which had been discovered three years previously. Charles VIII's army would be responsible for the early spread of this disfiguring and incurable sexually transmitted disease, which for this reason was initially known as the 'French Disease'.

By now the Holy League had assembled a powerful army of mercenaries, under the command of Gonzaga, Marquis of Mantua, and in July these confronted the French army on the banks of the River Taro outside Parma. The result was a fierce and bloody battle, which quickly turned into a rout as the French cannons and cavalry put the mercenaries to flight. Despite this, the Marquis of Mantua insisted that the victory was his, as he had diverted and captured half of Charles VIII's booty train, including Charlemagne's sword. Meanwhile the other half of Charles VIII's camp followers ran through the deserted battlefield slitting the throats of the wounded as they scavenged for anything of value.

In an attempt to encourage Florence to join the Holy League, Pope Alexander VI had sent a cordial letter to Savonarola inviting him to Rome, so that he could relate his wondrous visions and prophecies to his master the pope in person. Savonarola may have been something of a holy innocent, but he was no holy fool; he was not willing to surrender himself voluntarily into the clutches of a man like Alexander VI. The prior of San Marco thanked the pope for his kind letter, but pleaded an inability to visit him on account of illness.

As the months passed, the City of God gradually became more firmly established in Florence. Increasingly, wives and daughters began taking vows and entering convents, whilst in public none dared wear wigs or brightly coloured clothes. All who valued their position in the new society began making sure that their regular presence at church was noticed, yet it soon became apparent that Savonarola did not have the support of all the citizens of Florence. The bands of singing white-robed children found a number of the narrower streets barred to them by groups of sullen citizens who refused to move and let them pass. Some were now unwilling to surrender any more of their 'superfluous possessions' and 'vanities'; and amongst the leading families this opposition focused around a group who called themselves the *arrabbiati* ('the angry ones'). The members of this group referred to Savonarola's followers as the *capernostri* ('the nodders' – that is, those who were constantly bowing their heads in muttered prayer), regarding them all as *piagnoni* ('snivellers' of the working class). Yet Savonarola's supporters were not limited to the *popolo minuto* and common tradesmen; as we have seen, many of the Signoria, as well as the humanists Pico della Mirandola and Poliziano, and even the painter Botticelli, were all deeply affected by his preaching. They certainly obeyed Savonarola's call to 'change your life', as did a clear majority of Florentine citizens in the beginning. However, many people were now coming to see that this was not so easy, if they were to continue going about their daily business, maintaining the trade on which the city depended. It seemed all but impossible to live the life of the spirit demanded by Savonarola, yet at the same time continue with the necessary business of trading and earning a living – the two appeared irreconcilable.

Doubts were also beginning to creep in about Savonarola's support for Charles VIII, who had gone back on his promise to return the Florentine territory he had occupied. The border towns that he had seized had been sold off to Florence's enemies on the other side of the border; Genoa and Lucca had been only too willing to pay for the fortress towns to the north, while Siena had readily paid for the garrison castles to the south. Pisa had simply been left to its own devices, whereupon it had declared itself independent and immediately sided with the Holy League for protection. Florence's Tuscan territories were unprotected and its trade was beginning to suffer.

During these early years the opposition in Florence remained largely covert, though there were a number of rowdy disturbances during Savonarola's sermons, and even two bungled attempts to assassinate him. Meanwhile the *arrabbiati* sent a delegation to Rome, begging the pope to intervene. In 1496 Alexander VI responded in the way he knew best: he attempted to bribe Savonarola, offering him a cardinal's red hat, to which Savonarola haughtily replied that he wished only for a hat 'red with blood'. This has been seen by some as a reference to martyrdom. Had Savonarola foreseen this end for himself in his overheated visions? Or was he willing this fate upon himself? Or was he perhaps gradually coming to realise that this was the only outcome for him: one that might lead to sainthood and the posthumous furtherance of his cause? Whichever is true, such possibilities must have begun to loom increasingly large in his mind.

At the beginning of Lent in 1497, Savonarola's rule reached its apotheosis with the famous 'Bonfire of the Vanities'. The bands of 'blessed innocents', this time accompanied by armed guards, were despatched throughout the city to collect all the 'vanities' they could find, and these were stacked in a great pyramid in the Piazza della Signoria. At the base of the pyramid were placed wigs, false beards, pots of rouge, perfumes and trinkets. Next came piles of 'pagan books': works of the Ancient Greek philosophers, books containing poems by Ovid, Boccaccio and Petrarch, works by Cicero and Poliziano. Above these were drawings, busts and paintings of profane subjects (including some works by Botticelli). Higher up were piled musical instruments: lutes, violas and flutes; then came sculptures and paintings of naked women; and at a higher level figures of the ancient gods and heroes of Greek legends. This was finally topped by a hideous effigy of Satan, complete with hoofed goat's legs, pointed ears and a little beard — though according to one report, this was given the face of a Venetian dealer who had offered to buy all the works of art for 22,000 florins. Fortunately for his own skin, this dealer had been sent packing, yet his offering price indicates the value of the works of art involved, for even during Lorenzo the Magnificent's time very few painters received more than one-hundredth of this sum for a commissioned work.

On Shrove Tuesday, while the assembled Signoria looked down from the balcony of their palazzo, the bonfire was finally lit. As the smoke and flames rose from the massive pyre, which was now sixty feet high and almost 100 feet wide, the assembled crowd sang, '*Te Deum laudamus . . .*' ('We praise thee, God . . .') and other Latin psalms.

By this stage Florence was a riven city, and according to a contemporary diarist, the Florentine silk merchant Luca Landucci, opinions for and against Savonarola now 'divided fathers and children, husbands and wives, brothers and sisters'. Yet what might have been a tragedy began to enter the realms of farce. Shortly after the end of Lent, news reached the city that Piero de' Medici had left Rome with the blessing of the pope and was marching on Florence leading a column of 1,300 armed mercenaries. Encouraged by news of divisions within the city, and by the knowledge that the new *gonfaloniere* Bernardo del Nero was a secret Medici sympathiser, Piero saw this as his chance to regain power. But he had sorely miscalculated his chances; even amongst those who were against Savonarola, few wished for a return to the more politically restricted days of the Medici. Gonfaloniere Bernardo del Nero correctly gauged the feelings of the city and simply refused to open the gates to Piero and his men. So Piero decided to remain camped outside the city walls, waiting for the popular uprising that he had assured his men would take place; but the mercenaries soon decided they had waited long enough and simply marched back to Rome.

This humiliation proved too much for Piero, who took to a life of dissipation on his return to Rome. A former companion later described his daily routine: rising at noon, Piero would settle down to a long and bibulous lunch; afterwards he would return to bed once more, accompanied by a prostitute, male or female depending upon his inclination that day. After his energetic pleasures, he would start into a heavy gambling session with his cronies, which would last until after dark, when the company would set out on a riotous tour of the low taverns and bordellos of the city, returning the worse for wear at around sun-up, when the honest citizens were on their way to work. Piero the Unfortunate would meet a characteristically unfortunate end some six years later in 1503 whilst attempting to cross the River Garigliano in a boat, which capsized, drowning him. This would leave the twenty-eight-year-old Cardinal Giovanni as head of the exiled Medici family.

In June 1497 Pope Alexander VI finally issued a papal bull excommunicating Savonarola; but as no papal envoy dared enter the city to deliver the bull, Savonarola ignored his excommunication and continued to preach as before. Many were profoundly shocked by the sight of this excommunicated Dominican priest celebrating Mass in the cathedral, and on at least one occasion a riot broke out amongst the congregation, followed by another bungled assassination attempt. The Signoria was so incensed by these events that it forbade Savonarola to preach.

The city was now in a turbulent state; war had been declared on Pisa, and an attempt was being made to recover the city by force of arms, although this was proving a costly failure. The city's coffers were empty, and when the harvest failed that summer the population began to suffer from food shortages; soon there were rumours of people dying of starvation, then word began to spread that two people had died of the plague in the riverside Ognissanti district. The bands of hymn-singing children who roamed the streets were now seen as spies searching for evidence of heresy, as well as spreaders of disease. Doors were slammed in their faces, while their armed protectors were pelted with missiles and subjected to a rain of refuse, or worse, from the upper windows of the tenements.

By early 1498 things were rising to a climax. The Dominican prior of San Marco was subjected to a challenge by the rival Franciscans, who remained loyal to the pope. They demanded that Savonarola prove his special relationship to God by submitting to an ordeal by fire, along with one of their own priests. Only if Savonarola could walk unharmed along a path of burning brush in his bare feet would this show that he had divine protection. If he succeeded, he had every right to rule the city; if he failed, then he should go into exile. Once again, the Signoria was outraged; this resort to medievalism was a disgrace to the civilised city of Florence; why, they might just as well challenge Savonarola to walk across the Arno. Yet the Franciscans were not to be deterred, and duly selected one of their priests; but Savonarola refused the challenge, whereupon one of his more zealous disciples, Fra Domenico da Pescia, took up the challenge in his stead.

On the appointed day, a pathway of burning brushwood was prepared across the width of the Piazza della Signoria; the Signoria gathered reluctantly on its terrace as crowds filled the piazza, and heads craned from every window while the two priests prepared for their ordeal. There was a delay, while the two sides debated whether the contestants were allowed to carry wooden crucifixes in their hands, fearing that the crucifixes might be sacrilegiously burned. Then, in the midst of this intense theological debate, the heavens opened and there was a downpour that put out the fires. The ordeal had descended into farce, and reluctantly everyone returned home.

Things came to a head the next day, which was Palm Sunday. One of Savonarola's disciples attempted to deliver the Lenten sermon in the cathedral and was chased out by an angry mob. The disciple and his followers amongst the congregation ran and barricaded themselves in the San Marco monastery, whilst their pursuers gathered outside. As the day went on, the mob surrounding San Marco became larger and angrier. Their leaders began demanding that those inside hand over the prior, Savonarola, whom they knew to be inside; then the *arrabbiati* produced some missile-throwing machines and grappling ladders to scale the walls. Inside, Savonarola ordered his priests to refrain from violence, but to no avail; making use of candlesticks and heavy crucifixes, the priests began desperately knocking back those on the scaling ladders. An angry German friar started firing an arquebus (an ancient blunderbuss) into the crowd, which only served to further enrage the besiegers. The rowdy scenes continued after nightfall, becoming increasingly riotous, until at around two o'clock in the morning the mob finally burned down the wooden doors of the monastery and surged in. Savonarola was discovered in his cell at prayer, and was immediately set upon by armed men who dragged him outside. He was then led through the hissing, spitting crowds to the Palazzo della Signoria, where he was bundled up the stairs of the tower and locked in the Alberghetto. It was just sixty-five years since the same fate had befallen Cosimo de' Medici, an event that had heralded the golden age which had now come to such a bitter close.

Next day, Savonarola was removed to the notorious Bargello; unable to walk because of the irons that clamped his feet and hands, he was 'carried there by two men on their crossed hands'. Once inside the Bargello,

Fig 10 Execution of Savonarola on the Piazza della Signoria (1498)

he was subjected to Florence's ingeniously excruciating form of torture known as the *strappado*. The victim's wrists were bound behind his back with straps and tied to a rope, which was passed over a pulley; he was then hauled above the ground, his entire weight supported by his wrists yanked up behind his back. Then the rope was released, so that the victim plunged *almost* to the floor. The jolt of pain was agonising, with the possiblity of the victim's arms being wrenched out of their sockets.

After four drops on the *strappado*, Savonarola broke down and confessed to the heresies of which he was accused. Yet no sooner was he released from the straps and back on his feet than he promptly retracted his confession. This gruesome fiasco was repeated several times until Savonarola was in no state to withdraw his previous confession. He was then condemned to death, along with two of his disciples, including the faithful Fra Domenico, who had always been willing to die for him.

As Savonarola was a priest, he could officially only be tried and condemned by an ecclesiastical court, so the Florentine authorities sent to Rome for permission to carry out their sentence. Pope Alexander VI now decided it was time for him belatedly to assert his authority, and insisted on Savonarola being tried by his representatives. Two papal commisioners were despatched to Florence to carry out the trial, though as one of them would later confide, they 'arrived in Florence with the verdict in their bosom'. Savonarola was duly tortured and condemned once more; he was then ordered to be hanged along with his two disciples, their bodies weighted down by chains, in the Piazza della Signoria; their corpses were then to be burned. This duly took place on the morning of 23 May 1498, at the very spot where just a year previously Savonarola had conducted his Bonfire of the Vanities. According to the eyewitness Landucci, 'When all three had been hanged a fire was made upon the platform on which gunpowder was put and set alight, so that the said fire burst out with a noise of rockets and cracking. In a few hours they were burnt, their legs and arms gradually dropping off. Part of their bodies remaining hanging to the chains, a quantity of stones were thrown to make them fall, as there was a fear of the people getting hold of them.' After this, the bones were burned to ashes. 'Then they fetched carts and carried the last bit of dust to the Arno, by the Ponte Vecchio, in order that no remains should be found. Nevertheless, a few good men had so much faith that they gathered some of the floating ashes together, in fear and secrecy, because it was as much as one's life was worth, so anxious were the authorities to destroy every relic.' This was not the last that Florence would hear of the City of God.

Part 4

The Pope
and the Protestant

18

Il Gigante – A Statue of Biblical Proportions

D URING THE UNSETTLED days before the flight of Piero de'
Medici from Florence at the end of 1494, a friend of the
young Michelangelo had a nightmare. This 'friend's' dream was
so vivid that Michelangelo could still recall it in old age to his companion and early biographer Ascanio Condivi: 'Lorenzo de' Medici had
appeared to him with a black robe, all in rags over his nakedness, and
commanded him to tell his son that he would shortly be driven from
his house, never to return again.' This dream was almost certainly
Michelangelo's own, evoking as it does the closeness of his relationship
with Lorenzo de' Medici (it has even been claimed that Lorenzo's near-
nakedness suggests a homosexual attraction). Within a week of
Michelangelo having this dream, and even before Piero went into exile,
the nineteen-year-old sculptor fled the city – fearful of what he felt
sure was going to happen, and fearful that his close association with
the Medici would prove his undoing.

Michelangelo ended up in Rome, where a banker called Jacopo Galli
commissioned him to produce a full-sized statue of Bacchus, the Ancient
Greek god of wine and revelry. The result was a superb psychological study
– with, in the words of Condivi: 'the merry face, and the squinting lascivious eyes, such as are usual in those who have fallen excessively in love
with wine'. The youthful standing figure, holding a cup of wine, has a
swelling stomach and is daringly off-balance, supported by a diminutive
young satyr at his side, biting into a bunch of grapes.

Surprisingly, this profane work led to a commission for a work of the utmost sacredness, from the French Cardinal of St-Denis, who was living in Rome at the time. The result was Michelangelo's first masterpiece, his *Pietà*, which depicts the Virgin Mary cradling the all-but-naked figure of the dead Christ sprawled across her lap, just after he has been taken down from the Cross. Michelangelo's *Pietà* was completed in 1500, and has such technical virtuosity that it is difficult to imagine it being the work of a mere twenty-five-year-old. The problem of depicting the two separate figures in the same block of marble is overcome by contrasting Christ's smooth naked flesh with the voluminous folds of Mary's dress. Her serene yet suffering face is undoubtedly alive, while Christ's lolling dead face is still marked with the agony of his crucifixion. Michelangelo manages to convey a sense of tranquillity, at the same time evoking a profound spiritual emotion.

Not all were entirely satisfied with this work; many, including Condivi, questioned why Mary's face appeared no older than that of Christ. Michelangelo replied: 'Don't you know that chaste women remain far fresher than those who are not chaste?' Another contemporary, Giorgio Vasari, in his revealing *Life of Michelangelo*, hinted at a more hidden explanation of this anomaly. He claimed that Michelangelo's 'manner of speech was very veiled and ambiguous, his utterances having in a sense two meanings'; and what was true of his speech was also true of his work. Vasari explained that Michelangelo's deep-felt image of Mary's comparatively youthful motherhood may well have stemmed from the fact that both his mother and the nurse who looked after him had died when they were young. As we shall see, Michelangelo's personal psychology would often play a haunting role in his work.

By the time Michelangelo returned to Florence in 1500, Savonarola had been dead two years and the city was in a pitiful condition; once the capital of a proud state, its power was now much reduced and its people plunged into poverty. The war against Pisa had been conducted so ineptly by the Florentine military leader Paolo Vitelli that the Signoria had vented its frustration by arresting him for treason, having him tortured and then beheaded. The populace was disgruntled, and the streets were becoming increasingly lawless. Perhaps the most telling image is that of Botticelli: the glory days of his colourful and symbolic paintings long over, even his renunciation of worldly delights at the feet of Savonarola now a thing of the past, he shuffled on crutches through the streets beneath a drab thread-bare cloak, aged, sick and incapable.

The government was impotent, and its policy now altered every two months with the change of *gonfaloniere*. In an effort to halt the drift, it was decided to try another Venetian measure: the new *gonfaloniere* would be elected for life, just like the doge of Venice. This would at least enable the city to follow through a consistent policy – as it had not done since the days of the Medici, ironically. The first *gonfaloniere* elected for life was Piero Soderini, a member of the leading Florentine family that had produced Niccolò Soderini, who had tried to depose Piero the Gouty, and later Tommaso Soderini who became Lorenzo the Magnificent's right-hand man.

Piero Soderini was known to be a trustworthy character, but was of limited abilities; Florence had grown tired of men who saw themselves as exceptional leaders. However, he did have one unusual trait: he had noticed the talent of Michelangelo and had taken a liking to this promising, if difficult, young man. Soderini, in his wisdom, now decided that Michelangelo should be commissioned to sculpt a great work that would restore the civic pride of Florence.

The wardens of Santa Maria del Fiore had in the cathedral workshop a large block of white marble, which had been brought to the city some forty years previously from Carrara, near the Tuscan coast, where the finest marble in Europe was mined. Years earlier, an inept craftsman had begun hacking out blocks of stone in preparation for creating a sculpture, but this work had been abandoned; what was left was an eighteen-foot-high block of marble in a distressingly mutilated condition. Soderini suggested to Michelangelo that perhaps this could be carved into a giant statue of David, the brave symbol of Florence's republican pride. Only an artist of the ambition and self-confidence of the twenty-six-year-old Michelangelo would have accepted such a daunting commission.

Michelangelo set to work making preliminary sketches, on one of which he wrote a brief verse expressing his aim:

> *Davicte cholla fromba*
> *e io choll'archo*
> *Michelangelo*

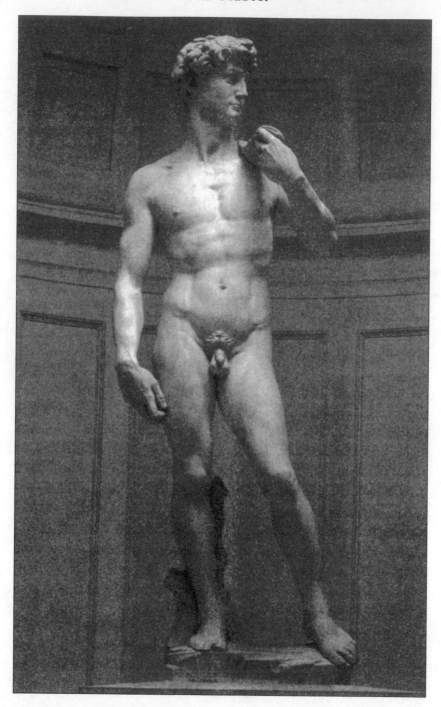

Fig 11 David by Michelangelo

(David with his sling
And I with my bow
Michelangelo)

The bow referred to was a curved wooden instrument for drilling into stone; the poem expresses Michelangelo's pride, as he likens himself to David setting forth to do battle.

Michelangelo was soon working obsessively on his *David*, chipping away in the seclusion of the cathedral workshop day and night. During the sweltering heat of summer he worked stripped to the waist, the sweat dribbling into his eyes; during the finger-freezing cold of winter he worked swathed like a mummy, the steam of his breath obscuring his vision. Despite the energy-sapping effort required by his task, as ever Michelangelo lived frugally; years later he would tell Condivi: 'However rich I may have been, I have always lived like a poor man.' He also insisted on working in secret, having a phobia about his work being seen before it was finished.

Astonishingly, it took Michelangelo just eighteen months to complete his sculpture, which was two times larger than life-size. As a physical feat alone, this was remarkable; as a work of art it proved a sublime achievement. The classical nudity and restraint of this standing male figure is filled with a living force; here the volatile physicality of his *Bacchus* is contained within the sheer presence of his *Pietà*. The result is profoundly humanistic, a magnificent celebration of what it is to be human, yet at the same time there is something transcendent in David's expression of the human ideal, and in this it achieves an almost Platonic ideality. The statue itself marks the emergence of a quality that was increasingly evoked by Michelangelo's work: the apt Italian word for this is *terribilità*, meaning awesome, almost dread-inspiring power.

According to one report, the statue was originally intended to stand on the roof of the cathedral; it was after all a religious work, the biblical figure of David the celebrated slayer of Goliath (though many in the republican faction would have understood the defeated Goliath as none other than the expelled Medici). The statue's possibly intended location may account for some of the exaggeration that gives it such power: it was intended to be seen from far below. Yet such a piece, such unadorned and unashamed nakedness, was hardly appropriate for a Christian church, even in Renaissance times, and it was decided that the statue should be placed instead on the raised platform outside the Palazzo della Signoria. Here, overlooking the piazza where the assembled citizens gave voice to their wishes for the future of the city, was the perfect location; and, curiously, beneath the façade and tower of the Palazzo, the statue's dwarfing size became almost human.

Yet moving the statue was to prove no easy undertaking. To begin with, the entire wall of the cathedral workshop had to be demolished simply to get it out. Then came the task of physically lifting the statue — nothing like this had been attempted before. Vasari described how the shrouded statue was contained within a strong wooden framework 'from which the statue was suspended by ropes so that when it was moved it swayed without being broken'. This contraption was moved by a number of winches, operated by more than forty men, which drew it slowly forward over planks laid on the ground. According to Landucci, who witnessed this event along with a large crowd of onlookers, it took four days for the statue to reach the piazza (a distance of a quarter of a mile).

Before it was unveiled, Soderini insisted on a private viewing. According to the legend recounted by Vasari, Soderini was highly pleased, but could not resist making a suggestion — perhaps the nose was a little too large. Though exasperated at this criticism of his work, Michelangelo controlled his anger; without a word he climbed the scaffolding, holding a chisel in one hand, whilst with the other he casually swept up some marble dust lying on the planks. Standing so that his back obscured what he was doing, he pretended to chip away at the nose, letting a trickle of marble dust fall from his hand as he did so. Then he stepped back, calling down to Soderini: 'Look at it now.' 'I like it better,' Soderini replied, 'you have given it life.'

Whether or not this story was true, it undeniably illustrates a growing trend that first came to the fore in the Renaissance: the belief in the autonomy of the artist in matters of taste concerning his own work. Earlier, when Donatello had knocked his statue from the parapet of the Palazzo Medici, this appeared more as an act of petulance; now, with Michelangelo, such behaviour was becoming an asserted right of self-determination. As ever in the Renaissance, it was art that led the way; in this respect, other aspects of the new humanism were hampered by their very articulacy. When Pico della Mirandola had set down the details of his humanist philosophy, he had found himself accused of heresy. The individual still had little freedom of action, and even less of speech; only in art and science (still interwoven, though becoming less so) was a more guarded freedom possible.

This is not to say that the artist and his art were above criticism, far from it; and Michelangelo's *David* was to prove no exception. Throughout Florence the statue soon became popularly known as '*Il Gigante*' ('The Giant'); but why was it so large, people wanted to know, for surely David's opponent Goliath was meant to be the giant? In fact, as many were quick to point out, the statue could have been seen as representing any number of ancient figures. It could just as easily have been Hercules, or even a youthful Samson; very little indicated that this was the biblical David, apart from the sling thrown over his left shoulder. (This was originally, and now remains, the only part of the body that was covered, though at the first public unveiling the Signoria insisted on the statue's rather blatant genitalia being hidden, and these were obscured by a brass garland containing twenty-eight copper leaves, which would continue to adorn the statue for another thirty years.) There was no denying that Michelangelo had made the description of the biblical David a secondary matter – the primary consideration being a display of his own superlative powers. This trait too would become increasingly evident in Michelangelo's ensuing work, as the near-perfection of his *David* gave way to an increasing mannerism. With a Michelangelo, there would be no doubting whose work it was; indeed, this mannerism is already partly visible in his *David*. The hands are enlarged and exaggerated, suggestively adding to the figure's power; and on closer inspection, the neck and features of the face too are enlarged. (Did Soderini have a point?) These distortions are justified by the fact that the spectator views the statue from beneath, which gives it a foreshortening effect. Michelangelo wished to make the statue appear as large as he could, and it was impossible for him to have made it physically any larger; as Condivi points out, Michelangelo calculated his block of marble 'so exactly, that as can be seen on the crown of the head and on the base, the old rough surface of the marble still appears'.

Having completed this supreme work, Michelangelo was now aggrieved to find himself in a similar position to David facing Goliath. In 1504 the authorities commissioned him to produce a large mural of a battle scene in the Palazzo della Signoria – on the wall directly adjacent to a mural that was being painted by his arch-rival Leonardo da Vinci. These two murals were intended to depict Florence's military triumphs, to expunge the memory of recent disasters, though all the citizens of Florence quickly realised that the painting of these murals meant much more than this. Here was the ultimate contest between the fifty-two-year-old maestro and the young emergent genius half his age: who would triumph in this battle between Florence's two greatest artists? Victory, and defeat, would both be permanent – there for all to see for years to come.

This element of competition has been seen as a trivialising of great art, but it was far from being the case. Here Florence was merely following the precedent set by the Ancient Greeks, whose regular pan-Hellenic competitions to choose the greatest tragedy produced Aeschylus, Sophocles and Euripides. This contest in Florence would have a profound effect on Michelangelo; although in his later years he would insist to Condivi that he was entirely self-taught, the influence of Leonardo is noticeable during this period. Like any ambitious competitor, Michelangelo studied his opponent and would learn from him a subtlety of emotional expression that is absent in his *David*. Unfortunately, the competition itself would result in little else: all that remains are the sketches for their murals produced by both artists. Leonardo probably went so far as to outline his projected scene on the wall, but characteristically found himself unable to bring his work to conclusion; Michelangelo was only able to produce a cartoon of his projected work before he was summoned to Rome.

In 1503 the seventy-two-year-old Pope Alexander VI finally died; despite his luridly degenerate life, he remained physically robust to the end – making many suspect that he had been poisoned. Although his son Cesare Borgia did his utmost to prevent Alexander VI being succeeded by his arch-rival Francesco Piccolomini, even going so far as to seize the Vatican, he could not prevent this and Piccolomini became Pope Pius III. However, within a month the new pope was dead; he had been physically frail and had not been expected to last for long, yet nonetheless the sheer brevity of his tenure led to further speculations concerning poison. Pius III was succeeded by Julius II, a rather more vigorous opponent of the Borgias, who evidently took greater care over his diet. Michelangelo's reputation was already known to Julius II, who had been particularly impressed by his *Pietà*, and he summoned Michelangelo to Rome to start work on a hugely ambitious scheme for his tomb, involving no fewer than forty large sculptures.

19

Rome:
The Medici's New Home

THE ROME TO which Michelangelo returned in 1505 had now taken over from Florence as the leading city of the Renaissance. This was a remarkable transformation, which was only partly assisted by the decline of Florence during the thirteen years since the death of Lorenzo de' Medici.

Just a century previously Rome had been little more than a medieval town of squalid alleys huddled amidst ancient ruins which were simply beyond the comprehension of most of its inhabitants. Indeed, popular local wisdom had it that the magnificent remains of the Claudia Aqueduct, with its 100-foot-high arches stretching more that forty miles south into the countryside, had been used for bringing olive oil from Naples. On winter nights wolves came down from the hills, howling amidst Rome's darkened shacks, while the old aristocratic families and cardinals barricaded themselves in their palazzi, living in a style that remained inconceivable beyond their walls. Even so, there had long been sufficient opulence behind closed doors to attract a thriving community of bankers; Giovanni di Bicci and Cosimo de' Medici both learned their trade here around 1400.

Though Rome remained officially under papal rule, during the fourteenth century the popes themselves (there was often more than one) tended to reside in Avignon or elsewhere. As we have seen, this situation was not resolved until the Council of Constance (1414–18), and it was not until 1420 that the new undisputed pope, Martin V, left Florence to resume permanent papal residence in Rome. The pope installed himself on the far side of the River Tiber in the Castel Sant'Angelo, which had first been constructed as Hadrian's tomb in AD 135. After Martin V, the succeeding popes gradually began imposing order on the unruly population, and it was said that during this period there were so many rotting bodies of executed criminals hanging from the battlements of the Castel Sant'Angelo that the smell made the bridge across the Tiber all but impassable. Many of the more powerful cardinals who now took up residence in the city began building themselves increasingly grandiose palaces, often using stones vandalised from the Ancient Roman ruins. The seven hills of the ancient city had long since returned to vineyards and gardens, whilst the Forum was still used for grazing cattle; in a tradition that remained since the glories of Ancient Rome, the city had no industry. Rome now depended on pilgrims and tourists; and the footpads and cut-throats of previous centuries were supplemented by ragged monks and dealers in fake relics, who set up stalls along the wider streets that were now beginning to replace the labyrinthine medieval quarters. Yet such improvements to the landscape were only gradual; when Cosimo de' Medici's contemporary, the poet and philosopher Leon Alberti, lived in the city during the 1450s, he counted more than a thousand ruined churches.

Rome's ascendancy over Florence as the centre of Italian culture is usually marked by the completion in 1498 of Cardinal Raffaele Riario's magnificent Renaissance palazzo (the Cancelleria), which was funded from the proceeds of a single night's gambling. The resurgent city of this period, where the exiled Piero the Unfortunate spent much of his last degenerate years, had doubled in population during the previous century to 50,000, equalling that of Florence. Yet beneath the veneer it remained business as usual; 7,000 prostitutes worked in a wide range of bordellos, all of which were required to pay a licence fee that ended up in the papal coffers. These houses and their inmates catered to the needs of the local clergy and the pilgrims who visited from all over Europe (thus ensuring that the so-called French Disease reached parts of Europe which had hitherto remained unaffected). Meanwhile a criminal underclass of similar numbers sought to relieve the populace of any remaining funds – or worse. Despite the continuing campaign to bring civil order to the city, the murder rate was around one hundred each week; many of those responsible were apprehended, though only the destitute ended up dangling from the battlements of the

Castel Sant'Angelo. As Pope Alexander VI astutely observed: 'Our Lord is not so much interested in the death of sinners, more that they are able to pay for their sins and continue living.'

This was the city in which Lorenzo the Magnificent's second son, the exiled young Cardinal Giovanni de' Medici, would make his home. The chubby, intelligent, but distinctly lazy child who had been educated by Poliziano had retained much of his teacher's humanist hedonism; and this attitude to life had continued, despite his father's efforts, even after Giovanni officially took up his cardinal's red hat. The young Cardinal Giovanni de' Medici was fulfilling a role that may well have been prepared for him some generations previously. Cosimo de' Medici had realised that Florence would one day tire of the Medici, but had ensured that the family would be remembered long after they had gone into exile, because of the buildings and churches he had erected. But Cosimo had not faced the question of what would actually happen to the Medici if or when they were forced into exile; it was either his son Piero the Gouty or his grandson Lorenzo the Magnificent who had come to a decision on the matter of the Medici fate. Florence would no longer be their centre of power, and with the decline of the Medici Bank they could no longer rely on money as their source of power – the only answer was to spread their power base and attempt to rise still further in the world. A crucial decision had been reached: instead of serving the Church as bankers, the Medici should now attempt to infiltrate it, and thus attain an even greater source of wealth and power. No record of such thinking survives, but the evidence suggests that those deathbed conversations, when the father passed on his advice to his son and heir, must have included such a strategy.

Lorenzo de' Medici tried to secure a cardinal's red hat for his beloved brother Giuliano, but Pope Sixtus IV was too busy filling any available senior posts with members of his own family. Only after Giuliano was murdered in the Pazzi conspiracy did Lorenzo transfer his hopes to his own second son Giovanni, whom he quickly perceived as being the more able of his offspring. Piero may have had good looks and presence, but Giovanni had brains; and though Giovanni was short-sighted, fat and lazy, Lorenzo noticed that he was quite the equal of his athletic older brother when they went riding together.

After Sixtus IV was succeeded in 1484 by the more amenable Innocent

VIII, Lorenzo de' Medici seized his opportunity. From the outset, he shamelessly cultivated Innocent VIII's friendship, writing him regular cordial letters and sending him barrels of his favourite Tuscan wine. This was of course also part of his peacemaking policy as the 'needle of the Italian compass'; as long as he could maintain the Milan–Florence–Naples axis, and keep the pope as his friend, peace in Italy was assured. In 1488, Lorenzo's relationship with Innocent VIII was cemented by the marriage of the pope's son Franceschetto to Lorenzo's daughter Maddalena. Meanwhile, Lorenzo had made sure that his son Giovanni took the tonsure – signalling his intended vocation in the Church – at the early age of eight. Lorenzo soon began obtaining rich ecclesiastical benefices for his son, many in France where it was easier to procure such items (though this may also be taken as the first evidence of a secret long-term project involving the Medici family in France, which we will not see coming to fruition until the following century).

The Lyons branch of the Medici Bank was ordered to scour the land for suitable 'vacancies'; such posts were held *in absentia* and brought with them a considerable income, as well as status within the Church. Yet even here there could be the occasional slip-up, for several months after Lorenzo had embarked upon the process of purchasing for Giovanni the arch-bishopric of Aix-en-Provence, it was suddenly discovered that the aged incumbent was still alive! All this cost money, and there is no doubt that a good part of it came from the Florence exchequer; unbeknown to its citizens, Florence was now funding a Medici future that might not involve the city. Lorenzo was by this stage unable to obtain sufficient funds from elsewhere, for the Medici Bank was already sinking fast, with the liquidation of its branches in Milan (1478), Bruges (1480) and Venice (1481).

Finally in 1489 Lorenzo had managed to persuade Innocent VIII to make his thirteen-year-old son Giovanni a cardinal. Even during these lax times such a youthful appointment was without precedent – so much so that Innocent VIII made Lorenzo promise that this appointment would not be made public until Giovanni was officially installed at the age of sixteen. There followed three long anxious years; Innocent VIII was old and ill – if he died before Giovanni was sixteen, the new pope would certainly annul this exceptional appointment. Then it became clear that Lorenzo himself was dying. However, in the spring of 1492 Giovanni at last came of age, and the dying Lorenzo, now confined to his litter, looked down proudly from the balcony of the Palazzo Medici at the banquet celebrating his son's appointment.

Immediately afterwards, the sixteen-year-old Cardinal Medici travelled to Rome to take up his appointment. Lorenzo, on his deathbed, wrote a long letter to his son, informing him of the seriousness of his position. His appointment was 'the greatest achievement of our house', and he reminded Giovanni that from his powerful position 'it will not be difficult for you to aid the city and our house'. The youthful Giovanni was advised to remain close to the pope, but without pestering him; and he was to behave himself. Lorenzo was well aware of Giovanni's character: growing up amidst Lorenzo's brilliant and entertaining circle, Giovanni had already developed a premature taste for the finer things in life – fine books, fine pictures, fine wine and fine cuisine. Yet this was more than mere precocity: the company of his father's exceptional companions meant that he had also developed a true appreciation of such things – though at the expense of some more priestly virtues. In Lorenzo's final letter to Giovanni, he stressed in the strongest possible terms: 'One rule above all others I urge you to observe most rigorously: *Rise early in the morning.*'

Lorenzo must have had an inkling that the future of the Medici fortunes now lay with the bright and slothful Giovanni in Rome, rather than with the arrogant and preening Piero, who was to succeed him in Florence, though he cannot have foreseen that disaster would strike so quickly. Months after Lorenzo's death, Innocent VIII too would be dead, succeeded by the Borgia pope Alexander VI, causing the perceptive young Cardinal Medici to remark: 'We are in the clutches of a wolf.' Then Charles VIII marched into Italy, and Cardinal Medici rushed to Florence in an attempt to help his brother Piero, but in vain; they were both exiled, with a price on their heads.

The eighteen-year-old Cardinal Medici realised that it was not wise for him to return to Rome; instead, he embarked on an extended tour of Europe. He could afford such luxury: he now had a range of benefices, including that of the celebrated (and hugely wealthy) Abbey of Monte Cassino. Giovanni's first visit was to Pisa to see his cousin Giulio, the illegitimate son of Lorenzo's beloved brother Giuliano, who had been born just weeks before his father's assassination in Florence Cathedral. Lorenzo had taken the infant Giulio into the Palazzo Medici, where he had been educated with his own sons; and like Giovanni, Giulio had been destined for the Church. The quiet young Giulio and the somnolent, slyly smiling Giovanni had long been close, sharing a sense of humour, as well as a love of learning and the good things of life. Giulio was now completing his education in the university at Pisa. There had been a university at Pisa since medieval times, but this had been considerably revived when Lorenzo the Magnificent had transferred most of the faculties of the University of Florence to Pisa in an attempt to cement the difficult relations between the two cities.

After a brief stay in Pisa, Giovanni left with Giulio for Venice. They then crossed the Alps into northern Europe, where they would spend another five years of travel. For the most part Cardinal Medici and his cousin Giulio travelled as private citizens, rather than as members of the Church, behaving much like any other wealthy young bachelors on a cultural tour. However, this was something of a front – it was what they wanted people, both in Europe and back in Italy, to think they were doing. In fact, their travels were not entirely dedicated to pleasure, and they certainly made sure they donned their Church robes when they visited the Holy Roman Emperor Maximillian I, who was so impressed by these two bright young churchmen that he gave them letters of recommendation to his son Philip, who was governor of the Low Countries. Cardinal Medici, and his young cousin Giulio, were making important friends who might prove useful political contacts for the future.

Later they would meet Cardinal Giuliano della Rovere, who owed his many appointments to having been a nephew of the celebrated nepotist Pope Sixtus IV; besides being a cardinal, he was also an archbishop and held no fewer than eight bishoprics. Like his uncle, Cardinal della Rovere had been brought up on the Ligurian coast near Genoa and remained a distinctly rough and ready character; he was stout, but physically tough and virile, and his long residence in Rome had already resulted in syphilis. He had little time for any kind of learning, and believed that a cardinal was better off being well versed in military tactics than in theology. He also enjoyed hunting and displaying his wealth. Such a powerful charac-ter had proved an evident threat to Alexander VI, and Cardinal della Rovere had chosen to absent himself from Rome before he was poisoned, or worse. The twenty-year-old Cardinal Medici visited the sixty-year-old Cardinal della Rovere at his estate in Savona on the Gulf of Genoa, and the two of them were soon commiserating about their common exile from Rome – discovering that they both, in their own very separate ways, had a love of beauty. Later they went hunting together, and the older cardinal was unexpectedly impressed at the tubby, short-sighted young cardinal's fearless ability to outride him.

When Alexander VI crossed swords with Savonarola in 1495, Cardinal Medici made a tactical return to Rome, where he was welcomed by the pope as the enemy of his enemy. Cardinal Medici now settled in Rome, establishing a reputation as an intelligent and good-natured host to a wide social range of artists, humanists and church dignitaries. He did his best to rouse his exiled brother Piero the Unfortunate from his dissipated despair, and also participated in schemes for the Medici return to power in Florence. When Piero died in 1503, Cardinal Medici assumed the leadership of the senior Medici faction, continuing to maintain covert links with Medici sympathisers in Florence. Alexander VI died in the same year, and Cardinal Medici was a member of the conclave to elect the next pope, Pius III, where he witnessed at first hand the factionalism and horse-trading involved in the election of a pope. Cardinal Medici was a little more experienced when a second conclave was called a few months later following the death of Pius III. He made sure that he was openly seen as an enthusiastic supporter of Cardinal della Rovere, who emerged as the successful candidate and succeeded as Pope Julius II. It soon became clear that the powerful but ageing Julius II looked upon young Cardinal Medici as something of a protégé. When news of this growing Medici influence in Rome reached Florence, it was greeted with some suspicion and many began to wonder what precisely the Medici were up to now.

20

Machiavelli Meets His Match

U NDER THE RULE of Piero Soderini, Florence was gradually becoming at ease with its more republican style of government – the
emphasis here being on style, rather than form, for apart from
the *gonfaloniere* being elected for life, the structure of the administration in
fact remained much the same. The Signoria and the separate committees
were still elected in the same fashion, and were still limited to members
of families who had previously provided office-holders (in practice, about
3,000 people). But the crucial point was that the elections were no longer
manipulated by the ruling families, or by a single ruling clique such as the
Medici. The remaining powerful cliques amongst the leading families were
now more evenly balanced and merely jockeyed for position. This situation was reinforced by Soderini's more permanent presence as *gonfaloniere*;
and though his political expertise continued to be somewhat limited, he
had sufficient astuteness to choose his advisers well. Amongst the most
talented of these was an ambitious dark-eyed young man called Niccolò
Machiavelli, a talented writer renowned amongst his friends for his sardonic
wit, who would exercise his brilliance as a diplomatic emissary for the
Florentine Republic and as a leading member of the Council of War.

Niccolò Machiavelli was born in 1469 and grew up in the glory days
of Lorenzo the Magnificent. His father was an impoverished lawyer, a
member of a long-established Florentine family that had been rich and
distinguished well over a century beforehand, during Florence's great banking era prior to the Black Death. Niccolò's mother died while he was still
a young man, but appears to have had a formative influence; she is known
to have read widely and to have written verse. Another crucial influence

was Niccolò's education; the Machiavellis were too poor to afford a humanist education for their son, so instead he learned Latin and absorbed the
medieval Aristotelianism that still pervaded fifteenth-century European
education, even in Florence. Only later would his friends introduce him
to the Roman poets, rhetoricians and historians who so inspired the humanist young men of Florence. It was through such authors that Machiavelli
became conscious of how Italy had once been the centre of a great empire
which had ruled the known world. The contrast with its present condition of squabbling city states and rampaging foreign armies was all too
plain to see.

But at the same time Italy was undergoing a cultural transformation,
and many were beginning to recognise this fact: it cannot have been long
after this that the word *Rinascimento.* (Renaissance) was first coined. And
as the effects of this cultural transformation permeated to countries further
afield, it became clear that Europe was entering a new age. This is more
than mere cliché or hindsight, for the intimation was widespread and
becoming pan-European: it is explicit in works from Pico della Mirandola
to the early sixteenth-century Dutch scholar Erasmus, all of which were
becoming widely available. The spread of printing meant that even a
comparatively poor young man such as Machiavelli could afford to buy
books of his favourite authors from one of the several booksellers that
had now sprung up in Florence. Machiavelli is known to have possessed
works by the Latin historian Tacitus, who described the lives of such
monstrous emperors as Caligula and Nero. Amongst the poets, Machiavelli
favoured Lucretius, whose recently rediscovered long philosophical poem
De Rerum Natura (On the Nature of Things) described how the world originated and also outlined the stark realities of the human condition.
Lucretius's assertion that man's life is decided by the disparate factors of
his own nature and chance would make a deep impression. Whatever belief
Machiavelli had in God fell into abeyance at an early age, and for the rest
of his life he would merely go through the motions of attending church
on major festivals and feast days. In this, he would not have been exceptional amongst his circle of lively intellectual friends.

The humanist world that had given birth to a renaissance in the arts,
and the early stirrings of a modern scientific outlook, had now been
affected by developments that extended far beyond the intellectual world.

The Portuguese had rounded the Cape of Good Hope into the Indian Ocean; in the very year that Lorenzo de' Medici died, Columbus had crossed the Atlantic to the New World, whose riches were now pouring into Spain, making it the most wealthy nation in Europe. Columbus may have been Genoese, but he worked for the Spanish; Italy benefited less than most from these new discoveries. Amongst the plethora of Spanish, Portuguese, English and Dutch names in the New World, Italian names are significantly the exception: Colombia, America, Venezuela (little Venice), but remarkably few others. And though named by Italian explorers, these did not become Italian colonies.

Meanwhile the parochial bickering of Italian inter-state wars had entered a drastic new phase with the arrival of French armies from the north, a situation further worsened by the arrival of Spanish troops in the south: the whole of Italy was increasingly being torn apart by war. Machiavelli would grow up amidst an atmosphere of political turbulence, both in Italy at large and at home in Florence. He was a boy of nine when Florence was convulsed by the Pazzi conspiracy; by the time he was twenty-five he had witnessed the rise of Savonarola, the banishment of Piero the Unfortunate, and the humiliation of Charles VIII's triumphal entry into his native city.

Little is known of this early period of Machiavelli's life, and he only emerges from the shadows in 1498, just a month after the execution of Savonarola, when he is elected as secretary to the Second Chancery. The twenty-nine-year-old Machiavelli appears as a rather unprepossessing, not to say curious, figure; he is described as slender, with beady black eyes, black hair, a small head, aquiline nose and tightly closed mouth. His biographer Pasquale Villari comments that 'everything about him conveyed the impression of a very acute observer and sharp mind, though not someone who was liable to influence people much'. Villari also mentions Machiavelli's 'sarcastic expression', 'air of cold and inscrutable calculation' and 'powerful imagination'. Hardly a sympathetic type: yet he was certainly popular amongst his circle of young intellectual friends, and Gonfaloniere Soderini seems to have favoured him highly. Machiavelli's new post as secretary of the Second Chancery meant that he was responsible for the administration of the Florentine territories beyond the city. Later he was to be made secretary to the Council of War, putting him in charge of the

Fig 12 Niccolò Machiavelli

foreign relations of the republic. Machiavelli would remain in high office for the next fourteen years, doing his best to further Soderini's policies.

During the course of this work Machiavelli would travel on diplomatic missions as far afield as France and Germany. His task was to maintain Florence's alliances amidst the ever-changing Italian political scene and beyond; as a result, he would encounter some of the major political figures in Europe, including Louis XII, the new king of France, the Holy Roman Emperor Maximilian I, and later the new Pope Julius II. As a relief from the seriousness of these long and arduous diplomatic travels, Machiavelli would write letters to his friends back in Florence detailing various ludicrous amorous episodes that had befallen him. His marriage, which took place in 1501 when he was thirty-two, appears to have been typical of the time and place, and when he went on his long diplomatic missions his wife was left behind to look after the children (there would be four). Meanwhile, his letters to his friends continued to detail his absurd peccadilloes, for despite his unprepossessing appearance, women seem to have found him attractive.

There was a curious dichotomy which ran right through Machiavelli's character. He was a serious admirer of the great men he encountered, and in many ways he sought to emulate them, at least in their ways of thought; on the other hand, he felt the need to make himself appear ridiculous to his friends. However, his admiration of great men was far from uncritical; and the joke element of his character was not displayed in public. With Machiavelli we begin to see aspects of humanism penetrating beyond the charmed circle of the Palazzo Medici and other similar houses of the rich and privileged. The sharp, sardonic eye of Machiavelli belonged to no elitist clique, and the conclusions to which this clear vision now led him were guardedly pragmatic, rather than openly celebratory of any privileged position. His political experience would lead him to understand what worked in one's dealings with the world. He learned to rely on empiricism rather than idealism — and like other creative expressions of humanism, this would rely on skill *and* science. But his field would be reality, rather than art. Machiavelli's humanism relied on human instincts and judgement of experience, rather than any idealistic or religious principles — and in this it was a direct descendant of the humanism practised by Lorenzo the Magnificent. But where Lorenzo's humanism was one of gesture, Machiavelli's would be one of hard-headedness; though both were based on the premise of a humanity living, and being responsible for, its own life, with little or no reference to any transcendent life. Lorenzo had realised that anything was possible, anything was worth trying. Machiavelli would read the implications of this: if anything was possible, anything was permitted — in order to survive one had to take into account the full range of human character, especially its treacherous elements. Cold calculation, rather than noble gesture, was what succeeded in the end.

Machiavelli's views gradually hardened as he experienced the constant devi-ousness and subterfuge of a diplomatic scene that he was impotent to control. Others might have despaired at the futility of it all; Machiavelli sought a remedy. If Italy was to become great again, as it had been in the days of the Roman Empire, it needed a leader who was willing to be utterly ruthless, and who would not shrink from adopting the most extreme measures.

One man, above all others, appeared to possess such qualities: this was Cesare Borgia, whom Machiavelli would encounter on two separate occasions. By 1502, at the time of Machiavelli's first mission, Borgia was acting as the military wing of his father Alexander VI's papal power. With the aid of inspired military strategy and well-disciplined troops, Borgia was carving out an expanding territory in the Romagna.

Cesare Borgia was born in Rome in 1475, the illegitimate second son of the man who would become Pope Alexander VI. Despite being born in Italy, Cesare's family life and culture were entirely Spanish; he was charming, highly intelligent and handsome, but he also inherited the amoral ruthlessness of his father, who intended him for high office in the Church. It soon became plain that Cesare was even more unsuited for such a career than his reprobate father, but Alexander VI insisted, making his son Archbishop of Valencia at the age of sixteen, and a cardi-nal a year later. Cesare's older brother Juan was intended by his father to become military commander of the papal forces, but Cesare decided to take matters into his own hands and poisoned Juan. Alexander VI prag-matically accepted that Cesare was now the only person he could trust to command his forces, and Cesare was permitted to resign from his cardinalate and renounce his holy orders. Alexander VI then arranged for Cesare to marry a French princess and receive the title of Duke of Valentinois from the French king Louis XII. With the French as his allies, and providing military support, Cesare was now ready to launch a mili-tary campaign in the Romagna.

By 1502, after three years campaigning, Cesare Borgia had successfully conquered vast swathes of central Italy as far as the Adriatic, and in recog-nition of his services Alexander VI created him Duke of the Romagna. When Borgia finally turned inland and took Urbino, on the borders of the Florentine Republic, Machiavelli was despatched on a diplomatic mission to try and discover Borgia's intentions. We know details of this meeting from Machiavelli's letters to the authorities back in Florence. The twenty-seven-year-old Borgia received the Florentine mission at night amidst the dramatic torchlight of the magnificent ducal palace (built thirty years previously by the retired *condottiere* Federigo da Montefeltro). Borgia's bearded, flickeringly illuminated face was intended to strike a chill in the hearts of the visiting delegates, and it succeeded. Unsettlingly, Borgia began by flattering the Florentine delegation with deceptive charm, saying how much he respected the Florentines for maintaining their neutrality during his campaigns. But if they were not willing to be his friends now – and here Borgia's manner abruptly changed – he would not hesitate to over-run the republic and reinstate the Medici, whose leader Cardinal Giovanni de' Medici was now a friend of his father, the pope. The Florentine delegation insisted that Florence had no intention of invading the territory held by Borgia; but Borgia was not satisfied with this. He told the Florentine delegation that he did not trust their republican style of government, and if they did not change it, he would change it for them. The Florentines stood their ground, bravely informing Borgia that the people of Florence were well pleased with their new republican government, and they were the only ones who mattered where this was concerned. Borgia just laughed in their faces. As a last resort, the Florentine delegation reminded Borgia that their city still remained in alliance with France; if Florence was attacked, Louis XII was bound by treaty to come to its rescue. Once again Borgia just laughed and said: 'I know better than you what the King of France will do. You will be deceived.' The Florentine delegation was well aware of the truth of what Borgia was saying, but their nerve held. They knew that Borgia was bluffing too; he had no wish to risk making an enemy of Louis XII. Next day, Machiavelli set off at full gallop back to Florence to inform the Signoria of the precariousness of the situation. His assessment was that Borgia would not attack; on the other hand, given Borgia's character, there was no telling what he might do.

Fortunately, Borgia was now distracted by more pressing concerns, for he learned that his commander Vitellozzo Vitelli and several senior offi-cers had revolted, taking their soldiers with them. This left Borgia vulner-able, so he immediately used money from the papal exchequer to hire French troops. Vitelli and his fellow conspirators then had second thoughts, and sent word to Borgia suggesting that they meet and resolve their differences, to which Borgia readily agreed.

It was now that Machiavelli was despatched on a second mission to Borgia, which would result in Machiavelli staying with the military commander for several months; and it was during this period that Borgia would demonstrate to Machiavelli the full scope of his abilities. In order to settle his differences with Vitelli, Borgia arranged for a reconciliation at the small town of Senigallia on the Adriatic coast. Borgia dismissed his French troops as a goodwill gesture to reassure Vitelli and the others, turning up at Senigallia with only a skeleton force. Here he welcomed Vitelli and his commanders 'with a pleasant countenance . . . greeting them like old friends'. As he did so, Borgia manoeuvred them so that they were separated from their troops, whereupon he had them bundled off and flung into a dungeon. That night, as they 'wept and begged for mercy, frantically blaming each other', Borgia had them strangled.

This incident proved inspirational to Machiavelli; he would write of it in his report 'The Treachery of Duke Valentinois Toward Vitelli and Others', and it would play an exemplary role in his masterpiece of political philosophy, *The Prince*. What Machiavelli described in these works was not some improving example of how politics should be conducted; instead, he described what we would recognise as realpolitik.

Yet we should not mistake Machiavelli's description of this realpolitik for reality. Machiavelli was an artist who believed in the skilful embodiment of his ideas. Despite Machiavelli's later report, we now know that Borgia did not in fact dismiss his French troops in order to reassure Vitelli – they were suddenly recalled, leaving Borgia badly exposed, with no alternative but to bluff his way through his plan. Machiavelli's delegation accompanied Borgia on his trip to the fateful meeting at Senigallia, and his original report tellingly describes how the news of the French flight 'turned this court's brains topsy-turvy'. Likewise, all the weeping and blaming as the victims were strangled was an embellishment: no mention of this was made in the original report. Machiavelli's intention was to heighten and deepen the character of Borgia, not to make the embodiment of his ideas appear to be a panicky double-crosser. Machiavelli was interested not in Borgia the man, but in his method; and this had been a science of action, independent of morals. Here was an entirely new science, the science of politics. What Machiavelli sought, and would describe in *The Prince*, was a formal method that could encompass both the gestures of Lorenzo the Magnificent and the ruthlessness of Cesare Borgia. This would be a science where such daring, such bluff, such opportunism and such viciousness were set down as rational courses of action, each to be applied when the circumstances dictated them. Successful politics was a science, and thus had no room for morality.

Intriguingly, whilst Machiavelli was staying with Borgia he met and became friends with Borgia's chief military engineer, who was arguably the greatest scientific mind of the period. This was still the age prior to the emergence of modern science, and this scientist was an artist – Leonardo da Vinci. Here was another man riven by dichotomies, and this may well have drawn Machiavelli to him; Leonardo had a horror of war, yet spent hours in his study designing military engines far in advance of his time. He also hated tyranny, yet saw nothing wrong in hiring out his talents to tyrants such as Lodovico Sforza of Milan, and now Cesare Borgia.

In the meeting of Machiavelli and Leonardo we see two embryo scientists, who believed in empirical method. Leonardo believed in looking closely at everything in the world, and trying to see how it worked; whilst in his own, political way Machiavelli did precisely the same. Yet with Leonardo and Machiavelli we also see the further development of the humanist spirit, to the point where it diverges: the humanism that had once informed art, poetry and philosophy was now extending into a divergent practical reality – into politics, and into embryo science.

When Machiavelli returned to Florence, Soderini secured a place for him as secretary to the Council of War, in charge of Florence's military strategy, which was now in disarray. Pisa had revolted in 1494, cutting off Florence's main route to the sea; the consequent Florentine siege of the city proved unsuccessful, mainly because the mercenaries hired to do the job were unwilling to submit themselves to danger. Machiavelli proposed that instead of hiring mercenaries, Florence should create its own standing army. This was a revolutionary suggestion, for previously no Italian city had maintained its own fully trained full-time militia. Soderini agreed, and Machiavelli was soon drilling his men in their new red uniforms with white caps and waistcoats, complete with red-and-white socks: an army that represented the pride of Florence had to dress accordingly.

Machiavelli decided to hire Leonardo da Vinci as his military engineer, and Leonardo immediately came up with an ingenious idea to defeat Pisa. If they diverted the Arno so that it flowed *around* Pisa to the coast, this would at a stroke bring two great advantages. Florence would have direct access to the sea via the diverted Arno, and the drying up of the river downstream would leave Pisa literally high and dry. Machiavelli, attracted as ever to the notion of bold action, was delighted; but Leonardo's scheme was to suffer from the fatal defect that hampered so many of his practical ideas. It was ahead of its time, and the contemporary technology was simply not up to the task; the result was a farce, with hundreds of soldiers in mud-splattered uniforms digging a large trench knee-deep in mud. Soderini quickly called a halt to this costly exercise, and Leonardo was encouraged to seek employment elsewhere. Fortunately, this tale would have a happy ending, and Pisa would finally succumb to Machiavelli's new militia; this was his greatest triumph, and he received word from Florence that bonfires were being lit to celebrate his momentous victory. 'You alone have restored the fortunes of the Florentine state,' wrote one of his admiring friends.

But Machiavelli and Borgia, both of whom in their own way sought to control history, would eventually find themselves swept away by it. In 1503 when Pope Alexander VI fell ill, Borgia hastened back to Rome; after his father died, Borgia seized the Vatican in an attempt to retain power, but was unable to prevent a papal election. However, the new pope Pius III agreed to retain Borgia as '*gonfaloniere* of the Papal forces', which virtually guaranteed him control of the territories he had overrun. Although Borgia himself was now seriously ill, he would remain Duke of the Romagna, both in fact and in name; but when Pius III died a few months later he was succeeded by Julius II, a sworn enemy of the Borgias. It looked as if Borgia's position was untenable, but Julius II unexpectedly chose to confirm him in his position, even using Borgia to pacify an uprising against papal authority in the Romagna. With a masterstroke worthy of Borgia himself, Julius II then arrested Borgia; in order to regain his freedom, he was obliged to surrender the Romagna cities to direct papal control. With no power base, or powerful backers, Borgia was forced to flee Italy and died three years later in Spain.

In *The Prince*, Machiavelli would attribute this drastic reversal of fortune to Borgia's illness and consequent lack of ruthless decisiveness. 'He should never have allowed the papacy to go to one of those cardinals he had offended, nor to someone who, once elected, had cause to fear him, for men attack either through fear or hate.' Having started in Machiavellian fashion, Julius II continued likewise. His first move was to ally with the French in order to drive out the Venetians from papal territory, which they had occupied after Borgia's flight. In keeping with his vigorous views on clerical behaviour, Julius II led the campaign himself, insisting that his twenty-four resident cardinals should accompany him. The result was a lamentable sight: aged and overweight cardinals were soon trailing far behind the papal troops and their enthusiastic commander. Only young Cardinal Giovanni Medici acquitted himself with valour; plump and near-sighted he may have been, but he certainly knew how to encourage the troops – and Julius II was highly impressed.

Having used the French to defeat the Venetians, Julius now revealed his underlying strategy, which was to rid Italy of the 'barbarian invaders' (that is, the French). He summoned another Holy League, which included Naples, the Holy Roman Emperor and a somewhat chastened Venice; Florence, which remained allied to France, prudently decided to remain neutral. The French king Louis XII was so outraged at the pope's volte-face that he ordered a convocation of French cardinals with the aim of deposing Julius II; and to the consternation of Florence, Louis XII decided to hold this convocation in the newly recaptured city of Pisa.

Pope Julius II chose to see Florence's neutral stance as a betrayal of Italy and the Holy League, for which he vowed Florence would pay dearly. But first he had to deal with the French, who still held Bologna and much of Lombardy. Julius II now despatched his papal army, which included both Italian and formidable Spanish troops, under the leadership of Cardinal Medici. The papal army consisted of no fewer than 3,000 cavalry supported by 20,000 infantry; and Julius II promised his faithful young cardinal that if he was successful against the French, he could then march on Florence and install himself as ruler of the city.

On Easter Saturday 1512 the large French army, under its dashing young commander Gaston de Foix, lined up in formation on the flat plain outside Ravenna, by the banks of the Ronco. Arrayed in line were 24,000 French infantry and 4,000 archers. Opposite them, the Spanish and Italian troops of the papal forces took up their positions under the shouts of their ensigns. Then Cardinal Medici, dressed in his red cardinal's robes, rode out on his white charger to address his massed troops. In a ringing voice, he called upon them to fight valiantly for the pope and pray to God for a glorious victory over the foreigners. (What did his Spanish listeners make of this, one wonders?) The troops then marched bravely into battle under the proud gaze of their commander, though as the contemporary historian Guicciardini records: 'For the more active part of warlike operations, the Cardinal Medici was, indeed, in a great degree disqualified by the imperfection of his sight.'

By now the papal troops, as well as the French, were equipped with a formidable array of cannons, and as the battle began the rows of advancing infantrymen on either side were soon being mown down by the constant volleys of cannonballs. The result was one of the worst slaughters in European history up to this date: 10,500 French were killed, but there were even more casualties amongst the Spanish troops. As a result the French claimed victory, and when this news reached Florence the relieved citizens lit celebratory bonfires in the streets.

After the battle, Cardinal Medici dismounted from his horse and passed amongst the fallen, attempting to give solace to the wounded and dying. This would have been all they received; there were no physicians wandering the battlefield as the spring daylight slowly failed over the howling, the groaning and the more fortunate dead. Even the French commander Gaston de Foix, lying in his death throes beside his horse, his tunic spattered with his own brains, could have expected no medical assistance. One can only imagine the feelings of Cardinal Medici as he for once fulfilled the true role for which he had been ordained; though it is easier to imagine his consequent feelings when a passing troop of French soldiers arrived on the scene and took him prisoner.

Despite their 'victory', the French decided to return north across the Alps; Cardinal Medici's object had been achieved, though ironically he was forced to accompany them – such a favoured cardinal would fetch a fine ransom. But there was always a lot more to Giovanni de' Medici than met the eye. Astonishingly he effected a daring escape: dressed as an unlikely foot soldier, he managed to slip past his captors, whereupon he is said to have eluded his pursuers by secreting himself in a pigeon house.

When Cardinal Medici arrived back at the headquarters of his Spanish troops, he received word from Julius II that he could now march on Tuscany and install himself as the ruler of Florence. Anxious to avoid bloodshed, Cardinal Medici sent a note ahead to Soderini, asking him to surrender. Soderini refused — though not without first calling a Parlamento and consulting the assembled inhabitants of the city. Soderini knew that he now had Machiavelli's militia of 9,000 men at his disposal; by this stage, Cardinal Medici's depleted Spanish troops numbered only just over half as many.

Machiavelli began preparing the city's defences as Cardinal Medici advanced towards the small town of Prato, some ten miles to the north-west. Unfortunately, at the approach of the dreaded Spanish troops, the Prato militia simply threw down their arms and ran away. Geared up to fight, the Spanish forces stormed the defenceless city and a scene of hideous mayhem ensued: for two days the Spanish soldiers went on a rampage of raping, looting and murder. According to a contemporary report: 'the nuns of the invaded convents were forced to submit to the unnatural as well as the natural lusts of the soldiers. In the streets, mothers threw their daughters into wells and jumped in after them . . .' The troops were well beyond the control of their commander, who did his best to alleviate the situation; in the midst of the panic and pandemonium, Cardinal Medici attempted to barricade as many women as possible in the local church for their own safety. In all, more than 4,000 people would eventually be killed during the sacking of Prato, one of the worst atrocities of the time.

When news of this reached Florence, terror spread throughout the city. A group of Medici supporters made their way to the Palazzo della Signoria and demanded Soderini's resignation. He complied at once, despatching Machiavelli to inform Cardinal Medici of his actions and requesting safe passage out of the city. This was granted, and Soderini fled. Later, papal agents were sent in pursuit of him, but he managed to escape across the Adriatic to the port of Ragusa (modern Dubrovnik), which was a Christian vassalate of the Ottoman Empire beyond papal reach, and here he began a life in exile.

On 1 September 1512 Cardinal Medici, accompanied by his cousin Giulio, entered Florence. After eighteen years, the Medici were back as rulers of the city. For the first few months Cardinal Giovanni himself would rule the city, before handing over to his younger brother Giuliano de' Medici, named after his uncle who had been murdered in the Pazzi conspiracy.

Surprisingly, it was two months after the Medici return before Machiavelli was finally dismissed from his post. He was then punished; stripped of office (for supporting Soderini), stripped of his citizenship (a deep public humiliation) and fined 1,000 florins (effectively bankrupted), he was banished from the city and exiled to the smallholding seven miles south of the city that he had inherited from his father. Just forty-three, his life was in ruins.

Yet worse was to come. Four months later, in February 1513, a plot to assassinate Giuliano de' Medici, the new ruler of the city, was uncovered. One of the conspirators was found to have a list of twenty leading citizens who might be in favour of their cause, if they succeeded. Machiavelli's name was on the list, and a warrant was issued for his arrest.

As soon as news of this reached Machiavelli, he hurried to Florence and surrendered himself to the authorities. He had wished to demonstrate his innocence, but to his consternation he was flung into the Bargello. Eventually he was subjected to torture: four excruciating drops on the *strappado* (which had proved enough to make Savonarola confess to heresy). Machiavelli was middle-aged and of no great physique, but nonetheless he bore up well; referring later to these events and to his torture, he stressed his pride that 'I have borne them so straightforwardly that I love myself for it.' This is probably no exaggeration: had he confessed to any knowledge of the plot – even falsely, just to put an end to the agony – he would certainly have been executed.

Fortunately, it was accepted that he was innocent; even so, this experience had a marked effect upon Machiavelli. When he came to write his political theory, it would emphasise the role of torture; in order to rule successfully, a prince must 'be held in constant fear, owing to the punishment he may inflict'. Machiavelli was speaking from first-hand experience here – laws and moral sanctions carried extra force when they were backed by fear of torture.

Machiavelli was detained in the Bargello for a further two months and then released, whereupon he returned to his country smallholding in despair. He would later tell of his life here, and of how amidst the Tuscan hills he cultivated his olive trees and his vineyard, supervising the husbandry of his few goats and sheep; when the sun went down at the end of the day, he retired to the local inn and played cards with the baker and the miller. A pleasant easy-going life, yet he hated it; he still dreamed of returning to politics.

Machiavelli began sending a stream of letters to the new rulers of Florence, but these make sad reading. He set his considerable literary talents to composing abject begging letters, as well as winsomely flattering poems, which would be interspersed with occasional snippets of advice on matters of the day, drawn from the wealth of his experience. But all his letters were ignored; enemies and former rivals now stood between him and the seat of power, and they made sure that his letters were never received – his expert and original advice would frequently be used, but only to further the career of someone else. Machiavelli's despair curdled into bitterness, and he wrote to a friend of his situation: 'Caught in this way among the lice, I wipe the mould from my brain and relive the feeling of being ill-treated by fate.'

In the autumn of 1513, Machiavelli sat down and began writing *The Prince*. Working in the white heat of inspiration, he had completed it by the end of the year. This contained the distillation of his life's experience in politics; all that he had learned in the service of Florence during one of the most difficult and dangerous periods of its history was boiled down to a series of simple but profound truths – each illustrated by telling examples from past history. This would be a new political philosophy of government, no less; and unlike all previous attempts, this would be practical, rather than theoretical or utopian. It would describe what *did* happen (and its consequences), rather than what *ought* to happen.

Machiavelli's despair had stripped bare the illusions of life; now, as if for the first time, he saw (and wrote down) the pitiless truth that underlay all political reality. What he claimed to describe was a clear and uncompromising picture of the world as it is, and always has been throughout history. *The Prince* addressed the ruler of a state, informing him of the best way to use his power, and maintain it, as long and as efficiently as possible. These pragmatic and efficient rules were Machiavelli's political science: 'A prince who desires to maintain his position must learn to be not always good, but to be so or not as needs may require.' A ruler had to learn to lie, to cheat, to deceive – in order to survive; he had to learn how (and when) to betray even his closest allies and friends. In this science there were no moral principles, only practical ones; ruthlessness was obligatory if one wished to stay in power, and a ruler was only a ruler as long as he was in power.

However, there were always events that remained beyond a prince's immediate control. The reality of politics was simply a struggle between two forces. One was *virtù*, which was not to be mistaken for virtue: in Machiavelli's Italian sense, *virtù* meant potency or power, deriving from the Latin *vir*, meaning 'man', and the exercise of *virtù* was control. The other force was *fortuna* – chance, destiny or fortune, which attempted to disrupt *virtù*, but was not entirely beyond its control. Reflecting the prejudices of his age, and the Italian language, Machiavelli characterised *virtù* as masculine and *fortuna* as feminine: his advice for dealing with *fortuna* was as politically incorrect (in our modern sense) as the rest of his philosophy: 'It is better to be impetuous than cautious, because *fortuna* is a woman, and if you wish to control her it is necessary to restrain and beat her.'

Machiavelli understood that science, as such, was neither ethical nor compassionate – it either worked or it did not. What he set down was filled with amoral psychological insight; what he sought was the most successful and ruthless way in which political science can be made to work. Machiavelli is often misunderstood here; his ultimate motive was to make Italy great again, as it was in Roman times, and his ruthless 'science' would enable a ruler to achieve that aim. His means would be justified by this end – though Machiavelli did not emphasise this aim sufficiently, and as a result we tend to concentrate on the means that he advocated.

The importance of *The Prince* would be profound, marking a crucial step in our European political self-understanding. Here was the necessary hypocrisy we needed to live as moral beings within an efficiently ruled society, one that sought to thrive (or simply survive) on the international scene. This remains the pluralism at the heart of Western culture: the inherent contradiction between spiritual and civil life, between the values of our principles and the values of our practice. Such pluralism involves the ability to accept this dichotomy and live with it, which in turn involves a logic-defying sophistication (or cynicism). Not always wittingly, the

Medici and Florence well illustrate the steps towards this Western self-understanding. First, Cosimo de' Medici wrestled with the contradiction between the sin of usury and the salvation of his soul, being willing in fact to give up neither. Next, Savonarola demonstrated the impossibility of religious fundamentalism in a commercially and politically viable society. Later Machiavelli showed the fundamental division between ethics and the science of government: the pluralism by which we have learned to live. This is the uncomfortable and unsettling truth, an unresolvable contradiction, which many see as the grit in the oyster that would in the coming centuries drive Western civilisation to its world dominance.

But Machiavelli's message would not bring him any success. Although he dedicated *The Prince* first to one member of the Medici family and then to another, they were not interested; such ideas win few friends. In his exile he would turn to literature, and his bitter black comedy *La Mandragola* (The Mandrake) is widely regarded as the first comic masterpiece written in the Italian language. Years later the Medici would relent slightly, and Machiavelli would be commissioned to write *The History of Florence*. This is an illuminating work, but is of course biased in favour of the Medici view of events, for Machiavelli hoped it would lead to a government appointment. He did receive two minor jobs — an unimportant mission to Lucca, and a post as a supervisor of the city walls — but never returned to high office, and in 1527 he died an impoverished and disappointed man. Five years later the first edition of *The Prince* would appear in Italian, and it would soon be translated into all major European languages. As a result, Machiavelli's name would become a byword for evil throughout the continent, which found his uncomfortable truth so difficult to accept. Despite this, *The Prince* has not been out of print in English for more than 400 years. The Medici's rejection of *The Prince* would be particularly ironic: here was the ideal handbook on how to be a godfather of the Italian Renaissance.

21

Rome and the Lion Pope

WHEN CARDINAL GIOVANNI de' Medici set about restoring Medici rule in Florence, he followed the example established by his father Lorenzo the Magnificent: a series of celebrations was organised. Pageants, which had been banned since Savonarola's time, were staged in the Piazza della Signoria, and tables dispensing free cakes and wine were set up in the Via Larga, outside the newly reoccupied Palazzo Medici. At the same time, a sweeping political transformation was also put in place: the likes of Machiavelli were systematically dismissed from their government posts and replaced by Medici men, and the republic's standing army was disbanded. The *gonfaloniere*'s term of office was reduced to one year and there was a reversal of foreign policy, with Florence joining Julius II's Holy League.

Yet in February 1513, within six months of the Medici reinstatement, news reached Florence that Pope Julius II was dying. By this time Cardinal Medici's health, never good at the best of times, had undergone a severe relapse as a result of his uncharacteristic exertions. He had begun suffering from a stomach ulcer, and still had an exceedingly painful anal fistula caused by his long period in the saddle during his military campaigns. Despite these disabilities, the cardinal knew that his presence in Rome was imperative if he was to have any influence on the conclave of cardinals that would be called to elect the pope's successor. He ordered that he be carried on a litter and was rushed in great pain along the bumpy 150-mile road to Rome, only to discover on his arrival in early March that Julius II had already died. However, by now Cardinal Medici was too ill to do anything but retire to bed for a week.

Meanwhile the conclave of cardinals that met to choose the next pope had already begun its traditional proceedings. In order that no outside influence could be exerted, the cardinals retired to sealed quarters, which they were not permitted to leave until they had reached their decision; even the windows were sealed, and only meals were allowed into the conclave. As the days passed, and the heat rose in the sealed chambers, the atmosphere and the need for a change of clothes became ever more conducive to an end to the bickering. When the proceedings became even more extended, the quality and quantity of the meals were reduced. By the time Cardinal Medici was admitted, the assembly of twenty-five stout cardinals in their malodorous red robes was down to one meal a day, of similar quality to that served to the novices in the strictest monasteries.

Throughout Cardinal Medici's earlier years in Rome, he had assiduously cultivated the friendship of the many powerful cardinals around Julius II. His cultured fun-loving nature, his great generosity and evident intelligence, as well as his closeness to the source of power, had stood him in good stead. Many of these friends were now willing to vote for him as a compromise candidate, while others were willing to vote for him for two main reasons. Despite his heroic efforts during papal campaigns, it was generally understood that Cardinal Medici was not by nature a belligerent character, and would therefore not involve the papacy in another endless series of military adventures, like Julius II. Many of those present had fond memories of the days when Cardinal Medici's father, Lorenzo the Magnificent, had done so much to maintain peace in Italy. The second point in Cardinal Medici's favour was that he was vastly overweight and quite obviously very ill; if choosing him did turn out to be a mistake, he would probably be dead in a couple of years anyway. But these arguments were implacably opposed by a faction headed by Cardinal Francesco Soderini, the brother of the deposed *gonfaloniere* of Florence, Piero; and despite the deteriorating domestic conditions, to say nothing of the increasingly meagre diet, the deadlock could not be broken. The conclave bickered and pleaded around the table, while secret horse-trading was attempted in the reeking latrines.

During an interval from the table, Cardinal Medici quietly approached Cardinal Soderini and began exercising his considerable charm. Evidence of the power of this can be seen in the fact that Cardinal Soderini finally decided to support Cardinal Medici's candidacy, though this charm had required the backing of certain promises. Piero Soderini, the exiled former *gonfaloniere*, would be recalled from his exile in Ragusa; and although Cardinal Medici was insistent that Piero would not be allowed to return to Florence, he would be permitted to settle in Rome, where he would be generously provided for until the end of his days. Also, Cardinal Medici's young nephew Lorenzo (son of Piero the Unfortunate) – a possible future ruler of Florence – was promised in marriage to one of Cardinal Soderini's nieces; in this way the Soderini family would be joined to the new rulers of Florence, and would be united to the family of the new pope, thus holding a position of considerable power and influence for the future.

To the great relief of the assembled long-suffering cardinals, Cardinal Medici was finally elected as the next pope. In keeping with the warlike names taken by his predecessors (Alexander VI, after Alexander the Great; Julius II, after Julius Caesar), he decided to take on the name Leo X. This was intended to show lion-like qualities of courage and magnanimity; it was also, as all citizens of Florence would have understood, a reference to the city's mascots, who still inhabited their cage in the Via dei Leoni.

According to a report that reached the Venetian ambassador, the new Pope Leo X exclaimed to his young brother Giuliano: 'God has given us the Papacy. Let us enjoy it.' This certainly set the mood of the new papacy, and such feelings quickly spread further afield. When Giuliano de' Medici, who now ruled Florence in his brother's absence, arrived home in the wake of the news, the city embarked on a series of celebrations that were to last several days. Though these were doubtless encouraged by Giuliano, there is little doubt that they were for the most part geniunely felt; Leo X was the first pope to have come from Florence, and as such brought great honour to his native city. To cries of '*Palle! Palle!*' and '*Papa Leone!*' ('Lion Pope'), bonfires were lit in the piazzas and cannons sounded, while the night sky was set ablaze with *fuochi d'artificio* (fireworks), which had arrived from China a century or so previously as a largely military device, but whose celebratory potential was now beginning to be exploited to the full in Italy.

The papacy that Leo X inherited had essentially three separate functions. Firstly, the pope was the successor to St Peter, the disciple whom Christ had chosen to fulfil his mission on earth, and as such the pope was the ultimate arbitrator, interpreter and creator of Christian doctrine.

It is ironic that this duty should fall to a man whose belief in God was far from being a central part of his life; indeed, his faith appears to have been of such a tenuous nature that, with some justification, it has been suggested that he was agnostic. His early education was humanist, concentrating on the pagan ancient classics, and this had been conducted by Poliziano, who showed little sign of any belief in God at this time; similarly, the young future pope's later exposure to the preaching of Savonarola had no positive religious effect whatsoever, and may even have tipped the balance the other way. If, as seems likely, Leo X was agnostic, he would surprisingly have been the first pope for whom the existence of the deity was not a matter of certainty. Villains like Alexander VI, and many roguish predecessors, were far too spiritually primitive and superstitious to think of questioning the existence of God; their hypocrisy was as ingrained as their orthodoxy in belief – in their view, heretic popes went to Hell. Leo X, on the other hand, was highly intelligent, yet well educated enough to know the rules; he went through the observances in a pious manner, and in public his personal behaviour exhibited many of the Christian virtues. Unlike some of his predecessors, the first agnostic pope was also an expert theologian, and fully understood what was required in doctrinal matters; it was only the strength of his faith in such doctrines that was lacking. In this aspect at least, he fitted the *ethos* of Machiavellian rule, and his papacy would be none the worse for it.

The second aspect of the papacy that Leo X inherited was his princely power as ruler of the Papal States, which now effectively occupied a large region of the Romagna. In Leo X's case, this temporal power also extended to the Florentine Republic, which he continued to govern despite his younger brother Giuliano de' Medici's nominal rule. All pretence of Medici subterfuge was now abandoned, and Leo X created his brother 'Captain General of the Florentine Republic'. Paradoxically, the pope's external rule of Florence was the main guarantee of the republic's continuing independence, for without him Florence would not have survived as a separate state.

In recent times, Florence had been most seriously threatened by Cesare Borgia, acting for the pope; Leo X's accession ensured not only that there would be no threat from the papacy, but that it could rely on the backing of the papacy. To ensure that this connection was reinforced, Leo X appointed his illegitimate cousin Giulio, his closest and most trusted confidant, as Archbishop of Florence.

The third aspect of the pope's rule was as head of the Catholic Church, an administration that spanned virtually all of Christendom. The Orthodox Church had survived the fall of Constantinople only in Russia and pockets of the Balkans, whilst Roman Catholic Christendom had by this stage expanded far beyond Europe to include the Americas, and would soon include dioceses in Africa, India and the Far East. Appointments, clerical dues and taxation now brought the papacy vast incomes from a world-wide domain.

Leo X quickly followed the administrative example of his predecessors by appointing members of the Medici family to lucrative posts, whose grateful occupants could then be relied on for support. Such apppointments were not limited to the Church; Leo X's nephew Lorenzo was created Duke of Urbino, with the intention that he would one day rule over a Medici kingdom to be created in the Romagna. Having risen to the papacy, the Medici would now begin to reveal even greater ambitions, the blueprint of which had surely been laid down by Lorenzo the Magnificent, the first Medici to take on a central role in Italian politics and thus understand its mechanisms from the inside. Here his huge ambitions curiously mirrored Machiavelli's ideas: power should be expanded by whatever means possible, where necessary by planning far in advance and using the utmost deviousness. Lorenzo the Magnificent must have passed on these ideas to his sons, though Piero the Unfortunate had been unable to fulfil them, owing to circumstances and character. Yet Lorenzo may well have foreseen such an eventuality, and have felt that he was in fact entrusting the fate of the Medicis to Giovanni, the future Leo X – to such an extent that Lorenzo the Magnificent's agenda may be regarded as the secret guiding hand of Leo X's political policy.

In the light of this, even seemingly minor examples of Leo X's policy can become illuminated as part of a grand strategy. Leo X had promised his cousin Giulio, the new Archbishop of Florence, that if he became pope he would make him a cardinal. Unfortunately, this was not possible on account of Giulio's illegitimacy; technically children born out of wedlock could not become cardinals. Admittedly, Alexander VI had made his illegitimate son Cesare Borgia a cardinal, but this had remained open to later dispute. For reasons that will only gradually emerge, Leo X wished there to be no grounds for dispute whatsoever in Giulio's case. He therefore set up a special Papal Commission to 'investigate' the matter of Giulio's illegitimacy; the implicit message was plain, and within a short time the commission returned with its finding that Giulio's father and mother had in fact been 'married in secret' at the time of his conception. As a result Giulio de' Medici, the son of Lorenzo the Magnificent's beloved murdered brother, received his promised cardinal's hat. And as we shall see, this seemingly trivial act of nepotism would in the years to come have repercussions that changed the course of European history.

Other promises by Leo X regarding members of the family were not always kept. Piero Soderini was recalled from his exile in Ragusa, but Cardinal Francesco Soderini waited in vain to hear of his niece's betrothal to Leo X's nephew Lorenzo de' Medici. The pope had other more ambitious plans for Lorenzo, which make it plain that he never had any intention of keeping the promise that brought him the papacy. Away in lowly exile in a farmhouse outside Florence, Machiavelli could only watch in silent envy.

Such were the matters within Leo X's political control, though he was quickly to be made aware that several important political matters lay far beyond his control. Within months of assuming the papacy, he was approached by emissaries of the powerful Ferdinand I of Spain (who now controlled Naples) and the English king Henry VIII, with the aim of forming an alliance against the French. Not wishing to upset Louis XII, Leo X diplomatically decided against this offer. No sooner had he done so than Louis XII crossed the Alps at the head of the French army to assert his long-standing claim to the Dukedom of Milan and the Kingdom of Naples. Once again, the whole of Italy was under threat. Leo X now demonstrated political skills of which his father would have been proud. Without officially joining the Milanese, who together with soldiers of the Spanish and English alliance now faced the advancing French army, Leo X succeeded in turning the balance entirely in their favour. Quickly and quietly he despatched the equivalent of 34,000 golden florins to the Milanese commander, so that he could hire an army of crack Swiss troops. At the ensuing Battle of Novara, twenty miles west of Milan, the French army was put to flight. Shortly afterwards, Leo X took the seemingly bizarre move of signing a new treaty with France, though it will become clear as events unfold that this too was part of Leo X's Machiavellian strategy for the advancement of the Medici.

Then on 1 January 1515 the fifty-three-year-old Louis XII died, and was succeeded by the twenty-one-year-old Francis I, a young man of considerable intellect and verve who had been brought up on chivalrous tales of French conquest in Italy. Inspired by dreams of glory, Francis I immediately began assembling a huge army in preparation for a full-scale invasion of Italy; in consternation, Leo X turned to his advisers.

One result of this was that Machiavelli's opinion was sought; the previous allusion to Machiavelli following Leo X's political activities in silent envy was no figure of speech, Machiavelli's expert opinion was still quietly sought on occasion. But apparently this only depressed him still further, emphasising how distant he was from the actual events taking place on the political stage where he himself had once played his part. His advice was never acknowledged, and seldom followed. On this occasion he advised that Leo X's only hope was to seek an alliance with the French, in an attempt to avoid any invasion of Florentine or the papal territories. The young Francis I could be persuaded that such diversions would only detract from his real purpose. But Machiavelli's advice was once again ignored; Leo X decided the only chance to save Italy was to form an alliance with the Spanish and the Holy Roman Emperor, and resist any invasion.

In the summer of 1515 Francis I crossed the Alps with an army of 100,000 men, the largest yet seen in Italy. They were confronted, at the Battle of Marignano just outside Milan, by the forces of the Papal Alliance, supported by the formidable Swiss. Francis I fearlessly charged into battle, leading the cavalry at the head of his vast army, and the opposing forces were simply swept aside. Leo X swiftly despatched a note to Francis I, suggesting an alliance, and it was arranged that they should meet for talks in Bologna.

On his way to Bologna, Leo X passed through Florence, where the new pope's first visit to his home city would be greeted with the greatest pageant the city had yet staged. Indeed, so magnificent were the planned festivities that when the pope arrived at the city gates, he was informed that the preparations were not yet complete. Would it be possible for him to retire to a villa at the nearby village of Marignolle for a couple of days, and wait? Leo X graciously acquiesced – while his younger brother Giuliano, Captain General of the Florentine Republic, frantically berated his citizens to finish their preparations.

Some days later, the pope in his bejewelled white robes and glittering tiara rode in triumph into the city, accompanied by his train of scarlet-clad cardinals and a procession of German papal troops in gleaming armour bearing their double-bladed axes. As the papal train passed beneath the succession of magnificent triumphal arches decorated by the city's leading artists, the rotund, beaming Leo X gazed about him at the cheering crowds, squinting at them through his eyeglass. The height of the procession was a display containing a statue of his father Lorenzo the Magnificent, with the motto '*Hic est filius meus dilectus*' ('Here is my beloved son'). When Leo X raised his eyeglass and read this he was seen to be moved to tears. According to the diarist Landucci: 'He ordered silver money to be thrown to the people as he passed through the streets.' The magnificence of the show, to say nothing of its cost, defied belief. 'Several thousand men laboured for more than a month beforehand, working days and holidays alike.' In all there were no fewer than fifteen triumphal arches: the fourth, by no means the most spectacular, occupied 'the whole Piazza di Santa Trinità, and made a circular building like a castle, with 22 square pillars round it, and in the spaces between were hangings of tapestry, and above the pillars was a cornice all round, with certain inscriptions in the frieze'. Landucci asserted: 'a cost of 70,000 florins or more was mentioned, all for things of no duration'. He reflected that for a similar sum 'a splendid temple might have been built in honour of God and to the glory of the city'. Landucci was probably right when he claimed: 'It is unimaginable that any other city or state in the world could have been capable of making such preparations.'

The procession was followed by a grand feast and a pageant, the central feature of which was a young boy painted in gold standing on a pedestal. This was intended to symbolise the rebirth of the golden age of Florence, but it was to be followed by an ominous and equally symbolic devlopment; no sooner had the curtain fallen than the boy was gripped by a sudden mysterious illness and died, inadvertently suffocated by the gold paint covering his body.

What Lorenzo the Magnificent had begun as displays to distract the people and keep them happy had now expanded into a display worthy of a Roman emperor. In Lorenzo's time, the likes of Botticelli and Michelangelo, Leonardo and Poliziano had all worked on such pageants; indicatively, the only celebrated artist who worked on this overblown display was Sansovino. What had once been the *joie de vivre* of genius had now descended into vulgar opulence. The leading poets and philosophers that Cosimo's Florence had nurtured were now dead; the ensuing great artists whom the Medici had sponsored were now only visitors to the city; the leading figures of the Renaissance and even its present godfather lived elsewhere.

Leo X's subsequent arrival at Bologna was a very different matter from his triumphal entry into his home city. The young and vigorous Francis I was not impressed by the waddling middle-aged pope, who took his place before him breathing heavily through his permanently open mouth. But the pope was wise enough to let himself be judged by appearances, whilst quietly exercising his political guile to ensure that this potentially disastrous meeting ended amicably. Leo X opened by baldly denying the 'rumour' that he was in the habit of financing the Swiss army to fight against the French, and Francis I appeared cautiously to accept this (though he knew otherwise). The alliance between France and Leo X was then confirmed, but Francis I extracted a heavy price. Leo X was reluctantly forced to concede to the French king the right to make senior church appointments in his own country, a concession that meant a large loss in papal revenue and influence; the man who had almost become Archbishop of Aix-en-Provence at the age of nine felt humiliated, but decided to put a brave face on it. With a show of magnanimity he appointed the king's tutor a cardinal, whereupon Francis I was so impressed that he made Leo X's brother Giuliano de' Medici the Duke of Nemours. Once again, a seemingly fortuitous result of Leo X's policy would one day have huge repercussions, for a member of the Medici had become aristocracy, and the family now had a foothold in the nobility of France. It is difficult not to see this apparent accident as part of Leo X's covert grand strategy for the family, which it was now becoming clear relied heavily on an alliance with France.

Leo X returned to Rome, and during the next few years he would establish a papacy that was very much a reflection of his remarkable if flawed personality. The city that had overtaken Florence as the centre of the Italian Renaissance would now enter a golden age such as it had not experienced since Ancient Roman times. What in Florence had given way to a grandiose, somewhat tinsel display would become artistic substance in Rome.

Julius II had instigated the large-scale rebuilding of Rome, driving so many wide streets through the ramshackle medieval dwellings that he became known as *'Ruinante'* ('The Wrecker'). The centrepiece of this new Rome was to be St Peter's, whose foundation stone was laid by Julius II in 1506; meanwhile the Urbino-born Donato Bramante had been appointed as architect, and had designed a suitably imposing basilica to house the tomb of St Peter. This was intended to be the papal place of worship, the central church of Christendom, the final destination of all those who set out on the pilgrimage to the Eternal City, and none but the finest artists would be commissioned to decorate its interior. It would also be the largest church in Christendom, a Renaissance masterpiece that was consciously intended to surpass and supersede the great medieval Gothic cathedrals of northern Europe.

Julius II's notorious impatience had forced Bramante to cut a few corners, but in doing so he had liberated architecture from some of its previous restraints. The use of moulded stucco, for instance, replaced painstakingly carved stone. In achieving this liberation, Bramante would found the architectural style now known as Roman High Renaissance – where in earlier years Renaissance architecture had consciously modelled itself on ancient classical buildings, with their restraint of line and form, it now began to develop a sense of confidence and bravura all its own.

When Bramante died in 1514, Leo X appointed the artist Raffaello Sanzio, now better known as Raphael, to succeed him. Raphael, another product of Federigo da Montefeltro's Urbino, would become the leading artist of the Roman High Renaissance. He would receive papal commissions to paint works in the Sistine Chapel, and would transform the art of portraiture. His portrait of Leo X would succeed in the difficult achievement of evoking a profound and serious likeness of its unprepossessing subject, at the same time managing both to gloss over his more preposterous physical features, yet still hint at their existence (see colour plates).

Raphael had been deeply influenced by Michelangelo, but his sunnier temperament softened the tortured muscularity of Michelangelo's style, giving his figures a relaxed poise and clarity of line that were unmistakably his own. His art would go beyond Botticelli's Platonic embodiments to a new level of humanist self-realisation. In his masterpiece *The School of Athens*, the Ancient Greek philosophers are pictured going about their business amidst the arched grandeur of a distinctly Roman Athens. Yet far from being overwhelmed by this imposing architecture, his figures appear completely at home, their physical strength and spiritual presence resonating with their surroundings. Raphael succeeds in making the philosophers utterly human, but at the same time possessed of a dignity which echoes the profundity of their thought.

Raphael would quickly become Leo X's favourite artist, and as the new architect of St Peter's he would transform Bramante's original Greek-cross structure, with four equal aisles, changing it to the present Latin-cross design, a T-shape with three aisles. These would meet at the central altar, beneath which lay the supposed tomb of St Peter; and above this would rise the magnificent soaring dome, a direct descendant of Brunelleschi's original Renaissance dome in Florence. This new dome would both outspan its predecessor and achieve a baroque grace of line that far outshone it.

Leo X and the urbane Raphael appear to have had a temperamental affinity, which cannot be said of his relations with the difficult Michelangelo, with whom he had grown up in the Palazzo Medici. When Leo X became pope, Michelangelo was still at work on Julius II's grandiose tomb; he would refer to this monumental waste of his time, which occupied him on and off for thirty years, as 'the tragedy of the tomb'. Later Leo X, encouraged by his cousin Cardinal Giulio de' Medici, would commission Michelangelo to create a suitably impressive tomb for the Medici, in the family church of San Lorenzo in Florence. This would result in the domed Medici Chapel, with its two pairs of Michelangelo's sculptures, representing 'Day and Night' and 'Dawn and Dusk'. Michelangelo intended the group as a whole to represent 'time, which consumes all things'; and these superb, if somewhat overwrought reclining statues, are filled with that *terribilità* that characterises so much of his best work.

Yet in effect Leo X did little to encourage Michelangelo's work; nor did he appear to appreciate the genius of Leonardo da Vinci. According to a story recounted by Vasari, Leo X gave Leonardo a commission, but when the artist immediately began preparing his varnishes and oils, the pope exclaimed: 'What can be expected of a man who attends to the finishing before he even begins his work?' After this there were no further commissions for Leonardo, and he was only employed on an ambitious but abortive scheme to drain the Pontine marshes. The sad fact is that Leo X, one of the greatest patrons amongst the Renaissance popes, had a rather shallow artistic taste.

In the Medici tradition he collected manuscripts, and added considerably to the Vatican Library, which until this time had remained a poor copy of the Medici Library back home in Florence. Leo X had a deep interest in the classics, and in imitation of his father he also dabbled in poetry; yet most of all he inherited his father's delight in extravagant display – but with a difference. Lorenzo the Magnificent's penchant for display appears as the overflow of a remarkable Renaissance man: here was the largesse of an exceptional human being who strove to emulate the humanist ideal. Leo X had many of his father's qualities – ambition, intellect, bouts of unsuspected energy – yet he was also cursed with an exaggeration of his father's flaws. What in Lorenzo appeared as the foibles of greatness, appeared in Leo X as ridiculous extravagances; he not only looked absurd, but he often behaved in a manner to match.

His extravagances were legendary, and were indulged on an imperial Roman scale, perhaps best exemplified by his favourite dish, which was peacocks' tongues. He enjoyed great banquets where the guests would be entertained by singers, jesters, tumbling dwarfs, even jousters, while the centrepiece feast would consist of dozens of courses, each served and eaten off different sets of silver and golden platters. Some of the dishes also incorporated trivial spectacles – nightingales flying from pies, young boys dressed as cherubs emerging from puddings. Curiously, these extravagances do not seem to have involved sexual misdemeanours; Leo X enjoyed watching the show, rather than taking part in it. He would clap his podgy hands in delight at the sight of revellers dancing in fancy dress beneath the light of a thousand candles at a masked carnival ball, unworried by the fact that many of the masked couples were cardinals dancing with their courtesans. Leo X particularly liked to go hunting, an activity for which he was especially ill-equipped; he may have been a skilled and fearless rider, but unfortunately he could not see where he was going. Eventually a wild boar would be netted and dragged towards him, whereupon Leo X would ride in for the kill, brandishing his pike in one hand, with the other holding his eyeglass pressed to his squinting eye.

Leo X's good-natured but distinctly overblown character is best illustrated by his relationship with his favourite pet: an Indian elephant called Hanno. This animal caused a great stir, being the first of its kind seen in Italy since Hannibal's invasion more than one and a half millennia previously. Hanno had been sent to Leo X as a present by the King of Portugal, along with several exotic birds, two leopards and a number of Persian stallions, all of which had been transported from Asia to Europe by Portugal's merchant-explorers, who were now opening up trade to the Far East. The pope was said to have loved his pet elephant dearly, being particularly touched by the fact that when it entered his presence it would kneel down and trumpet loudly. When Hanno fell ill, Leo X was filled with sorrow; he summoned doctors, and offered to pay the equivalent of 4,000 golden florins to anyone who could cure him. In the end, the ailing Hanno was administered an elephantine purgative, which was said to have weighed 400 ounces, but this had no effect and he soon died, much to the distress of Leo X, who grieved deeply. A vast grave was dug, and the pope commissioned Raphael to paint a full-size portrait of Hanno on the wall above it, while Leo X himself composed a heartfelt Latin epitaph, which was incorporated in the painting.

Yet this good-natured buffoonery was deceptive, for when threatened Leo X was capable of swift and ruthless action. In 1517 a number of cardinals, led by the powerful Cardinal Petrucci and including the resentful Cardinal Soderini, hatched a plot to murder the pope. The intended method of assassination was particularly devilish and painful: the renowned surgeon Battista da Vercelli was hired to poison the bandages used to dress Leo X's anal fistula. In order to establish his innocence, Cardinal Petrucci then left Rome, but Leo X's spies intercepted one of his letters, which hinted at a plot. Vercelli was arrested and put to the rack, where he soon revealed what Cardinal Petrucci had intended; Leo X then sent for Petrucci, guaranteeing him safe conduct, on the honour of the Spanish ambassador. The moment Cardinal Petrucci presented himself before the pope, he was seized by armed men; shrieking curses at the pope's treachery, he was hauled off and flung into the dungeons of Castel Sant'Angelo. The Spanish ambassador, who had been present at Petrucci's seizure, protested loudly and furiously at this outrage to his honour. But Leo X presented a theological argument to defend his action: the pope's promise could not be valid on a guarantee of safe conduct, if this guarantee did not specifically mention that its bearer had intended to murder him. The Spanish ambassador was not impressed by this spurious argument, but was deterred from further comment by the pope's visibly mounting anger.

Leo X now summoned a meeting of his cardinals in full consistory; shouting at the assembled cardinals, he demanded the names of the other conspirators. By now his rage was all but uncontrollable: no one had ever seen the pope display such uncharacteristic passion before – though some present remained unconvinced, feeling that his behaviour was so out of character that it must have been an act. One by one the cardinals were made to step forward and swear, in the name of God, that they were innocent. When it came to Cardinal Soderini, he at first denied all knowledge of the plot, but when Leo X angrily questioned him further, he eventually gave way to tears and confessed, flinging himself to the ground at the pope's feet, begging for mercy and beseeching Leo X to spare his life.

Upon witnessing this abject display, the other guilty cardinals reluctantly came forward and confessed. To the surprise of many, Leo X decided to be magnanimous, and the assembled cardinals were merely ordered to pay a large fine, being required to raise a sum equivalent to 20,000 golden florins.

The grateful cardinals departed, and between them found little difficulty in raising such a sum – only to be informed that there seemed to have been a misunderstanding, for they were required to pay 20,000 florins *each*. This news was greeted with widespread consternation: some grudgingly paid up, while others fled in fear of bankruptcy. The total collected sum was then used to pay off the mounting debts that Leo X's extravagances had incurred. But lest there be any further misunderstandings, the ringleader Cardinal Petrucci was strangled in the dungeons by the pope's Muslim executioner, who was specifically retained for such duties (no Christian executioner would have risked his soul by executing a cardinal).

The surgeon Vercelli was protected by no such niceties: gobbets of flesh were wrenched from his body by red-hot pincers, before he was dragged by horses through the streets to be hanged from a gallows on the bridge of Castel Sant'Angelo.

In order to secure his position, Leo X then took the unprecedented step of creating thirty new cardinals, all relations or proven Medici supporters. Those amongst the new cardinals who could afford it were expected to contribute lavishly to the papal exchequer, whose funds remained alarmingly low, despite the enforced contributions from their guilty predecessors, who had all been stripped of office to make way for the new Medici cardinals. Yet by this stage there were other family matters that needed Leo X's attention: his younger brother Giuliano de' Medici, created Duke of Nemours, had died without producing any legitimate heir. The Medici connection to the French nobility, which Leo X had seen as essential to his master plan, had taken a severe blow. The pope now turned his attentions to his nephew Lorenzo de' Medici, Duke of Urbino, who had succeeded Giuliano as Leo X's proxy ruler of Florence. The young Lorenzo, Duke of Urbino, had begun to assume airs and graces to go with his title; he was the first Medici ruler of Florence to require the deference shown to a ruling prince – the *gonfaloniere* and his Signoria were expected to doff their caps and bow in his presence. The new Captain General of the Florentine Republic seemed to go out of his way to offend the republican sensibilities of his subjects: he even wore a beard, the mark of an aristocrat in the rest of Italy, an affectation which was scorned in Florence. His older and wiser cousin Cardinal Giulio, the Archbishop of Florence, tactfully counselled him to change his ways, but the Duke of Urbino was not interested in the advice of his illegitimate relative.

Regardless of Lorenzo's character, Leo X was forced to accept that the future of the Medici family lay with this arrogant young man. The senior members of the family – Leo X himself, and Cardinal Giulio – were both men of the Church, and as such unable to have recognisable legitimate heirs. There was even a danger that the line might die out, for although the Duke of Urbino was only twenty-five, he had already begun to suffer from tuberculosis and was rumoured to have contracted syphilis. Leo X opened negotiations with his French ally Francis I, and a marriage was arranged: Lorenzo, Duke of Urbino, would take the hand of the

Bourbon princess Madeleine de la Tour d'Auvergne, who was Francis I's cousin. This meant that Medici were now marrying into royal blood; but it soon became clear that there might be a last-minute hitch to Leo X's plans. When Lorenzo, Duke of Urbino returned from France with his new young bride, it was evident that he was mortally ill, and Princess Madeleine too appeared frail and far from well.

In April 1519, Madeleine, Duchess of Urbino, died in childbirth, and within days her husband too had succumbed – yet their child survived and was christened Caterina. This babe-in-arms succeeded to the Duchy of Urbino, and might have succeeded as the infant ruler of Florence, if the Medici had been intent upon founding a strictly hereditary dynasty. But Leo X decided that the time was not right for this, and Cardinal Giulio, the Archbishop of Florence, took over the reins of power in the city. Caterina was brought to Rome; the Medici now had a child of royal blood, and their ambitions had received a powerful boost.

When Leo X had acceded to the papacy, he had inherited the Fifth Lateran Council, which had been summoned in 1511 by his predecessor Julius II. This council had been intended to combat the rival council of French cardinals at Pisa, which had been called by the French king with the object of deposing Julius II. It was widely recognised at the Fifth Lateran Council that the pervasive decadence of the Church put it in great need of reform. Certain measures were discussed over the years as the Lateran Council dragged on, but Leo X showed little interest in these; he was more concerned with papering over the schism which had threatened to develop with the French cardinals, and when this matter was dealt with the council was finally dissolved in 1517. At the council's closing ceremony a missive from the pope was read out announcing a solemn excommunication of anyone who questioned, or put forward their own interpretations of, the findings of the council, without the pope's special permission. Any 'interpretations' that might have allowed for reform were stopped in their tracks.

The papal exchequer was by this stage practically empty, with the finances of the holy see rapidly spiralling beyond control. All the pope's exorbitant entertainments, generous gifts, gambling debts and expensive artistic patronage had to be paid for somehow; yet when the need arose, Leo X would simply sell off a few more ecclesiastical appointments, or call in his bankers and demand another loan. By now even the papal bankers were becoming worried: the papacy appeared to be heading for bankruptcy. In order to cover further loans, the bankers soon began demanding rates of interest up to 40 per cent, to which Leo X blithely signed up, then continued as before.

But there was one project that the papal bankers could not continue financing: the cost of building St Peter's was proving enormous, ruinous even by papal standards. Julius II had realised that the only way to pay for such a vast project was through the widespread sale of indulgences, and now Leo X decided to embark on a further sales initiative in this sphere, on a massive scale. Soon papal agents and licensed priests were journeying from town to town throughout Europe, cajoling and bullying the faithful into paying out hard cash for the scrolls of paper that constituted indulgences. The purchase of such a scroll reduced the various terrors and agonies of Purgatory, through which all Christian souls had to pass in order that their sins be 'purged' so that they could enter Heaven. Indulgences were sold on a sliding scale according to the magnitude of sins; and the higher the price paid, the less time spent in Purgatory.

Indulgences touched a deep nerve throughout Christendom. During the medieval era the notions of Hell and Purgatory, of fearful punishment in the afterlife, had become very real to all Christians. Hideous scenes from these nether regions were depicted in churches, dramatised in holy plays and horrifically evoked in sermons. The prospect of hellfire, or the torments of Purgatory, were a secret fear in every heart, and this was very much a part of the deep psychological hold which the Christian faith exercised over the whole of Europe.

Indulgences both exploited this fear, and at the same time trivialised it, as the notorious call of the indulgence-seller, with his metal collecting bowl, soon became known to all:

> As the coin in the basin rings,
> The soul to Heaven springs!

Indulgence-sellers became the object of widespread resentment; many saw their faith cheapened by such unscrupulous practices – which all knew went to support a church hierarchy whose extravagances had become the tattle of Christendom. In the end, one young German priest decided that he could tolerate it no longer and determined to take action. His name was Martin Luther, and on 31 October 1517 he nailed to the door of Wittenberg Castle church ninety-five Theses demanding reform of the Church.

22

The Pope and the Protestant

THE RENAISSANCE HAD by now reached north of the Alps, permeating all of Europe. The spread of rediscovered ancient learning and the ideas of the new humanists were particularly aided by the European discovery of the ancient Chinese art of printing. The first press had been set up by Johannes Gutenberg in around 1450 at Mainz in Germany; when the city was sacked in 1462 the early printers fled into exile, and printing began to disperse, reaching the Low Countries (1463), Italy (1465) and Paris (1470). The greatest of the northern European humanists was Desiderius Erasmus, who was born in 1469 in the Low Countries. His influential *The Praise of Folly* satirised stale Aristotelianism (as Dame Stultitia), showing that this was not the only way to achieve wisdom; there were different ways of interpreting the world, and many different types of learning.

With the lateral spread of printing through the continent came the vertical spread of literacy down into layers of society that had not previously encountered intellectual stimulation; and a new self-confidence emerged, encouraged by the financial self-confidence of a rising merchant class. What had happened to the Medici in Florence now took place on a minute scale in many rich bourgeois households in all major commercial centres. In the Low Countries, in England and throughout Germany painting and reading flourished; in other countries, such as France, this change was more limited to the courts, yet it even had its effect in conservative gold-rich Spain. As a result, many educated people began in private to question the corrupt and essentially medieval hegemony of the Church, and this criticism took a significant step with Luther, who as a priest was questioning the Church from the *inside*.

Luther had been born in 1483 at the small town of Eisleben in Saxony (now part of Germany), where his father had been a copper miner, but rose to become a town councillor. The young Luther grew up in a pious household and went to the University of Erfurt; it was his father's intention that he should study to become a lawyer, but to his father's anger Luther entered an Augustine monastery, becoming a priest at the age of twenty-four. Three years later, in 1510, Luther was sent on a mission to Rome, where the earnest intellectual young German priest was horrified by the laxity and corruption of the Church. As a result of his ensuing spiritual uncertainties, Luther began reading the Bible with fresh eyes, and this led him back to what he saw as the original spiritual message of Christianity. In his view, this clear and simple faith had been obscured by the teachings of the Church, with its overlaying doctrines and interpretations; for Luther, the soul's salvation lay in its direct faith, not in the teachings of the Church. The pope had no right to claim that he could forgive sins (the very purpose of indulgences), for this could be done by God alone.

Luther's deep faith was allied to a tempestuous character, which made him a moving preacher, but also made him unable to tolerate things in which he could not believe. Eventually he could contain himself no longer, and angrily nailed his ninety-five Theses to the door of the castle church at Wittenberg in 1517; these questioned not only the validity of indulgences, but also the authority of the Church and its leadership by the pope. According to one of the Theses: 'The Pope is richer than Croesus, he would do better to sell St Peter's and give the money to the poor.' Another even questioned the pope's theology: 'Those who believe they can be certain of salvation because they have bought Indulgences will be eternally damned.'

Luther then translated his Theses into German, so that they could reach a far wider audience than Latin-speaking scholars, and it was not long before an enterprising printer started publishing copies of this translation. People far beyond Wittenberg were soon reading Luther's sensational Theses demanding reform of the Church – though even at this late stage Luther insisted that he was not against the Church, only against the practices of the papacy. But the momentum of events would soon overtake this distinction: the movement now known as the Reformation had begun.

When news of Luther's defiance finally reached the pope in 1518, Leo X ordered Luther to Rome to explain himself; but Luther was well aware of the danger that lay in such a journey, and made a series of excuses. Leo X ordered a papal legate, Cardinal Cajetan, to interview Luther, and the result was an angry confrontation; but by now Luther's teaching had struck a chord with many in Germany, and he was protected by the Elector of Saxony, Frederick III.

The Holy Roman Emperor Maximilian I had died that year, and Frederick III was one of the seven 'elector princes' who were to choose the new emperor. Leo X was anxious not to offend him, as he wished for an ally of the papacy to be elected to this powerful position. What had begun as a minor incident at Wittenberg now began to take on wider political consequences. Meanwhile, Luther continued preaching his ideas, and during the summer of 1519 he took part in a series of public debates at Leipzig, which were attended by the Duke of Saxony (the elector's cousin), theologians from the universities at Leipzig and Wittenberg, and many state and Church dignitaries.

The parallels between Luther's ideas and those of the humanist Erasmus were apparent, and many Germans were becoming sympathetic both intellectually and theologically. Erasmus had embarked upon a programme of classical scholarship, returning to the origins of Western civilisation; Luther returned to the Bible as the sole source of theology and spiritual certainty. The humanism that was sweeping through northern Europe would have a considerable effect upon the Reformation, though not on Luther himself, who remained very much a medieval believer. What drove him to challenge the authorities of the Church was not new philosophical ideas; his confrontation was entirely religious, its aim nothing more or less than the search for salvation. All these new ideas were leading some to question the very structure of European society, where the Church stood at the centre of intellectual life and held every aspect of it together – from science to philosophy, from morality to art. Across Europe many were beginning to see a new hope in Luther's ideas, though the situation of the priest himself remained precarious.

During the course of the Leipzig debates Luther was skilfully tricked into supporting the heresies of Jan Hus, who had been burned at the stake after his appearance at the Council of Constance in 1414. When Leo X heard of Luther's support for Hus, he sent a papal bull condemning Luther as a heretic. This would surely be the end of the matter, just as it had been for Jan Hus; but still Luther remained protected by several German nobles.

By now the nineteen-year-old Archduke Charles of Austria, grandson of the deceased Emperor Maximilian I, had been elected as the Holy Roman Emperor Charles V. This was the very man Leo X had not wanted to be elected. King Ferdinand of Spain and Naples had died in 1516, and Charles V had inherited these titles, along with the Spanish Netherlands; add to these the Holy Roman Emperor's territories in Germany, and it was evident that the power of Charles V threatened the whole of Europe. His domains almost completely encircled France, the only other major power, to whom Leo X was allied.

Luther's teachings, and the sympathy of several German princes, were now threatening the Church's hegemony in Saxony and elsewhere in Germany. Leo X knew that the new emperor Charles V was a staunch believer in Church doctrine, and asked him to intervene; the domain of these German princes was after all part of his empire. Charles V was hesitant to stir up trouble in his far-flung empire by overruling the German princes, yet the pope insisted that the emperor had to act on this matter. Finally Charles V agreed, but struck a hard bargain in the process: if he was to condemn Luther, he would in return require the pope's backing for his forthcoming move against Milan, which remained in the hands of the French king Francis I. This meant that Leo X would have to betray his ally.

In 1521, Leo X finally issued a papal bull excommunicating Luther, but this only served to make matters worse. Luther responded by publicly burning the papal bull before an audience of appreciative citizens and university doctors. Frederick III of Saxony placed Luther in his castle at Wittenberg, more for his own protection than to detain him. Luther now began translating the Bible from Latin into vernacular German; the people would no longer require priests to interpret the word of God for them, since they would be able to read it directly for themselves. He also had time to collate his ideas into a coherent alternative doctrine, and much like his celebrated sermons this was filled with rousing words: 'Neither Pope nor bishop nor any ordained man has the right to impose one sylla-ble of law upon any Christian believer . . .'

It was just four years since Luther had nailed his Theses to the door of the castle church at Wittenberg, but already his ideas had begun to spread as far afield as Hungary, France and Bohemia (where many still remembered Jan Hus, secretly regarding him as a national hero and a martyr). When word reached England, Henry VIII was horrified, and wrote *A Vindication* denouncing Luther's ideas; this he dedicated to Leo X as 'a declaration of faith and friendship', and he sent the pope a copy. Leo X was so deeply touched by this loyalty that he despatched a message back to England granting an indulgence to every person who read Henry VIII's tract; he also awarded Henry VIII the title '*Fidei Defensor*' ('Defender of the Faith'), a title which to this day appears beside the monarch's head on British coins, in the abbreviated form of 'FD'.

But Leo X now found that he had more pressing matters to deal with. At the end of November 1521 the Spanish troops of the Holy Roman Emperor Charles V marched north to Milan, where they defeated the French army of Francis I, whose scattered remnants fled back across the Alps. As soon as news of Charles V's victory reached Florence, its ruler Cardinal Giulio de' Medici despatched a messenger to his cousin Pope Leo X, who had gone hunting at his villa outside Rome. That night Leo X sat at an open window of his villa benignly presiding over the bonfire that had been lit in celebration of Charles V's great victory. At last the French had been driven from Italy, which was now back where it had been at the beginning of his papacy. No one quite knew what would happen next; but for a pope who had sworn to enjoy his papacy, no opportunity for celebration would be lost.

According to the official report, the cold November night air affected the pope's chest and he retired to bed suffering from a chill; this quickly became a fever, and within days he was dead. As he died, Leo X was said to have exclaimed: 'Oh God! Oh God!', which has been seen as a definitive contradiction of his alleged agnosticism, though others have seen it as an empty blasphemy that merely confirms it.

Nothing about this incident was what it seemed. Leo X's death was probably murder: the physicians who attended the pope would later report that his death was due to poison, though who was responsible remains unclear; during his eight years as pope Leo X had made many enemies, both in Rome and further afield. Although assassination by poisoning was alien to Francis I's knightly character, he must certainly be considered a strong suspect, for after years of alliance, during which the Medici had even married into the French royal family, Leo X had betrayed him. Whoever was responsible, Leo X was dead – leaving the papal exchequer all but bankrupt, Italy in a state of unresolved confusion, and the Roman Catholic Church falling apart.

23

The Papacy Stays in the Family

ITHIN A MONTH of Leo X's death at the end of 1521, the conclave to elect the next pope was held in Rome. His cousin Cardinal Giulio de' Medici was widely expected to succeed him; it was common knowledge that he had been Leo X's most able adviser, as well as manager of the pope's financial affairs. The fact that Leo X had blithely ignored his cousin's advice, on so many occasions, was widely seen as being responsible for the plight of the papacy – not the influence of Cardinal Giulio de' Medici. On the contrary, Cardinal Giulio appeared to be everything that Leo X was not: he was handsome, thoughtful, saturnine and gifted with good taste. Despite this, many remained steadfast in their opposition to his candidacy.

Cardinal Giulio's candidacy may have had powerful backers, for the Medici cousins had over the years cultivated influential friends in Rome, but they had also made powerful enemies. Cardinal Francesco Soderini for one was determined that there should not be a second Medici pope; and he was unexpectedly supported by Cardinal Pompeo Colonna, one of the thirty-one cardinals created by Leo X, who saw this as his own chance to be elected. When these two were supported by all the French cardinals, who were unwilling to forget Leo X's treachery to their king, there was a stalemate.

Cardinal Giulio now chose to make an astute tactical move. He declared modestly that he was unworthy of such high office; instead, he suggested the little-known Flemish scholar Cardinal Adrian Dedel, an ascetic and deeply spiritual man who had been tutor to the Holy Roman Emperor Charles V. Cardinal Giulio was sure that Cardinal Dedel would be rejected

– on the grounds of his obscurity, his lack of political expertise and the fact that he was not Italian. The selfless suggestion that had been made by Cardinal Giulio de' Medici would then demonstrate to all that he was in fact the ideal candidate. But this move backfired badly, Cardinal Giulio's bluff was called and Cardinal Adrian Dedel was elected as Pope Adrian VI. When the name of the new pope was announced to the waiting crowds outside the papal conclave, the news was greeted with astonished disbelief – there were none of the usual cheers, just silence, followed by a mounting tumult of jeers and catcalls.

The common people had evidently known better than the cardinals what this election would entail, and the appointment of a pope who behaved just as a pope was meant to behave would prove a disaster for the city of Rome. There were no lucrative appointments, no carnivals and pageants, no lavish spending sprees; the pious Adrian VI took up residence in a minor chamber of the papal apartments and proceeded to live on a florin a day, rising to pray before dawn, and eating only a thin gruel served by his fierce old Flemish maidservant. The pope's exemplary lifestyle was viewed by cardinals and citizens alike as barbarism; in their view this was typical northern European behaviour, just the sort of thing one would expect of an unsophisticated non-Italian. But worse was to come: the pope ordered all the cardinals and archbishops resident in Rome to leave the city and take up residence in the dioceses they represented (many of which they had never seen before). There followed a grim exodus from the Eternal City.

Economic life in Rome soon ground to a standstill; and as Vasari put it, many artists were left 'little better than dying of hunger'. With the artists so reduced, other less privileged members of society were inevitably far worse off: cut-throats were reduced to beggary, pickpockets resorted to charity, prostitutes starved, and even the priests were forced into abstemious piety. Not unexpectedly, Adrian VI was to die in 1523 within two years of taking office; the official cause of death was recorded as kidney disease – almost certainly a euphemism for poisoning, an occupational hazard that had now probably accounted for six popes in succession.

This time Cardinal Giulio came to the conclave well prepared; but so also did his sworn enemies Cardinal Francesco Soderini and Cardinal

Pompeo Colonna, who now had the public backing of Francis I as well as all the French cardinals. The result was another deadlock; bribes were offered and received, the usual covert promises were given – but still the stalemate remained. Days turned into weeks, then into a month, then into another, whilst outside the common people began to riot. Nobody could communicate with the cardinals in their sealed conclave, yet somehow news reached them that the rulers of Europe were growing increasingly dissatisfied at this hiatus. The Holy Roman Emperor and Henry VIII of England had made it known that they favoured another Medici pope; and now even Francis I of France agreed with them (convinced that Cardinal Medici would betray the emperor soon enough, and return to an alliance with France). After sixty days, the longest conclave in history, Cardinal Medici was duly elected and became Pope Clement VII.

Clement VII had been brought up in the Medici Palace, and had received the finest humanist education that Medici money could buy. At forty-five, he was old enough to remember dining at table with Lorenzo the Magnificent, sitting alongside the young Michelangelo and the future Leo X as they listened to the likes of Poliziano and Pico della Mirandola discussing philosophy and reciting poetry. Clement VII had inherited his murdered father's good looks, though these tended to lapse into a dark scowl rather than a smile (see colour plates). He had also inherited something of his great-grandfather Cosimo de' Medici's skill with accounts, as well as a strong inclination to his legendary caution, making the new pope hesitant when it came to taking important decisions; and unlike his cousin Leo X, he possessed a deep understanding of art.

While Leo X's lavish patronage had made Raphael rich, his younger and more careful cousin had encouraged the artist to extend himself. It had been Cardinal Giulio de' Medici who had commissioned Raphael's final masterpiece *The Transfiguration*, which had remained unfinished on his premature death at the age of thirty-seven in 1520. In this work Raphael went beyond his habitual grace and elegance to depict a vibrant and multifarious humanity awed by the miraculously transfigured Christ. It is a work of inner tension and brilliance, its lower darkness enclosing the airy lightness of the airborne Christ; and as such, it may be seen as an echo of Clement VII's own spirituality, for despite his worldly indecisiveness and often saturnine appearance, his inner life was illuminated by an unwavering faith.

Such characteristics may well account for his affinity to Michelangelo, who despite his deep and evident faith remained a problematical and unpredictable artist at the best of times. In the years before his papacy, Cardinal Giulio had supervised Michelangelo in his work on the Medici Chapel in Florence, and during his papacy as Clement VII he would commission Michelangelo to paint his *Last Judgement* in the Sistine Chapel. According to Condivi, Clement VII was of the opinion that 'the variety and grandeur would give a wide field for [Michelangelo] to prove the power that was in him'. Clement VII knew what he was doing, though he would not live to see this overwhelming fresco in all its completed glory (see colour plates). The hordes of judged humanity, some ascending, many cast down towards Purgatory and the fires of Hell, are recognisable as Renaissance figures. But this is no simplistic fire-and-brimstone medieval depiction; here is humanity, in all its guises, from saints to the most angst-ridden sinners. The painting stands as a reminder that even strong and self-confident humanists will have to face the final judgement; the Renaissance, for all its transformations, remained essentially religious, while the ideas that would begin to change this still remained in embryo.

Yet Clement VII was in surprisingly close contact with these ideas, and even more surprisingly he was deeply sympathetic towards them. It is known that his secretary Johannes Widmanstadius introduced the pope to the ideas of Copernicus, even delivering a lecture on the new cosmology in the Vatican Garden, which was attended by Clement VII and a number of his senior dignitaries. The contents of this lecture came from Copernicus's *Commentariolus*, which was circulating privately at the time and contained 'Theories of the Motions of Heavenly Objects from Their Arrangements'. Copernicus suggested that the movement of the stars and the planets was best explained by a stationary sun circled by the earth and the other planets, with only the moon circling the earth. This had profound implications, for it meant that the earth, and thus also human beings, were not the centre of God's creation. The medieval idea that man was a microcosm of the macrocosmos (the universe) no longer held; the wealth of interpretation that had gone into this idea, and the meaning it gave to human life, vanished at a stroke. Also, Copernicus's theory was significant in being the first major challenge to the ideas of ancient classical learning which had resurfaced with the Renaissance. This new theory opened the way forward for a novel way of thinking based on observation and experience: what would become scientific thinking.

Clement VII had no difficulty in accepting Copernicus's heliocentric idea, and appeared to see no challenge to his faith in its implications; his Renaissance humanism was open to such progressive theories. Ironically, it would be Luther who rejected Copernicus; although the Reformation represented a progression beyond the constrictive hegemony of the Church, it also preserved many earlier Christian ideas. The Protestant faith that was born out of the Reformation retained intact many medieval notions of faith and learning, and when Copernicus's ideas challenged those of Aristotle, Luther remained heavily on the side of Aristotle.

In the days before his papacy, the future Clement VII had been close to Leonardo da Vinci. He was too young to have witnessed Leonardo's hypothetical stay at the Medici Palace in Florence, but he had certainly known Leonardo during his comparatively lengthy stay in Rome, which began in 1513 at the outset of Leo X's papacy, when the new pope installed Leonardo in his own apartment within the Vatican. These were not good years for Leonardo, who was by now in his sixties and growing old grumpily; he was suffering from hypochondria, which was hardly helped by his extreme mistrust of doctors. He also became highly suspicious of the two German assistants whom Leo X provided for him, and was convinced that they were stealing his ideas. They in their turn reported Leonardo to the pope for 'necromancy', which was not strictly true, though they probably thought otherwise. In fact, Leonardo had merely been conducting anatomical researches, but the dissection of cadavers was not a pursuit that the Church wished to encourage, so Leo X banned Leonardo from this practice. It is also possible that Leonardo was having second thoughts about his youthful, though undeclared, atheism. His notebooks became filled with depictions of great deluges, which were prompted by his forebodings about a second Flood 'that the wrath of God will visit upon the human race'. Even a towering Renaissance mind like Leonardo's was vulnerable when it came to religion. The humanism of Poliziano, Pico and Botticelli had proved fragile, and they had all succumbed to Savonarola; Leonardo, on the other hand, seems to have succumbed to his own conscience, or to the quirks of his own psychology. During this period the simple mirror-writing code which he had used in his notebooks retreated into a more cryptic script, while even some of his more open remarks remained ambiguous. One particularly puzzling entry from this time reads: '*i medici me crearono edesstrussono*', which translates as 'the Medici created and destroyed me'. It would be very revealing if this was what Leonardo actually thought of the Medici, and one wonders how they could have destroyed him. Was this perhaps a temporary irritation, connected with Leo X's ban on dissection, or was it a considered assessment? The trouble is that the word *medici* is also the plural of *medico*, the Italian for doctor, and the latter meaning seems more likely. Leonardo's well-known distrust of doctors could easily have led him to imagine they were destroying him; and if his birth had been difficult, he might also have regarded doctors as 'creating' him – even so, this interpretation too remains problematical.

Yet this period of Leonardo's life was not all clouded with negative thoughts. It was now that he saw the work of Raphael for the first time, which deeply impressed him and would have a marked effect upon his art. Another happy occasion came in 1515, when Leonardo accompanied Leo X on his triumphant entry into Florence, and to his subsequent difficult meeting at Bologna with Francis I, the new young king of France. Leonardo was brought along to amuse, delight and astonish Francis I, and he certainly succeeded. At Leo X's suggestion, Leonardo had constructed a mechanical lion that walked forwards a few steps and then opened its chest to reveal the French fleur-de-lis in the place of its heart, which was intended to symbolise the heartfelt friendship between Leo (the lion) and Francis. The delight caused by this toy may well have smoothed their edgy encounter and contributed to Giuliano de' Medici being created Duke of Nemours. This would have proved a fitting recompense of fortune, for Giuliano had long been close to Leonardo and may well have been his most auspicious patron: there is a possibility that he commissioned the *Mona Lisa* – who may well not have been the wife of the Florentine dignitary Francesco del Giocondo, but instead Giuliano de' Medici's mistress.

Leonardo was certainly commissioned by Leo X, and produced a madonna for the future Clement VII, two of only a few dozen paintings that can be firmly attributed to him. The Medici would be a considerable influence on Leonardo's life, and Leo X's introduction of Leonardo to Francis I at Bologna would prove particularly fateful.

The twenty-one-year-old French king, besides seeing himself as an embodiment of knightly virtues, was also a scholar; as a result, he and Leonardo would establish a deep and lasting rapport. When Francis I returned to his homeland he established a Renaissance court, to which he invited Leonardo. Disgruntled with his life in Rome, the ageing Leonardo accepted and travelled to France, where after less than three years he would die at the age of sixty-seven – according to the sometimes unreliable Vasari, he even died in Francis I's arms.

Another very different artist who was patronised by Clement VII was the goldsmith and sculptor Benvenuto Cellini, who also left a colourful but unreliable account of his times. Cellini was born in Florence in 1500, and early in life made a name for himself as a superb craftsman in gold. As a result of a brawl, he was condemned to death, but fled the city, the first of a series of violent and bloody incidents which punctuated his life.

Cellini arrived in Rome at the age of twenty-three, in the very year that Clement VII ascended to the papacy. The new pope was quick to recognise Cellini's exceptional abilities and gave him a number of commissions, which brought Cellini great renown in Rome. In his *Autobiography* he would later recall how he worked industriously, producing a cornucopia of objets d'art – including coins, altarpieces and a clasp with a papal heraldic device, all of which were brilliantly executed, in his own modest estimation. He also describes how he would often retire to the countryside with his fowling piece and favourite hunting dog Barucco, where he was apparently capable of bringing down two geese with a single shot at a distance of one hundred yards. Cellini's wide-ranging but immovably centred *Autobiography* reveals its author as a braggart, a liar, a thief and even a murderer, but it also contains much illuminating detail concerning the many important figures with whom he came into contact, including Clement VII. Although the series of intimate conversations which he claimed to have had with Clement VII are palpably untrue, there is no doubt that he was close to the pope, and as we shall see he was also present at some of the most crucial events in his life.

Unfortunately, owing to the material in which Cellini so often worked, a large number of his artefacts were later melted down by avaricious vandals, ranging from kings to common thieves. The only fully accredited extant example of his work in gold is a large salt cellar, with reclining male and female nudes, executed for Francis I, which demonstrates beyond question that a promiscuous bisexual braggart and murderer can also be possessed of genius.

Even the quiet and patient Clement VII could become exasperated beyond measure by Cellini. On hearing of yet another escapade, in which he had fatally cracked open a notary's skull, Cellini recalls: 'Livid with rage, the Pope ordered the Governor, who happened to be in the room, to seize me and hang me on the spot where the murder was committed.' Fortunately, before the governor could apprehend Cellini his victim made a miraculous recovery, whereupon the pope pardoned Cellini, allegedly remarking that 'he would not like to lose me for all the world'.

If this incident is to believed, it recounts one of the few occasions when Clement VII acted passionately, swiftly and decisively. Under most circumstances he appears to have been a man of almost icy self-control, but in him the Medici trait of self-contained caution had deepened into a flaw. When the Venetian ambassador reported on the new pope, he remarked: 'He speaks well and sees into everything, but is very timid.' This is perhaps too harsh a judgement; if anything, Clement VII had too much understanding – he could always see both sides of any particular argument. This had made him an excellent close adviser to his cousin Leo X, but hampered his ability to take matters into his own hands. When he had been running Florence, this had not mattered so much, for the party machine took care of most decisions, and his rule had been for the most part competent and astute. But as pope he would have to make decisions that reached far beyond city politics, decisions that required leadership, informed by self-certainty and self-confidence – qualities which may have been undermined by his illegitimacy. Clement VII's psychology seems to have been severely affected by his lack of a true father; Lorenzo the Magnificent may have cared deeply for him, even noted and encouraged his talents, but for Lorenzo his own children always came first. Indicatively, it was not Lorenzo but his son Leo X who brought about the first major advances in the future Clement VII's career.

This flaw of indecisiveness in Clement VII would be noticeable from the very outset of his rule as pope; whether it had fatal consequences for his papacy, or whether these consequences were in fact inevitable, is another matter. The difficulties facing Clement VII on his accession were formidable, and were not helped by his lack of a coherent vision; his moderate way of life may have reformed the behaviour of the papacy at home, but it was the papacy as a whole that stood in desperate need of reform.

Clement VII appeared hampered whichever way he turned. Whilst his enemy Cardinal Colonna continued to plot his downfall, the pope found it all but impossible to buy friends, owing to the emptiness of the papal exchequer. Things looked even more ominous beyond Rome, where Christendom faced the external threat of the formidable Sultan Suleiman the Magnificent, the ruler of the Ottoman Empire, which now occupied the Balkans as far as the Adriatic and was beginning to extend north into Hungary, threatening the whole of central Europe. As if this was not bad enough, Christendom also faced the internal threat of the Protestant movement unleashed by Luther, which was now beginning to spread alarmingly, whilst closer to home, the conflict between the powerful French and the Holy Roman Emperor threatened to tear Italy apart.

Francis I was soon back on Italian soil, leading his army once more towards Milan. Ten years earlier, Leo X had just managed to survive an identical situation at the start of his papacy, and Clement VII's handling of the situation would attempt to be much the same, although fortune and character would work against him. Clement VII joined forces with the Holy Roman Emperor Charles V, together with his Spanish army, and in February 1525 these forces met the French at Pavia, just twenty miles south of Milan. The Spanish army inflicted a crushing defeat and many of the French noblemen-commanders were killed, while Francis I himself was captured and carried off to Spain. He would only be released a year later, having been forced to cede to Charles V the whole of Burgundy, as well as having to renounce his claims to Naples and Milan.

Clement VII quickly understood that the Emperor Charles V now posed a direct threat to the whole of Italy, to say nothing of the rest of Europe, and immediately opened secret negotiations with the newly released Francis I. In 1526 this resulted in the League of Cognac, which joined France, Venice, Milan, and the Papal States, as well as Florence, all in an alliance against the Holy Roman Emperor.

The Emperor Charles V was incensed; but news now reached Rome of a great battle between the Hungarians and the Ottoman army of

Suleiman the Magnificent at Buda, on the banks of the Danube. The historian Guicciardini, who was in Rome as the pope's councillor, relates how they heard that 'the army, gathered of all the nobility and brave men in Hungary, was shattered, a great many killed, and the King himself was slain, together with many of the leading prelates and barons of the realm'. Clement VII at once appealed for 'a universal peace amongst Christians' and for the formation of an armed alliance against the invading infidels, whereupon he summoned his college of cardinals and told them to gather their forces in preparation for a march against the Turks.

Heedless of the greater threat, Cardinal Colonna saw this as his opportunity to strike at Clement VII, and immediately set off for his fortified estates in the foothills of the mountains forty miles south-east of Rome, where he succeeded in raising an army of 800 horsemen and 5,000 foot soldiers. He then marched them to Rome, where according to Guicciardini: 'the Pope had neither his own forces to defend himself; nor did the people of Rome, partly happy at his misfortune and partly judging that public disturbances would not affect them, make any sign of moving in his support'. As a result, Cardinal Colonna quickly overran the city. 'Ready to die', Clement VII took 'his place on the pontifical throne, vested in his pontifical garb and ornaments, following the example of Boniface VIII' (who had been similarly attacked by a Colonna in 1303). However, Clement VII's cardinals eventually managed to persuade him to take refuge in the Castel Sant'Angelo, which certainly saved his life; though in the event Cardinal Colonna was able to extract a humiliating agreement from the pope 'because there were no victuals in the Castello to maintain him'. Clement VII was forced to repudiate the League of Cognac against the Holy Roman Emperor; at the same time Cardinal Colonna and his fellow conspirators were to be granted a special papal pardon granting them immunity from reprisal.

Clement VII's position was now virtually untenable; with his authority undermined and his political strategy in ruins, he appeared to lapse into his habitual state of indecision. Yet on this occasion the appearance belied the reality: acting with some stealth and uncharacteristic speed, the pope arrived at a hasty decision, one that would later be seen as amongst the worst of his life, though its initial effect certainly caught Cardinal Colonna by surprise. Clement VII despatched a large contingent of papal troops to Cardinal Colonna's estates, with orders to lay waste his domains and its fortifications, scatter to the hills those who lived on his estates, and burn his castles to the ground. To add insult to injury, the pope also decreed that Cardinal Colonna himself be stripped of all his Church offices and titles, and be branded as an outlaw, even going so far as to put a price on his head (which added further insult by being disrespectfully low, owing to the lack of funds in the papal exchequer). It was reported that when Cardinal Colonna heard of this, he was plunged into such a fury that the very mention of the pope's name made him shake with rage. Without further ado he marched the remainder of his men south towards Naples, where the Holy Roman Emperor's viceroy was already following the orders of Charles V and assembling an army to 'teach the Pope a lesson he would never forget'.

Meanwhile north of the Alps, Charles V had ordered another of his generals to assemble a vast army to march on Rome. This consisted of *Landsknechte* (mercenaries) recruited from Bavaria and Franconia, mostly Protestants of peasant stock all filled with religious zeal for the march on Rome and further inspired by tales of rich booty. These were led by the formidable but ageing German commander Georg von Frundsberg.

Clement VII's desperate situation was only slightly relieved when papal forces south of Rome managed to check Cardinal Colonna and the Neapolitan troops at Frosinone, the gateway to Colonna's ravaged estates. But by now von Frundsberg's army of *Landsknechte* had begun to make its way south through the Alps. Undeterred by torrential rains, and then the first snowstorms of winter, they forced their way through the ravines of the upper passes, heaving and manhandling the portly von Frundsberg over rocks and snowfields, until finally they made it to the plains of Lombardy. Ragged and hungry after their ordeal, the *Landsknechte* joined forces with the troops of the other imperial commanders, the dashing Philibert, Prince of Orange, and the Duke of Bourbon, who led more Spanish forces. In all, the imperial army in the north now numbered 30,000 men.

By this stage Clement VII was in an agony of indecision, unable to make up his mind whether to defend Rome or sue for a humiliating peace, to brazen out his position by asserting his right as the spiritual leader of Christendom or throw himself on the mercy of Charles V – or simply

Fig 13 Three *Landsknechte*

flee and hope that the Church hierarchy would come to his rescue.
Eventually the pope was persuaded to despatch emissaries, who managed
to negotiate a temporary peace with the Duke of Bourbon and his advancing army. Yet when the motley German *Landsknechte* were informed of this
they were literally up in arms; their payment was dependent on them fighting, and having survived their alpine crossing they were in no mood to
attempt another one empty-handed. Even the continuing rain failed to
douse their ardour, and they shouted down any attempt to address them
by Georg von Frundsberg, who became so outraged at this insubordina-
tion that he had a fit of apoplexy and had to be carried off in a cart to
recover in Ferrara.

The Duke of Bourbon now took charge of the *Landsknechte*, but found himself unable to control the increasingly mutinous and bedraggled elements of his army. Still it continued to rain, supplies were running short and the heavy artillery was becoming bogged down; soon even the disciplined Spanish troops were against the peace, and the Duke of Bourbon caved in, giving the order to march south across the Apennines towards Rome. With a cheer, the Germans surged forward, followed by the more orderly ranks of grim Spaniards.

The torrential rains continued as the army moved rapidly south through the mountains. Contemporary reports speak of the ragged and starving *Landsknechte* accompanied by fanatical Spanish troops storming over the passes and the ravines. In gangs of thirty men with clasped hands, they made their way through the cascading torrents of the swollen mountain streams, driven on by dreams of the gold and plunder that lay ahead.

In Rome, Clement VII was so terrified by the turn of events that he is said to have lapsed into a state of near-deranged apathy from which he could not be roused, his dark hollow-eyed face fixed in an immobile stare. Some of his cardinals were now fleeing the city, while others were barricading themselves in their fortified palaces and burying their valuables. Finally the pope stirred himself into action, only to find that the papal exchequer was empty – there was no money to pay for the defence of the city. In a desperate move to remedy this, Clement VII quickly appointed six of the richest remaining citizens as cardinals, thus raising just over 15,000 florins; but this only plunged him into a state of further indecision. According to Guicciardini: 'The Pope's conscience was more deeply upset over this flagrant bribery than he was at the prospect of the end of the Papacy and Christendom in ruins.' By now 3,000 people had taken refuge in the all but impregnable Castel Sant'Angelo, which this time had been properly provisioned for a siege. Yet still Clement VII dithered in the papal palace, refusing all entreaties to save himself, as the imperial army swarmed down the approaches to the Eternal City.

On the morning of 6 May 1527 the imperial army arrived at the walls of Rome, where overnight a thick mist had risen from the Tiber. Inside the papal palace, Clement VII had been on his knees since the early hours, praying frantically for divine intervention. As the enemy emerged through the mist and began to scale the walls, the defenders rushed to the ramparts. Cellini, who was present, describes the scene: 'When we got up onto the city walls we could see below the formidable massed ranks of the Duke of Bourbon's army, which were battling their utmost to break into the city. The fighting was particularly bitter where we were, and already many young men had been killed by the attackers. The whole place was covered in the thickest fog and the fighting was desperate.' Cellini described how his companion-in-arms panicked and desperately begged him to flee, but the brave goldsmith managed to rally his friend. By now the imperial troops had a number of ladders secure against the walls; Cellini and the defenders fired down at them with their arquebuses, and amidst the mist and shouts and gunfire there was chaos. Several sources report how at the beginning of the assault the Duke of Bourbon stood at the forefront of his troops bravely rallying them and urging them on. At one stage a pocket of swirling mist cleared, and Cellini described how, up on the ramparts: 'I pointed my arquebus at the thickest and most packed group of the enemy, aiming directly at a man I could see standing out from the rest. It was so foggy I could not even see whether he was on foot or on horseback.' If Cellini is to be believed, this was how he shot dead the leader of the imperial troops; and indeed, other historical sources confirm that the Duke of Bourbon was shot by an arquebus as he stood below the walls, though none specify who did this deed.

The assault troops were now joined by the forces of Cardinal Colonna, and the defenders found themselves outnumbered; as the walls were scaled, the inhabitants of the city panicked, fleeing for the pope's fortress at Castel Sant'Angelo. The tumult was so great that many were trampled to death on the approaching bridge over the Tiber; under such conditions it was impossible to blow up the bridge to prevent a river crossing by the imperial troops into the heart of Rome. As the populace besieged Castel Sant'Angelo, a last cardinal was to be seen being hauled up the wall in a basket. Cellini and his companions fled the city walls and made their way as best they could through the fleeing throng towards the Castel. 'It was difficult for us to flee for the Castel, because our officers were wounding or killing anyone who fled from the fighting at the city walls. The enemy had already broken into the city and were chasing after us by the time we managed to reach the gate of the Castel. Luckily the castellan had cleared the crowd as he wanted to drop the portcullis, so the four of us were able to rush in at the last moment and push our way inside.'

Fig 14 Castel Sant'Angelo

Amazingly, at this stage Clement VII was still on his knees in the oratory of the papal palace; in between imploring him to leave, his weeping attendants informed him of the latest news of the fighting. When the pope heard that the Duke of Bourbon had been killed, he was momentarily emboldened. Assuming an air of majesty he ascended to the papal throne, drawing his episcopal robes about him; once again, he declared that he would confront his enemies like Boniface VIII. From outside, there was a sudden tumult of roars and cries as the enemy troops arrived and began hacking their way through the streets of terrified citizens huddled around the papal palace. Clement VII became distraught, weeping; at the last moment he was persuaded to rush for the safety of the Castel, making his way along the raised stone passage that linked it to his palace (a feature prudently installed by the Borgia pope Alexander VI). With Clement VII's attendants holding up his long pontifical robes behind him so that he could run faster, he hurried along the passageway over the street, while through the apertures in the passage wall the *Landsknechte* could be seen below butchering the priests and the citizens with their halberds. At this point, in the words of the papal historian Paolo Giovo, who was running alongside the pope: 'I flung my own purple cloak about his head and shoulders, lest some Barbarian rascal in the crowd below might recognise the Pope by his white rochet, as he was passing a window, and take a chance shot at his fleeting form.' Thus Clement VII finally made it to the safety of the Castel Sant'Angelo.

By the end of the day the city was overrun and 8,000 people had been killed. But this was only the beginning; on the morning of the next day the Sack of Rome began with a vengeance. Inflamed after a night's carousing, the *Landsknechte* began ransacking the churches and breaking into the convents to attack the nuns. Spanish troops were seen conducting vicious tortures and mutilations on their hapless victims, while the impoverished southern Italian troops were said to have pillaged even the hovels of the watermen, carrying off everything down to the pots and nails. Other reports tell of holy relics employed for target practice, piles of ancient manuscripts used as litter for horses, Martin Luther's name scratched by a pike in large letters across a Raphael fresco. The palaces of the cardinals and dignitaries were broken into and pillaged, the women raped, the masters stripped, subjected to gross indignities and then ransomed for huge sums. Those not worth a ransom were lucky to die. According to a contemporary eyewitness: 'Hell hath nothing to compare with the present state of Rome.'

Cellini tells of a man standing beside him on the ramparts of the Castel Sant'Angelo, crazed with grief 'tearing at his face and sobbing bitterly', as he watched the soldiers below dragging his family from his house. It comes almost as light relief to hear Cellini bragging how he became such a brilliant shot with his cannon on the walls that on one occasion he 'sliced a Spanish officer in two with a single cannon ball'. On another occasion: 'I fired the arquebus, dealing out death and destruction. The man I hit was the Duke of Orange, who was carried away . . .' Miraculously, the prince seems to have survived this episode, for as we shall see he continued to play an energetic role as an imperial commander.

Cellini's *Autobiography* also records Clement VII's profuse and frequent admiration for his brave exploits: 'The Pope was highly delighted [with me] . . . The Pope sent for me; we shut ourselves in a room together and he asked me what to do about the Papal treasures . . . hotly defended my action . . . thanked me warmly . . .' and so on. In fact, the pope was a broken man; as the siege continued, he would daily rise at dawn and trudge to the ramparts, searching the northern horizon for the French troops he imagined were being sent to rescue him.

The Sack of Rome brought about a transformation in the character of Clement VII. His previous honesty was replaced by an incurable deviousness, and he trusted no one; his hesitancy remained, but now it masked a scheming mind rather than an understanding one. Never had a pope been so humiliated, and news of the Sack of Rome spread quickly throughout Europe – such a thing had not happened for more than a thousand years, since the Dark Ages and the invasions of the Vandals and the Visigoths. The Emperor Charles V hypocritically ordered his court into mourning; Luther saw it as God's wrath visited upon the worldliness and corruption of the Eternal City; and Erasmus was caused to remark: 'Truly, this is not the ruin of one city, but of the world.'

The siege of Pope Clement VII in the Castel Sant'Angelo would last for five weeks, during which the thousands of inmates endured the growing heat and were soon reduced to near-starvation. Not until 7 June would the Emperor Charles V allow the siege to be lifted, but first Clement VII was made to sign a treaty surrendering vast swathes of papal territory – from Civitavecchia and Ostia on the coast, to Parma, Modena and Piacenza in the north. At a stroke, the papal territories were reduced to a fraction of their former size; they no longer had access to the sea, or much land beyond the Apennines.

Even after this, Clement VII himself was not permitted to leave the Castel Sant'Angelo, where he lived as a virtual prisoner, whilst around him the remnant citizens of Rome lived in misery amongst their desecrated dwellings, suffering from hunger and plague. Carrion crows circled in the sky above the ruins, and even the few imperial troops left encamped outside the Castel Sant'Angelo became disheartened as the long hot summer months gave way to autumn. With the advent of winter, hordes of German *Landsknechte* and Spanish mercenaries who had spent the summer pillaging the countryside of the Romagna returned to Rome. They had yet to receive any money and issued an ultimatum: if they were not paid, they would break into the Castel Sant'Angelo and slaughter the pope.

In the early hours of 7 December, the pope and his retinue were permitted to escape. Disguised as a servant, Clement VII made his way north with his attendants; sewn into the linings of their clothes were strips of gold that Cellini had made from melted-down papal treasures. After travelling for several days the ragged papal entourage finally stumbled up a solitary mule track into the Umbrian mountains, the only approach to the isolated and deserted Episcopal Palace at Orvieto. Here at least Clement VII was safe – from his enemies, if not from the elements, for according to eyewitness reports the palace was 'ruinous and decayed', and to reach the pope's privy chamber one had to pass through three large rooms 'all naked and unhanged, the roofs fallen down'. Partly for warmth, but probably more as a reflection of his dejection and transformation of character, the pope now grew a moustache and beard: the man who on his accession to the papacy had widely been acclaimed as the most handsome man ever to hold this office was now reduced to a haunted figure with a black saturnine beard. By this stage he had developed the Medici heavy-lidded eyes, which had passed through Cosimo *Pater Patriae* to his grandson Lorenzo the Magnificent; but in Clement VII's case he looked half-asleep, or scheming.

In Orvieto, the pope attempted to continue with the business of administering the papacy, and was soon beset with further political problems. A delegation arrived from Henry VIII of England, seeking papal dispensation for a divorce from his wife Catherine of Aragon. This placed Clement VII in a particularly difficult situation: he had no wish to alienate his ally Henry, but on the other hand Catherine of Aragon was the aunt of the Emperor Charles V, on whom the very future of the papacy now depended. Clement VII prevaricated – for the moment he appeared incapable of making *any* decision. The English delegation returned home, bringing dire news of the pope's circumstances: 'all things are in such scarcity and dearth as we think has not been seen in any place', and they spoke of 'hunger, scarcity, ill-favoured lodging, ill air', and of how the roofless chambers of the pope's palace were filled with 'rif-raf and others, standing in the chambers for a garnishment. And as for the Pope's bedchamber, all the apparel in it was not worth twenty nobles [less than seven pounds], bed and all.' This description of the pope's humiliation and powerlessness would have crucial repercussions: the first seeds of doubt were sown, and Henry VIII would begin to have his suspicions about the power of the man he was dealing with.

*

Clement VII had not only lost vast swathes of papal territory, but he had also lost the Medici power base Florence. On being elected to the papacy, he had appointed as his successor to rule Florence a papal emissary, Cardinal Passerini, who had been instructed to coach the two teenage Medici heirs Ippolito and Alessandro in the business of government. The main branch of the Medici family now had precious few heirs, and both of these youths were in fact illegitimate; Ippolito was the bastard son of the deceased Giuliano, Duke of Nemours, whilst Alessandro was officially the bastard of the deceased Lorenzo, Duke of Urbino. In reality, the swarthy and uncouth Alessandro was almost certainly the illegitimate son of Clement VII himself, the result of a liaison with a Moorish slave girl whilst he had been living at the Palazzo Medici in Florence. The only legitimate offspring was Caterina de' Medici, daughter of the Duke of Urbino and Francis I's cousin Princess Madeleine de la Tour d'Auvergne, the first Medici with royal blood. From the start of his papacy, Clement VII had nursed plans for Caterina that went far beyond Florence. As we shall see, even in his extremity he continued to harbour this secret and highly ambitious plan – which he almost certainly inherited from his uncle Lorenzo the Magnificent, by way of Leo X.

Clement VII's choice of Cardinal Passerini as his representative in Florence had been ill-judged; the historian Francesco Guicciardini, acting as a papal councillor at the time, reported back to Clement VII during a visit to Florence expressing his forthright views on Passerini. According to Guicciardini, Cardinal Passerini was a 'eunuch who spent the whole day in idle chatter and neglects important things'. The presence of an outsider in the Palazzo Medici was deeply resented in the city, and Passerini's two illegitimate charges were regarded with contempt. There were outbreaks of civil unrest, and during one of these the Palazzo della Signoria was seized by anti-Medici demonstrators. In the course of the ensuing siege, the demonstrators hurled from an upper window a heavy wooden bench, which hit Michelangelo's *David* in the piazza below. The statue's raised left arm was snapped off and fell to the ground, shattering into three pieces. These were rescued by the sixteen-year-old Vasari, who placed them in a nearby church for safekeeping; the arm would later be restored, though the joins can still be seen to this day.

When news of the fall of Rome reached Florence, the people once again took to the streets, causing Cardinal Passerini and his two charges to flee in fear of their lives. A new administration took over, and appointed as *gonfaloniere* for a period of twelve months the anti-Medici Niccolò Capponi, the son of Piero Capponi, the *gonfaloniere* who had stood up to the French king Charles VIII during his occupation of the city.

For the third time, the Medici had been ousted from Florence. The first time Cosimo de' Medici had made a triumphant return after just a year; the second time the Medici exile had lasted for eighteen years; but now, with Medici money, power and popularity all but dissipated, it appeared doubtful whether they would ever return. Citizens who had been friends of the Medici were persecuted, all Medici insignia on buildings were destroyed and other evidence of Medici rule was defaced; at the same time the eight-year-old Caterina de' Medici was seized and held in the convent of Santa Lucia as a hostage.

Reflecting the unstable situation in the rest of the country, the situation within Florence remained unsettled. To begin with, an oligarchy manipulated by the old families remained nominally in control, but this was soon opposed by more popular republican forces. Instability brought about a resurrection of the ideas of Savonarola, who had now been dead almost thirty years. People flocked to the churches in religious fervour, Jesus Christ was proclaimed King of Florence, and moves were made to establish once more a City of God – this time known anomalously as the 'Republic of Christ'. Laws were passed against gambling, carnivals and pageants, as well as immodest or extravagant dress and behaviour, whilst wealthier citizens took the precaution of hiding their books, paintings and other finery. As before, the aim was to expunge the Medici past and all it stood for; the blend of social envy and justifiable resentment, which never lay far beneath the surface of the city, again possessed its citizens. However, the worst excesses of the Savonarola era were avoided, largely owing to the actions of Francesco Carducci, a man of principle and a confirmed democrat, who took over as *gonfaloniere*. While others succumbed to piety, he ensured that autocratic measures introduced by the Medici were repealed and more republican laws enacted in their place.

By the summer of 1528, Clement VII felt it safe to return to Rome and take up residence once more in the papal palace. His main concern was now Florence, for he knew that without that city the Medici were

Fig 15 The siege of Florence

homeless and all but powerless: what little influence they had would disappear with the end of his papacy. For the Medici to return to their power
base in Florence, Clement VII realised that he would need a strong ally.
It quickly became clear that he could not rely on the French, who in 1529
once again seized the opportunity to launch an offensive in Italy, sweeping all before them until they reached Naples. Here they were ravaged by
plague, suffered from over-extended supply lines and were forced to retreat.

Clement VII now made overtures to the Emperor Charles V, who
decided that it was in his interests to make friends with the pope, and

early in 1529 they signed the Treaty of Barcelona. For his part, Pope Clement VII agreed to crown Charles V as Holy Roman Emperor at Bologna. This ancient ceremony originated with the first Holy Roman Emperor, Charlemagne, who had been crowned by the pope in 800; the ceremony had not lapsed until Charles V's predecessor Maximilian I, whose territorial ambitions had led to him being prevented from entering Italy by the Venetians. Charles V was anxious to revive this tradition, and in return promised to aid Clement VII in returning Medici rule to Florence.

Yet still the French king Francis I remained a threat; ever since his

release from humiliating captivity by Charles V, Francis I had been determined to avenge himself. Unfortunately, this required some delicacy – for
Charles V still held the French king's sons as hostages, which ruled out a
direct attack on Charles V in Spain. The offensive on imperial Naples had
proved a fiasco, as had the issue of a personal challenge to Charles V to
meet Francis I in knightly combat, which had simply been dismissed with
scorn – such things were for knights and princes, not kings and emperors. Finally it became clear that there was only one recourse; in August
1529 Francis I of France and the Holy Roman Emperor Charles V signed
the Treaty of Cambrai, whereby Francis I was handed back his heirs in
return for a ransom equivalent to one million florins.

By now Charles V had sent orders to his commander in Italy, the
Prince of Orange, to offer his services to the pope. In order for Clement
VII to fulfil his plans to reinstate the Medici in Florence, the pope would
now have to endure the further humiliation of employing the Prince of
Orange, who two years previously had imprisoned him in the Castel
Sant'Angelo. The Prince of Orange marched into Tuscany with an army
of 40,000 mainly Spanish troops, who began laying waste the towns under
Florentine control; and on 24 October his vast army appeared on the hill-
sides overlooking Florence itself.

The city had long since prepared itself for such an eventuality. When
Cardinal Passerini and his youthful Medici charges had fled Florence,
Michelangelo had been working on the Medici Chapel in the church of
San Lorenzo, and the authorities had immediately appointed him to
Machiavelli's old post: Supervisor of the City Walls. The paths of art and
science may by now have begun to diverge somewhat, but artists were still
regarded as technicians; just as Leonardo had been employed by Cesare
Borgia, so Michelangelo was now employed by the city of Florence – as
a military engineer.

Reluctantly, Michelangelo abandoned his creative endeavours and set
to work on the fortification of Florence. He ordered that the city walls
be extended south to include the hill of San Miniato, which overlooked
the city centre, making it a key site for a besieging army to position its
cannons. He also ordered that the tower of the church at San Miniato
should be strapped with mattresses of tightly packed straw to protect it
from cannonballs. All this was long since completed by the time the Prince

of Orange arrived and his army pitched their thousands of tents across the surrounding hillsides to begin the siege of Florence.

All roads in and out of the city were blocked, the countryside and villages around were laid waste, and the besieging cannons began sporadically firing into the city. Yet it soon became clear that the citizens of Florence were in no mood to surrender. They were also considerably aided, and heartened, by the exploits of one of their military officers, Francesco Ferrucci. At night, Ferrucci would sally forth from one of the city gates with a band of armed men, attacking whichever point he had noticed was the weakest in the besieging army; before reinforcements could arrive, a convoy of fresh supplies would be rushed into the city under cover of darkness. In this way autumn passed into winter, and still Florence held out.

In February 1530 Clement VII travelled to Bologna to crown Charles V as Holy Roman Emperor of the German nations. The coronation had been fixed for 24 February, Charles V's birthday: amidst suitable pomp the two great leaders of Christendom, both dressed in their magnificent ceremonial robes, approached one another. The pope then crowned the emperor with the iron imperial crown, in a ceremony dating back more than 700 years (though this was in fact the last time that the ceremony would take place). In the course of these proceedings a personal rapprochement of sorts was established between Pope Clement VII and Emperor Charles V; the spiritual and political powers of Europe were now united, and the peace of the continent seemed assured.

Yet still the siege of Florence continued; winter passed into spring, then summer. Despite Ferrucci's efforts, the populace was now all but starving, and cases of plague were being reported. Ferrucci decided upon a desperate but brave measure: under cover of darkness he led a troop of armed men out beyond the besieging forces into the Tuscan countryside; he then began riding from town to town, gathering up an army of volunteers. When he returned to Pistoia, twenty miles north-west of Florence, his volunteer army numbered 3,000 foot soldiers and 500 cavalry.

By now the Prince of Orange had received intelligence of what was happening, and together with a large detachment of Spanish soldiers he went in pursuit of Ferrucci, finally managing to surprise him resting in the mountains above Pistoia at the village of Gavinana. Ferrucci and his men were quickly surrounded, hunted from house to house, and more than 2,000 of them were slaughtered. In the midst of this bloody mayhem, the Prince of Orange was felled with two shots from an arquebus, but Ferrucci himself fought to the last, and was captured only when he was mortally wounded. He was then carried on a litter before the new commander, a Neapolitan called Maramaldo, who was so outraged that he set upon the dying man in a frenzy with his dagger.

When news of Ferrucci's brutal death reached Florence, the population was in despair; bands of starving *popolo minuto* took to the streets, crying out pitifully: 'Give us the Medici, who can give us bread.' Six days later the *gonfaloniere* despatched a delegation to surrender to the enemy, while the population barricaded themselves in their cellars or took sanctuary in the churches, in fear of the imperial soldiers. After ten long months the siege was over; but there was no massacre, as Clement VII had insisted to Charles V that the population be spared. The Swiss and Spanish soldiers of the imperial army moved in, and the Medici faction quickly took control of the city. The *gonfaloniere* was merely imprisoned, though the previous incumbent Francesco Carducci was executed; the Medici recognised the democrat as their true enemy. At the same time, a number of the leading families who had supported the republican regime, such as the Strozzi, were banished to exile.

When Medici rule had once again been firmly established, and the imperial army had withdrawn, Clement VII sent his twenty-year-old illegitimate son Alessandro to take over the reins of power. (The other illegitimate claimant, Ippolito, was consoled by being made a cardinal.) The day after Alessandro entered the city, he was declared Head (*Capo*) of the Florentine Republic. This title was suitably significant, but also suitably vague; the main ruling councils were retained, but the head had a seat on all of them, and the head was also *gonfaloniere* for life.

The godfathers of the Renaissance now provided the officially recognised godfather (the aptly named *Capo*) of Florence, and the gauche and fractious Alessandro de' Medici soon lived up to his title. Within two years the Signoria was abolished; and in an act whose symbolism resonated throughout the city, the bell in the tower of the Palazzo della Signoria, the famous *vacca* that summoned the people to a Balìa, was thrown from its tower. It crashed to the ground in the piazza, smashing to pieces;

Alessandro then ordered the pieces to be melted down and cast as medals celebrating the Medici family.

But the Emperor Charles V was still concerned about Florence; he insisted to Clement VII that what he now required of his new Florentine ally was a consistency of foreign policy, which could only be achieved by consistency of rule. There must be no further uprisings, no more changes of government, no more switching of allegiances: what was required above all else was stability. With some reluctance Clement VII took the necessary steps: acting in his power as pope, he bestowed a title on Alessandro de' Medici, sending word to Florence that Alessandro 'is henceforth to be called the Duke of the Florentine Republic'. This was a crucial step: the Medici had now become the noble rulers of the city – the title of duke was hereditary, and whoever inherited it inherited the city. The last semblance of democracy, or even the pretence of it, had disappeared.

Clement VII was only fifty-five years old, but he had become ill and was ageing rapidly; even so, he was still determined to pursue the fulfilment of his ambitions for the Medici family. Florence was now allied to both the Emperor Charles V and Francis I of France, and Clement VII made it known that he wished to seal these alliances by marriage. Despite his illness, in 1533 he travelled in some discomfort to Bologna for another meeting with Charles V, at which he suggested that there should be a marriage between Alessandro de' Medici, the new Duke of Florence, and the emperor's natural daughter Margaret. Charles V agreed, whereupon Clement VII carefully introduced the subject that was his main concern, asking the emperor if he had any objection to him arranging a marriage between the young Caterina de' Medici and one of Francis I's sons. The emperor reluctantly gave his permission, convinced that Francis I would never permit one of his royal sons to marry 'one who was little more than a private gentlewoman'.

But Clement VII had already taken the precaution of approaching Francis I on this matter, and had received his assent; by the time Charles V realised that he had been tricked, it was too late. In October 1533, the petite pale-faced fourteen-year-old Caterina disembarked from Tuscany for the south of France. Clement VII himself travelled to Marseilles to conduct the marriage ceremony, and Caterina de' Medici, Countess of Urbino, was duly married to Francis I's second son Henri de Valois, Duke of Orléans.

The ceremony was suitably magnificent, with the bride attended by no fewer than twelve maids of honour, and it was to be followed by nine days of lavish banquets, pageants and festivities. As tradition demanded, the expense of all this was met by the bride's family; in preparation, Clement VII had imposed punitive taxes on Florence, and special new taxes had been introduced in Rome. The father-in-law Francis I was particularly impressed by his present of a casket containing twenty-four panels of rock crystal framed in silver, each carved with a biblical subject, while the casket itself was engraved with Clement VII's papal insignia. For this ultimate occasion – the entry of a Medici into the very heart of the leading royal family of Europe – the Medici once again displayed their legendary generosity; Lorenzo the Magnificent, who had taken the first steps towards this day, would have been proud of his favoured nephew.

But 1533 was also marked by the final disgrace of Clement VII's reign. Henry VIII of England, created Defender of the Faith by Leo X, at last lost patience with the pope over his prevarication concerning the divorce from Catherine of Aragon, and in an unprecedented move the Church of England severed its links with the Roman Catholic Church. Previously a number of German states had broken from the Church, as well as remote Sweden and some Baltic states, but now for the first time a major European power had declared itself Protestant. After this there could be no disguising the fact that Europe was tearing itself apart as never before; with Leo X and Clement VII, the Medici unwittingly became very different godfathers – this time to the Protestant Reformation.

It soon became clear that Clement VII was dying. His liver was failing and his skin turned yellow; he also lost the sight of one eye and became partially blind in the other. The irrepressible Cellini describes a visit to the pope. 'I found him in bed, at a very low ebb. Still, he welcomed me affectionately.' Cellini had brought some medals he had designed for the pope, but the pontiff's eyesight was now so bad that he was no longer able to see them. 'He began feeling my work with the tips of his fingers for some time, and then he gave a deep sigh.' Three days later, on 25 September 1534, Clement VII died after having been pope for ten years. A few days later Cellini put on his sword and went to pay his last respects to Clement VII, who was lying in state: 'I kissed his feet, and could not restrain my tears.'

However, Cellini appears to have been the only person in Rome who mourned Clement VII's passing, for by this stage the pope was reviled throughout the city. After he was buried, St Peter's was broken into on several nights; his tomb was desecrated with graffiti and smeared with excrement. His conduct during his papacy has been likened to that of a dedicated but clumsy disciple of Machiavelli: he was ruthless, but at the wrong time; he felt strong enough to scorn popularity, but did so when he most needed it; and though not afraid to betray his friends, he succeeded in alienating them all at once. In Clement VII's defence, it must be said that no pope ever presided over the Church at a more unfortunate time, though it must also be said that he did little or nothing to avoid the greatest calamities of his reign: the Sack of Rome, and Christendom dividing against itself.

Yet there remains one sphere in which Clement VII's life can be seen as an unalloyed success: his actions marked perhaps the most significant turning point in the history of the Medici family – the ascent into nobility in Florence, and the joining of the French royal family. Without the guiding hand of Clement VII, the Medici would never have been able to achieve the pinnacles of greatness that were yet to come.

Part 5

The Battle for Truth

24

A Grim Aftermath

THE CITIZENS OF Florence had been outraged when Alessandro de' Medici was made Duke of Florence in 1533, and this resulted in some sporadic civil unrest, though there was no attempt at armed rebellion. The siege and the fighting had taken their toll; Guicciardini tells of 'all the houses around Florence destroyed for many miles, and in many towns of the Florentine dominion the peasant population immeasurably decreased'. It is reasonably estimated that in Florence and throughout Tuscany well over 10,000 must have died during the invasion of the imperial troops under the Duke of Orange and the consequent year of siege. As Guicciardini points out, during this period 'there had been neither harvest nor seed time . . . with the result that more money left the city, afflicted and weakened as it was, for the purpose of buying grain in distant places and livestock outside of the dominion'. On the insistence of Charles V, the city now also had to support a standing army of Spanish soldiers, whose orders were to see that the present administration was not overthrown.

The new ruler of the city, Alessandro de' Medici, Duke of Florence, was a curious mixture, both physically and mentally. He had a dark Moorish complexion topped by frizzy North African hair, he was ill-educated and was generally regarded as uncouth; yet in his own erratic way he was not without certain political skills. He held regular audiences at the Palazzo Medici where he listened sympathetically to the grievances of the poor, and he became known for his spontaneous generosity; his mother had been a slave, and in his dealings with the needy and downtrodden he was always

Fig 16
Alessandro de' Medici

mindful of the hardships she had endured. He was also in the habit of dropping in unannounced on his political supporters, asking without ceremony what they thought of the way things were going; he would listen to their replies, but in such an impassive way that it was difficult to tell how much he was taking in.

On the other hand, there is no denying Alessandro's deep unpopularity amongst most classes of the run-down citizenry, though how far this extended to the *popolo minuto* cannot be judged. There is also no denying his firm hold on power. One of his early moves was to impound all weapons, even those hanging in the churches as votive offerings; and in a manner more reminiscent of the tyrants of Milan, he demolished the ancient convent of San Giovanni Evangelista by the northern wall of the city, and in its place began erecting the Fortezza da Basso. This large and forbidding castle was to house the Spanish garrison imposed by Charles V, and it would overlook the city centre as well as the city walls – its cannons could be used to subdue the city, as well as protect it.

Although Alessandro was seen in Florence as being responsible for this fortress, the idea for its construction undoubtedly came from the Emperor Charles V. Indeed, he made it a condition that it be completed before he would let Alessandro marry his natural daughter Margaret. When Clement VII died in 1534, Alessandro lost his chief adviser, and chief restrainer. His already well-developed penchant for wanton sexual behaviour now became extravagant in the extreme; aided and abetted by his young favourite, Lorenzino de' Medici, a distant cousin, Alessandro embarked on a succession of escapades that soon became the horrified gossip of the city. Convent walls were scaled at night, young girls of good family debauched, and even wives of prominent citizens compromised. Such tales were obviously coloured by his unpopularity, which certainly included elements of snobbery and racism, yet his unsavoury reputation was not entirely undeserved. Those who spoke against Alessandro on the government committees, or opposed his views, were liable to find themselves financially ruined by an exhaustive tax investigation followed by a swingeing bill (admittedly, a method favoured by the Medici since the early days of Cosimo *Pater Patriae*). But Alessandro often spiced such punishment by letting it be known that it could be reduced in return for sexual favours. (Again, such things were not unknown under previous rulers, such as Lorenzo the Magnificent.) Alessandro soon found it expedient to move out of the Palazzo Medici on the Via Larga and take up residence in the more heavily guarded Palazzo della Signoria – now renamed the Palazzo Vecchio (Old Palace), since the disbanding of the Signoria. He would also have been aware of the deep symbolic significance of this move, as indeed would all the citizens of Florence: the Medici had made the time-honoured seat of the city's power their home.

Within a year of Clement VII's death, the leading citizens of Florence decided that they had put up with enough, and a delegation was despatched to the Emperor Charles V. This was supported by powerful Florentine exiles living in Rome, such as the Pazzi and the ancient banking family of the Strozzi; it was even covertly encouraged by Francesco Guicciardini, Clement VII's former councillor, who was now acting as Alessandro's adviser. The Emperor Charles VII was in Tunis, at last having decided to lead a campaign against the advancing Ottomans in North Africa. (In 1534, his brother Ferdinand had halted the Turks at the gates of Vienna.)

It was decided that the Florentine delegation to Charles V should be led by Cardinal Ippolito de' Medici, who was extremely jealous of his cousin's rise to sole power in Florence. Ippolito was also seen as the obvious replacement for Alessandro, having already shown himself to be both more intelligent and more malleable, as well as being of slightly better moral character. In August 1535 Cardinal Ippolito set off south to take ship for Tunis, but he only got as far as Itri, seventy miles south of Rome, before he fell ill and died, almost certainly poisoned on Alessandro's orders.

When the Emperor Charles V returned from Tunis, he summoned the Florentine delegation, and Alessandro himself, to meet him at Naples. The new leader of the Florentine delegation, the historian Jacopo Nardi, put his case to the emperor, citing particularly how the newly constructed Fortezza da Basso was being used 'as a prison and slaughter-house for the unhappy citizens'. When he had finished, the emperor asked Guicciardini, Alessandro's adviser, to put the opposing case. The Florentine delegation expected the skilled orator subtly to undermine Alessandro's case, damning him with faint praise and obviously empty denials; but to their consternation, Guicciardini used all his powers of persuasion to refute the allegations of the Florentines, referring favourably to Alessandro's virtues and to the high regard in which he was held in Florence. He ended with a flourish: 'I see no point in trying to refute all these charges concerning women, rapes and such slanders, when all that are referred to are generalities, without a single particular case being mentioned.' Guicciardini was a skilled politician, who had no wish to be on the losing side and thus lose his job. He had realised that Charles V had no intention of deposing Alessandro, who was on the point of becoming his son-in-law; the emperor wanted Florence to be ruled firmly, no matter how, for political stability was his only concern.

The chastened Florentine delegation returned north, and in the summer of 1536 the Emperor Charles V arrived in Florence, bringing his daughter Margaret for the wedding with Alessandro. As a sop, he also brought with him several families of Florentine exiles, specially pardoned to mark the occasion. Yet as soon as the festivities were over and the emperor left, life continued as before, both for the Florentines and their ruler: marriage appeared to have no effect on Alessandro's monstrous sexual appetite.

In this he was certainly encouraged by his boon-companion Lorenzino de' Medici, though these two roisterers made an odd pair. Lorenzino (meaning 'Little Lorenzo') was undeniably short in stature, but his nickname had further connotations: it implied that Lorenzino was a person of little consequence, who would never amount to much, whereas in fact he was highly ambitious and determined to show the world that he represented a lot more than his name suggested. This combination made Lorenzino a complex and volatile character. As a Medici, he could trace his lineage directly back to the brother of Cosimo *Pater Patriae*, and he saw himself as the scion of a great house; yet his mother was a Soderini, from a family that prided itself on its democratic sympathies. These elements too played their part in his contradictory character.

Lorenzino had grown up in Rome, where he had acquired a wide-ranging humanist knowledge; he could quote extensively from Cicero and Machiavelli, and enjoyed showing off his learning. At the same time he also acquired a reputation as a hell-raiser; when drunk, his favourite trick was to decapitate an ancient statue in the Forum with his sword – boasting that he was striking a blow against 'imperial power'.

These exploits were eventually brought to the attention of Pope Clement VII, who was so outraged that he banished Lorenzino de' Medici to Florence. Here his hell-raising soon brought him into the company of Alessandro, Duke of Florence, and the two became bosom pals, as Lorenzino did all in his power to endear himself to Alessandro. But in fact Lorenzino hated and despised Alessandro, becoming increasingly jealous of him, though he took care never to show this. Here was an ignorant half-caste bastard, just three years older than himself, who had all the power and money that he wanted – while he, Lorenzino, a true Medici, had a brilliant mind and yet was penniless and powerless. The closer Lorenzino became to Alessandro, the more this drove him to a deep unbalancing resentment; meanwhile Alessandro affectionately christened Lorenzino 'the philosopher', and Lorenzino repaid this friendship by pimping for him.

When Alessandro had their cousin Cardinal Ippolito de' Medici poisoned, Lorenzino's hatred deepened into psychotic fantasy. Lorenzino began to see himself as Brutus to Alessandro's Julius Caesar, the emperor who had despoiled Ancient Rome's democratic tradition; and, like Brutus, he would avenge Alessandro's injustices by assassinating him. With this noble act, he would no longer be seen as 'little Lorenzo' – he would become somebody, he would be a hero. The more Lorenzino brooded, the more his fantasy deepened: if he delivered Florence from this illegitimate tyrant, he would then become the obvious successor – he was, after all, a noble and legitimate Medici.

This fantasy soon become so strong that it took on a reality, and Lorenzino began plotting the details of Alessandro's murder. Yet unlike other previous assassination plots in Florence, this would be no conspiracy, for Alessandro was determined to work on his own, with the aid of just a single hired assassin. The plot was cunningly contrived: Lorenzino began goading Alessandro about a woman called Caterina Soderini Ginori, who was married to an elderly husband. Caterina was known to be a somewhat shallow woman, but nonetheless virtuous; according to Lorenzino, if Alessandro could seduce Caterina, then this would prove that he was a *real* man. At the same time Lorenzino assured Alessandro that as a true friend he had begun putting in a good word for the duke with Caterina (who happened, in an interesting psychological twist, also to be Lorenzino's sister).

Just after New Year's Day 1537, Lorenzino assured Alessandro that Caterina was now definitely interested in him, and that he had arranged an assignation for the two of them the following Saturday, which was Twelfth Night, a time known for its revelry. Alessandro was to go to Lorenzino's house and wait for him to bring Caterina, then Lorenzino would slip away on a pretext, leaving the two of them together.

Alessandro duly arrived at Lorenzino's house and slipped in unnoticed amongst the street celebrations, telling his bodyguard to wait ouside the house. As usual at this time of night, Alessandro was somewhat the worse for drink; he staggered into the bedroom, unbuckled his sword, loosened his clothes and stretched out on the bed ready to receive Caterina – but soon fell asleep.

What happened next was recorded by Lorenzino, who also told slightly different versions to others; the details vary, but the central facts remain the same. Some time later that night Lorenzino stole into the room where Alessandro was asleep, accompanied by a hired assassin known locally as Scoronconcolo (a nickname that may well have had gruesome imaginative connotations, but in fact literally meant 'the nut sheller'). Lorenzino made his way towards the bed, whispering 'Are you asleep?', and when Alessandro rolled over towards him, Lorenzino held him down and Scoronconcolo began stabbing him. As Alessandro struggled frantically, screaming, Lorenzino forced his fingers into Alessandro's mouth in an attempt to silence him, while Scoronconcolo continued plunging his dagger into him. In his frenzy, Alessandro bit through Lorenzino's fingers to the bone, until eventually Scoronconcolo managed to stick his dagger into Alessandro's neck, twisting it as it gouged through his throat. Alessandro's body convulsed for several moments, and then lapsed into stillness amidst the blood-drenched sheets.

Lorenzino now covered the body with a blanket, pinning a note to it on which was written a quote from Virgil's *Aeneid*: '*Vincit amor patriae laudumque immensa cupido*' ('Love of one's country and great desire for glory shall conquer') – this was intended to be seen as the heroic act of a sophisticated assassin. After the two murderers had left the room, Lorenzino locked the door and pocketed the key; he did not want the body discovered until he was well clear of the city. He then clambered on his horse and quickly rode away. (At least one witness later testified to seeing Lorenzino galloping through the streets, mentioning that his hand was bound, or gloved, but visibly oozing blood.) Lorenzino fled, taking a circuitous route through northern Italy so that it was several days before he reached Venice, by which time news of his deed had preceded him. He was welcomed with open arms by the exiled Filippo Strozzi, the head of the banking family. Lorenzino knew that it might take some time for things to settle down, but he confidently awaited the call from Florence: he would return as a hero and a ruler.

Back in Florence, events had not unfolded quite as Lorenzino expected. Owing to the locked door, the body of Alessandro was not immediately discovered; only when Alessandro's bodyguard began demanding how much longer he was required to wait were suspicions aroused. Cardinal Cibò, the Emperor Charles V's representative in Florence, was informed that the duke, Alessandro, appeared to have gone missing. Eventually, on Sunday evening, the door was broken down and Alessandro's body discovered amidst the bloodied blankets.

Cardinal Cibò, who besides being the emperor's representative was also a Medici, consulted with Francesco Guicciardini. They both agreed it was imperative that the murder be kept secret, and the body was conveyed under cover of darkness to be concealed in the Medici vault in San Lorenzo. (When Alessandro's body was exhumed some 350 years later, its stab-wounds appeared to confirm Lorenzino's account.) Both Cardinal Cibò and Guicciardini felt sure that if word of Alessandro's murder became known there would be a popular uprising; republicans would take over the city, and when the uprising was put down, as it surely would be, the consequences would be dire. Florence would definitely lose her independence this time, for if the Emperor Charles V took the city he would undoubtedly install a viceroy, as he had done in Naples. At the same time, it was known that the new pope Paul III also had his eyes on Florence, so it was imperative that action be taken at once, and a new ruler installed, before there could be any outside interference.

The question now arose as to who should be the new ruler. The only direct legitimate heir was Caterina de' Medici, who was now living away in France, which meant that it was necessary to turn elsewhere if a ruler was to be installed at once. Alessandro and Margaret had left no heir, though Alessandro did have an illegitimate child called Giulio, who was now four years old; Cardinal Cibò proposed that Giulio be installed, with himself as regent. However, this was opposed by Guicciardini, who favoured the seventeen-year-old Cosimo de' Medici, son of the dashing Florentine military hero Giovanni de' Medici delle Bande Nere (of the Black Bands), who had died defending the republic against the forces that had sacked Rome, and who had married his distant cousin Lorenzo the Magnificent's daughter. Cosimo seemed the ideal choice; also, Guicciardini saw this as his chance of taking over power, acting in the name of the inexperienced Cosimo and cementing this arrangement by marrying Cosimo to his own daughter.

It was decided to call a meeting of the city council at the Palazzo Vecchio, to decide the matter; here Cardinal Cibò promoted his protégé, while others remained in favour of declaring a republic, and Guicciardini pleaded for a decision to be taken quickly as time was running out. In fact, Guicciardini had already sent word to Il Trebbio, the Medici villa in the Mugello where he knew Cosimo to be staying, summoning him to Florence at once. Guicciardini had also had a word with Alessandro Vitelli, the captain of the guard, who was on duty with his men outside in the piazza, suggesting a plan.

After hours of wrangling, the negotiators in the Palazzo Vecchio became aware of a commotion outside in the piazza amongst the soldiers: raised voices could be heard through the open window of the upstairs council chamber. Some soldiers began calling out: 'Vote for Cosimo! Cosimo must be Duke of Florence!'; they then began chanting: 'Cosimo! Cosimo! Cosimo!' In accordance with Guicciardini's plan, Vitelli now called anxiously up to the window: 'Hurry up! I can't hold the soldiers back much longer!' Guicciardini's choice quickly won the day, and Cosimo de' Medici was voted in.

Alessandro had represented the last of the major branch of the Medici family descended from Cosimo *Pater Patriae*, through Lorenzo the Magnificent, which had included the two popes Leo X and Clement VII. The branch to which Cosimo, the new Duke of Florence, belonged was descended from Lorenzo, the younger brother of Cosimo *Pater Patriae*, who had helped to run the Medici Bank and had rallied support for Cosimo in the countryside when he had been locked in the tower of the Palazzo della Signoria. This branch also included Lorenzo di Pierfrancesco, the rich cousin of Lorenzo the Magnificent who had commissioned Botticelli's *Primavera*, and who had later opposed Piero the Unfortunate, inviting the French king Charles VIII into Florence. Technically, the assassin Lorenzino de' Medici was senior in years and bloodline to Cosimo de' Medici in this branch of the family, but significantly no one had thought to suggest Lorenzino as a candidate for the dukedom. He may have rid Florence of the detested Alessandro, but he was too closely associated with him. All were agreed that what was needed was a fresh start to Medici rule.

25

Aristocratic Rule

COSIMO DE' MEDICI now became Duke of Florence, and Guicciardini prudently made sure that the new young ruler took up residence in the Palazzo Medici. Cosimo had been just seven years old when his heroic father Giovanni de' Medici delle Bande Nere died in battle, after which he had been brought up by his mother Maria, née Salviati, at Il Trebbio in the Mugello. He had later followed a peripatetic education in Venice, Bologna, Naples and Genoa. His ambition had been to follow in his father's footsteps and become a soldier; temperamentally he was very much the opposite of his romantic, dashing father, but Cosimo would always retain something of the military about him. He was stiff of bearing, gave orders rather than instructions, and believed in respect for rank, rather than cultivating popularity. Where his father had cut a poetic figure, Cosimo remained distinctly prosaic: a moderately good-looking young man, with his hair cut short, displaying little by way of personality.

Yet in many ways Cosimo was what Florence needed, and during his early years as duke he would quickly grow in stature from an inexperienced young man into a determined ruler. He would listen carefully to the advice of Guicciardini, but followed this less and less as he developed his own ideas.

The first challenge to Cosimo's rule came in 1537, the year of his accession, when Filippo Strozzi led an army supported and financed by the exiles in a march on Florence. Strozzi had made the mistake of judging that Cosimo's rule would be no more popular than that of his predecessor Alessandro; in fact Cosimo was not particularly popular, but the citizens of Florence were now in the mood for a period of stable rule.

Fig 17 Cosimo I Duke of Florence: bust by Cellini

When Strozzi's army reached Prato, he confidently expected the Florentines to rise up spontaneously against their Medici ruler; but there was no uprising, and instead Vitelli was despatched at the head of the Florentine militia, considerably strengthened by the Spanish garrison from the Fortezza da Basso. The opposing forces met at Montemurlo, outside Prato, the result being a swingeing defeat for Strozzi and the army of the exiles. Many members of the leading exiled families were captured and paraded humiliatingly through the streets of the city before the jeering populace, though this was only the beginning, for the captives were now tried and sixteen of them were summarily executed. The rest, including Strozzi himself, received lengthy prison sentences; as it turned out, few would finish their terms, for many quickly disappeared, while others died after torture. Filippo Strozzi fell on his sword, in the Roman fashion, leaving behind a note quoting Virgil: '*Exoriare aliquis nostris ex ossibus ultor*' ('Some avenger will arise from our bones').

Cosimo and his adviser Guicciardini were determined that this would not happen, and set in motion a process of hunting down enemies in exile. Some years later Lorenzino de' Medici would be stabbed with a poisoned knife in Venice; and the remaining Strozzi, Pazzi and other exiled families soon learned to watch their backs at all times. At home, Cosimo quickly began establishing his own autocratic rule. It did not take him long to decide that Guicciardini's advice was not needed any more, and his adviser was encouraged to retire to his country villa near Arcetri, south of Florence. During Guicciardini's remaining years he would write the work for which he is remembered, his justly celebrated *History of Italy*, one of our main windows on the age, through which he lived. Here the author unexpectedly reveals himself as a patrician who perhaps ultimately believed in democratic rule in the Ancient Greek style, such as he had encountered in his humanist education. Guicciardini's conclusions have the seasoned insight one would expect of a man who had served as an ambassador, had been the closest councillor of two popes (Leo X and Clement VII) and had advised two rulers (Alessandro and Cosimo). As such, his *History of Florence* is not only more reliable but superior in judgement to that produced by Machiavelli, his earlier contemporary. Guicciardini was not entirely scrupulous, either in his life or in his *History*, but his advice (and his writing) was not Machiavellian. Nonetheless, it was the Machiavellian approach that Cosimo de' Medici now chose to adopt, regardless of the advice of his experienced former mentor; and this was precisely what was needed if Florence was to survive in the world of sixteenth-century Italian politics.

Cosimo was determined to establish himelf as *ruler* of Florence, rather than merely rule the city: a subtle but fundamental shift. Previously those who had ruled the city, either well or badly, had emerged more as leaders than as rulers; they were the head of an efficient party machine, which supported them. Cosimo, Duke of Florence, would establish himself as a sovereign ruler, who was supported by an efficient professional bureacracy consisting of institutions rather than councils. Again, the transformation is subtle, but represents a distinct sea change. Previously, the administration consisted of factions, jockeying for power; now it became a bureacratic monolith; others had previously delegated, while Cosimo took an intense and detailed interest in the workings of his administration. Initially, his rule would be one of cold calculation. He was not afraid to instil fear, for he felt himself above popularity; and it seemed that the time was ripe for such rule. The citizens of Florence had suffered deeply: they had been shamed, bewildered and humiliated — the Republic of Christ had been followed by the siege, then had come a decadent tyranny. A beaten populace acquiesced to Cosimo's autocracy: the republican spirit of old was now a spent force.

Guicciardini had already begun to fall out with Cosimo before he was encouraged to retire. For him the last straw had been Cosimo's willingness to accept that Florence was now little more than a vassalate of the Emperor Charles V, its defence and even its government dependent on the Spanish troops in the Fortezza da Basso, who received their orders from elsewhere. But the young Cosimo was wise enough to see that there was little alternative for the moment; instead he would bide his time – the ruler who had ascended as an inexperienced young man was quick to mature. A later description of Cosimo by the Venetian ambassador indicates the man he was rapidly becoming: 'He is unusually large, very sturdy and strong. His expression is gracious but he can make himself terrible when he wishes. In toil or in taking exercise he is indefatigable and delights in recreations that call for agility, strength or dexterity . . . he recognises no one, [has a] habitual severity . . . he is never familiar and keeps himself aloof save when business makes this impossible.'

Cosimo's policy resided in several closely interlinked ideas; his prime intention was always the greater glory of Florence and the Medici (which he saw as largely identical). In foreign policy, this would require the gradual withdrawal from control by the Emperor Charles V. Internally, it required an efficient government by a civil service, rather than the jealousies of ruling factions and families who hoped that one day they might rule; once this hope was extinguished, the families worked together to support Cosimo, competing only to serve him. Such an administration also introduced the spread of efficient rule throughout the region under Florentine control. Cosimo would preside over a Florence that gradually transformed itself from a city state to a full-blown sovereign territory with an integrated administrative structure. His period as ruler marked a rite of passage for Florence's government – a transformation that was taking place to a greater or lesser extent throughout Europe, for now it was government's turn to experience a Renaissance. Certain ancient civic ideals, such as those of Cicero, were indeed adopted by some administrators; and many (including Cosimo, Duke of Florence) would strive for an autocracy mirroring the Roman Empire. But in reality the practice of government also underwent a Reformation: outmoded medieval attitudes and practices were discarded, in favour of a reformed administration working according to a fixed agenda. In Cosimo's case this may be seen quite clearly;

what in the time of Lorenzo the Magnificent had been a series of gestures, designed to further Medici rule, now became a recognisable policy, designed to further the inseparable interests of the duke and his dukedom.

Despite Cosimo's wish for independence, he saw that Florence's interests were for the time being best served by continuing the close alliance with Charles V, and with this in mind he approached the emperor with a suggestion that he be allowed to marry Charles V's daughter Margaret, Alessandro's widow. This was seen by Cosimo as a purely dynastic match, undertaken to give an element of continuity and to retain a beneficial alliance. Yet Charles V had other ideas; he knew that he could rely on Florence, though he was less sure of the new pope Paul III, so instead he married Margaret to Pope Paul III's grandson.

Cosimo next approached Don Pedro of Toledo, Charles V's viceroy in Naples, requesting permission to marry his only daughter, the seventeen-year-old Eleanor of Toledo; this request was granted. Don Pedro had acquired vast riches from the New World, and Eleanor brought with her a suitably munificent dowry; though as the Medici only continued to act as bankers in private trading, there are no *libri segreti* available to put a precise figure on this dowry, whose bounty would have included particular articles of treasure beyond exact price. The marriage in 1539 at the Medici family church of San Lorenzo in Florence was a suitably lavish occasion, and the people of the city were encouraged to participate with free cakes and wine; this was the first big public celebration that Florence had witnessed in many long years.

After his marriage, Cosimo moved from the Palazzo Medici on the Via Larga to the Palazzo Vecchio in the centre of the city. Cosimo had two reasons for taking up residence here: not only would he and his family be more easily guarded by the Florentine militia, but he would also be able to supervise more closely the administration that was housed in the same building.

In 1542 the uneasy truce between Francis I of France and the Holy Roman Emperor Charles V once again gave way to open hostility. Cosimo was quick to pledge his support for Charles V, who made known his need for money to hire an army; at once Cosimo made available a large sum from his dowry, and in return the grateful emperor withdrew his Spanish garrison from the Fortezza da Basso, as well as from similar garrisons at

Livorno and Pisa. Cosimo immediately began integrating the administration of these cities with that of Florence, at the same time building up the Tuscan defences. As Charles V's ally, he also undertook to march on Siena, Florence's long-standing enemy to the south, where Strozzi's son Piero had taken up residence with the intention of using the city as a base to launch another attack on Florence.

The war between Siena and Florence would result in a bitter three-year conflict. Piero Strozzi eventually fled to France; imperial Spanish troops, nominally under Florentine control, laid waste much of Siena's surrounding countryside; and the city was then besieged. By the time Florence was finally victorious, the population of the city of Siena was reduced from 16,000 to 6,000; slaughter, disease, flight and banishment had all but destroyed this small city and its surrounding territories.

Many in Florence saw this victory as futile, when the city was worth less than 60,000 florins a year to the dukedom. Cosimo thought otherwise, for this was the largest addition Florence had ever made to its territory, and it was even guaranteed by Charles V. Siena's complex and ramshackle 'democratic' government had for centuries been the cause of crippling internal strife and external foreign adventures, usually at Florence's expense, but now the city's government was integrated into the stable and efficient Florentine administration. In effect, on a small scale, Siena became part of a Florentine empire; to this growing empire was also added the island of Elba, off the southern Tuscan coast, which Cosimo purchased from Genoa in 1548, with the intention of turning it into the dukedom's naval base. Cosimo's ambitions included Florence becoming a sea power, while the mercantile navy was also developed, with the expansion of the port city of Livorno. In a move to recruit new citizens and attract international trade, Cosimo I (as he was now significantly known) declared Livorno to be a city where all forms of religious worship would be tolerated; as a result, the city began to attract Turks, Jews and even persecuted English Roman Catholics. (By the following century, Livorno would have the largest Jewish population in the western Mediterranean.)

Unlike any Medici since Cosimo *Pater Patriae*, Duke Cosimo I set himself a strict daily routine. This would begin with him rising before dawn to study the latest reports from various councils and other city administrations. Cosimo was a great believer in keeping files and records, frequently instigating statistical surveys, censuses and reports suggesting future developments. One result of this would be a network of canals that soon began spreading through the Tuscan countryside, both for irrigation and for navigational purposes. He also revived the flagging fortunes of the universities at Florence and Pisa, introducing sweeping reforms; in a significant move, he particularly encouraged study of the sciences. Even in humanist studies, these were still known as natural philosophy, though in fact learning was now on the brink of the great divide that would one day separate humanist studies (the humanities) from the sciences.

Cosimo would often work through the heat of midday, but in the late afternoon he insisted on taking regular exercise. In winter, he would go riding; in bad weather, he would train at weight lifting; but in summer, his routine would include a swim in the Arno. On one occasion this nearly cost him his life, when unknown assassins had placed rows of spikes and blades beneath the surface of the water at the very spot where he usually dived into the water; fortunately one of his attendants caught sight of a blade glinting in the sunlight. There were various assassination attempts, and Cosimo never went out without several accompanying bodyguards, who were taken from the city's brigade of Swiss Guards, which had replaced Charles V's Spanish garrison. In another significant change, these troops were moved from the Fortezza da Basso to a barracks right by the Piazza della Signoria, a building that became known as the Loggia dei Lanzi (the last word being the Italian corruption of *Landsknechte*, as the Swiss were misleadingly known). A trumpet call from the guards at the ducal apartments in the Palazzo Vecchio, and the Swiss Guards would come running.

However, Eleanor of Toledo quickly tired of the poky rooms and chambers of the Palazzo Vecchio; she had no wish to live in a miniature palace next to a barracks of drunken mercenaries. Worse still was the cage of lions behind the palazzo in the Via dei Leoni; these would frighten her by roaring in the night, and in hot weather their stench was unbearable. Eleanor was a proud Spanish aristocrat, who had grown up in a genuine Neapolitan palace, furnished with all the accoutrements and treasures of viceroyalty, and she was unwilling to settle for less simply because she was married. There was only one residence in Florence that lived up to such expectations, and this was the vast, incomplete Palazzo Pitti – the grandiose folly which had witnessed the ruin of the ambitious Luca Pitti in the time of Piero the Gouty. In 1549, Eleanor of Toledo purchased the Palazzo Pitti, paying a mere 9,000 florins out of her personal fortune; whereupon architects and designers were immediately set to work to make a palace fit for a duchess of viceregal blood. Cosimo himself supervised the laying out of the gardens on the large plot of land at the back, which had been purchased from the Bogoli family. In a corruption of this name, these gardens would become known as the Boboli Gardens – remaining to this day a green haven of shady walks, statues and distant hillside views, all within a mile of the city centre. These still bear the impact of Cosimo's interest in botany, for he not only encouraged the study of science, but practised it in his own small way himself.

Cosimo and Eleanor, together with their growing family, eventually moved into the Palazzo Pitti in 1560, whereupon its official title became the Ducal Palace. Cosimo was as much a family man as was possible for a person of his cool, aloof temperament, and Eleanor accepted these very Spanish characteristics. The only difficulty was Cosimo's mother, Maria de' Medici, née Salviati, who insisted on maintaining her own apartment in the Ducal Palace; Cosimo would become incensed at her fussing interference, while she and Eleanor simply could not get on with each other.

Together Cosimo and Eleanor would have half a dozen children, of whom they were both very fond in their different ways. Eleanor established a distinctly Spanish ambience in the Ducal Palace, and her three daughters were brought up in chaste seclusion, rarely leaving the confines of the building. In keeping with Medici tradition, Cosimo took great pains to cultivate the friendship of a series of popes, ensuring that his second son Giovanni was made a cardinal at seventeen, while his third son Garcia became one some years later. But despite this large family the atmosphere behind the vast austere façade of the Ducal Palace had none of the spontaneity and *joie de vivre* that had characterised the Palazzo Medici in its heyday.

Yet not all was autocratic gloom, and Cosimo did his best to continue the Medici tradition of providing novel entertainment for his citizens, both to amuse them and to distract them from any rebellious inclinations. Perhaps reflecting his Roman aspirations, Cosimo introduced chariot-racing in the large open space in front of the Santa Maria Novella church, and this quickly proved a popular success.

Also in the Medici tradition, Cosimo established himself as a patron of the arts, though this was evidently more through a sense of duty than aesthetic pleasure. For the most part, artists were simply given commissions as the need arose, rather than ones that showed any understanding of their talents. It was Duke Cosimo I who commissioned the posthumous portrait of Cosimo *Pater Patriae* by Jacopo da Pontormo, which took its place in the portrait gallery of the Ducal Palace (see colour plates); and to this was added the duke's own formal and curiously characterless portrait painted by Bronzino: the aim was to establish a Medici tradition, reflecting the greatness of a dynasty. Botticelli, Leonardo and Raphael were long dead; and Michelangelo, whose fame had made him the richest artist of them all, was now a crotchety old man in Rome, constantly revising his final unfinished sculptures. The High Renaissance was over, and art was now entering a period of more mannerist baroque.

The atmosphere of the artistic scene in Florence would be enlivened by the return of Cellini to the city early in Cosimo's reign. According to Cellini himself, he was very close to the duke and his Spanish duchess, and Cosimo's 'usual reserve and austerity' would melt in the artist's company. For once, it appears that Cellini's claims are true; something about this incorrigible and not altogether charmless braggart seems to have penetrated Cosimo's reserve, though even Cellini concedes that there were occasions when Cosimo was less than amused by his antics, with the result that he received several severe reprimands and warnings.

The work that Cosimo commissioned from Cellini would prove amongst the artist's best. To begin with, there was the obligatory grand bust of Cosimo as an Ancient Roman, complete with armour; though despite its evident flattery, this bronze head does hint at something of Cosimo's emotional coldness and contained anger (see page 331). But Cellini's finest work for Cosimo was undoubtedly his full-length bronze of the Ancient Greek Perseus, the slayer of Medusa, the mythical female Gorgon, whose gaze turned men to stone. Cellini depicts Perseus in his winged helmet, sword in hand, holding aloft the freshly decapitated head with its dribbling entrails. This was a popular Renaissance subject, and its mythical resonance is open to wide interpretation; for Cosimo, it represented not only Florence's victory over its enemies, but also how authority would slay the hideousness of public disorder and dissent.

Work on this masterpiece was interrupted by a typical escapade, when Cellini was forced to flee Florence to evade a charge of immorality, involving an outraged mother and her handsome young son. Unusually, this appears to have been a false charge, cooked up by some of the artist's many enemies; and Cellini returned when things had blown over, made his humblest apologies to the sorely tried Cosimo, and completed his *Perseus* as speedily as possible.

The other renowned artist to be befriended by Cosimo was Giorgio Vasari, who had trained under Michelangelo. Vasari would also paint a self-serving portrait of Cosimo, this time surrounded by the artists who enjoyed his patronage, all in somewhat subservient positions. This was at least better than the portrait that Vasari was commissioned to paint celebrating the victory over Siena. He produced an initial design, showing Cosimo surrounded by his councillors planning the victorious campaign, but Cosimo was dismissive, using the royal 'we' to inform Vasari: 'We acted entirely alone in this matter. You can fill up the places of these councillors with figures representing Silence and some other Virtues.' Such megalomaniac claims are given the lie by Cosimo's major commission to Vasari: to design a grand building to house the administration of the Florentine state. This was the Uffizi (meaning 'Offices'), whose imposing colonnaded wings would enclose a long courtyard leading from the edge of the piazza beside the Palazzo Vecchio; this is now the world-famous Uffizi Gallery, which houses so many of the Renaissance masterworks commissioned by the Medici.

Of lesser architectural importance, but some historical interest, is the work Vasari attached to this building. This is the raised and enclosed passageway now known as the Corridoio Vasari, which linked the Uffizi and the Palazzo Vecchio to the duke's new residence nearly half a mile away across the river in the Ducal (Pitti) Palace. It crossed the river by way of a roofed corridor above the shops of the Ponte Vecchio, giving the duke speedy and unimpeded passage to his administrative offices: a means of checking up on things at any moment, as well as a handy escape route.

However, Vasari's masterpiece was undoubtedly his *Lives of the Artists*, a literary work that gave vivid contemporary descriptions of so many of the great Renaissance artists, as well as deep insights into their work and character. The first edition of Vasari's *Lives* appeared in 1550, and the acclaim that greeted it made Cellini so jealous that he immediately began work on his own rather less reliable *Autobiography*. Vasari's *Lives* contains a portrait gallery of genius, warts and all, but in passing it also shows the pervasive effect of Medici patronage, which to a greater or lesser extent affected so many of these artists. This was of course intended; Vasari dedicated the book to Cosimo and meant it to be a glorification of the Medici family, whom he served in so many capacities. Vasari was responsible for almost the entire extensive artistic and architectural programme of Cosimo, acting virtually as his minister of arts. Besides glorifying the unique contribution of Florence (and the Medici) to the creative flowering that we call the Renaissance, Vasari's *Lives* was also the earliest attempt to come to terms with the Renaissance itself: what it meant, what it had achieved and *what in fact it was*. This was just the first in a long process of definition and reassessment that has continued to this day – for this was the age which in so many ways gave birth to our modern world, and how we see ourselves remains reflected in how we see this beginning. This surely is the most pertinent distant mirror of our age.

Cosimo's last years were to be very different, for in his forties his temperament began to mellow, and this made it particularly difficult for him to endure the succession of personal misfortunes that suddenly befell him. In 1562 the forty-year-old Duchess Eleanor, and her two sons Cardinal Giovanni and the teenage Garcia, all died during a malaria epidemic. As if this was not enough, Cosimo's two teenage daughters also died, one of whom was Cosimo's favourite, Maria. In 1564 Cosimo himself became ill and handed over the reins of power to his twenty-three-year-old heir Francesco. Yet there was some good news: in 1569, Cosimo's cultivation of Pope Pius V finally reaped its hoped-for reward, and he was raised to the rank of Grand Duke of Tuscany. The choice of Tuscany, rather than Florence, was his own, intended to indicate that Florence was now a sovereign *territory*. Cosimo's new rank entitled him to be addressed as *Vostra Altezza* ('Your Highness'): the Medici in Florence were now sovereigns, just one rank below royalty. The extension of Florentine power was also demonstrated two years later, when the Turks were defeated by the navies of the Holy League at the Battle of Lepanto, in the southern Adriatic. The new Florentine navy, created by Cosimo, played a vital role in this great battle, which checked Turkish naval power in the region.

Yet the victory proved of little comfort to the new grand duke, who had by this stage shut himself away in a chamber of his huge empty palace, where he lived in grief-ridden isolation, often staring for hours on end at the sole picture on the wall, a portrait of his beloved daughter Maria. However, this spell of self-imposed solitude would not prove permanent; in an effort to rouse himself from his sorrows, Cosimo gradually resumed his sporting habits: hunting, swimming and weight lifting. But now that he had relinquished his power, there was nothing else to occupy his mind – so he took to womanising.

Eventually Cosimo decided to marry a young woman called Camilla Martelli, who had become one of his mistresses. His remaining family was horrified; no sooner had the Medici become grand dukes than the leader of the family was undermining their status by marrying a commoner. The marriage proved a disaster, as Camilla turned from a loving mistress into a shrewish, nagging wife, and life in the Ducal Palace soon became a succession of inelegant shouting matches involving all of the family. Cosimo retired once more to his solitary chamber, and in April 1574 he finally died of apoplexy, at the age of fifty-five. His official reign had lasted thirty-seven years, longer by far than any of his Medici predecessors; he had not been popular, but he had left a flourishing and prosperous Tuscany, whose capital city was a rather dull and provincial Florence. The high artistic drama of the Italian Renaissance had now come to an end, and a hiatus would ensue before the next momentous stage, which would see the Medici returning to their role as godfathers.

26

Medici – European Royalty

B Y THIS STAGE Florence was no longer the main seat of Medici power and influence. When the fourteen-year-old Caterina de' Medici had married Henri de Valois, the second son of the French king Francis I, at Marseilles in 1533, none would have guessed at her auspicious future. Not even Pope Clement VII, who had sought to foster Medici ambitions by marrying her into a royal family, could have imagined that within thirty years she would be dominating that family, and ruling France. By the time of her death Catherine de Médicis (as she became in France) would have been married to one king of France (Henri II) and given birth to three more (Francis II, Charles IX and Henri III). Such was her personality that for almost thirty years Catherine de Médicis would be the virtual ruler of France. While the Grand Dukes of Tuscany ruled over a comparatively peaceful population of 75,000, Catherine de Médicis was attempting to impose her will on the fifteen million people of France during one of the most turbulent periods of that country's history.

Having been orphaned within days of her birth, Catherine's upbringing was entrusted largely to nuns; but this was no tranquil otherworldly life, for all too audibly beyond the walls of the Santa Lucia convent in Florence, the troubled days of the 'Republic of Christ' were unfolding. During this period of Medici exile, Catherine herself was a valuable hostage, and as such, she was lucky to survive the siege of Florence.

The fourteen-year-old Catherine who arrived in Marseilles to marry the fourteen-year-old Henri was a quietly self-possessed, rather dull little girl. But her plain exterior masked a considerable intelligence combined with a character of extreme tenacity; and as she grew up she would increasingly exhibit many of the qualities of her exceptional great-grandfather, Lorenzo the Magnificent, though ironically his almost feminine charm and love of gesture would in Catherine's case be supplanted by a distinctly masculine desire for control.

After her marriage, Catherine and her husband took up residence at the French court of her father-in-law Francis I. The effect of the Italian Renaissance had arrived here early, largely imported by Francis I himself, and his court was a haven of dazzling sophistication amidst a large, somewhat backward rural country. Leonardo da Vinci had spent his final days at the court of Francis I, dying just fourteen years before Catherine arrived. The king still had great ambitions, and in 1546 decided to pull down his old palace in Paris, so that he could begin erecting in its place a vast new edifice for the housing of his family, his court and his art collection — this would be the Louvre.

Despite living amidst such a recognisably Italianate court society, Catherine's early years were difficult. In a court filled with nobles, some of whose domains were larger than Tuscany, it was generally considered that Henri de Valois had married beneath his station. Catherine was sniffily dubbed 'the tradesman's daughter', and as she grew into young womanhood she hardly blossomed; according to a contemporary description: 'She is small and thin; her features are not delicate, and she has bulging eyes, like most of the Medici.'

Matters were not improved when Francis I's eldest son Francis, Duke of Orléans, died in 1536, and Henri de Valois became heir to the throne. Henri de Valois was a deeply damaged young man, who had never fully recovered from his childhood period as a hostage in Spanish captivity. When his father had been released, he had left his two sons behind in captivity; the abandoned Henri had never forgotten this. After his eventual release he returned to hang about his father's court, a silent, brooding figure amongst the witty and sophisticated nobles. He made no secret of the profound resentment he felt towards his father, and this malevolent streak dominated his obstinate character; having absorbed little education, Henri remained intellectually backward and displayed none of the facility of speech required for court life and its cultural activities. Indeed, he largely ignored these, appearing to be little interested in anything but violent pursuits such as hunting and jousting.

Being married to such a man was not easy for Catherine, and it now became imperative that she and Henri produce an heir to perpetuate the royal line, but their marriage remained childless. After several years, court gossip began to suggest that a divorce was in the offing, but Francis I assured Catherine that he would not allow this to happen. Throughout this difficult period, Francis I became very much the father she had never known; Catherine imbibed his ideas, becoming in the process a firm believer in the power of the monarchy. For his part, the ageing Francis I admired Catherine; he enjoyed watching her dancing and hunting, and appreciated her energy and intelligence, as well as her slowly blooming confidence. This was doubt-less encouraged by the presence of a number of Italian artists at the courts in Paris and Fontainebleau. Cellini himself briefly visited Paris in 1537, and would return for a four-year stay in 1540; in his *Autobiography* he mentions meeting Catherine on a number of occasions, but is more interested in describing the impression he made on the king. Cellini mentions how 'the very flower of the French court came to visit me'; and in another chapter he modestly recalls: 'The King returned to his palace, after bestowing on me too many marks of favour to be here recorded.' 'What a miracle of a man!' the king exclaimed on seeing Cellini's work, and so on . . . It was during this period that Cellini produced his justly celebrated gold salt cellar. Catherine too was gradually emboldened by Francis I's appreciation of Italian culture, which was accorded increasing respect as the Renaissance took hold amidst this privileged realm in France.

Then in 1544, after eleven years of marriage, Catherine finally produced her first child at the age of twenty-five. In all, she would eventually have ten children, with four boys and three girls surviving infancy. Three years after the birth of Catherine's first child, Francis I died and her husband ascended to the throne of France as Henri II. But by now the awkward twenty-nine-year-old Henri II was more interested in his forty-eight-year-old mistress, Diane de Poitiers; her maturity had cast a spell over the child-ish Henri, but as she aged and her looks faded, she became increasingly uncertain of her position. As a result she did her best to assert herself over Catherine, even to the extent of organising the education of her chil-dren; meanwhile Catherine de Médicis' self-control was remarkable – uncannily so to many observers. The new queen never lost her dignity, remaining quietly confident of her husband's feelings for her, despite his defects of character; and in this she appears to have been justified, inasmuch as it is possible to judge such intimate matters.

By now Catherine had begun to introduce her own Italian innovations into life at the French royal court. Perhaps the most radical of these was her effect on French cooking, which brought about such a transformation that Catherine de Médicis is widely credited with the origin of French cuisine as such. Prior to Catherine's arrival, French cooking had been largely medieval: thick, sickly sauces were used to disguise the taste of tainted meat, heavy dishes included sweet-and-sour elements, and pungent spices were regarded as the ultimate delicacy. When Catherine had arrived in France, she had brought with her a number of Florentine cooks, who were well versed in the nuances of Italian cuisine, which was much lighter and more subtle than its French counterpart; it was also better balanced, as the Renaissance had seen the inclusion of a wide range of healthy vegetables, which were no longer regarded as simply fodder for the poor.

The Italian attitude towards cuisine would transform the French table, even to the extent of affecting those who sat at the table; prior to this period, the French nobility still regarded eating itself as very much a rough and ready affair, with the man of the house admitting women to his table only on special occasions. Italian meals, on the other hand, had always involved the whole family: men, women, children and even servants all sat down at table together. With the advent of Catherine de Médicis, women now became a regular feature at the dining table in the French court. Likewise, the table itself became a sight of some elegance; Cellini's sumptuous salt cellar, an artistic masterpiece, was symptomatic of the change in table-dressing, and other novelties included fine wine glasses and decanters, rather than beakers or tankards. Before Catherine's time, the French would cut up their food with a knife, but eat it with their fingers; Catherine introduced the Italian refinement of eating from the prongs of a fork, which was regarded by the French as highly effete (to such an extent that this Italianate extravagance would be dropped soon after Catherine's time, and forks would not make a comeback at the French table until the late eighteenth century). The range of French cooking was also extended by Catherine with the introduction of such novelties as aspics and sweetbreads; new vegetables were imported from Italy, including artichokes and truffles; also imported were such sensational treats as

ice cream, and a blend of whipped egg yolk, sugar and Marsala wine called
zabaglione. It is little wonder that in middle age Catherine put on a considerable amount of weight, which even the flattering court portraitists were
hard put to disguise (see page 350). However, for many years she managed
to preserve her waistline by energetic dancing, which she particularly
enjoyed; it was Catherine who also introduced the art of ballet to the
French court, importing specialised Italian dancers and ballerinas.

Throughout the reign of Henri II, Catherine played little part in the
running of the kingdom, and her skills were exercised in organizing the
court. But this difficult task appears to have sharpened her political and
social acumen. She listened to her husband's policy, but said nothing; at
home, Henri II was determinedly opposed to the creeping Protestantism
that was now spreading through France, as Luther's ideas began to take
hold throughout Europe. (England had declared itself Protestant in the
year Catherine arrived in France.) In foreign affairs, Henri II pursued an
anti-Spanish policy, a vindictive legacy of his imprisonment in Spain,
though at length this policy proved futile and was finally ended by the
Peace of Cateau-Cambrésis in 1559.

A great tournament was held to celebrate the signing of this treaty,
and the forty-year-old king insisted on playing a vigorous role in the jousting. In the course of this, a wooden lance rammed through his helmet,
splintering as it entered his skull. The finest physicians in Europe were
summoned, including the great Andreas Vesalius, but nothing could be
done. Within a few days Henri II was dead.

Catherine's sickly fifteenth-year-old son ascended the throne as Francis
II, but was little more than a nominal ruler, for the power lay in the hands
of two noblemen, the Guise brothers. Cardinal Charles Guise looked after
foreign affairs, while Francis, Duke of Guise, controlled the army; the
Guise brothers were fanatically anti-Protestant and were supported in this
by Spain and the papacy.

As Protestantism had spread through Europe, it had begun to attract
increasing numbers of the disaffected and down-trodden peasantry;
exploited in feudal conditions since the earliest medieval times, this class
had found its own spiritual Renaissance in the Reformation of Luther.
As such, Protestantism had taken on a distinctly political edge, and this
element had become more pronounced when over-taxed shopkeepers and

tradesmen began converting to Protestantism as it spread to the cities of France. The Huguenots (as the largely Calvinist French Protestants became known) began to view the Catholic authorities as the enemy; the religious divide now became a political divide, as the Huguenots spoke out against the Crown and the government, although in the event such protests were quickly suppressed.

Matters began to take on a different tenor in 1559, when the Huguenots were joined by disgruntled nobles, who felt themselves stifled by the increasing power of the monarchy and the aristocratic government. The disunited lower classes now had leaders, and the revolt became open; secret congregations in the households of converted tradespeople now became large public meetings in town squares, addressed by Huguenot noblemen.

The Huguenots petitioned Catherine de Médicis, as queen mother, to restrain their persecution by the Guise brothers, which was being enacted in the name of her young son. Catherine began to use her moderating influence, but in 1560 Francis II died and was succeeded by his ten-year-old brother, who became Charles IX. If Catherine's first son had proved a disappointment, then her second son was even more so; the genetic inheritance from his father, combined with that of Catherine's father, the syphilitic Lorenzo, Duke of Urbino, had proved an inauspicious mix. Like his older brother, Charles IX was physically weak, but on top of this he also suffered from mental instability.

This time Catherine was determined to take charge, and made sure that she was appointed regent; her aim was to preserve peace at all costs. The Protestants now had some legal rights, but in practice these were largely ignored in the increasingly hostile climate that was sweeping the country. Catherine could create laws, but had not the power to enforce them, and in 1562 the country collapsed into civil war. A year later Francis, Duke de Guise, was shot by a spy whilst besieging the Protestants at Orléans; when the spy was tried, he confessed that he had been hired by the Protestant leader Admiral de Coligny.

At the termination of the civil war in 1563, Charles IX was declared of age to rule at the Parlement of Rouen, and for the next two years Catherine conducted the young king on a long tour of France, so that he could show himself to the people and gain their loyalty. But the Guise faction and their extremist Catholic supporters were bent on civil war, which broke out again in 1567 and 1568. Catherine did her best to bring about a reconciliation; she conducted negotiations with the Guise faction, and even invited the dashing Admiral de Coligny to meet the king. It so happened that when Coligny arrived in Paris, Catherine was away attending to her daughter Claude, Duchess of Lorraine, who was ill. Coligny used all his charms on the gauche and impressionable young Charles IX, and they would sit up talking into the early hours in the royal chambers at the Louvre. It appeared that Coligny was attempting to usurp Catherine's influence over the king, and when word of this reached her, she returned to Paris in a fury, quickly reasserting her power over the weak-willed Charles IX.

Finally, in an effort to seal a reconciliation between the two factions, Catherine arranged for her daughter Marguerite to marry the young Protestant leader of Bourbon royal blood, Henri of Navarre; and in August 1572 the Catholic and Protestant leaders gathered in Paris to witness the marriage. Despite the signs of public rejoicing, with the bells ringing out from Notre Dame and church towers throughout the city, the atmosphere on the streets below remained uneasy, as Paris sweltered in a summer heat-wave. The pope had made it known that he opposed the marriage, announcing that there could be no union between Catholics and Protestants; as a result the ceremony itself could not be held in Notre Dame, but took place in the square immediately outside. In the midst of this the Protestant leaders ostentatiously 'went for a walk' at the point in the ceremony where Mass was celebrated by the newly wed couple.

Four days later, at the climax of the celebrations on Wednesday 20 August, an assassination attempt was made on Coligny. An arquebus was fired at him from an upper window as he walked along the rue de Béthisy (now the rue de Rivoli), but at the opportune moment Coligny happened to bend down to fasten his shoe and was merely wounded. The house from which the arquebus was fired was found to belong to a retainer of the Guise family; evidently they were seeking to avenge the murder of Francis, Duke of Guise.

Catherine and Charles IX hastened to Coligny's bedside, and the admiral asked to speak alone with the king. On their way back to the Louvre, Catherine browbeat Charles IX into revealing what Coligny had said in their secret conversation – apparently he had warned the young king not to trust Catherine. By now Paris was in a turmoil: 200 Huguenots occupied the Guise house on the rue de Béthisy, and armed bands of Huguenots roamed the streets. The markets closed and the shops were shuttered as the citizenry took refuge in their homes.

Prompt action was necessary, or the situation in the capital was liable to get out of hand, in all likelihood sparking another civil war throughout the country. Next day Charles IX was shown proof that Coligny had in fact been plotting to attack him, and on learning of the treachery of his new friend he is said to have become unhinged. Whether Charles IX now acted alone, or on the encouragement of his mother, is unclear, but in the early hours of Sunday 24 August, the feast of St Bartholomew, members of the Swiss Royal Guard led by one of the Guise faction broke in on Coligny and stabbed him to death, tossing his body out through the window into the street below. This was a signal for the massacre of the Huguenots by the royal forces, aided by the Catholics of Paris. Huguenots — men, women and children — were dragged from their beds throughout the city and murdered in an orgy of killing that lasted two days, during which as many as 2,500 were killed. As news of the St Bartholomew's Day Massacre spread throughout France, similar slaughters took place in Orléans, Rouen, Lyons, Bordeaux and Toulouse; in all, as many as 8,000 may have died. This marked the beginning of a series of wars of religion that would plague France for the next thirty years.

It seems likely that Catherine de Médicis was at least partially responsible for the St Bartholomew's Day Massacre. Whether she panicked, or saw this as the only course, is uncertain; though there can be little doubt that if she had not struck first, her life, as well as that of the king, would have been gravely endangered. Either way, Catherine de Médicis was certainly blamed for this bloody settling of scores, one of the most infamous acts in French history. And from now on she would be regarded as the leader of Catholic France in its struggle against the Huguenots.

Reports vary as to the effect of this event on Catherine de Médicis herself. According to some, she never fully recovered; now in her fifties, her manipulative temperament took on a harder cynical edge, while her previously stout middle-aged figure became flabby and repulsively fat. Other reports indicate that she remained active, hunting and dancing and talking as wittily as ever — France was irreconcilably divided, even down to the way it saw its ruling queen.

Fig 18 Catherine de Médicis

In 1574 Charles IX died at just twenty-four years of age, and Catherine's favourite third son now ascended to the throne as Henri III. Catherine had placed little confidence in Charles IX, but she had high hopes for the twenty-three-year-old Henri, despite being well aware of his weaknesses. Henri III kept aloof and made few friends outside his close-knit immediate circle, who were known as the *mignons* (cuties); in the words of a contemporary: 'They all dress alike in coats of many colours and they are sprinkled with violet powder and other sweet perfumes.' Catherine seemed to accept this homosexuality as perhaps inevitable in the weak son of such an overbearing mother. However, Henri III's pathological extravagance, together with his interest in zealous religious flagellants, appeared to hint at deeper deviancy from the norm. Two days after his coronation, he was married to Louise of Lorraine, with the aim of ensuring a much-needed heir for the house of Valois, although for the time being no heir appeared.

Catherine de Médicis remained virtual ruler of France, but even during these difficult years she still found time to extend her cultural influence over her adopted country. It was she who brought the final legacy of the Italian Renaissance to France: Catherine was responsible for the building of the Tuileries, the great royal palace adjoining the Louvre on the right bank of the Seine. (This would be burned down in the 1871 Commune, leaving only the present Tuileries Gardens in the centre of Paris.) Catherine would also design and build several of the great French chateaux, including the most enchanting of them all, which spans the river at Chenonceaux. This marks the ultimate coming together of the Italian and French styles, being a blend of northern European Gothic and southern Renaissance, shot through with a vision of pure fairyland. (Not for nothing is one of the chateaux along the Loire said to be the setting of the original Sleeping Beauty.) This was Florence north of the Alps, yet it was also the Medici north of the Alps; here the Medici spirit had blossomed. These chateaux were not palaces for the ruler of a city state, but the fairytale extravagances of supreme majesty; in France the Medici had become sovereigns, leaving all notions of democracy far behind, just as they had done in Florence.

Yet the question remained as to how all this could continue, for still Henri III and his unfortunate bride Louise failed to produce an heir. This left the Protestant Henri of Navarre as the heir presumptive, and the fact that he was married to Catherine's daughter Marguerite now appeared as yet another piece of characteristic Medici foresight. In 1586 Catherine travelled south-west to Cognac to meet Henri of Navarre and secure the succession; at the same time she also made a final attempt at a reconciliation between the Protestants and the Catholics, although this failed. France was descending further and further into chaos and it appeared that nothing could be done to avert this. Bloated and worn out by her efforts, Catherine de Médicis finally died in 1589 at the age of sixty-nine.

As much as anyone, Catherine had ruled France during the fourteen-year reign of her son Charles IX, and for the fifteen years she had lived during the reign of her son Henri III. She had been the dominating presence, though precisely how much she had in fact guided France's destiny remains open to question. The internecine chaos over which she presided had almost certainly been inevitable, yet it is fair to say that, but for her influence, the country might well have collapsed into chaos earlier and for longer than it did.

During the last years of the fifteenth century, France – in the form of Charles VIII – had brought military might to Italy. By the early decades of the following century, Italian culture had begun to percolate back into

France, and would continue to do so throughout the sixteenth century. Catherine de Médicis was to encourage a late flowering of this, leaving permanent cultural monuments ranging from chateaux and the ballet to the founding of a great cuisine. But she also brought elements of the dark underside of the Italian Renaissance; hers was the politics of Machiavelli, for even if she had not read *The Prince* she had certainly imbibed its message – through her life in Florence, and through her very existence as a Medici. She would have known by heart the stories of her great-grandfather Lorenzo the Magnificent; and like him, during times of travail her rational, calculating humanism had succumbed to the irrationalism that was also reborn with the Renaissance. When all else failed, she fell back on astrology; it is known that on several occasions she consulted the great French seer Nostradamus, who answered her questions with characteristically enigmatic prophecies. On one occasion, a vision in a mirror led him to prophesy that the line of Valois would die out (though precisely when this event would occur was not mentioned). However, when the need for action arose, Catherine chose to rely on the methods of Machiavelli rather than on magic, and as such she remains one of the great figures of French history: respected and reviled by many, loved by few. The little orphan, abandoned amidst the siege of Florence, had not known love: the legendary stories of her ancestors and the sound of the guns surrounding the city were all that she had heard of her family during her impressionable childhood years.

Within three months of the death of Catherine de Médicis, the Catholic League had seized Paris and attempted to depose her son Henri III, on account of his alleged leniency towards the Huguenots. In the course of the siege the king was assassinated by a fanatical priest, and Henri of Navarre succeeded to the throne as Henri IV, with Catherine de Médicis' daughter Marguerite as his queen. In 1593 Henri IV converted to Catholicism in a desperate attempt to reunite France; seven years later he wished to sever the French royal connection with Catherine de Médicis by divorcing his wife Marguerite, who had failed to produce an heir. Besides needing an heir, Henri IV also required a rich wife to refill the royal coffers, which had become sorely depleted during his conflict against the Catholic League.

On hearing of this, Ferdinando I, Grand Duke of Tuscany (son of Cosimo I) contacted his distant cousin Marguerite; he impressed upon her that the future of the Medici dynasty was at stake, and that this should be placed above her own personal interests. As a result of this consultation Marguerite agreed to divorce Henri IV, but on one condition – that he married her cousin Maria de' Medici, the niece of Ferdinando I. At the same time Ferdinando I contacted Henry IV, saying that if he agreed to this arrangement, Maria de' Medici would be supplied with a handsome dowry of 600,000 florins – sufficient to equip an army with which the French monarchy could defend itself. In October 1600 Henri IV married Maria de' Medici, and in the following year she gave birth to a son, who was christened Louis: the succession was secured.

Maria de' Medici had been born in Florence in 1573, and by the age of five she had to all intents and purposes become an orphan. Her mother had died, whereupon her father quickly remarried and moved out of the Palazzo Pitti, leaving Maria, together with an older brother and two sisters, in the care of governesses supervised by the palace chamberlain. Within four years her brother and a sister had died, and the other sister had moved out with her new husband. From the age of nine, Maria was brought up amidst the large emptiness of the Palazzo Pitti, with its scores of furnished but largely unoccupied rooms, salons and chambers. (Although the Palazzo Pitti would not be enlarged to its present vastness until 1616, it was already an imposing edifice at this time.) Amidst the desolation of her loneliness, Maria formed a deep attachment to a girl called Leonora Dori, who was the daughter of her wet-nurse. Leonora was three years older than Maria, and was to become the first of several such favourites on whom Maria grew to depend.

Maria herself was a rather stolid, strong-willed child with mousy hair and a snobbish sense of her own lineage; her mother had been a Habsburg, her father a grand duke, and no one was allowed to forget this. When crossed, she displayed a passionate temper, but would quickly seek a reconciliation when this had been directed at one of her favourites. Much like her distant cousin Catherine de Médicis, her Medici predecessor on the French throne, Maria was a forceful personality, but this personality had distinct flaws. Unlike Catherine, she was not intelligent, witty or energetic; indeed, she was often mentally slow and given to bouts of lethargy.

Marie de Médicis (as she now became) had been married to Henri IV by proxy, and she arrived in France, a bride at the rather late age of twenty-seven, to find herself married to a forty-seven-year-old French philanderer. Henri IV was offended by her plainness, and Marie found the king uncouth and malodorous (the Italians had retained the Roman habit of bathing frequently, whereas this custom had lapsed during the Dark Ages in the colder climates north of the Alps). Marie, who was short and stout, was disappointed to discover that her grey-bearded husband was even shorter, though despite his aged appearance Henri IV relished his court nickname of 'the Green Gallant', a reference to his ever-green lust.

Marie de Médicis brought two favourites with her to France: her attendant Leonora Dori was accompanied by a homosexual social-climber called Concino Concini, who had married her in an unscrupulous mutual arrangement to better themselves. Unlike the Medici splendours of the Palazzo Pitti in Florence, the royal residence of the Louvre was in a sorry state, and the adjoining Tuileries started by Catherine was still far from complete. The Louvre had been badly ravaged by the civil war, and the royal coffers had been too depleted to afford repairs – with the result that many rooms were deserted, and some sections even remained without roofing. Marie immediately began spending some of her considerable Medici inheritance on refurbishing the royal residence, while Henri IV responded to this by moving in his mistress Henriette, whom he had created Marquise de Verneuil. Shortly after Marie de Médicis produced a royal heir, Henriette also produced a male offspring, and he too was brought up in the Louvre, along with the rest of the king's gaggle of illegitimate children, who also inhabited the palace. Henriette immediately commenced plotting to have her son declared heir to the throne, but to Marie's relief this eventually resulted in a charge of treason. A farcical court case ensued, and Henriette was sentenced to death; after a suitable interval, she returned once more to the Louvre, but refrained from any further dynastic ambitions.

Unexpectedly, the leading participants in this hectic royal household developed a genuine familial feeling for one another, with only occasional domestic spats. As Marie began producing more children on a regular basis, Henri IV began to overlook her plainness; indeed, he gallantly informed one and all that if Marie had not been his wife, he would have had her as his mistress. Marie evidently decided to regard this as something of a compliment, and did her best to create a happy home for her errant royal husband; meanwhile, the new Italian cooks whom Marie had brought with her from Florence ensured that all ate well at the royal table.

Like Catherine de Médicis, Marie would also made her contribution to French cuisine. Catherine's cooks had strongly influenced French cooking, but it was during Marie's time that modern French cuisine emerged as a recognisable entity, and this only occurred when French chefs had absorbed the rationale that lay behind Italian cooking. The central idea of Italian cuisine was to enhance the flavour of the meat or fish, rather than smother it; sauces were intended to emphasise elements that were already present, drawing them out, thus meat was garnished with a sauce made from its own juices, while fish was cooked in a stock consisting of discarded elements such as the head and tail. Previously French cooks had merely copied Italian recipes; now that they understood the theoretical basis of Italian cooking they quickly began creating their own national cuisine.

The first outstanding chef of this kind was François La Varenne, who trained in the Italian kitchens of Marie de Médicis, and twenty years later would write *Le Cuisinier français* (The French Chef), the first systematic and comprehensive guide to the preparation of French cuisine. La Varenne is remembered particularly for his innovative use of mushrooms to accentuate the taste of beef and lamb, and it was in the royal kitchens that the classic dish Tournedos Médicis, steak with a Madeira sauce, was invented and named after Marie de Médicis.

In 1610 Henri IV was assassinated on his way to campaign against the Spanish, and Marie became regent for her eight-year-old son Louis XIII. Marie had always disliked her husband's anti-Spanish policy, and now countermanded this with the aid of her favourite Concino, whom she had raised to the status of Marquis d'Ancre, and who now became her close adviser. In 1614 Louis XIII came of age to reign, but the regent and her adviser chose to ignore this; the immature twelve-year-old was easily browbeaten into acquiescence, and Marie continued to rule France in his name. Power began to encourage her naturally extravagant nature, which had the effect of warping her judgement so that she made a number of ill-advised concessions to enemies amongst the nobility; but she was shielded from her growing unpopularity by her circle of Italian sycophants.

Soon Louis XIII also had a favourite, the manipulative and increasingly powerful Charles d'Albert de Luynes, and together they schemed to wrest power from Marie. In 1618 the Marquis d'Ancre was assassinated and Marie de Médicis was exiled to Blois, where she unsuccessfully attempted to foment rebellion against her son. She now turned to a new adviser, a talented and aristocratic young clergyman named Armand Jean du Plessis de Richelieu, who approached Louis XIII and used his considerable political skills to affect a reconciliation between the king and his mother.

Louis XIII was soon in conflict with the Huguenots, together with their foreign allies, and when his adviser de Luynes was killed in battle, Richelieu took his place. By this stage the ongoing struggle between Catholics and Protestants had begun to stir up all manner of dynastic and territorial conflicts further afield, and Europe was plunged into the vicious and destructive Thirty Years War, with armies clashing from Russia to France, from Austria to the Baltic. Richelieu used his skills as best he could to protect France, yet was only marginally successful; in 1622 Louis XIII ensured that Richelieu was made a cardinal, in recognition of his services. Marie de Médicis bitterly resented Richelieu's 'treachery' to her, as she saw it; not only had he deserted her for her son, but he was also reversing her pro-Spanish pro-Catholic policy, in favour of tactical alliances with Protestant powers.

Thwarted in other fields, Marie de Médicis now diverted her energies to cultural matters, and in this field her influence would be almost as pervasive as that of Catherine de Médicis. As early as 1615 Marie had commissioned the finest French architect Salomon de Brosse to build the Luxembourg Palace on the left bank of the Seine. This was intended to be a replica of the Palazzo Pitti, and Marie even sent to Florence for plans of the Pitti; de Brosse graciously accepted these, and then continued with his own design. Marie would also commission works by a number of artists, including the young French painter Nicolas Poussin, though her favourite artist was undoubtedly the Dutch Baroque painter Peter Paul Rubens, whom she invited to Paris in 1622.

By now the High Renaissance in art had given way to the extravagances of Baroque, where brilliance of surface technique carried art beyond the structural understanding that had once united it with science. Art had outgrown its scientific phase, just as science was beginning to emerge from being a mere 'art'; a century after the death of Leonardo, the existence of a Renaissance man whose genius both spanned and integrated the arts and sciences was no longer conceivable. In Leonardo's studio, his assistants had frequently hung about unemployed, whilst the master ground his own newly discovered combinations of pigments, or secretively filled his coded notebooks with art-science. By contrast, Rubens's studio was a hive of collective activity, with industrious assistants, 'collaborators' and apprentices all working away under the master's direction; here was the division of labour and co-operative effort required to produce the vast canvases that made Rubens's studio a thriving industry and its master a millionaire. Rubens too was multi-talented, and was in many ways the Baroque evolution of the Renaissance man; but his talents spilled out into diplomacy and scholarship, rather than the discoveries of science, and it was his extravagance of character rather than his intellect that informed his work. The baroque Renaissance man blossomed as an impresario expressing the fullness of his nature, rather than as an explorer of the secrets of nature. As we shall soon see, this investigative strain of Renaissance endeavour would require its own distinct quality of genius for it to be fully developed.

Rubens was set to work by Marie de Médicis to decorate two large galleries of the almost complete Luxembourg Palace, and for this he produced more than twenty vast canvases depicting the main events of her long career, all suitably glorified into mythological or legendary context. Rubens's ability to depict large fleshy women as objects of ethereal beauty was ideally suited to the requirements of Marie de Médicis, and the artist flatteringly fulfilled his duty to his royal patron (see colour plates); despite such weighty requirements, these paintings would be amongst Rubens's finest works.

In 1629 Richelieu persuaded Louis XIII to invade Italy, a move that antagonised the Catholic Habsburg powers (Austria and Spain); as a result, Marie demanded that Louis XIII dismiss Richelieu, at the same time urging her second son Gaston, Duke of Orléans, to rebel against the king. Faced with such opposition from within his family, Louis XIII at first dithered, and then plumped for Richelieu. In 1631 Marie de Médicis was banished, and fled to the Spanish Netherlands, where she lived in increasingly lonely exile. Rubens, who was probably her only real friend, died in 1640. After this she travelled to England, where one of her daughters had married Charles I, but quickly discovered that no one wanted her here, and was forced to return to the Netherlands. Wherever she went she was an embarassment; even her presence in the Spanish Netherlands became ill regarded in Spain, as its king sought to amend matters with the French king. In 1642 Marie finally died at Cologne in Germany, alone and unloved, at the age of sixty-nine. Her extravagances of personality had left her bankrupt, both financially and spiritually, and Medici power outside Italy was dissipated, though her children would ensure that Medici blood now passed into all the major royal houses of Europe.

27

Godfathers of the
Scientific Renaissance

I N THE SUMMER of 1605, five years after Marie de Médicis had left
Florence to join her husband King Henri IV of France, Grand Duke
Ferdinando I required a temporary tutor for his son Cosimo. The
fifteen-year-old Cosimo was a lively, personable young man, but there was
no getting away from the fact that he was indolent; although intellectually gifted, he seemed to prefer entertainment to education. The tutor who
commended himself most to Ferdinando I was the forty-year-old professor of mathematics at Padua University; this was Galileo, the man who
was to become the first great scientist of the modern era.

The family of Galileo Galilei were citizens of Florence who had originated in the Mugello, the mountain valley north of the city that also
produced the Medici. Galileo himself was born in Pisa on 15 February
1564, just three days before the death of the eighty-nine-year-old
Michelangelo, the last hero of the High Renaissance. This juxtaposition
is significant: the vanguard of the Renaissance would now pass from art
to science. Galileo's father Vincenzo was a formative influence on the young
scientist and a man of some interest in his own right. He was descended
from a noble family of dwindling fortune, had little money, and possessed
a combative temperament which would ensure that he remained in this
situation. Yet he was also a man of genuine musical talent, playing the
lute and writing compositions that involved an unmistakable mathematical ability.

When the Galilei family returned from Pisa to Florence in 1572,
Vincenzo was employed at the grand-ducal court in the Palazzo Pitti as

a musician. He also renewed an association with the Camerata Bardi musical circle, a group of talented performers and theorists who were given hospitality by the ancient banking family. Vincenzo had his own original ideas about musical theory, and rebelled against the straitjacket of counterpoint, which had been favoured in medieval music; instead, he insisted that music should please the ear in practice, rather than conform to formal mathematical beauty on the page. The freer compositions preferred by Vincenzo and others in Florence at the time were to bring about a renaissance in music.

Most notably, the musicians of Florence were responsible for the birth of opera, which arose from two distinct sources. On the one hand, there was medieval liturgical drama: holy plays enacted publicly at various times in the Church calendar. Quite separate from these were the classical Greek dramas, with their choric interludes, which were revived and staged by the Florentine humanists. When these two forms were combined, the result was opera: non-religious work incorporating music and drama. The term takes its name from the Italian expression *opera in musica* (work in music); and the settings of these early operas were usually either legendary or mythical, requiring a new freer musical form such as that favoured by Vincenzo Galilei.

The first opera is generally accepted as *Dafne*, a drama by the Florentine poet Ottavio Rinuccini, which was set to music by the singer and composer Jacopo Peri, who was musical director at the court of the Medici; and this work was performed at the pre-Lenten carnival in Florence in 1598. The text is largely lost, but significantly the oldest *surviving* opera, a setting of Rinuccini's *Euridice*, is known to have been performed at the Palazzo Pitti in 1600. Astonishingly, the Medici seem also to have been godfathers of Renaissance music.

By the turn of the seventeenth century the Renaissance was beginning to make itself felt in a range of increasingly disparate fields. The times were changing, even in the most literal sense: when it was noticed that the seasons were beginning to drift away from their customary position in the ancient calendar, Pope Gregory XIII abandoned the ancient Julian calendar dating from Julius Caesar in 46 BC, and in 1582 introduced a new Gregorian calendar, at a stroke advancing the date by ten days. Yet many remained highly suspicious of such transformations, and as the new calendar was introduced over the years throughout Europe, it provoked riots, with indignant mobs demanding back the ten days that had been robbed from their lives. After centuries of medieval stasis and certainty in so many fields, change was seen by many as a threat and was far from being universally welcomed.

The red-headed young Galileo Galilei was a boisterous rebel who inherited many of his father's characteristics; but unlike his father, he was also self-confident and quickly convinced of his own brilliance, though quite where this brilliance was to be applied was another matter. At the age of seventeen he returned to the city of his birth to study at the University of Pisa, but soon became disillusioned by what he was expected to study; stale medieval scholasticism was taught by rote – and was expected to be learned as such, to be repeated in exams. There was no room for imagination, independence of thought, new ideas – the Renaissance may have transformed art and architecture, and may have begun to transform much more, but the arid ideas of Aristotle's natural philosophy still prevailed in the universities.

It was not in Galileo's nature to suffer fools gladly, and he made no attempt to hide his contempt for his teachers; he would interrupt their lectures by posing ironic questions designed to show them up. Why, for instance, did all hailstones regardless of their size hit the ground at the same speed, when Aristotle said that heavier bodies fell faster than lighter ones? The lecturer would reply that the lighter hailstones evidently fell from lower in the sky, so that they *appeared* to fall at the same speed. Such explanations were derided by Galileo, but he was making himself few friends; it soon became evident to all, including his fellow students, that he was too clever for his own good. With nothing else to challenge his mind, Galileo began seeking stimulus elsewhere, in the taverns and bordellos of Pisa.

Fortunately, provincial Pisa came to life between Christmas and Easter when the Grand Duke of Tuscany transferred his court to the city, a tradition that had been inaugurated by Grand Duke Cosimo I, in an attempt to draw the cities of Tuscany together and unite the grand duchy. For a brief season, Pisa would become the social hub of the dukedom, with all manner of stimulating entertainment, ranging from music to chariot-racing and lectures on a wide variety of subjects. On one occasion Galileo managed to sneak his way into a private lecture being given by Ostillion Ricci, the court mathematician (a new post introduced by the scientifically sympathetic Cosimo I). Galileo was captivated by what he heard; he had long been intrigued by abstract calculation, but mathematics was dismissed as irrelevant by the university authorities – several years prior to Galileo's arrival at Pisa, the professor of mathematics had died, but his position would remain unfilled throughout Galileo's student years.

Galileo soon began to study under Ricci, who introduced him to the Ancient Greek mathematicians, leading him through the proofs and arguments of Euclid and Archimedes. The traditional scholastic arguments taught in the universities looked to authorities such as the writings of Aristotle to confirm the truth of what they said. Galileo was intrigued to learn that the arguments of Euclid used only the irrefutable reason of proof to establish their truth. After Ricci and the court moved back to Florence, Galileo continued studying on his own at Pisa.

Much to the anger of his father, Galileo returned to Florence in 1585 without either a degree or the prospect of a job. Eventually Vincenzo managed to pull a few strings at the grand-ducal court and Galileo secured some occasional lecturing at the Florentine Academy. Then in 1589 he managed to secure the post of professor of mathematics at his old university; this was a curious appointment for someone with Galileo's qualifications, but here it seems that he benefited from medieval laxity. Another factor may have been the salary, which was just sixty florins a year, less than the income of a shopkeeper; Galileo was outraged when he discovered this, but there was nothing he could do about it, for he desperately needed any money he could get. His aged father could no longer work, and Galileo now had to support the entire family; to provide further income at Pisa he took extra tutoring, but also found time to continue with researches of his own.

These researches were conducted with characteristic flair. According to the celebrated legend, Galileo mounted the leaning Tower of Pisa and dropped two objects of differing weight, and in this way demonstrated to the assembled students and professors that both objects fell through space at the same rate, thus contradicting the Aristotelian view that heavier bodies fall faster than lighter ones. Whether or not this experiment actually took place (and most now think it did not), the anecdote serves as a perfect illustration of how Galileo's method differed from Aristotelian practice. Galileo did an experiment to discover the truth, while the Aristotelians believed their truth because that was what was said in the writings of Aristotle. Of course, if two bodies of different weight *are* dropped from the same height, they will not in fact hit the ground at precisely the same moment. This is because of differing air resistance; and the Aristotelians maintained that this discrepancy proved their point, which forced Galileo to conjecture that the two objects would indeed fall at the same rate if they were dropped in a vacuum. (It would be almost 400 years before Galileo's conjecture was dramatically vindicated before a huge audience. In 1969, whilst standing on the surface of the moon, the astronaut Neil Armstrong dropped a hammer and a feather; both hit the surface at the same moment, at which Armstrong remarked: 'You see, Galileo was right.')

As a result of Galileo's experiments, he came up with certain laws of motion, such as: 'When falling, the final velocity of a body is proportionate to the time it has fallen.' This incorporated a crucial step: Galileo was applying measurement to physics, an innovation that would eventually lead him to conceive of the fundamental notion of 'force'.

Galileo's stroke of genius was the application of mathematics to physics; this may seem obvious to us now, but in Galileo's time these were two separate and seemingly disparate subjects. The moment when maths and physics were combined – giving rise to such notions as measurable force – modern physics was born. Things could be weighed, distances measured, times recorded, all in precise numbers, and this application of mathematical analysis to physical phenomena brought into being the notion of experiment. Such things could only be determined and measured *in practice*, and this was the beginning of experimental science. Concrete practical experience could be abstracted into numerical and conceptual terms, results could be recorded, then compared with other results recorded under similar conditions, and in this way general laws could be formulated. The name Galileo gave to such practical tests was *cimento*, which in Italian means 'ordeal'; similarly, the word we use today – experiment – derives from an Old French word meaning 'to put on trial'. Galileo's insight and practice laid the basis of modern science; it was he who said: 'The book of Nature is written in mathematical language. Its characters are triangles, cubes and

Fig 19 Galileo Galilei

other geometrical figures, without whose help . . . one wanders in vain through a dark labyrinth.'

In Ancient Greek times, there had been inklings of this, and Pythagoras had even stated: 'The world is made of number.' But he had not envisioned this in practical terms; Galileo was the first to *apply* mathematics in this fashion, and in doing so he discovered an entirely new way to understand the world. The Renaissance in the fields of ancient philosophy and art had given rise to the self-confidence and beliefs of humanism; the Renaissance of ancient science showed how this humanism could realise itself in practical application. Renaissance humanism had created a new way of seeing ourselves, Renaissance science would create a new way of seeing the world.

Galileo soon became a popular figure at Pisa, with the students idolising their rebellious and rumbustious young lecturer, though with the authorities it was another matter. Most of the other lecturers at Pisa were friars, and in Galileo's publicly expressed opinion the ideas of his friar colleagues were as mediocre as they were orthodox. He had similar contempt for academic dress, refusing to wear a gown, and even composed a student ditty to express his view:

> Only wear gowns
> if you're a dim-wit who frowns,
> it's the uniform for schools
> who have to obey rules;
> not allowed in the bordello
> if you're that sort of fellow . . .

Inevitably the Pisan authorities soon grew tired of their disruptive young colleague, and in 1592 Galileo was told to seek employment elsewhere. Fortunately, the chair of mathematics at the prestigious University of Padua had fallen vacant, and Galileo applied. By now his scientific work had begun to attract the attention of several important scientifically minded figures throughout Italy, and his renown was even brought to the attention of Grand Duke Ferdinando I, who referred to him as 'one of Tuscany's finest mathematicians'. Aided by this recommendation, Galileo was accepted for the post at Padua, in the republic of Venice.

Galileo was soon enjoying himself at Padua, where his salary was the equivalent of 500 florins a year. As disrespectful of convention as ever, he set up house with a fiery young mistress called Marina Gambia, by whom he would eventually have three children. His researches were soon producing equally unorthodox results. It was during this period that Galileo began corresponding with the German astronomer Johannes Kepler, who was living in Prague. Galileo confessed to Kepler that he believed Copernicus's theory about the earth and the planets circling the sun, but was afraid to admit this in public for fear of becoming a laughing stock, as his colleagues at Padua remained almost exclusively Aristotelians. In fact, although Galileo did not realise it, Kepler was by this stage both confirming and improving upon Copernicus's heliocentric idea. Making use of the most accurate astronomical observations available in this pre-telescopic age, Kepler was coming to the conclusion that the planets passed around the sun in elliptical orbits, rather than the circular ones suggested by Copernicus.

In 1604 Galileo noticed that a new star had appeared in the sky; this was in fact a nova (an exploding star), only the second of its kind to appear since 134 BC. The arrival of this star caused great consternation amongst orthodox thinkers, for according to Aristotle there could be no such thing as a new star, any more than an old one could disappear. Aristotle had taught that the earth consisted of four elements (earth, air, fire and water), while the heavens were separate from the earth and consisted of 'quintessence', the fifth element or essence, the finest of them all, which was perfect and unchangeable. Objects such as comets, which seemed to contradict this view, were ingeniously explained away as not belonging to the heavens at all; they existed in the sub-lunar region closest to the earth, and were thus meteorological events and not stars.

Never one to shirk an argument, Galileo began a series of lectures on this new star, pointing out how it disproved Aristotelian notions about the heavens. As a result he became involved in a public feud with Cesare Cremonini, the professor of philosophy at Padua. Cremonini maintained the orthodox Aristotelian view that physical laws and measurements only applied on earth; they did not apply to the heavens above the earth, which contained all the planets and stars. Being composed of quintessence, these were unchanging and not subject to the same laws as applied to earth, air, fire and water. When measurements of the heavens were made, they only *appeared* to contradict the laws of Aristotle; in fact, they did nothing of the sort, because such laws were simply inapplicable in this realm. Galileo was frustrated by his inability to deny such arguments on his own terms – he could provide no experimental scientific proof that they were wrong. He was unaware that Kepler was doing just this, as he calculated mathematically the elliptical orbits of the planets, thus demonstrating that mathematics applied to the heavens, just as it did to earth.

By now the ambitious Galileo was becoming impatient; already he was forty, but somehow the fame and fortune that he felt to be his due continued to elude him. Even Cremonini's salary was double his, and others had made a name for themselves without displaying half his originality. Galileo had conceived of all manner of original ideas; he had even produced a number of ingenious inventions – including agricultural devices, military machines and medical instruments – but none of them brought success. After he had done all the work, others simply purloined his ideas and made money out of them. Yet every day his need for money became greater; he now had to support a mistress and three children, to say nothing of his family back in Florence – and his debts were mounting.

As a last resort, Galileo decided to write to Grand Duke Ferdinando I of Tuscany, asking for an official post at court. His letter arrived at an opportune moment, for Ferdinando required a tutor during the summer months for his fifteen-year-old son and heir Cosimo. Galileo was appointed, and took up residence with his young charge in the Medici villa at Pratolino in the hills outside Florence. Here he spent a pleasant few months, living a life of ease and luxury, at the same time endearing himself to his young charge with his exciting scientific experiments and brilliant ideas. But then the summer was over, and it was back to Padua and his creditors.

In 1609 Galileo was once again commissioned by the Medici family, but this time it was Ferdinando I's wife, the Grand Duchess Christina, who required his services. Unfortunately she was under the impression that Galileo was a renowned astrologer, rather than a renowned astronomer, and asked him to cast her husband's horoscope. Ferdinando I was seriously ill: she wanted to know if he would survive this illness, and if so how long he would live. Galileo had no wish to fall from favour and set to work at once, producing a highly optimistic horoscope; he assured the grand duchess that according to the stars all boded well for Ferdinando I, who would soon recover from his illness and live for many years to come. In the event, Ferdinando I died within the week; the prospects of further employment by the Medici seemed bleak.

That same year word reached Galileo in Padua of a new invention: this was the telescope, which had been developed in Holland. Before he had even seen a telescope, Galileo quickly grasped the principle behind what was essentially a two-lensed tube, and immediately produced his own version, which was more than ten times more powerful than any previous telescope. With some political astuteness, he then donated his new 'invention' to the Doge of Venice. The immense importance of the telescope to a sea power such as Venice was quickly realised; it meant that invading ships could be detected on the horizon, giving the city valuable extra hours in which to prepare its defences. The grateful doge extended Galileo's professorship at Padua for the rest of his life, though unfortunately the extra cash he was hoping for did not materialise: he still remained saddled with debts.

Galileo had quickly seen how to make a better telescope, and eventually he would make one thirty-two times more powerful than the original. More importantly, he quickly realised how to make better use of this magnifying instrument, raising it to the night sky, where to his amazement he saw a new universe opening up before him. It was like Columbus discovering an entirely unsuspected continent, and soon Galileo was making a series of sensational discoveries.

Essentially, nothing new had been discovered about the heavens for around three and a half millennia; astrological observation by the naked eye had been taken to its limit by the ancient Babylonians standing atop their ziggurats plotting the patterns of the stars. The moment Galileo raised his telescope to his eye and focused it on the moon, everything changed. Previously the moon had appeared to be nothing more than a radiant disc, which waxed and waned; now it became transformed into a large and mysterious spherical body. Instead of waxing and waning in size, it was seen to be a sphere divided into light and shadow; upon closer inspection it became clear that the surface of this sphere contained craters, mountains and even what appeared to be seas. Galileo knew that this marked the final demise of Aristotelian astronomy: the heavenly bodies were certainly not perfect spheres created out of unchanging quintessence – they were entirely new worlds, with all the imperfections and features of the one inhabited by humanity.

Galileo described his discoveries in a book he entitled *The Starry Messenger*, which he dedicated hopefully to his former pupil, who had now succeded as Grand Duke Cosimo II of Tuscany. Galileo's book would cause a sensation throughout Europe; amongst his many discoveries was the fact that Jupiter had satellites, and in honour of the book's dedicatee, Galileo christened these new moons *Sidera Medicae* (The Medici Stars). The Medici were now immortalised in the heavens! More significant in scientific terms was Galileo's observation of the 'phases of Venus': the planet waxed and waned in precisely the same way as the moon. Its surface, as viewed from the earth, moved from shadow into light, and then back again. This was incontrovertible evidence that Venus, as well as the earth, orbited the sun; there could be no other possible explanation of such a phenomenon.

Galileo also observed the sun (using smoked glass to protect his eyes), and found that it had black spots, which took on all kinds of shapes 'like clouds' that 'appeared to consume themselves'. Here was further proof that the heavens were not timeless and changeless, as Aristotle had claimed. Inevitably Galileo's observations provoked fierce opposition from many Aristotelians and members of the Church. The most characteristic observation came from a Bavarian abbot who declared: 'I have read all the works of Aristotle and have found nothing resembling what you describe . . . Your spots on the sun are defects of your optical instruments or eyes.' Ominously, it was impossible for Galileo to contradict such critics, for the reason that *they simply did not recognise his point of view.*

Galileo's response was equally characteristic: the Aristotelians, the Church, his enemies, his creditors – they were all in league against him. As his ideas became more far-reaching and original, so did his paranoia. His replies to his critics became increasingly implacable and dismissive; Galileo was making himself more and more enemies in important places.

But *The Starry Messenger* also brought success, for the nineteen-year-old Grand Duke Cosimo II was flattered that his former tutor had remembered him, and honoured Galileo in generous fashion. He immediately offered Galileo the post of 'first philosopher and mathematician' in Tuscany; the job carried a handsome salary and included luxurious accommodation at the Villa Bellosguardo on a hill south of Florence, ideally situated for making astronomical observations. Galileo left Padua at once, bringing with him his three children; his mistress Marina was abandoned in Padua, apparently by mutual consent – though Galileo did leave her with a suitable dowry so that she could get married, which she did a year later.

This period would prove to be the apex of Galileo's life; it would also represent the height of Medici influence on the scientific Renaissance. Here the Medici were becoming godfathers of a new scientific age, and under their patronage and protection Galileo was able to extend his scientific researches unhindered by his critics. In direct consequence, news of his discoveries would spread and be absorbed by intellectuals through-out Europe. In Holland, the philosopher and mathematician René Descartes would begin a study of Galileo's work, which inspired him to write his ground-breaking *Discourse on Method*, in which he outlined a rational and scientific method of thought for the discovery of truth, providing the philosophical basis for all that Galileo had begun.

Galileo now launched himself into a programme of unhampered research, at the same time embarking on a series of wide-ranging theo-retical speculations. His ideas on the close relationship between mathe-matics and physics led him to make a distinction between two different qualities of objects. First there were those physical qualities that could be measured, such as length, weight and so forth; these belonged to the objects themselves. Then there were qualities that could not be measured, such as the smell of an object, its colour and its taste; these did not belong to the objects themselves, but were the impressions caused by the objects on the people who observed them. This crucial distinction would later be taken up by the English philosopher John Locke, and would form the basis of his philosophy of empiricism, the first genuinely scientific philo-sophy, which stated that all truth must be based on experience.

The philosophies of Descartes and Locke would bring about a revival in philosophical thought, and are generally recognised as the beginning of modern philosophy. Both of these philosophies – the rational and the empirical – owe a crucial debt to Galileo, who in turn relied so heavily on Medici patronage and protection. Galileo himself would also bring about the renaissance of an ancient philosophical idea that would trans-form science, rather than philosophy. As a result of his experiments, Galileo began speculating on the ultimate nature of matter, and this led him to revive an idea first proposed by the Ancient Greek philosopher Democritus in the early fourth century BC. Democritus had stated that all matter ulti-mately consisted of indivisible entities, which he called 'atoms' (a word that comes from the Greek *atomos*, meaning uncuttable, or indivisible). In time, this idea would permeate physics and chemistry, putting paid to the ancient Aristotelian idea that all matter consisted of a mixture of earth, air, fire and water.

Although it would be many centuries before atoms could actually be observed or counted, this idea goes to the very heart of the new scientific revolution. Atoms, as individual entities, are theoretically able to be counted, whereas a mixture of earth, air, fire and water is a matter of qualities, rather than numbers. The new scientific revolution was shifting from a qualitative world to a quantitative world, one where mathematics could be applied.

Galileo began pondering the implications of the new heliocentric theory, and speculated that the inertial path of a planet around the sun must be caused by some form of magnetic force between the two objects. His papers reveal that he was on the brink of formulating a notion similar to that of gravity, and of conceiving of this a universal force that applied throughout the heavens. Galileo's application of physics to the motion of the planets was an epochal step; Kepler had applied mathematics to the universe, and now Galileo showed that the earth's laws of physics were also universal. Boldly he declared: 'Earthly laws apply in the heavens.'

By now he was treading on dangerous ground, and the Vatican authorities were beginning to take an increasing interest in Galileo's revolutionary new ideas. But there was no stopping him. In 1611 he was invited to the papal court to demonstrate his new telescope, and his ideas made a surprisingly favourable impression. Emboldened by this, Galileo decided to reveal the full extent of what he had discovered, demonstrating once and for all the truth of the heliocentric solar system. He wrote a book describing sun spots; he exploded the idea that the earth was the centre of the universe; and he showed how science could explain the heavens. His book was soon being distributed throughout Europe, and its ideas started to catch on amongst students at the universities.

The Aristotelians began to see the enormity of the threat posed by Galileo, and belatedly mounted a devastating counter-attack. They pointed out that Galileo's Copernican ideas not only contradicted the teachings of the Church, but also flatly denied what was written in the Bible. The Church decided it was time to act: Galileo's ideas were undoubtedly heretical.

Yet even at this late stage Galileo still had his friends and advocates amongst the Church hierarchy. Popes and cardinals had played their part in furthering the ideas of the Renaissance, and many powerful figures in the Church remained sympathetic to consequent intellectual progress.

(Tellingly, the magnificent new dome of St Peter's – the pride of the Catholic Church, which had been completed twenty years earlier – had been understood as a product of art *and* science.) Amongst those interested in the latest scientific ideas was a fellow Florentine, the influential Cardinal Maffeo Barberini, who informed Galileo that as long as he limited himself to speaking purely as a mathematician, he would not get into trouble. This advice was unwittingly ironic, for the Church regarded mathematics in the Platonic sense, as essentially an idealistic and abstract matter, which had no relevance to the real world; Galileo's major scientific insight had been to recognise the contrary.

With hindsight, this conflict between the Church and science can be seen in context: it was both historically inevitable, and in an intellectual sense utterly unnecessary. Its origins lay in the part Christianity had played in preserving Western civilisation. During the Dark Ages after the collapse of the Roman Empire, ancient knowledge had survived only in remote Christian communities. With the coming of more settled times in the medieval era, this knowledge had spread throughout the countries of western Europe, but had remained the preserve of the Church. This process had reached its apotheosis in the comparative intellectual stasis of the high medieval era, when the Church had still regarded all philosophy, all knowledge, all learning as its own: knowledge and the teachings of the Church were one. With the revival of intellectual enquiry prompted by the Renaissance, the Church found itself in a difficult position. Unwilling to relinquish its monopoly on knowledge, the Church decreed that any new knowledge must agree with its teachings, which meant paradoxically that the new discoveries of science were acceptable to the Church only when they were the same as what was already known! Progressive thought was harnessed to static intellectual practice, and as the tension built up it was inevitable that something would give; Galileo's misfortune was to find himself at the centre of this increasingly destructive process.

In 1616 the Church placed the works of Copernicus on the Index of banned books, and Galileo was warned that he must not 'hold or defend' such ideas, or he would be brought before the Inquisition. This body had been set up as part of the Counter-Reformation that was now actively combating all opposition to the Catholic Church. The aim of the Inquisition was to seek out heresy, by means of torture if necessary; in this way, any seeds of Protestantism in Catholic territories would soon be eliminated.

Desperately Galileo wrote letters to Cardinal Barberini, the Grand Duke of Tuscany and other influential friends. To the Dowager Grand Duchess Christina he wrote pertinently: 'To ban Copernicus now would seem in my judgement to be a contradiction of truth.' But these pleas were to no avail, and Galileo retired to his villa at Bellosguardo, where he remained under the protection of Grand Duke Cosimo II.

Seven years later Galileo's friend Maffeo Barberini became Pope Urban VIII, and Galileo journeyed to Rome filled with optimism to argue his case. Urban VIII remained to a degree sympathetic, and gave Galileo permission to write a book about 'the systems of the world'. In this he could put forward both the Copernican point of view of the universe and that of the Church, so long as he made it quite clear that the Church's was the correct one. Galileo now wrote *Dialogue Concerning the Two Chief World Systems*, in which he propounded the Copernican view in the mouth of the witty intellectual character Sagredo, while the Church and its Aristotelian viewpoint was represented by a character called Simplicio. Unfortunately, Galileo once again became carried away, and as a result Simplicio was made to look a little bit too simple. Worse still, many thought they recognised in Simplicio a characterisation of the pope himself. Urban VIII was furious, and his advisers egged him on by insisting that such ideas only served to undermine the entire Counter-Reformation. Europe was now in the midst of the Thirty Years War, involving ruinous conflict between Catholic and Protestant armies throughout the continent; and in the hysteria of the moment Galileo's ideas were judged to be worse 'than Luther and Calvin put together'.

Unfortunately for Galileo, his protector and former pupil Grand Duke Cosimo II had died in 1621. With no one to defend him, Galileo was ordered to Rome in 1633 to stand trial for heresy. Only thirty years previously, the philosopher and scientist Giordano Bruno had been similarly charged in Rome, and had ended up being burned at the stake. Galileo realised he was in mortal danger; now sixty-eight years old and in deteriorating health, he made his way to Rome. Faced with the prospect of being tortured by the Inquisition, he soon caved in. He was made solemnly to declare that he 'abjured, cursed and detested' his view that the earth moved around the sun, though according to legend he could not help muttering under his breath, 'But it still moves.'

Galileo was sentenced to life imprisonment, but on account of his age and ill health he was allowed to return to Tuscany. Here, under the benign guardianship of the new Grand Duke Ferdinando II, he served his term under house arrest on his small estate at Arcetri just south of Florence. Four years later he began to go blind; but he was far from being the broken man he appeared. His fame ensured that he was visited by several distinguished travellers from northern Europe, including the English philosopher Thomas Hobbes and the poet John Milton. In the very month before Galileo finally succumbed to complete blindness, he discovered by telescopic observation that the moon oscillated on its axis as it orbited the earth. A short time later he completed his final masterpiece, *The Two New Sciences*, which summed up his ideas; and the manuscript was smuggled to Holland, where it was published and distributed to scientists throughout Europe. Galileo finally died at the age of seventy-seven on 8 January 1642, just a few months before the birth of Isaac Newton in England; 350 years later the Vatican would finally concede that, in the case of Galileo, 'errors were made'.

This 'pardon' marked a considerable climbdown, for at the time of Galileo's death the Church was in no mood to forgive his transgressions, and his erstwhile friend Urban VIII remained particularly vindictive. When Grand Duke Ferdinando II ordered that Galileo should be buried in Santa Croce, which contained the tombs of such great Florentine figures as Ghiberti, Machiavelli and Michelangelo, the pope forbade this. Galileo would not to be permitted a Christian burial inside Santa Croce until seventy-five years after his death.

Grand Duke Ferdinando II had taken a keen interest in Galileo's activities, and after he had come of age and ascended to the dukedom in 1632 there had been regular orders from the Palazzo Pitti to Galileo asking him to procure the most up-to-date telescopes for his highness. Ferdinando II took particular pride in the Medici Stars, which he would proudly show to distinguished visitors through his latest telescope. In 1635, after Galileo's *Dialogue Concerning the Two Chief World Systems* had been condemned by Urban VIII, Ferdinando II played a significant role in ensuring that this work was preserved and disseminated. He made sure that his younger brother

Mattias de' Medici smuggled a manuscript copy of the work out of Florence to northern Europe, where it was translated and published in several languages. As a result, when Hobbes visited Galileo during his period of house arrest, he was able to inform the ageing scientist that he had seen an English translation of his *Dialogue*.

So why did Ferdinando II not protect Galileo after the initial publication of the *Dialogue* in 1632? And why had he allowed the ailing Galileo to be summoned to Rome in fear of his life? Ferdinando II had come to power at the age of ten in 1621, on the death of his father Grand Duke Cosimo II, and during his minority Tuscany had been ruled by the formidable Dowager Grand Duchess Christina and her daugher-in-law, Cosimo II's wife. At the age of seventeen Ferdinando II had been sent on a tour of European capitals to broaden his education, but even after he assumed full power in 1632 he had remained under the domination of the Dowager Grand Duchess Christina until she died in 1636. At the time of Galileo's summons to Rome in 1632, Urban VIII had contacted the young Ferdinando II and advised him not to interfere, warning that to do so would provoke a major diplomatic upset. The Dowager Grand Duchess Christina had allowed Tuscany to fall increasingly under papal influence, and Florence witnessed an influx of priests during this period. The many monasteries in Florence, some of which had been almost empty, were now filled to overflowing. Under Christina, priests had been allowed to take up important posts in the administration, an unprecedented development, which had in fact been specifically forbidden by Grand Duke Cosimo I when he extended the permanent bureaucracy.

Ferdinando II was a plump, easy-going young man with flowing dark hair and a dashing winged moustache. Even in his early portrait by Sustermans he cuts a slightly absurd figure, dressed in shining armour, his hand on his sword: a somewhat dandified and unlikely warrior (see colour plates). But his languid, affable exterior masked unexpected abilities, though these remained for the most part latent on account of his laziness. He appeared to treat his duties more as a pastime than as a serious pursuit; yet during his rule Tuscany would manage to maintain the difficult balance between the often conflicting demands of Austria, France, Spain and the pope.

In 1638 Ferdinando II was married to Vittoria della Rovere, with the expectation that they would soon produce a male heir to ensure the Medici succession. Yet this task did not prove so easy; Vittoria della Rovere was a large, prim, domineering woman, but despite her ample physique she found childbearing difficult. Her first son died at birth, and two years later she produced a similarly ill-fated daughter, whose birth almost killed Vittoria. Many began to suspect that there would be no heir, especially when they noticed that Ferdinando II seemed to prefer the company of the handsome young men of the court to that of his overbearing wife. Fortunately this pastime did not distract him entirely from his dynastic duties, and a male heir was born in 1642.

Meanwhile Ferdinando II's mother Maddalena remained a powerful presence behind the throne, making the morals of Tuscany her particular concern, and the grand duke appeared quite content with this arrangement. However, shortly after the birth of his son, who was christened Cosimo, the Dowager Grand Duchess Maddalena confronted Ferdinando II with a long list of all those holding high office in the grand duchy who were homosexuals. She demanded to know what her son proposed to do about this. Ferdinando II quietly took the list, read the names on it and then added his own. Maddalena refused to be disconcerted, saying that he had only acted in this fashion to save these sinners from the punishment they deserved. Ferdinando II asked her what this punishment was, and she replied that they should all be burned. Whereupon Ferdinando II tossed the paper into the fire and exclaimed: 'Voilà, your command has already been accomplished.'

This anecdote is indicative, for it shows Ferdinando II's growing determination beneath his easy-going manner; but perhaps more importantly, it gives a sign of the prevailing moral climate in Florence. Despite the relaxed and more prosperous ambience of the city under the grand dukes, there remained those who wished it otherwise; the forces that had given rise to Savonarola, and the Republic of Christ, might yet be summoned once more.

Like many Medici before him, Ferdinando II enjoyed putting on pageants for the people. Florence still prided itself on its artistic accomplishments, but these were a pale imitation of its greater days; peace and prosperity were somehow not capable of inspiring the genius that the city had produced during times of violence and instability. Even the city's celebrated taste lapsed – uncertainty had given it edge, while normality required only entertainment and fond memories of the 'good old days'. This is perhaps best typified by the most popular artist of the period, Luca Giordano. For once, Florence's favourite was not even a Florentine: Giordano was a Neapolitan, whose talent was firmly allied to his facility. At an unprecedented rate, he turned out copies of paintings by Michelangelo, Raphael and other great Renaissance predecessors. Gone were the days when Florence was an artistic force, and the leading centres of art were now scattered through Europe – in Rome, Paris and Amsterdam. The High Renaissance copied by Giordano was long past, but Florentines preferred his anachronistic fakes to the Baroque style that now prevailed in the leading artistic centres of Europe.

It has been claimed that the Baroque style, with all its melodrama, pathos and love of grandiose gesture, was temperamentally alien to Florentine taste, which preferred clarity of line and classical form. But this view is highly contestable. Florence had produced, and taken to its heart, Michelangelo, whose works were filled with drama and torment and had in fact paved the way for the exaggerations of the Baroque. Florentine taste had evolved from Masaccio to Botticelli through to Michelangelo; but now this glorious fluency of taste had finally petrified. The city's inability to remain abreast of artistic development was due to a failure of its taste altogether, rather than to any particular blind spot regarding the Baroque style.

Yet not all the art produced during this period in Florence was unoriginal. Ferdinando II's younger brother, Cardinal Giancarlo de' Medici, employed the Neapolitan Salvator Rosa, a painter and poet of considerable talent who never quite fulfilled his promise. As opposed to the hindsight of Giordano, Rosa was an artist *before* his time; some of his poetry, together with his dramatic landscapes and portraits, can now be seen as unmistakable precusors of a Romantic era that had not yet dawned. On his darkly brooding *Self-Portrait as a Philosopher* he inscribed the words:

Aut tace
Aut loquere meliora
Silentio.

(Either remain silent,
Or speak better than
Silence.)

Unfortunately Rosa himself did not live up to this, producing all manner of ephemeral satirical dramas and paintings of battle scenes to meet popular demand. Reflecting the times and place in which he lived, he seemed uncertain of himself; as an artist he was willing to try anything, and even had a spell as a comic actor. Only a fraction of his work is significant, but this spoke better than the artistic silence of his lesser work and the absence of artistic taste that surrounded him in Florence.

Ferdinando II's youngest brother Leopoldo would also become a cardinal, but before he left to take up his post in Rome he would inaugurate the last significant flowering of Medici Renaissance patronage, which would be in the scientific sphere. In 1657 Leopoldo de' Medici founded the Accademia del Cimento, a direct reference to Galileo's favoured scientific method of *cimento* (test, or experiment). Leopoldo's 'Experimental Academy' would seek to continue this scientific work; its motto was 'Try and try again', and its emblem was a furnace such as those used for assaying metals. The Cimento met at irregular intervals in the Palazzo Pitti, moving to Pisa when the court took up residence there, and its dozen or so enthusiastic participants included Ferdinando II himself.

Experiments were carried out in the palace and in a furnace in the Boboli Gardens. Strictly speaking, the Cimento had no actual members, or rules; it simply consisted of those who participated in its informal meetings. These participants passed on their findings in correspondence with scientists throughout Europe; at the time this was the only way in which news of the latest scientific discoveries was disseminated. During the Renaissance various societies had come into existence for the furtherance of philosophical, literary and theological discussion, but it was not until the seventeenth century that exclusively scientific societies were formed. The first of these appeared in Italy, with the Accademia dei Lincei (lynxes) being founded in Rome in 1603. Galileo had been invited to become a member in its inaugural year, and at one of their meetings it was decided that his *occhiale* (eyeglass) should be named a 'telescope'. But after the condemnation of Galileo, the Lincei was disbanded. The founding of the

Accademia del Cimento in 1657 was thus a brave move, as well as a pioneering one. The Royal Society in London was not founded until 1662, with the Académie des Sciences in Paris following four years later, and the Berlin Academy opening in 1700.

But the Cimento was more than just a loosely conducted club for aristocratic amateur scientists interested in the latest developments; amongst its active members was Evangelista Torricelli, the great Italian physicist. In 1641 the thirty-three-year-old Torricelli had journeyed to Florence to take up the post of Galileo's assistant, a rare accolade indeed; and on the death of Galileo the following year, Torricelli was appointed professor of mathematics at the University of Florence.

In 1643 Torricelli investigated an idea first put to him by Galileo. He took a U-shaped tube sealed at one end and filled it with mercury; this was then inverted, with its open end placed in a bowl of mercury. The mercury flowed into the bowl, but only so far, causing a space to appear at the sealed end of the tube. This was a vacuum, and Torricelli was the first to produce a stable vacuum in this way. Whilst studying this vacuum, Torricelli noticed that the height of the mercury varied from one day to the next. He concluded that this was due to changes in the air pressure — he had invented the first barometer.

Not all ideas produced by members of the Cimento were of such exceptional calibre, yet even some of its apparently more whimsical ideas were pursued with enthusiasm. Ferdinando II continued the family interest in biology started by his great-grandfather Cosimo I, and developed an interest in exotic animals; as a result he decided to import some camels from India, which were initially kept in the Boboli Gardens. Ferdinando II was convinced that the patience and endurance of the camel made it a superior pack animal to the mule, and intended to introduce camels into the local haulage trade. To the delight of the locals, camels were soon observed on highways throughout Tuscany, although it eventually had to be conceded that these were more of an exotic curiosity than a commercial practicality. The idea may have failed, but the camels themselves did not, and evidence of this doomed enterprise would persist until well into the twentieth century in the form of a herd of around 200 camels in the grand-ducal park at San Rossore on the coast near Pisa.

Ferdinando II was determined that his son Cosimo should be given a scientific education, but this was vetoed by the Grand Duchess Vittoria, who regarded science as heretical. Instead Vittoria insisted that her son should receive a strictly religious education. This proved an unwise choice, as it only served to accentuate the young boy's inclination to pious melancholy — an inclination that deepened during his adolescence into an unhealthy fixation with Christian martyrs. Ferdinando II was somewhat disturbed by this, but chose not to interfere; his preference for the quiet life invariably overrode any other considerations. Many saw this as evidence of an inherent weakness of character, and on some occasions there is no denying that Ferdinando exhibited this flaw. His abandonment of Galileo in his time of need, for instance, as well as his unwillingness to prevent the descent of his son into religious morbidity, are difficult to view as anything other than failures of character. Yet in the larger scheme of things, Ferdinando II's overwhelming desire for the quiet life would prove of benefit to Tuscany. During the course of his long reign — which would last just a year short of half a century — Tuscany saw little of war. However, these years were not entirely untroubled, and the opening of Ferdinando II's reign was beset by natural disasters. The complete failure of the harvest in 1621, after three years of bad harvests, brought Florence close to starvation; and during the three years up to 1633 the city suffered from outbreaks of plague that accounted for almost 10 per cent of the population. Ferdinando II's personal appearance distributing charity in the badly hit Santa Croce district during this period gained him early popularity.

From then on he presided as a benign despot, ruling over a grand duchy that gradually settled into a long, slow economic decline, as cheap foreign competition began to undercut the local cloth and silk industries. But there were compensations: Florence now began to receive its first tourists on a regular basis. In northern Europe, the spread of Renaissance art and ideas had resulted in a revival of interest in classical Rome and the Italian Renaissance. As part of their education, rich young men would now be sent to Italy on the Grand Tour, and Florence — with its Renaissance architecture, public statues and art treasures — became a traditional stopover on the way south to Rome.

During the reign of Ferdinando II, Tuscany would be involved in just one military campaign, when Pope Urban VIII occupied the small quasi-independent state of Castro on Tuscany's southern border in 1641. Ferdinando II put out cautious diplomatic feelers, and was informed that neither Spain nor France would intervene if he acted. So in 1643 Ferdinando II donned his shining armour and led a numerous but somewhat ragtag army of volunteers and mercenaries to Castro, where the papal forces were quickly put to flight. The citizens of Florence rejoiced, but were less pleased when it was discovered that paying for the army had left the grand duchy's exchequer all but empty. The grand duchy could no longer afford to pay interest on its government bonds, which accounted for the savings of many citizens, great and small. It seemed likely that the grand duchy would go bankrupt, but the expected rush to sell government bonds did not materialise; the economy was now so slow that there was simply nothing else in which it was worth investing. Out in the country, the consequent lack of currency was overcome by a resurgence of the barter system for paying agricultural wages, whilst in the city the growing influx of tourist money enabled the economy to continue ticking over.

By this stage much of the Medici family's income came from church benefices; and during this time of need, Ferdinando II established a number of charities to provide for the unemployed. The money extracted from the poor in church collection plates was thus returned to them. But the Medici family fortunes inevitably suffered, for their finances were identified heavily with the state. Lorenzo the Magnificent may have dipped into the city exchequer to finance his extravagant entertainments, but Ferdinando II had no need to resort to such pilfering of public funds, as the grand duchy's exchequer was his exchequer. This meant, for instance, that the ongoing additions to the Pitti Palace were carried out by public works, rather than by privately hired contractors. Long gone were the days when the Medici relied upon the family bank for their income, and it was during this period that Ferdinando II finally wound up the last of the Medici banking activities; the Medici were aristocrats, joined to the royal houses of Europe, and had no wish to be reminded of their origins in commerce.

In a brave attempt to get the economy restarted, Ferdinando II sponsored a number of public-works programmes, the most ambitious of which was an extensive new building project at Livorno, which was in desperate need of new housing. As a result of Cosimo I's freedom-of-worship decree, the port had expanded to become a thriving cosmopolitan city – to the point where in 1634 a British consulate was opened in Livorno, whose mellifluous name was vandalised in English to become Leghorn. The city had begun attracting all manner of traders, religious refugees, itinerant tradesmen, sailors, deserters, escapees from the galleys and other outlaws. Its trade was free from taxation, but it indirectly generated considerable income for the grand duchy in the form of the many ancillary trades that grew up around the port. On the other hand, the city had also gained the unsavoury reputation of being the main slaving port of the northern Mediterranean. The English diarist John Evelyn, visiting Livorno in 1644, saw 'such a concourse of slaves, Turks, Moors and other nations that the number and confusion is prodigious; some buying, others selling, others drinking, others playing, some working, others sleeping, fighting, singing, weeping, all nearly naked and miserably chained'. As part of Ferdinando II's public policy, new houses were now laid out beside the canals in the district that became known as New Venice; meanwhile undesirables were rounded up and deported to Algiers.

During his fifties, Ferdinando II began to suffer increasingly from dropsy, also becoming prone to fits of apoplexy. In 1670, at the age of fifty-nine, he was forced to take to his bed, where he received the finest medical treatment available at the time. As reported by an eyewitness: 'The Grand Duke's medicine did not work, so his physician bled him, and extracted a further ounce of the stone from his bladder . . . Later a cauterising iron was placed to his head, but to no avail, and powder was inserted in his nostrils . . . [Then] four live pigeons were ripped open and applied to his forehead.' Not surprisingly, he soon died. Ferdinando II had not been loved, but the citizens of Florence had grown used to his benevolent autocratic rule, and his passing was widely – if not deeply – mourned.

28

Godfathers No More?

FERDINANDO II WAS succeeded in 1670 by his twenty-eight-year-old son, who became Grand Duke Cosimo III. His reign would be distinguished only by its longevity – lasting for fifty-three years, longer than that of any other Medici – though during this period little of historical import would take place, other than the long, slow and occasionally pitiful decline of both Tuscany and its ruler. Cosimo III had been the second son, and would probably have been better off following the usual course for Medici second sons into the Church; but his elder brother had died at birth, and as a result Cosimo had become the unsuitable heir.

All who met the young Cosimo stressed his gloom and piety; indeed, the ambassador from Lucca went so far as to claim that the grand duke was 'never seen to smile'. His dominating mother Vittoria encouraged his religiosity, which appears to have been more a psychological ailment than genuine spirituality. All Cosimo spoke about was martyrs and salvation; all he read was theology and descriptions of miracles, all he seemed to do was attend daily Mass and go on pilgrimages to shrines around the countryside. By the time he was nineteen, even his unassertive father realised that something had to be done – the obvious answer was to get him married.

Ferdinando II began making enquiries, and finally managed to arrange a highly advantageous marriage to a niece of King Louis XIII of France. The separate French and Italian blood lines of the Medici were now becoming worryingly close: Ferdinando I's French wife Christina had been a granddaughter of Catherine de Médicis; and now Ferdinando I's great-grandson was marrying a granddaughter of Marie de Médicis, who had been Catherine de Médicis' distant cousin. Other Medici had already married into the great royal houses of Europe – the Habsburgs, as well as the Valois and the Bourbons (both of France). These too had many intermarriages, and the shadow of inbreeding hung heavily over all such families who wished to preserve their high pedigree by marrying only royalty, which frequently meant marrying amongst themselves. Madness, degeneracy and odd physical features (such as the notorious Habsburg chin, where the lower teeth overlapped those of the upper jaw) were now becoming a recurrent feature of all European royal families, and of lesser, often related families, such as the Italian grand-ducal branch of the Medici who wished to marry into them. In aspiring to greatness of lineage, the Medici were playing a dangerous game.

Cosimo's bride-to-be was Marguérite-Louise of Orléans, daughter of Gaston, Duke of Orléans, and the marriage was arranged through Cardinal Mazarin, chief adviser to the French king Louis XIV (who had succeeded in 1643, on the death of his father Louis XIII, son of Marie de Médicis). Cardinal Mazarin had an ambition to be pope, and had quietly informed Ferdinando II that the price for this marriage was Medici support for his candidacy when the occasion arose.

Word reached Florence that the fifteen-year-old Marguérite-Louise had 'brown hair, greenish-blue eyes, and a sweet, gentle temperament'. As regards her temperament, nothing could have been further from the truth. Marguérite-Louise was a wilful, utterly spoilt teenager, who was used to having her own freedom and getting her own way. By this stage she had become infatuated with her eighteen-year-old cousin Charles of Lorraine and wished to marry him. Even Marguérite-Louise's mother, the Duchess of Orléans, was against her daughter marrying a distant, unseen Italian, but Cardinal Mazarin bribed her to support his case.

The marriage contract was signed in January 1661, with a proxy marriage ceremony due to take place in April of that year. Arranged royal marriages of the period were the reverse of modern practice, and must have involved some peculiar psychological procedures at the best of times; following her proxy marriage, Marguérite-Louise would be expected to depart for Italy to meet her unknown bridegroom, take up married life, and only then get to know him.

From the start Marguérite-Louise put up spirited opposition to her arranged marriage. Then in March 1661 Cardinal Mazarin died, whereupon the Duchess of Orléans immediately petitioned the king to call off the marriage. But Louis XIV would not hear of this, so Marguérite-Louise went to see the king herself; kneeling before Louis XIV, she begged him forcefully not to make her marry Cosimo de' Medici. However, the king remained adamant, the proxy marriage was 'celebrated' in the Louvre and Marguérite-Louise departed for Florence, 'weeping openly for all to see'. It was a hard fate for a fifteen-year-old girl, made even harder by her obdurate character. She cheered up briefly when she arrived in Marseilles, where Charles of Lorraine came unexpectedly to bid her farewell, but in the end this only made matters worse. When Marguérite-Louise embarked on the galley decked with garlands and coloured ribbons, which was to row her to Livorno, it must have seemed like a fairy tale without a happy ending.

Back in Florence, Ferdinando II had been pleased to notice certain changes in his son's demeanour. Cosimo started taking care about his appearance, and even began dressing in the French syle, preparing to make a good impression on his French bride. Yet beneath this uncharacteristically fashionable attire, it was all too plain that Cosimo remained a fat and gloomy nineteen-year-old, with heavy-lidded Medici eyes and bulbous lips.

The young married couple set eyes on each other for the first time on 15 June at the Villa Ambrogiana, the Medici hunting lodge near Empoli, just fifteen miles from Florence. It was an inauspicious meeting; Marguérite-Louise was morose, which proved a discouragement to Cosimo, who could not even be induced to kiss the bride. Despite the unprepossessing character of both the bride and the groom, it is hard not to feel sympathy for them both in this impossible situation (which would have had its echoes in every family of consequence throughout western Europe).

Such were the two figures who would star in one of the most glorious celebrations that Florence had ever witnessed. The festivities commenced five days later, in a city whose every street had been transformed for the occasion; not since the entry of Pope Leo X, a century and a half previously, had Florence been so decorated. The Piazza San Gallo was lined with banks of seats, and triumphal arches bordered the route to the cathedral. Preceded by columns of Swiss Guards, Cosimo rode into the piazza resplendent in a black tunic laced with glinting diamonds, accompanied by 100 men-at-arms all dressed in the Medici colours. Following him, reclining in an open carriage drawn by white mules, came Marguérite-Louise, wearing a wedding gown of embroidered silver cloth overlain with 'a chain of diamonds, and forty tapering pearls hanging between them, the whole attached to the shoulders by two pearls the size of a small pigeon's egg'. Shielding her from the sun was a large gold canopy fringed with more pearls, held aloft by thirty-two young scions drawn from all the ancient families of Florence. The procession was followed by no fewer than 300 carriages, containing the remaining members of the city's ancient families. The bride and groom dismounted and proceeded towards the cathedral, and at the entrance they were sprinkled with holy water by the Bishop of Fiesole, as twelve massed choirs sang out the *Te Deum*. In the midst of it all, the bridegroom's face was fat and expressionless, his bride unable even to raise a smile.

After the ceremony the citizens of Florence celebrated as only they knew how, and the festivities would continue intermittently throughout the summer. Chariot races at the Piazza Santa Maria Novella were followed by jousting tournaments in the Piazza Santa Croce; horseraces preceded nights of fireworks; and in between there were costume balls at the Pitti Palace on such themes as historic heroes and ancient Greek legends. Even Marguérite-Louise appeared impressed by the sumptuous masque performed before 20,000 spectators in the amphitheatre of the Boboli Gardens, where tableaux enacted historical events, ballet dancers performed on horseback, and finally Cosimo himself appeared in bejewelled armour as the figure of Hercules. Yet no sooner were the celebrations over than Marguérite-Louise sank into an increasingly sullen depression, and Cosimo retreated into his customary pious gloom. Gossip amongst the palace servants was that the bride and groom were so averse to each other that they could not even bring themselves to consummate the marriage. Yet this must eventually have proved untrue, for after two years of marriage Marguérite-Louise finally gave birth to a son, Ferdinando, in August 1663.

By now the marriage was all but over. Marguérite-Louise did all within her power to antagonise and embarrass Cosimo, while for his part Cosimo withdrew into the consolation of prayer. When on one occasion he approached his wife's bed, she snatched a bottle from her bedside table and threatened to break it over his skull if he did not leave her chamber. Marguérite-Louise surrounded herself with her French servants, moving her residence from chamber to chamber in the vast palace so that her husband could not find her. Early on, she browbeat him into giving her the Medici crown jewels, which she immediately ordered her servants to take back to France. (Ferdinando II managed to have the servants intercepted before they reached the coast.) After the birth of her child, Marguérite-Louise began writing a stream of letters to Louis XIV, begging him to arrange for the pope to annul the marriage. Louis XIV ignored her pleas, ordering her to cease writing such letters; so instead she wrote to Charles of Lorraine saying how much she loved him, imploring him to come and visit her. In the end he relented and paid a brief visit to Florence, but nothing came of this and a further stream of love letters followed him back to France. Ferdinando II then got wind of what was happening and had her letters intercepted. Early in 1667 it became clear that Marguérite-Louise was pregnant for a second time, whereupon she took to setting off on long gallops in the hope of inducing a miscarriage. This was to no avail, and in August 1667 she gave birth to a daughter, Anna Maria Luisa.

Still the misery continued: Marguérite-Louise ranged between violent anger and comatose despair, while Cosimo sank into a state of almost permanent holy depression, and the only enjoyment he appeared to gain was from eating extensive meals. Ferdinando II began to find his son's marriage intolerable, and in pursuance of his wish for a quiet life he suggested to Cosimo that he set off on a tour of Europe – alone. Besides providing an escape from his domestic difficulties, this would also enable Cosimo to make useful diplomatic contacts in preparation for when he succeeded to the grand duchy.

In 1668 Cosimo set off on an extended summer tour of Austria, Germany and the Netherlands, but when he returned home matters remained just as before. So the next year Ferdinando II despatched Cosimo on another tour, this time to Spain, Portugal and London. His appearance in London was noted by Samuel Pepys in his Diary, where he described Cosimo as 'a comely black fat man in a mourning suit'. Cosimo was entertained by King Charles II, and himself entertained many members of London society at a series of lavish dinner parties, which – according to those invited – were enjoyed by all present, including the host. On his way home through France, Cosimo visited Paris, where it was noted that he 'spoke admirably on every topic and he was well acquainted with the mode of life at all the courts of Europe'. These trips seem to have taken Cosimo out of himself, his novel surroundings causing him to forget his piety and simply enjoy himself. But this carefree interlude was not to last, for shortly after he returned from his second trip his father Ferdinando II died. At twenty-eight years old, his son succeeded as Grand Duke Cosimo III.

To the surprise of the court, the new grand duke began his rule by launching into an ambitious plan to reform the grand duchy's finances, in an attempt to revive Tuscany's flagging economy. However, this operation soon proved more complex than expected, so Cosimo III turned to his mother Vittoria for advice. As he lost interest in the problems of his administration, the formidable Vittoria gradually took over the reins of power, and it was not long before the grand-ducal cabinet was holding its meetings in her private apartments.

In 1671 Marguérite-Louise produced a second son, who was named Gian Gastone, after his French grandfather Gaston, Duke of Orléans. A year later Marguérite-Louise wrote a letter to Cosimo: 'I declare I can live with you no longer. I am the source of your unhappiness as you are of mine.' She informed her husband that she had written to Louis XIV asking for permission to enter a convent in Paris.

Cosimo III was outraged by this news, and ordered the grand duchess to leave Florence forthwith. She was commanded to take up residence in the Medici villa at Poggio a Caiano, twelve miles east of the city at the foot of Monte Albano, and remain there until further notice. Making a great show of her displeasure, Marguérite-Louise set out from Florence taking with her more than 150 servants, cooks, grooms and sundry attendants. Cosimo III gave orders that his wife was not allowed to leave the villa except to take walks or rides in the grounds, when she was to be accompanied at all times by a detachment of men-at-arms.

News of this situation reached Louis XIV, who entered into correspondence with Cosimo III on this matter of his wife's incarceration; Louis was not in the habit of allowing a cousin of the royal blood to be treated in this fashion. Eventually, in December 1674, it was decided that Marguérite-Louise should be allowed to journey back to France, where she would enter a convent at Montmartre, just north of Paris. This plan appeared to suit everyone: Cosimo III kept his three children, as well as his pride; Louis XIV was heartily relieved; and Marguérite-Louise embarked on the monastic life after her own fashion. No sooner had she taken up residence at her convent than she wrote and attempted to take up once more with Charles of Lorraine, but she discovered that he was now happily married to someone else. So instead Marguérite-Louise instituted dancing lessons at the convent, and 'indoor games' involving the guardsmen who had been set to watch over her. Occasionally, dressed in a blonde wig with her cheeks heavily rouged, she would set off for Versailles, where she enjoyed herself gambling. When she had lost all her regular allowance from Cosimo III, she would write to him for more, interspersing her demands with such endearments as: 'There is not an hour or a day when I do not wish someone would hang you.' Eventually the abbess of the convent could endure Marguérite-Louise's behaviour no longer and complained to her superiors. Marguérite-Louise responded by threatening to burn down the convent, whereupon Louis XIV arranged for her to be moved to the smaller convent of Saint-Mandé, east of Paris. Here, at the age of fifty-one, Marguérite-Louise learned to her delight that she had inherited a small fortune from a distant cousin. The mother superior of Saint-Mandé, who enjoyed dressing as a man on trips outside the walls, eventually absconded; whereupon Marguérite-Louise took over, running the convent as she saw fit. Her fiery temper began to mellow in her later years, and as mother superior she settled down to a life of quiet domesticity with a renegade priest and her community of frequently absconding nuns. In old age she would enjoy reminiscing about her glorious years as Grand Duchess of Tuscany, before she finally died in 1721 at the age of seventy-six.

No sooner had Marguérite-Louise departed in 1675 to begin her monastic life in Paris than Cosimo III found that he began to miss his wife. Despite the fact that his domestic loneliness was punctuated by letters from her heartily wishing him dead, something within him remained inconsolable. He sank further into depression, comforting himself with ever larger meals; and as these gastronomic marathons began to develop heroic proportions, so did their main participant. Feasts would be arranged on a national theme, with attendants dressed in appropriate national costumes. Oriental nights involved robes and tarbooshes; English feasts were served by men in black leggings and wigs; and on Moorish nights, attendants were required to black their faces. Similarly there could be no skimping on the food: joints and roasted fowl had to be weighed in Cosimo III's presence before they were allowed to grace the table, and those that failed to pass the test of the scales were despatched back to the kitchens. Ice creams were sculpted into swans or boats, jellies came in the form of fortresses, their battlements cleverly incorporating exotic fruits such as pineapples. Cosimo III's particular favourite was crystallised fruits, a delicacy that he had encountered in London, and one of his cooks was despatched to England to discover the secret of manufacturing this delight.

Such indulgence appears to have been driven by factors involving psychological displacement, rather than sheer greed, for it was not accompanied by other forms of overtly decadent behaviour or sensual licence. On the contrary, despite his increasing girth, Cosimo was a convinced — if somewhat unconvincing — puritan; he remained deeply pious and was determined that the morals of Tuscany should reflect his devout behaviour. Here he retained the domineering influence of his mother Vittoria, with the result that the fun-loving citizens of Florence, who had so enthusiastically celebrated his wedding, now began to experience a distinct chill in the city's moral climate, which would become more extreme as Cosimo's long reign continued.

The University of Pisa, whose scientific reputation throughout Italy was second only to that of Padua, was informed by official decree: 'His Highness will allow no professor . . . to read or teach, in public or private, by writing or by voice, the philosophy of Democritus, or of atoms, or any saving that of Aristotle.' There was no avoiding this educational censorship, for at the same time a decree was issued forbidding citizens of Tuscany from attending any university beyond its borders, while philosophers and intellectuals who disobeyed this decree were liable to punitive fines or even imprisonment. Gone were the days when the Medici were the patrons of poets and scientists; Florence, once one of the great intellectual and cultural centres of Europe, now sank into repression and ignorance.

Such decrees defended the moral teachings of religion; and further decrees would safeguard its moral practices. The annual May Festival was banned because of its pagan origins, and girls were forbidden to sing the joyous songs of May in the streets, on pain of whipping. The practice of young men calling up to young women leaning from the windows, a long-established exercise in flirtation and courtship, was also forbidden because 'it led to rape and abortion'. There was even a futile attempt to revive the canon law that forbade actresses. Likewise, it was found impossible to banish prostitution, but from now on this practice was strictly supervised. All prostitutes had to buy an annual licence costing the equivalent of six florins (at the time a month's wage for an orthodox unskilled worker); they were also required to wear yellow ribbons in their hair and to carry a lantern in the street at night. Failure to comply would result in the offender being stripped to the waist and whipped through the streets. Those accused of sodomy were beheaded; and as Cosimo III's reign extended from years into decades, there was an ever increasing number of public executions for all manner of offences. Even comparatively minor misdemeanours could result in the offender being sentenced to the galleys, a fate from which only a few spectral, broken figures ever returned.

As is so often the case where social purity is concerned, the new laws soon began to take on a racial element. For many years there had been prohibitions on Jews living in Florence, and these were now much more strictly enforced throughout the whole of Tuscany. Anti-Semitism became institutionalised, with Jews forbidden to marry Christians, or even to live in the same household. Jews were also forbidden to visit Christian prostitutes, and any woman found guilty of prostituting herself to a Jew was whipped before being sent to jail. The effect of these laws was most strongly felt in Livorno, where the Jewish colony had reached 22,000; many Jews began to seek refuge elsewhere, and tax revenues gathered from trade between the free port and the Tuscan hinterland slumped. In such a climate any xenophobic prejudices were given licence, and the new laws represented the tip of the iceberg where daily social intercourse was concerned, especially in such a time of general austerity and need. As a result, the thousand or so Jews, Turks and Balkan nationals remaining in Florence found themselves becoming persecuted minorities. The benign despotism of the early grand dukes now became out-and-out tyranny, and while Cosimo III glumly stuffed himself in his palace, the night streets of an impoverished Florence were dark and silent.

As the economy of the grand duchy continued to decline, Cosimo III imposed further taxes, which were required in order to support the bureacracy that continued to run the country for him. Left entirely to its own devices, this administration might well have proved the saviour of Tuscany, yet it too was affected by the heavy hand of repression; the administration was efficient, but it was not permitted to initiate the necessary reforms to revive the economy. Only the Church thrived; priests and religious institutions were for the most part exempt from tax, and Florence became ever more a city of priests and nuns. During the reign of Cosimo III the number of nuns rose to the point where they accounted for 12 per cent of the female population.

Measures taken to raise money from the few remaining lucrative elements of the commercial sector only had the effect of stifling enterprise. Merchants were sold monopolies on staple commodities such as salt, flour and olive oil, but traders were then permitted to buy an 'exemption', which provided limited immunity from a monopoly. Despite this, such monopolies were not taken lightly. The salt monopoly was a case in point: the extraction of salt by illegal means, such as boiling down fish brine, became a capital offence.

The small traders and craftsmen, upon whose businesses the prosperity of the grand duchy so depended, fell into decline, while in the countryside outlying fields of arable land returned to wilderness. There are no precise reliable figures, but all the indications are that the population of Tuscany as a whole may well have declined by over 40 per cent during Cosimo III's long reign. The English Bishop of Salisbury Gilbert Burnett, travelling through Italy in 1685, noted: 'As one goes over Tuscany, it appears so dispeopled that one cannot but wonder to find a country that hath been the scene of so much action, and so many wars, now so forsaken and poor.'

Cosimo III must also have seen this, for he too travelled about Tuscany on a regular basis, though the purpose of his tours was not to observe the state of the grand duchy. Cosimo III was a great believer in pilgrimages to the many obscure shrines dotted about the countryside, and when not engaged in such spiritually nourishing journeys, he would spend hours on his knees in the dimness of his personal chapel in the Palazzo Pitti.

Cooks were not the only members of Cosimo III's staff who were despatched abroad on errands; he also had a team of agents who roamed Europe in search of holy relics. These were purchased with sums from the ever-decreasing exchequer; and when this became depleted, Cosimo III would make inroads into the Medici family fortune. The purchase of expensive religious knick-knacks, many of which were no longer required by Protestant states, may be seen as the last gasp of ruling Medici patronage, though such patronage at home in the old style had not yet entirely dried up. Cosimo III did indulge in direct patronage of his favourite artist, Gaetano Zumbo, a Sicilian who produced intricate lifelike works in wax depicting the sufferings of the damned in Hell, saints undergoing excruciating martyrdom, and luridly imaginative depictions of plague victims. In the same vein, Cosimo III maintained a collection of drawings depicting with great verisimilitude various freaks of nature, including double-headed calves and dogs, misshapen dwarfs, as well as imaginative drawings of exotic creatures and medical drawings of diseases. These last catered to his increasing tendency to hypochondria, which he nursed with pampering cures and obscure elixirs. Fortunately these did not affect his physical health, which was remarkably robust, given his overweight frame and unhealthy lifestyle; his mind, on the other hand, was said to have become increasingly obsessed with a fear of death.

It had taken the Medici just over two and a half centuries to reach this pitiful state of decline. Compare this state of affairs with that which had prevailed during the time of Cosimo III's original namesake, Cosimo *Pater Patriae*. This first Medici ruler of Florence *was* racked by painful and debilitating illness, and lived in fear of hellfire for disobeying the Bible's prohibition of usury. Yet his fear of death and damnation had produced churches and orphanages, libraries filled with ancient learning, many pioneer scholars of humanism and masterpieces of early Renaissance art.

In 1694 Cosimo III's formidable and pious mother Vittoria finally died, leaving her son with the prospect of running the grand duchy on his own. He now had to take at least a passing interest in the affairs of state; the administration may have virtually run itself, but foreign policy required decisions that lay beyond the scope of the bureaucracy. Here Cosimo III proved unexpectedly adroit in following the policy of inert neutrality maintained by his father Ferdinando II, and the continuance of this policy meant that Tuscany was now largely disregarded on the international scene. Formerly courted (and threatened) by kings of France and Naples, consulted (and coerced) by Holy Roman Emperors and popes, the ruler of Tuscany was now considered an irrelevance. Fortunately his territory was also disregarded, which meant that Tuscany was not involved in such major upheavals as the War of the Spanish Succession, which lasted from 1701 to 1714, during which northern Europe was torn apart as the French, the English and the Dutch Republic fought over the German, Spanish and Austrian territories of the Holy Roman Empire. In Italy, Savoy and Naples became involved, but Cosimo III did nothing to jeopardise the fate of Tuscany, largely by doing nothing.

Neutrality was not only wise for Tuscany, it was also a necessity, for during these years the grand duchy would have been incapable of military action. A glance at the detailed military records kept by the ever-efficient bureaucracy is revealing. The garrison at Livorno is listed as containing 1,700 men, though closer inspection reveals that many of the soldiers on the payroll were more than seventy years old, some even more than eighty. Descriptions of their able-bodied readiness descends into farce, with such entries as 'has lost his sight' and 'does not see owing to advanced age and walks with a stick'. As for the once-great Tuscan navy, this was reduced to three galleys and a few support craft, manned by a company of just 198 men.

However, Cosimo III's policy was never entirely neutral. With suitable diplomatic secrecy, during the early years of his rule he began a covert but persistent correspondence with the Holy Roman Emperor Leopold I, who was by now ill and ageing. Leopold I's long reign was degenerating into the struggles that presaged the War of the Spanish Succession, but Cosimo III was more interested in another matter. He was insistent that the Grand Dukes of Tuscany should be promoted to royal status, so that instead of being addressed as 'Your Highness', Cosimo III could be addressed as 'Your Royal Highness'. In order to terminate this seemingly interminable correspondence, Leopold I finally agreed to license this '*trattamento real*' (treatment as royalty) for the Grand Dukes of Tuscany in 1691. Armed with this pedigree, Cosimo III could now concentrate on the problem of the Medici succession. This involved trying to marry his offspring into European royalty so that they could produce male heirs, though this proved a somewhat difficult task, largely owing to the genetic heritage at his disposal.

At first glance, Cosimo III's eldest son Ferdinando seemed promising dynastic material. Despite having his early childhood disrupted by the wilful and unpredictable behaviour of his mother Marguérite-Louise, he had grown into a young man of high intelligence who was also a genuine connoisseur of art, becoming arguably the most discerning of all the great Medici collectors of paintings. The previous great Medici collectors had always used patronage for a purpose: as a means of political aggrandise-ment and control, as a salve to their conscience or to win friendship. There had invariably been an ultra-artistic motive in the commissioning of an artist. Ferdinando, on the other hand, collected paintings purely because they appealed to his taste, though unfortunately the art, the artists and the funds available to him were all of a lesser magnitude than those of his predecessors. As a result, the collections in his apartments at the Palazzo Pitti and the Medici residence at Poggio a Caiano consisted of exquisite minor masterworks – rather than, say, the self-glorifying bravura of the Botticellis inspired by Lorenzo the Magnificent and his court. Ferdinando's collecting would remain a triumph of pure taste, rather than an expres-sion of political patronage.

Ferdinando also played a considerable role in the musical flowering that took place during this period – an event that can be seen as a direct cultural consequence of the earlier renaissance in other arts. Ferdinando's most renowned achievement in this field was the close association he formed with the Sicilian-born operatic composer Alessandro Scarlatti. Since its birth in Florence over a century and a half previously, opera had spread far beyond Italy to the courts of Louis XIV in France and the new Holy Roman Emperor, Joseph I, in Vienna. But Italian opera remained supreme, especially in Venice and Naples. Scarlatti was the leading prac-titioner of his time, extending opera beyond its early Baroque manifesta-tion into the new musical era now known as Pre-classical. He gave a form to opera, making it revolve around recitative and arias, during which the drama stopped while the singer gave operatic vent to his emotions, often at some length. This ushered in the era of the virtuoso leading singers, with the female roles usually sung by castrati. In character and role, these were the first prima donnas – to such an extent that they soon succeeded in appropriating most of the leading male roles!

In 1702 Ferdinando invited Scarlatti to Florence, where he composed five operas for performance in the Medici villa at Pratolino (where Galileo had once tutored the young Cosimo II). These operas were highly regarded at the time, though all but fragments of them are now lost. After two years Scarlatti moved on to Rome and then Venice, but he corresponded regularly with Ferdinando over the next decade or so, to such an extent that these letters are now the main source for Scarlatti's life during this period.

As a young man, Ferdinando had soon become aware of his father's lack of interest in the governance of the grand duchy, but when he approached Cosimo III in the hope of taking on some of these duties, he was firmly rebuffed. This produced a predictable psychological reaction, and from then on the capable and intelligent son did all he could to outrage his doltish, bigoted father. Unfortunately this involved increasingly self-destructive behaviour, and what had begun as wilful rebellion quickly degenerated into a roistering dissipation to which his Medici temperament proved all too enthusiastically suited. Ferdinando took himself off to Venice, where there was more scope for such behaviour, and returned some time later with an arrogant castrato opera singer called Cecchino in tow.

After the joys of Venice, Florence proved a distressing anticlimax; the streets were filled with sanctimonious priests and nuns, whilst every corner had its wretched beggar. In an effort to liven things up (and further outrage his father), Ferdinando organised a great jousting contest for the pre-Lenten carnival of 1689, which took place before an enthusiastic crowd in the Piazza Santa Croce. The theme of the joust was a battle between Europe and Asia, and with a burst of energy and organisation worthy of Lorenzo the Magnificent himself, Ferdinando produced two teams of exotic jousters. One was dressed as Eastern warriors, with some members even in authentic armour captured from campaigns against the Ottomans; the other team was outfitted as European knights. Was this perhaps a sign of things to come, when Ferdinando succeeded as grand duke? Or would it prove just a final flourish of the old Medici ways?

Ferdinando continued in his erratic behaviour. One moment he would be corresponding with the German composer Handel, trying to persuade him to visit Florence, or involved in efforts to save a decaying Raphael altarpiece from one of the city's churches; the next he would be setting off with Cecchino for a further bout of debauchery in the fleshpots of Venice, where he contracted syphilis, allegedly from Cecchino. Undeterred,

Cosimo III doggedly continued with his enquiries around the courts of Europe in search of a prestigious wife for his son, one who would produce further male heirs to ensure the continuance of the Medici dynasty. Eventually he managed to secure Princess Violante of Bavaria, who on her arrival in Florence turned out to be a dull and rather intimidated sixteen-year-old girl. At Cosimo III's insistence she was married to Ferdinando nonetheless, though by now Ferdinando's dissipated behaviour and homo-sexual inclinations made it almost certain that he would prove incapable of producing an heir.

When Cosimo III realised that his obsession with male heirs had probably been thwarted in this direction, he turned his attentions to his second child, his daughter Anna Maria Luisa, a tall, bony, rather mascu-line and awkward girl with long black hair. Approaches for a suitable husband were made to a string of royal families. The Spanish were not interested, nor were the Portugese; the French and the House of Savoy politely but firmly turned him down; and he was then rebuffed by the Spanish (again). Finally Cosimo had success in Germany, managing to secure Johann Wilhelm, the elector palatine, as a prestigous bridegroom; though it turned out that he had syphilis, and as a result Anna Maria Luisa would produce only a series of miscarriages.

With increasing urgency, Cosimo III turned his attentions to his final child, his second son Gian Gastone, an intellectually gifted, aesthetically inclined young man who preferred his own company to that of his fellow human beings. Gian Gastone was to prove even less of a catch than his elder brother; he was both obese and immoderately sensitive, and the harsh-ness of reality had by now driven this touchy colossus to drink. His posi-tive abhorrence of female company soon made it clear that he was also homosexual. Even these hindrances might just have been overcome, if Cosimo III's choice of a bride for his thin-skinned offspring had not been so disastrous.

Princess Anna Maria Francesca of Saxe-Lauenburg, who had recently been widowed by the death of Count Palatine Philip of Neuberg, was considered a great catch by Cosimo III. She brought with her further titles, and her claim to the Saxon electorate through her dead father meant that her husband might one day become a prince of the Holy Roman Empire. On the other hand, Anna Maria Francesca of Saxe-Lauenburg was

Fig 20 Gian Gastone de' Medici

described as being 'of enormous weight, immense self-will and no personal attractions'. Her overbearing behaviour was said to have driven her husband to drink himself to death after just three years of marriage. In contrast to her aesthete husband-to-be, Anna Maria Francesca was uneducated, wifully philistine in her attitudes, and enjoyed rural life. According to the near-contemporary Medici historian Jacopo Galluzzi: 'Her favoured forms of exercise had long been riding, hunting and conversing with her horses in her stables.'

The merest rumours concerning his future bride were enough to drive Gian Gastone into a fit of trepidation, but his father was adamant that the wedding should proceed. Dejectedly and resignedly Gian Gastone made his way north across the Alps to marry his dynastically endowed German bride. On his arrival at Düsseldorf he was taken aback to find that his future wife was as fat as he was; and in her own way, she was also just as physically unappealing. Yet where Gian Gastone was simply unattractive, his bride was formidably ugly; apart from their mutual physical monstrosity, it soon became clear that neither had anything whatsoever in common.

In July 1697 the ill-matched couple were married by the Bishop of Osnabrück in the chapel of the elector's palace at Düsseldorf; both were said to be twenty-five years old, though the formidable bride looked somewhat older. The wedding celebrations included a lengthy programme of peasant dancing; the rural attire, clashing music and raucous tenor of this entertainment proved excruciating to Gian Gastone's classically attuned ears, though his wife applauded boisterously.

The bride insisted on leaving Düsseldorf as soon as the wedding celebrations were over, informing her husband that she could not abide urban living or sophisticated company of any sort. Gian Gastone accompanied his new bride in the royal coach down the long rutted highway across Bavaria, through the Bohemian Woods to Prague and on to the village of Reichstadt, where above the hovels and crooked rooftops rose the gloomy battlements of the bride's ramshackle castle. Pleased to be home, Anna Maria Francesca quickly disappeared to the stables, which seemed far better equipped than the damp and chilly human living quarters, where the bridegroom was left to his own dispirited devices. It soon became clear that there was no prospect of any offspring, male or otherwise. Anna Maria Francesca renewed her interrupted equine dialogues, and Gian Gastone began dolefully consoling himself with an Italian groom called Giuliano Dami. After a while he and Giuliano began making occasional sorties into Prague, where they would enjoy the low life. According to a contemporary memoir: 'There was also no small number of palaces at Prague belonging to great and opulent nobles. These had regiments of retainers about them in their households, footmen and lackeys of low birth and humble station. Giuliano induced His Highness to seek his diversions with these, and to mingle freely in their midst, so as to choose any specimen that appealed to his singular sense.'

In time, Gian Gastone became bolder, on one occasion even taking a trip to Paris. When Cosimo III got to hear of this he was deeply vexed, and wrote a letter to Gian Gastone bemoaning his lack of attention to producing an heir and upbraiding his son for his impious behaviour. By now Cosimo III had become even more devout and austere, and he had learned to moderate his eating habits. According to the English traveller Edward Wright, who stayed in Florence: 'For the last twenty years of his life, his constant beverage was water. His food was plain: he ate but one dish, and always alone, except upon the festivals of St John, and other peculiar days, when his family were summoned to join him.'

Florence was undergoing a similar austerity. The population of the city had now declined by 50 per cent and was down to around 42,000. Weeds grew up between the stones in the back alleys, and houses lay derelict, fallen in on themselves. The slump in Florence's fortunes affected all levels of society; beggars did their best to live off the tourists, meanwhile the great families were reduced to camping out in their empty palazzi, collecting their meals from local taverns. Their dismissed cooks and servants hung about the gateways of the palazzi that had formerly employed them, indicating the quality of people for whom they had once worked and the fact that they were for hire. During cold winters and times of sparse harvest, groups would gather beneath the windows of the Palazzo Pitti, calling pitifully for bread. Cosimo III would retire to his personal chapel to pray for them, while the palace guards chased them away. By 1705 the Tuscan exchequer was to all intents and purposes bankrupt.

News of this state of affairs soon began to circulate abroad. By now the Austrians had begun making inroads into northern Italy, staking a claim to Parma and Ferrara, and it soon became clear that the Austrian Holy Roman Emperor, Joseph I, had plans to extend his territory still further and annex Tuscany. The prospects for the continuation of Medici rule looked bleak: Cosimo III's son and heir, Ferdinando, was by this stage in alcoholic decline, suffering alternately from delusions and amnesia, though the public remained largely unaware of this because he rose only at night and seldom went out. Likewise, it was becoming evident that Gian Gastone was simply incapable of ruling the grand duchy. The Emperor

Joseph I was convinced that under Austrian rule, Tuscany could be turned into a thriving province once more, and at the same time Austria's central European empire would benefit greatly from such a revitalised economic force.

Joseph I entered into diplomatic negotiations with the ageing Cosimo III, whose son Ferdinando had by now developed epilepsy – it was evident he would soon die. The population had placed great faith in Ferdinando, believing that his accession to power would bring about a return to better days, and to many he was seen as a 'good Medici'. The Emperor Joseph I warned Cosimo III that Ferdinando's death could well spark anti-Medici riots amongst the disillusioned population, and that these might even lead to the overthrow of the Medici. If Austrian troops could be garrisoned on Tuscan territory, this catastrophe could be avoided.

Cosimo III resisted this suggestion, but Joseph I now made plain his objective, informing Cosimo III that his imperial lawyers had made a study of the family trees of the major royal houses of Europe, and this had led them to conclude that Tuscany in fact belonged to the Holy Roman Empire. (One of Ferdinando II's daughters had married Ferdinand Karl of Austria, while another had married the Duke of Parma, whose territory was now Austrian.) All of Italy was shaken by this news: spurious or not, Joseph I's claim could lead to the entire peninsula becoming embroiled in a war, with Tuscany being ravaged in the process.

Pope Innocent XII, whose domains would have been next under threat, urgently contacted Cosimo III telling him to buy off the Emperor Joseph I. But Cosimo could only reply that he had no money; whereupon Innocent XII immediately authorised him to withdraw the clergy's immunity from tax in Tuscany. As a result, Cosimo III was able to raise the equivalent of 150,000 florins, which was then used to buy off Joseph I, inducing him to withdraw his claim.

Even so, the Austrian occupation of Parma and Ferrara meant that Tuscany remained under threat, although by this stage Austria was not the only danger, for Tuscany was now menaced on all sides. The Tuscan navy, in its pitiful state, was incapable of defending the coast against any French invasion, and Spanish troops were garrisoned menacingly close across the border to the south. Only the prospect of Austrian troops entering Tuscany appeared to be keeping these other powers at bay. Cosimo III continued to dither, and in the end this lack of policy miraculously paid off. In 1711 the Emperor Joseph I died, and this was followed by a lull in the War of the Spanish Succession and the empire's territorial ambitions. Two years later Cosimo III's son and heir Ferdinando died, but the expected riots did not materialise; by now the population was too cowed and dispirited even to take to the streets.

Cosimo III's reign tottered on, and by 1720 it had lasted for fifty years. The English traveller Edward Wright described Cosimo III in the same year:

> His Highness was about eighty years old: his state of health was then such as would not allow his going abroad; but whilst he could do that, he visited five or six churches every day. I was told he had a machine in his own apartment, whereon were fix'd little images in silver, of every saint in the calendar. The machine was made to turn so as still to present in front the Saint of the day; before which he continually perform'd his offices. His hours of eating and going to bed were very early, as was likewise his hour of rising.

By now Cosimo's religious obsessions made him easy prey to his narrow-minded advisers, most of whom were priests. All naked statues were removed from the streets and galleries, on the grounds that they were 'an incitement to fornication', and even Michelangelo's *David*, the great symbol of Florence, was hidden beneath tarpaulin. Cosimo III rarely ventured beyond the precincts of the Pitti Palace; though when he did, crowds of curious citizens gathered in sullen silence to catch a glimpse of their detested ruler. In September 1723 he was overcome by a curious fit of trembling whilst sitting at his desk, and this spasmodic affliction lasted for two hours, leaving him drained and filled with foreboding. By October Cosimo III was on his deathbed; and daily he prayed, beseeching God to forgive him for his sins – though he still managed to sign a decree further raising the ruined grand duchy's income tax. On 31 October, at the age of eighty-one, he finally died – bringing to an end the longest and most ruinous Medici reign.

29

Finale

THERE BEING NO alternative heir, in 1723 Cosimo III's second son
became Grand Duke Gian Gastone. He was now fifty-two years
old, and it appeared that he would be the last of the Medici line,
for all his father's exhortations to produce a male heir had proved in vain.

In the years following his marriage to the redoubtable Princess Anna
Maria Francesca of Saxe-Lauenburg, Gian Gastone had been forced to
remain in residence at her forbidding castle in Bohemia, as his wife refused
even to contemplate moving to Florence. She had got it into her head that
the Medici were in the habit of poisoning their wives. According to
contemporary reports, Anna Maria Francesca was wont to stride about
the chilly halls of her castle in her coarse leather hunting gear and riding
boots, berating her hapless husband. When she went hunting wild boar
in the woods, he would stand at the window, gazing out over the smoking hovels of Reichstadt; and as the rain coursed down the distorting
mullioned widows, so tears of self-pity would course down his chubby
cheeks. He took to gambling with his paramour, the Italian groom Giuliano
Dami, and his companions, losing heavily as they cheated him. To pay off
his debts he would surreptitiously pilfer his wife's unworn jewellery and
pawn it on his increasingly frequent trips to Prague. Here he took his
pleasures: 'Setting forth in disguise, he would join the ribald company of
lackeys and tatterdemalion wretches that lolled about half-drunk in low
haunts and taverns of the town . . . In these resorts he grew accustomed
to wallow and debauch, smoking tobacco and chewing long peppers with
bread and cumin-seed, in order to drink more strictly in German fashion.'

By this stage Cosimo III had become exasperated; he needed his son
and heir back in Florence. When he heard that Gian Gastone's wife refused

to accompany him to Italy, he embarked on a scheme to coerce her from her castle. In 1707 Cosimo III contacted Pope Clement XI, who despatched the Archbishop of Prague to Reichstadt, where he sternly reminded the princess that it was her duty as a wife to accompany her husband to Florence. The princess built herself up into a towering rage, finally describing to the archbishop in the most coarse and intimate manner why there was no point in her accompanying her husband, because he was 'absolutely impotent'.

In 1708 Gian Gastone returned home, leaving his wife behind. They would never set eyes on each other again, and Princess Anna Maria Francesca of Saxe-Lauenburg would remain living alone on her remote Bohemian estates for the rest of her life. Until well into middle age she continued to be an enthusiastic hunter, but in old age she became increasingly headstrong and reclusive; she would die in 1741 at the age of seventy. Other branches of her family would go on to produce kings of Prussia, as well as kings and queens of England; but as her direct line came to an end, so did that of the Medici.

Gian Gastone took up residence in Tuscany, accompanied by his favourite Giuliano Dami, who looked after his domestic arrangements. Gian Gastone's extreme sensitivity meant that he still experienced a great need for extended periods of solitude; at night he would sit alone for hours on end, drinking and gazing up at the moon. Otherwise he spent much of his time moving from Medici villa to Medici villa, to avoid coming into contact with members of his family. He detested his father's religiosity, and he disliked his sister-in-law, Princess Violante (his older brother Ferdinando's widow), because she would lecture him on the need to reform his ways. Later, his loving sister Anna Maria Luisa de' Medici, electress palatine, returned to Florence after the death of her syphilitic German husband; but Gian Gastone now disliked her intensely, blaming her for his disastrous marriage. (As electress palatine, she had cast her eye over the German courts for Cosimo III, eventually recommending Princess Anna Maria Francesca of Saxe-Lauenburg.) In this way, the heir to the grand duchy skulked in Florence, living in trepidation of the day when his father would die and he would be faced with the responsibilities of rule.

The renowned French traveller Guyot de Merville, who resided in Florence during this period, remarked of Gian Gastone and 'his singular apathy. He carries this so far that it is even said he never opens a letter, to avoid having to answer it. This course of life might bring him to a very advanced age, did he not suffer from asthma and aggravate his infirmity by the quantity of potent cordials he consumes. Some fear he will prede-cease his father, which would not be surprising.' But this was not to be.

By the time Cosimo III died in 1723, Gian Gastone had become a vast physical wreck. In many ways he had aged far beyond his fifty-two years; yet his bloated frame retained an oddly youthful chubbiness. He would often spend days on end in bed, and such was his constantly befuddled state that it sometimes appeared as if he was prematurely senile. Giuliano Dami had collected a group of hangers-on to entertain him; these were usually good-looking young men from impoverished Florentine families, and became known as the *Ruspanti* – after the *ruspi* (coins) they were paid, although the word also has connotations of scavenging, or chickens scratch-ing about a yard – and the avarice of these hangers-on overcame all moral restraint. Gian Gastone would lie in his vast bed, with two or more of his *Ruspanti* tucked in beside him, whilst their colleagues enacted lewd impromptu fancy-dress dramas, encouraged by Giuliano Dami. Gian Gastone would bellow obscenities at them, encouraging them to fornicate with each other in the most promiscuous fashion, and then fall asleep with his small, thick-lipped mouth sagging open over his bulbous double chins.

To the surprise of all, the new Grand Duke Gian Gastone began his reign with a burst of energy; he even took his duties seriously. Well aware of how his father's long reign had blighted the grand duchy, he did his best to set things right by instituting a number of reforms. Public execu-tions were discontinued, the power of the clergy was drastically reduced, and anti-Semitic laws were repealed. In an attempt to restart the stagnant economy, taxes were heavily reduced for labourers, artisans and other crafts-men, while beggars were rounded up and put to useful public work. The University of Pisa was permitted to extend its curriculum beyond mori-bund Aristotelianism, and teaching was even permitted from the works of Galileo, many of which still remained banned by the Church.

Inevitably it took some years for all these reforms to be put into place, but gradually Florence began to return to a semblance of its former liveliness. Gian Gastone's scandalous private life had long since become public knowledge, but this was now regarded with a certain amused tolerance. He was better than his sanctimonious father; at least there were no longer spies seeking out irreligious behaviour. After his own fashion, the new grand duke achieved a measure of popularity: he was doing his best.

Unfortunately, Gian Gastone's best was not good enough. Gradually he sank back into his old slothful ways, and the stream of reforms began to peter out. Tuscany remained impoverished enough for the visiting French writer Montesquieu to remark: 'There is no town where men live with less luxury than in Florence.' Yet paradoxically he also noted: 'There is a very gentle rule in Florence. Nobody knows, or is conscious, of the prince and his court. For that very reason, this little country has the air of being a great one.'

The lack of awareness of the prince and his court was hardly surprising, for Gian Gastone now frequently took to his bed for weeks on end. His daily routine was hardly public: he would wake in mid-afternoon, and there followed a brief period when his councillors might attempt to visit him on official business. Usually Giuliano Dami was given orders to have them turned away at the palace entrance, but sometimes one would manage to bribe his way in through a side-entrance. The ensuing audience was liable to be brief, and at cross purposes, until Gian Gastone managed to find his handbell amongst the bedclothes and ring for Giuliano to escort the official from the premises. At five o'clock a lengthy dinner was served, and this would be followed by 'entertainments' performed by the *Ruspanti*, while the grand duke lay back on his pillows belching and bellowing ribaldries. A hearty supper would be served at around two in the morning; the grand duke would dress for supper by adorning himself with a long muslin cravat, which soon became besmirched with spillings, dribblings and clouds of snuff that he insisted upon taking – and sneezing – between courses. After this, Gian Gastone would sometimes ask for the shutters to be opened, and would order all to leave; he would then contemplate the moon as it bathed the rooftops, towers and cathedral dome of Florence in its pale ethereal light. The crash of a bottle rolling from his bed onto the floor around dawn signified to his attendants outside the door that he had fallen asleep.

In an effort to make Gian Gastone put in some public appearances, his sister-in-law Princess Violante organised a number of formal banquets, at which the grand duke was expected to preside. Her aim was to wean Gian Gastone from his *Ruspanti* and introduce him to civilised society. Princess Violante's witty and charming circle of aristocratic friends would watch cautiously, their fans fluttering, as the grand duke was assisted to his chair at the head of the table. Unfortunately, his sensitivity at being in such company would drive him to consume vast quantities of wine, whereupon he would become so 'relaxed' that he began behaving as he would amongst the *Ruspanti*. His wig askew, he would bellow enthusiastic obscenities, which fortunately remained for the most part incomprehensible. The end of Princess Violante's social experiments came on the occasion when, halfway through the meal, the grand duke copiously brought up into his napkin the previous half of the meal he had just consumed, and then proceeded to wipe his mouth with the flowing curls of his periwig, oblivious to the scraping of chairs and flurry of departing ladies.

When Gian Gastone retired all but permanently to his bed, not surprisingly word eventually began to spread through Florence that he was in fact dead. To put an end to these rumours, his sister Anna Maria Luisa, electress palatine, insisted that he make a public appearance at the 1729 St John the Baptist's Day horseraces, which took place at the Prato Gate. Having fortified his nerves sufficiently for him to face his subjects, Gian Gastone was loaded with difficulty into a coach in the yard of the Palazzo Pitti. This then set off across the large piazza in front of the palace, with the whale-like mass of the grand duke rolling from side to side inside. The effect on the passenger's stomach was perhaps inevitable, and the assembled curious citizens watched as the coach proceeded down the road, with the grand duke occasionally poking his head from the window to vomit into the street. By the time the coach reached the western gate, Gian Gastone had recovered somewhat; after taking the place of honour in the stand, he was soon enjoying the races, bellowing jovial obscenities at the cream of Florentine society seated around him. Finally he fell into a deep slumber and had to be carried back to the Pitti Palace on a litter – so that those in the streets who watched him pass were able to see for themselves that their groaning, prostrate grand duke was not dead, just unconscious.

It was by now quite evident that there could be no male Medici heir. But who would lay claim to the grand duchy of Tuscany? This was a potentially dangerous state of affairs, and the European powers recognised it as such. Following the War of the Spanish Succession, the thrones of Europe that fell vacant without an incontestable heir were now being distributed on a more or less even-handed basis amongst the two great continental powers, the Bourbons of France and the Habsburgs of Austria. In 1731 an international conference was held in Vienna to decide upon who should succeed as Grand Duke of Tuscany when Gian Gastone died, an event that seemed imminent according to diplomatic reports. The conference was attended by representatives from England, Holland, Spain and Savoy; Gian Gastone himself was neither invited nor consulted. Eventually the powers that be decided that the fifteen-year-old Spanish-born Don Carlos of Bourbon should inherit the grand duchy, and should take up residence there as soon as possible, so as to ensure a smooth succession. This was ratified by the Treaty of Vienna.

The ensuing rule of Tuscany had now to all intents and purposes been taken out of Gian Gastone's hands, although for the sake of appearances he was appointed guardian to the young Don Carlos, and was asked to sign a document confirming this. Gian Gastone appeared quite content, and on signing the document he remarked lightly: 'I have just got an heir by the stroke of a pen. And yet I could not get such a thing in thirty-four years of marriage.'

In 1732 Don Carlos arrived in Tuscany, accompanied by 6,000 Spanish troops, who led him into Florence unopposed. The young Spanish prince was cheered through the streets by the citizens of Florence, who appeared relieved that there would be no war of succession; most of all they appeared pleased to have a leader whom they could celebrate. (Ironically, this was a tradition that had originally been encouraged amongst the republican citizens of Florence by the Medici.) Don Carlos was also welcomed by Gian Gastone, who presented his heir with a little velvet-upholstered carriage pulled by two white donkeys, and a gold embroidered parasol to protect him from the sun. Here was the ultimate token of the famous Medici generosity: an absurd child's toy for driving about the Boboli Gardens. Don Carlos was no longer a child — by now the teenage prince was a keen hunter — but he accepted this inappropriate and somehow demeaning gift with good grace.

However, the problem of the Tuscan succession was not yet over, for events in Europe would now intervene. Not all dynastic successions were to be so easily arranged, and the continent was soon once again on the brink of catastrophe. In 1733 the King of Poland died, precipitating the War of the Polish Succession, whereupon the French and the Spanish tore up the Treaty of Vienna and moved into conflict with Spain. Fortunately the war was quickly brought to an end, and this time the ruling powers signed the Treaty of Turin, which resulted in another round of the musical chairs of royal succession. The young Don Carlos now became King of Naples, and his younger brother Francis of Lorraine succeeded him as heir to the grand duchy of Tuscany. Francis of Lorraine was betrothed to Maria Theresa, heiress of the Habsburg throne, so Tuscany now passed from Spanish into Austrian hands. As a result, in 1737 Don Carlos and his 6,000 Spanish troops marched out of Tuscany, and later in the year Florence was occupied by 6,000 Austrian troops, commanded by the Prince de Craon, the representative of Francis of Lorraine.

Gian Gastone was irritated by this change of arrangements, for he had developed a sentimental attachment Don Carlos; but there was nothing Gian Gastone could do about the change, other than sign another decree of succession as dictated by the Treaty of Turin. The Prince de Craon wrote to Francis of Lorraine describing Gian Gastone: 'I found this prince in a condition worthy of pity. He could not leave his bed. His beard was long, his sheets and linen very dirty, without ruffles. His sight was dim and enfeebled, his voice low and obstructed. Altogether, he had the air of a man with not a month to live.' One can all but smell the scene: not for nothing was the air of Gian Gastone's bedchamber invariably suffused with a heavy pall of incense at this stage of his life.

The citizens of Florence for their part were also upset by the heavy-handed appointment of Francis of Lorraine; and they took against his Austrian troops, referring to them disdainfully as 'Lorrainers'. The new occupying forces were very different from the tactful Spaniards, and soon began taking an active role in the city's affairs, with 'Lorrainers' displacing Florentines in key posts of the administration. Token occupation by a foreign power had now become a deeply resented fact, and when the French scholar Charles de Bosse visited Florence in 1739, he recorded: 'The Tuscans would give two-thirds of their property to have the Medici back, the other third to get rid of the Lorrainers. They hate them.' Public holidays that celebrated the Medici were now banned, a move that struck at the very heart of all that Florence held dear: its unique history, achievements and tradition. These public holidays had marked the birthday of Cosimo *Pater Patriae*, Giulio de' Medici's ascension as Pope Clement VII, and the election by the Signoria of Cosimo I, the first Grand Duke of Tuscany. The Austrian troops occupied the Fortezza da Basso, and the guns defending Florence were transferred to the battlements overlooking the city.

Gian Gastone was now virtually the last survivor of the Medici line. His sister-in-law Princess Violante had died, but his elder sister Anna Maria Luisa, electress palatine, continued to live on in her own apartments at the Palazzo Pitti. By this time she was in her seventies: an aristocratic old lady who insisted on maintaining the Medici dignity. Although Gian Gastone had forbidden her to enter his apartments, she took to visiting him regardless, whereupon forceful lectures were delivered to the recumbent grand duke, pointing out the error of his ways. Gian Gastone was taking a long time to die, but there was no denying (even to himself) that he *was* dying. Anna Maria Luisa finally managed to persuade her brother to embrace the faith which all his life he had rejected. The enfeebled, bloated figure of the grand duke held a crucifix before his wispily bearded, grey-skinned face and sighed: '*Sic transit gloria mundi*' ('Thus passeth the glories of this world'), and on 9 July 1737, after an ignominious reign that had lasted thirteen years, he died. He might have left Tuscany better than he had found it after the tyranny of Cosimo III, but his impotence, in all senses, had cost the grand duchy its independence. Thus passed the last of the Medici rulers of Florence.

When Gian Gastone died, Francis of Lorraine was away in the Balkans campaigning against the Turks; as a mark of courtesy, the Prince de Craon offered Anna Maria Luisa the post of regent until Francis of Lorraine returned. This would have been a purely token title, with the Prince de Craon and his appointed men holding all semblance of real power. Anna Maria Luisa proudly declined the post.

For the next six years she continued to live in the Palazzo Pitti; although she had no power, she was still in possession of the Medici fortune and very conscious of her role as the last of a long and glorious line. In her old age she was rarely seen; she left the Palazzo Pitti only to attend church, or for an occasional brief excursion on a summer evening, when she would be driven through the streets in her eight-horse carriage, with her personal guard in attendance. The British diplomatic representative, Sir Horace Mann, reported: 'In the latter part of her life she was the reverse of that good-humoured sloven, her brother. Then, indeed, she never so far lost her dignity as even to smile . . . The furniture of her bedchamber was all of silver: tables, chairs, stools and screens.' This allegedly struck those who saw it as more 'singular . . . than handsome'. When rare visitors called at the Pitti Palace to see her, Anna Maria Luisa, electress palatine, would receive them standing beneath a large black canopy; the last of the Medici lived out her days a stiff and haughty grande dame.

Late in 1742 she developed a slight fever, which left her very frail; and in February 1743 Anna Maria Luisa finally died. Sir Horace Mann wrote: 'The common people are convinced she went off in a hurricane of wind; a most violent one began this morning and lasted for about two hours, and now the sun shines as bright as ever, this is proof . . . Nothing can destroy this opinion which all people think they have been eyewitness to. All the town is in tears, many with great reason, for the loss of her.'

After her death, it was discovered that Anna Maria Luisa had made a will disposing of all the Medici 'galleries, paintings, statues, libraries, jewels and other precious things', stating that 'for the benefit of the people and for the inducement of the curiosity of foreigners, nothing shall be alienated or taken away from the capital or from the territories of the grand duchy'. The Medici treasures and their cultural heritage would remain for ever in Florence, the city which had in so many ways contributed to them, and had in so many ways already paid for them.

Acknowledgements

I WOULD PARTICULARLY like to acknowledge the assistance provided to me in the writing of this book by Jörg Hensgen, whose meticulous editing contributed so much to the style and content of this work. I would also like to thank his readers, whose advice on matters of fact proved invaluable. Any remaining infelicities of style or content remain my own doing.

I would also like to take this opportunity to offer long overdue thanks to the ever-helpful and friendly staff of the British Library, and the Science Museum Library on Imperial College Campus, who have for many years assisted me in my researches.

P. S.

Sources

Because this is intended as a popular book, I have not included a comprehensive list of sources. Quotes in the text are generally attributed, and many relevant works are mentioned. Listed below are sources for each chapter, which may prove of interest for further reading.

Prologue: High Noon

My description of the events that took place during the Pazzi conspiracy draws on several contemporary and historical sources. The best eyewitness account is that of Angelo Poliziano, which is drawn upon by all who describe this event in any detail. Unfortunately, this has not been translated. *April Blood* by Lauro Martines (Cape, 2003) is a scholarly, but highly readable, account of the entire conspiracy.

Part 1: Origins of a Dynasty

Chapters 1–2

The best authority on early Florence is *Renaissance Florence* by Gene A. Brucker (Wiley, 1969). Raymond de Roover's *The Rise and Decline of the Medici Bank* (Harvard University Press, 1963) is the classic work on the subject and is filled with all manner of unexpected gems, details of the accounts, tales of misdeeds by errant managers of far-flung branches, and so forth. It gives a fascinating picture of Medici banking during the period from 1397 to 1494.

Chapter 3

The most perceptive work on this period is Dale Kent's *The Rise of the Medici* (Oxford University Press, 1970). For sources nearer the period, try Francesco Guicciardini's *The History of Italy and the History of Florence* (abridged) (Brown, 1966) and Niccolò Machiavelli's *The History of Florence* (Bell, 1995).

Neither is utterly reliable, but they give the flavour of the period and paint a vivid picture of many vital incidents. I have drawn extensively on these books throughout.

Chapters 4–5

Try *Cosimo de Medici pater patriae* by Curt S. Gutkind (Oxford University Press, 1938) for a good, authoritative account of Cosimo's early period up to 1464.

Part 2: Out of the Darkness

Chapters 6–7

Cosimo de' Medici by K. D. Ewart (Hale, 1989) remains a good read despite its age. Marcel Brion's *The Medici: A Florentine Family* (Elek, 1969) has been translated from the French, and also covers this period well, especially the artistic influence. *Two Renaissance Book Hunters* by Phyllis W. G. Gordan (Columbia University Press, 1974) fills in the fascinating background to a number of Cosimo's scholarly humanist friends.

Chapter 8

The Council of Florence by Joseph Gill (Cambridge University Press, 1959) is the fascinating and probably definitive account of this event. It contains all manner of exotic details, and draws a compelling picture of a little-known period, as well as explaining the truly Byzantine theological disputes.

Chapter 9

A highly readable and deservedly popular book, which goes into this subject matter in some detail, is *Brunelleschi's Dome* by Ross King (Chatto & Windus, 2000). *The Life of Brunelleschi* by Antonio Manetti (Pennsylvania State University, 1970) is perhaps the best modern source for his life and times.

Chapters 10–11

Florence and the Medici by J. R. Hale (Phoenix, 2001) is the best scholarly work on the politics and power shifts of this period. It is also highly readable and filled with many intriguing insights.

Part 3: The Prince and the Prophet of Doom

Chapters 12–13

The classic biography is *Lorenzo the Magnificent* by W. Roscoe (Bohn, 1872), though it does not adopt a modern approach; for the Pazzi conspiracy, see the Prologue. *The Penguin Book of the Renaissance*, ed. J. H. Plumb (Penguin,

1982) has a wide range of excellent essays on this period of the Renaissance. Those interested should try *Lorenzo de' Medici: Selected Poems and Prose*, ed. John Thiem (Pennsylvania State University, 1991).

Chapter 14

Surprisingly, there are no good biographies of Pico della Mirandola in English. For an example of his work, with some good explanatory notes, see the classic reprint *Pico Della Mirandola*, ed. Sir Thomas More (Nutt, 1890). The best early study of the period remains the celebrated *The Civilization of the Renaissance* by Jacob Burckhardt (2 vols, Torch Books, 1958).

Chapter 15

By far the most readable work on the Renaissance artists remains Giorgio Vasari's *Lives of the Artists* (Penguin, 1991). Though not all the stories he tells are true, they are seldom less than illuminating. He has chapters on the major artists mentioned in this work. A good biography of Botticelli is Wadia Bettina's *Botticelli* (Hamlyn, 1968). For Michelangelo's life, try Howard Hibbard's *Michelangelo* (Penguin, 1998) or Herbert Von Einem's *Michelangelo* (Methuen, 1973), which is translated from the German. There are several good editions of Michelangelo's *Sonnets*. The best popular work on Leonardo da Vinci is the recent biography by Michael White, *Leonardo the First Scientist* (Little Brown, 2000).

Chapters 16–17

Savonarola by Roberto Ridolfi (Routledge & Kegan Paul, 1959) is the most extensive work on his life. Although it is something of a whitewash, it is easy to see one's way around much of his special pleading.

Part 4: The Pope and the Protestant

Chapters 18–19

The best popular work on Michelangelo's *David* is undoubtedly Anton Gill's *Il Gigante* (Review, 2003), which is in English, despite its title. Those wishing to know more about this aspect of the artist's work should try Martin Weinberger's *Michelangelo the Sculptor* (2 vols, Routledge & Kegan Paul, 1967).

Chapter 20

The most interesting and readable popular modern biography of Machiavelli is *Niccolò's Smile* by Maurizio Viroli (Taurus, 2001). For a more detailed, but almost equally readable study of the themes in Machiavelli's life try the award-winning *Machiavelli in Hell* by Sebastian De Grazia (Papermac, 1996).

Chapter 21

Biographies of popes are few and far between these days. *Leo X* by W. Roscoe (2 vols, Bohn, 1883) may be comparatively ancient, but it contains much fascinating detail.

Chapter 22

Martin Luther: An Illustrated Biography by Peter Manns (Crossroad, 1982) gives an intriguing picture of the life, religion and times of this always interesting figure. For a popular biographical approach, try *Luther the Reformer: the Story of the Man and His Career* by James Kittelson (Augsburg, 1986).

Chapter 23

The best popular life of Clement VII appears in the classic *The Medici Popes* by Herbert M. Vaughan (Methuen, 1908), which contains a mine of information and remains highly readable throughout; worth reading for Leo X as well. The highly readable and highly unreliable *The Autobiography of Benvenuto Cellini*, trans. George Bull (Penguin, 1998), remains a classic of its kind; one of the first autobiographies, it paints a lively picture of Renaissance Italy, as well as all kinds of scrapes and unlikely victories achieved by its unscrupulous but endearing author.

Part 5: The Battle for Truth

Chapters 24–25

The turbulent period covered by these chapters is best described in the more comprehensive works on the Medici. The earliest classic is G. F. Young's *The Medici* (2 vols, Murray, 1909), which has very fixed and exultant views on the art. Some may find it a little old-fashioned for their taste. A more modern work is *The Medici* by James Cleugh (Hale, 1976), which remains consistently interesting and covers much background family material.

Chapter 26

The two formidable and much-maligned figures of this chapter are long overdue a critical reassessment. At the moment the most comprehensive biographies remain *Catherine de Médicis* by Paul Van Dyke (2 vols, Murray, 1923) and *Marie de Médicis* by Julia S. H. Pardoe (3 vols, Samuel Bagsten & Sons, 1902), which concentrates on her time in France. For a good illustrated life, try *Catherine de Médicis* by Hugo Ross Williamson (Michael Joseph, 1973).

Chapter 27
Stillman Drake's *Galileo at Work* (Chicago University Press, 1978) remains the classic biography of this always fascinating subject. He also relates the man and his scientific development to the age around him.

Chapters 28–9
The final decline in all its lurid splendour and squalor is lovingly depicted in Harold Acton's *The Last Medici* (Methuen, 1973). Another general work on the Medici that catches this period well is Christopher Hibbert's classic *The Rise and Fall of the House of Medici* (Penguin, 1995).

Index